BEFORE AND AFTER GENDER

HAU
BOOKS

BEFORE AND AFTER GENDER

SEXUAL MYTHOLOGIES
OF EVERYDAY LIFE

Marilyn Strathern

Edited with an Introduction by Sarah Franklin

Afterword by Judith Butler

Hau Books
Chicago

Cover and layout design: Sheehan Moore
Cover photo printed with permission from the Barbara Hepsworth Estate and
The Art Institute of Chicago: Barbara Hepworth, English, 1903-1975, Two Figures
(Menhirs), © 1954/55, Teak and paint, 144.8 x 61 x 44.4 cm (57 x 24 x 17 1/2 in.),
Bequest of Solomon B. Smith, 1986.1278

Typesetting: Prepress Plus (www.prepressplus.in)

ISBN: 978-0-9861325-3-7
LCCN: 2016902723

Hᴀᴜ Books
Chicago Distribution Center
11030 S. Langley
Chicago, IL 60628
www.haubooks.com

Hᴀᴜ Books is marketed and distributed by The University of Chicago Press.
www.press.uchicago.edu

Printed in the United States of America on acid-free paper.

The Priest Sylvester, in Russia in the sixteenth century, writes to his son:

The husband ought to teach his wife with love and sensible punishment. The wife should ask her husband about all matters of decorum; how to save her soul; how to please the husband and God; how to keep the house in good order. And to obey him in everything. . . . And no matter how guilty the wife is, the husband should not hit her eyes or ears, nor beat her with his fist or feet under the heart. . . . But to beat her carefully with a whip is sensible, painful, fear-inspiring, and healthy. In the case of a grave offence, pull off her shirt and whip politely, holding her by the hands and saying: "Don't be angry; the people should not know about it; there should be no complaints." (Quoted in Catlin 1929: xvi)

Lord Kames, *Loose hints upon education* (1781):

"To make a good husband is but one branch of a man's duty; but it is the chief duty of a woman to make a good wife." (Quoted in Catlin 1929: xx)

From George Gissing, *The odd women* (1893):

"I don't think, Edmund, there's much real difference between men and women. That is, there wouldn't be, if women had fair treatment."

"Not much difference? Oh, come; you are talking nonsense. There's as much difference between their minds as between their bodies. They are made for entirely different duties." Monica sighed.
"Oh, that word Duty!"

From Wilkie Collins, *The woman in white* (1859–60):

"Human ingenuity, my friend, has hitherto only discovered two ways in which a man can manage a woman. One way is to knock her down—a method largely adopted by the brutal lower orders of the people, but utterly abhorrent to the refined and educated classes above them. The other way (much longer, much more difficult, but in the end not less certain) is never to accept to provocation at a woman's hands. It holds with animals, it holds with children, and it holds with women, who are nothing but children grown up."

From George Gissing, *The odd women* (1893):

[Miss Barfoot, talking about her uncle:] "I have heard him speak bitterly, and very indiscreetly, of early marriages; his wife was dead then, but everyone knew what he meant. Rhoda, when one thinks how often a woman is a clog upon a man's ambition, no wonder they regard us as they do."
"Of course, women are always retarding one thing or another. But men are intensely stupid not to have remedied that long ago."

Table of Contents

Original Acknowledgments

The purpose of this book is to apply some of the findings of social anthropologists to a topic which they do not often treat on its own, male-female relations. It is intended to suggest a point of view rather than offer an original synthesis, and the ideas in it are drawn from many sources in addition to those specifically given reference. But although the point of view is one which an anthropologist might be expected to follow, it in no way amounts to an orthodoxy. At the same time, I have both taken much anthropological analysis for granted and been free with the material I quote. I hope the authors whose works I cite will find there has not been too much distortion.

Several parts of the book were written in collaboration with Joyce Evans, my mother. I thank her for her help in this way, especially for the reading she did and for perusing the manuscript. Joyce Evans has for many years lectured on women's roles and "the woman question" to historical studies and literature classes, and any perspective I can lay claim to on the topic derives largely from what she has taught me.

Marilyn Strathern

Port Moresby, 1974

Editorial Note

In the quoted material, paragraphs follow the original text, with occasional elisions, but not necessarily in the original order. Intervening or missing text is indicated by ellipses (. . .), while square brackets ([ ]) supply explanatory or linking material, or else an English term substituting for a vernacular. All original footnotes have been ignored.

Gratitude is offered to all of the authors and publishers who kindly gave consent for material to be reproduced in this volume: Robin Morgan, Wiley Publishers, Shirley Ardener, Stanford University Press, The CS Lewis Company LDT, International African Institute, Ann Oakley, Pearson UK, Taylor and Francis Group (UK), Fabian Society, Aboriginal Studies Press (with particular thanks to Kim Johnston), and the American Anthropological Association. The author, editor, and publisher would also and especially like to thank Gavin Stevenson for his invaluable assistance.

The Riddle of Gender

Sarah Franklin

Written in Port Moresby in the early 1970s, Marilyn Strathern's remarkable missing book makes an invaluable contribution to gender scholarship on several fronts.[1] It would have had an immense effect on the questions it addresses had it been published sooner, and has for too long lacked a wider audience. It reads, like many feminist writings from the 1970s, with vivid contemporary relevance to questions of sex, sexuality, and sexual inequality. This is a classic 70s feminist text with a difference, however, as it offers a more complete theory of gender as a social and cultural form than any other writing from this era and interrogates how "woman" came to be a question at all. The intervening four decades since it was written allow us to appreciate the insights *Before and after gender* offers into changing forms of feminist argumentation, as well as their objects. These transforming frames of feminist thought cannot be aligned within an orderly genealogical sequence: the issues are too vast, too intertwined, and too important to be understood to have "evolved" in the manner we often associate with

1.   I would like to thank Marilyn Strathern for agreeing to publish this book as well as Judith Butler for generously providing the Afterword. Hau Books has been an assiduous partner in this effort, and I am also grateful to the many authors and publishers who have agreed to allow lengthy citations from their work to be reprinted here.

this word—namely to progress. The thick palimpsest of debate that allows the twenty-first century reader to parse Strathern's early engagement with the gender concept through the present lens of trans activism, queer theory, and cyborg feminism means that this text, in a sense, has not aged at all.

Indeed, the text remains extremely lively. The decision to retitle a work commissioned and written for a general audience concerning "men and women" to mark instead the many transformations in how gender is conceptualized expresses not only an intellectual, scholarly, and political ambition. There is another reason, too. Throughout this text the art of demonstration is at a premium, and it turns out to reveal even more than was originally intended. Part of the reason for this amplitude is that we get the several layers of icing hindsight allows to us add on top of what was a very impressive cake to begin with. We can slice this satisfaction several ways—in terms of how prescient so many of the insights offered here remain, in terms of the dexterity of argumentation and the quality of writing, and through the fascinating glimpses of how gender began to be rethought that flash past in the snapshots Strathern provides of the texts that influenced her thinking.

The manuscript was produced under commission for a series to be edited by Jean La Fontaine in association with the Royal Anthropological Institute. But the series fell through. The neatly typed completed manuscript was carefully labeled, wrapped in card, bound with string, tucked into a red box, and shelved. When the decision to publish this long waylaid manuscript had been taken, and the editing begun, it was an easy decision to agree not to make any other than minor and mainly typographical corrections because this is a beautifully written and argued book. It will undoubtedly be reintroduced into teaching not only because of its intellectual rigor and craft, and its vivid account of how gender works, but because the book could be used as a writing manual. The use of lengthy extracts from a wide range of sources—including ethnographies, songs, poems, feminist manifestos, novels, court transcripts, and scientific, literary, and sociological studies—reflected the original aims of the series for which the manuscript was commissioned, but they also allow the author to showcase her renowned skills of expression, interpretation, and analysis to great advantage. And they have the added advantage now of reminding us what a busy scene of debate feminist theory encountered in the 1970s.

I had the good fortune, I should declare at the outset, to have Marilyn Strathern as my first employer when I worked in the Manchester University Social Anthropology Department from 1989 to 1993 where she was then Chair.

A favorite occupation of my social group during this period was to religiously watch the Wimbledon Ladies singles finals every year in June, frequently featuring Martina Navratilova, whose exceptional athleticism earned her a reputation as one of the finest competitors of the twentieth century. In departmental seminars I was often struck by the similarly unbelievable speed and power with which Marilyn's mind operated when she asked a question that began in one place, flipped over, was respun at yet another level, and ended up flying off the table at an unexpected angle before gently coming to rest at the feet of its recipient. These vivid and memorable displays of intellectual agility were never labored or lavish: they were neat, precise, polite, and carefully targeted. But as in a great rally on court, the thrill lay in the accumulation of momentum as the ideas whizzed back and forth and took on new dimensions in mid-air, all in the seemingly vast playground of a single person's mind.

I felt a similar appreciation of the brilliant kinetic qualities of Strathern's writing when I first read this book, which presents gender to us as a mechanism, argues it can be put to various kinds of use, and then pursues this idea in volley after volley of shot-perfect play. We might mistake the premise as an easy forehand lob: "relations between men and women may stand for other things." We see the great control of pacing as Strathern demonstrates how many different ways that gender relations can be used to represent other things, and vice versa. This tactical display is both engaging and provocative, while maintaining an exemplary (and characteristic) level of composure and control. It would seem that one accomplished set piece after another is being played out in front of us as we move through chapters exploring symbolism, stereotypes, roles, marriage, the family household, personhood, sexuality, property, and individual freedom. It is only about mid-way through the book we begin to notice there are several other dimensions of the performance occurring simultaneously, and these become apparent—again in traditional Strathernian fashion—as the relation of the content to the form, the reader to the text, the texts to each other, and thus the whole apparatus of relationality as a game in play.

Ultimately, this book suggests, the instrumentality of relationality is not only isomorphic with gender—it *is* gender. It is this insight that animates the book initially, and throughout, at an increasing number of levels, which, cumulatively perform as well as explain what gender is and does. The form of the argument—its composition, pacing, and shot-reverse-shot reveals—is a crucial part of the way Strathern seeks to present gender relations to us. Her meticulously choreographed account reminds us that, like sociality, gender is still a riddle: yet her version of its devices and extensions intersects remarkably closely with themes that have become more prominent today, and will inspire others. Along the way, as we watch and learn the moves, our reading skills change, and with them our perceptions of not only how gender works but also what its workings reveal about how the world is made.

BEFORE GENDER

Gender, at the time the book was written, was only just coming into view. Strongly linked to the concept of "roles," and practically oriented toward clinical issues of sex reassignment, the terms "women," "female," and "feminine" were much more common in both the anthropological and feminist literature of the time. Kate Millett ([1969] 1971) wrote of "sexual politics," following Simone de Beauvoir's (1972) account of "the second sex." Germaine Greer (1970) described the plight of "the female eunuch," and Betty Friedan ([1963] 1965) "the feminine mystique," while Shulamith Firestone (1971) described "the dialectic of sex." Feminist authors in the texts Strathern cites use "males and females," "women's subordination," "female emancipation," and of course "sex roles" and "sexual revolution." Ann Oakley's (1972) pioneering work on sex and gender is cited and extended in this book, which would have offered the most comprehensive definition of gender yet published if it had appeared in 1975—the same year that saw publication of *Towards an anthropology of women*. In particular, Strathern's account of gender as a symbol of relations, and thus a model of society itself, is unprecedented, as is her emphasis on the uses of gender as a social lever, instrument, or tool. Gender relations, Strathern argues, offer a way of thinking through other social categories, while intervening in them too. Gender relations not only "stand for" other kinds of relations but also make explicit fundamental features of relationality itself—including both its lively unpredictability and its intransigent continuities. Strathern goes so far as to suggest that gender is a verb masquerading as a noun in its capacity to "provide models of boundaries and relationships." The concept of gender, she states in her conclusion, "itself assures a relationship." When this symbol becomes an instrument, a means, and a mechanism to recast and contest other relations, the world is its canvas, and gender becomes a means by which "society can use the world to talk about itself."

Unusually, Strathern's model of gender, in addition to replacing "women" and "men," is used "globally" in the sense that it is seen as an elementary form of sociality. This de-sexed, scaled-up model of gender is further distinguished by the way it is put to use in the text to do extensive analytical work. Gender relations, Strathern repeatedly shows us, are indexical of both social organization and its ambivalence, or undoing. Gender is one of the principal cultural forms of activating social agency—but one that is fraught with tensions that are both intimately personal and inherently political. The implications of these observations are presented both descriptively (using examples) and analytically (by using the gender concept to establish a new premise for "the woman question"). Strathern not only argues but stages her points, setting off deliberately opposed examples against each other, and then reversing the effect of contrast by revealing unexpected connections and similarities. Thus, what is remarkable, timely, and also timeless about this book is not only its bold take on the gender concept but the kinetic effects that it generates throughout between its content and its form. Fittingly, this style itself—of using gender as a performative analytic principle—offers a demonstration, and imitation, of what Strathern argues gender is, means, and does.

The set up for this thickly layered account of what gender is by way of imitating what it does initially takes the form of a familiar call-and-response sequence, in which questions are posed followed by observations to reach what appear to be conclusions. However, less conventionally, the conclusions are initially very brief: the first four chapters unfold like pleasantly unwinding paths of enquiry that seem to be heading for a conclusive ending, but instead appear to withhold the final "answer" that was their intended destination, leaving the curious reader to wander (and wonder) on independently, unaccompanied by the author, and encouraged to think things through for themselves.

The lessons in form here are important—politically, pedagogically, and analytically. In relation to what she calls "gender thinking," and gender "as a way of looking," Strathern distinguishes two levels of perception: conscious views and opinions about what men and women are like, and what she calls "mental operations," which are less conscious, institutionalized frames of reference—including stereotypes, normative conventions, ideas of what is "natural" or customary, or assumptions about what is biologically innate. These devices are clearly explained in the opening chapters, which contain a condensed introduction to sociological analysis. Crucially, however, from the start, the text also withholds—it cautions and doubles back, it points to implications it refuses, and it hesitates. A constant theme is our own embeddedness in the subjects we are analyzing. Ultimately, then, the text cannot help but return to the fact that we are analyzing ourselves. This is the riddle of gender that has made it so attractive to so many analysts for so long—the two-way traffic of its formative effects, the shapes it makes and unmakes, the patterns we both can and cannot see because we are part of them.

RIDDLED WITH GENDER

Chapter One concerns "the seductive symbol"—the title itself a play on words. The seductions of symbolism play a key role in the "sexual mythologies of everyday life" the book sets out to analyze and deconstruct. The seductively symbolic role of gender has two parts: we can analyze what is said about men and women—how they are depicted and symbolized—and then locate such descriptions in relation to behavior, action, social structure, et cetera (as in any typical anthropologist's descriptions of "men's and women's roles"). But this is only part of the story, Strathern is keen to emphasize, because it is "only half the sexual mythology" (or not even half, as it turns out). We are not only concerned, she explains, with how people depict the sexes or their interactions: we miss the point of gender if we do not also consider "the many ways this interaction is used to talk about, becomes an idiom for, other things." There is a third part too, it turns out, in terms of how gender messages are sent and received.

The first riddle of gender Strathern presents, then, concerns its complex functions as a symbol: the symbolic capacity for relations between men and women to "stand for something else," she points out, may appear to be simple and ordinary but it is both arbitrary and ambiguous. Consequently, gender symbolism necessarily involves an ambivalent and often uncertain transfer of meanings. The qualities associated with gender (men are strong/vulnerable/dominant, women are fragile/dangerous/subordinate) can vary, and since the means by which these are expressed can take different forms and produce a range of effects, the uncertainties accumulate. Using a relation as a symbol, she notes, raises complex issues because it is ambiguous to begin with and can become even more so through the process of transfer. In symbolism of this kind, both the quality being transferred (as a value) and its meaning remain highly arbitrary. This means that gender symbolism frequently contains so much noise it "obscures the identification of a single direction."

A key point for Strathern, developed through a complex series of examples at the outset of her text, is that part of the riddle of gender is that it is not about men and women: gender is everywhere, and we are everywhere riddled by it (as Shakespeare knew well). This is a difficult point to begin with, and it is established through careful steps that instruct us not only in terms of descriptive content—concerning rituals and beliefs associated with wedding ceremonies in two very different cultural settings—but how to read the ways in which anthropologists have reported and interpreted their observations of such events. Amid these examples Strathern adds another: a feminist critique of sexual mythologies that subordinate women. This illustration introduces yet another strand of her argument throughout—that we need a kind of ethnography of the feminist understanding of "the woman question." It is not only a feminist anthropology she is after but also an anthropology of feminism.

The first chapter ends abruptly with a quotation from Simone de Beauvoir—whose women "dream the dreams of men." This is directly preceded by an extract from Edwin Ardener (1972), whose men cannot hear the dreams of women at all because they don't know how to communicate with them. This provocative contrast sets up two of the most important themes of *Before and after gender*, in which the terms "myth" and "mythology" are often used as if they meant "model" or "modeling." Indeed this same conflation is the subject of both de Beauvoir's and Ardener's arguments about gender. For de Beauvoir, men are both the model and the modelers, whereas for Ardener the case is more one of two sets of irreconcilable models. Strathern's presentation of gender as a relation that models relations—both in the sense of representing and intervening—is her first object lesson that gender is about much more than "women."

GENDER IS RIDICULOUS

Chapter Two introduces the concept of the stereotype—a complicated term that is often oversimplified in a nonironic exemplification of the social process it names. Greek in origin, combining "stereos" meaning "firm or solid" with "typos" meaning "impression," the term derives from the printing industry, and was introduced in 1850 to mean "image perpetuated without change." It entered the human sciences through its modern psychological sense, introduced in the 1920s, of an adaptive response to a complex reality that takes the form of simplification. The stereotype connects an inner cognitive order to "the world outside"—the title of Strathern's Chapter Four. Here, we are returning to the theme that "sex is a peg on which other things can be hung," only with an eye to parody, caricature, and ridicule.

Under the subheading "making men and women" we are introduced to Gregory Bateson's ([1936] 1958) account of gender "buffoonery" along the Sepik River in New Guinea. Men's affectation in important public settings of an "overemphasis" of masculine pride, combined with a "clowning" and "theatrical" attitude, is considered both "superficial" and "normal," he reports. This exaggerated and parodic performance of masculinity reaches its peak in the men's house in displays that are at once "noisy, angry and above all ironical" combining "violence with histrionic gesture" and working up to a "high pitch of . . . excitement." In contrast, the women seem "jolly," "cheerful," "cooperative," and "unostentatious." Strathern notes these "marked contrasts in the reported behavior of men and women" and cheerfully proceeds to the next example. This is again from Bateson, describing the ways that men imitate women:

> They put on the most filthy old tousled skirts such as only the ugliest and most decrepit widows might wear, and like widows they were smeared with ashes. Considerable ingenuity went into this costuming, and all of it was directed towards creating an effect of utter decrepitude. On their heads they wore tattered old capes which were beginning to unravel and to fall to pieces with age and decay. Their bellies were bound with string like those of pregnant women. In their noses they wore, suspended in place of the little triangles of mother-of-pearl shell which women wear on festive occasions, large triangular lumps of old sago pancakes, the stale orts of a long past meal.
>
> In this disgusting costume and with absolutely grave faces . . . the two "mothers" hobbled about the village each using as a walking stick a short shafted paddle such as women use. Indeed, even with this support, they could hardly walk, so decrepit were they. The children of the village greeted these figures with screams of laughter and thronged around the two "mothers," following wherever they went and bursting into new shrieks whenever the "mothers," in their feebleness, stumbled and fell and, falling, demonstrated their femaleness by assuming on the ground grotesque attitudes with their legs widespread. (Bateson [1936] 1958: 12)

The parody of gender Bateson describes is part of the *Naven* ceremony through which Iatmul maternal uncles celebrate the achievements of their nephews, and he continues:

Finally they came to the big canoe which [their nephew] had made—the achievement which they were celebrating. They then collapsed into the canoe and for a few moments lay in it apparently helpless and exhausted . . . with their legs wide apart in . . . attitudes . . . found . . . amusing. Gradually they recovered and picked up their paddles, and sitting in the canoe in the bow and stern (women sit to paddle a canoe, but men stand), they slowly took it for a short voyage on the lake. When they returned they came ashore and hobbled off. The performance was over and they went away and washed themselves and put on their ordinary garments. (Bateson [1936] 1958: 13–14)

Women also perform parodic gender imitations along the Sepik River, and these, too, are described by Bateson:

The majority of the women, when they put on the garments of men, wear the smartest of male attire. . . . [On one occasion] their faces were painted white with sulphur, as is the privilege of homicides, and in their hands they carried the decorated lime boxes used by men and serrated lime sticks with pendant tassels whose number is a tally of men killed by the owner. This costume was very becoming to the women and was admired by the men. In it the women were very proud of themselves. They walked about flaunting their feathers and grating their lime sticks in the boxes, producing the loud sound which men use to express anger, pride and assertiveness. Indeed so great was their pleasure in this particular detail of male behaviour that the husband of one of them, when I met him on the day following the performance, complained sorrowfully that his wife had worn away all the serrations on his lime stick so that it would no longer make a sound. (Bateson [1936] 1958: 14–15)

Bateson interprets these reciprocal instances of gender ridicule as part of a conversation between women and men about their respective roles. But Strathern wishes to push the form of the stereotype to reveal more about what gender is and does. She describes the stereotypical caricature as a "manipulation" of gender that works both because it is a rigidly defined form, and isn't: it may appear to describe a familiar reality but instead *comments* on it, and *evaluates* it, and therefore intervenes in this reality in an instrumental way. As Bateson's examples so effectively illustrate, the stereotype, in the context of a parody, is not reductive at all: indeed it is eloquent, and can evoke a whole range of emotions, in the way theater releases the imagination from the real—not through reduction but amplification. Mockery, parody, caricature—these are complex forms of commentary that undo precisely the forms they imitate. To ask here what the "messages" of such exaggerated gender performances might be is to introduce a very open-ended question indeed.

In turning next to the work of Margaret Mead (1935), Strathern introduces a more somber aspect of gender ridicule—the harsh, shaming, and destructive consequences for individuals whose gender is not "correctly" made. Why do such rigid gender expectations exist, Mead asks, and to what cost is this "dichotomy of social personality" enforced?

> Any society that specializes its personality types by sex, which insists that any trait—love for children, interest in art, bravery in the face of danger, garrulity, lack of interest in personal relations, passiveness in sex-relations [. . .]—is inalienably bound up with sex, paves the way for a kind of maladjustment of a worse order. . . . In addition to, or aside from, the pain of being born into a culture whose acknowledged ends he can never make his own, many a man has now the added misery of being disturbed in his psycho-sexual life. He not only has the wrong feelings but, far worse and more confusing, he has the feelings of a woman. . . .
>
> Thus the existence in a given society of a dichotomy of social personality, of a sex-determined, sex-limited personality, penalizes in greater or less degree every individual born within it. Those whose temperaments are indubitably aberrant fail to adjust themselves to the accepted standards, and by their very presence, by the anomalousness of their responses, confuse those whose temperaments are the expected ones for their sex. So in practically every mind a seed of doubt, of anxiety, is planted, which interferes with the normal course of life. (Mead 1935: 290–306 passim)

And so the riddle of gender continues: we are riddled with gender, but gender is ridiculous. It is absurd to expect so large a group of people as half the population to share the same qualities that radically demarcate them from the other equally large and diverse group of people who are supposed to be their polar opposites. The premises that stereotypes operate as a kind of filter of variation in order to ease social function, or dampen the sharp edges of social complexity, are illogical in the context of gender. In this context, stereotypes—like myths—are cultural forms that can be manipulated to depict, to comment, to evaluate, to mock, to shame, to play, and to entertain. As these examples show, gender can be rigidly prescriptive but also meaningfully opaque: its rationalities of conformity can themselves stand for absurdity and rupture.

On these points, Strathern returns to her dialogue with de Beauvoir, citing at length her trenchant critiques of male solipsism and its crushing subordinations. But in her pursuit of a more anthropological feminism, she also carefully raises her doubts:

> De Beauvoir has given an analysis of why females as a sex should be so endowed with conflicting attributes that they appear ambiguous. She is concerned to show how these myths about the nature of women define for men a concept of the individual. She is concerned with the limits of personal freedom and identifies women as a primary medium through which men see themselves as acting on the world, on nature. These concerns undoubtedly draw heavily on European tradition, on philosophies which have been preoccupied with notions of individuality, free will, mortality, and such like. It is illuminating in this regard to consider the prominence which sexual intercourse has in her account. It is women's sexuality she suggests, which allows for so much play on the theme of ambiguity. (p. 55)

In the end, Strathern suggests, "one might suggest that de Beauvoir is really dealing with the place (and use) of sexuality in Western thought, and not, as she would suggest by some of her examples, human thought in general." For it is in the European tradition especially, she notes, that sexual relations are used to symbolize other types of encounters—and this is not the case in all societies.

> Carnal knowledge, possession of the flesh, mortality and release of the spirit, boundaries of freedom, domination of the natural world—some of these themes can be traced in European thought back to Medieval times and beyond. Sexual intercourse flows through these notions as a symbol of the ultimate ambiguity: it is a means of subduing Nature, and makes Nature yield forth her blessings; it is also the means by which Nature subdues man, for insofar as he is prey to the temptations of the flesh, he is not in control of his own destiny. But I am not sure whether sexual intercourse holds quite the same symbolic place in, say, Iatmul thought. (p. 57)

Indeed it is particularly unlikely that European, British, English, or Anglican models of sexuality would approximate those of the Sepik peoples given that they are not even shared among the travelers on a London double-decker bus.

As we have seen over the forty years since this book was written, the symbolic role of both sexuality and sexual intercourse has undergone significant and rapid change. In Chapter Three, Strathern addresses a perennial feminist theme in which such dramatic changes have not been so evident, namely the housewife and her labors. This chapter too is about the form of forms, and here it is the contents of models that will concern us.

MODEL HOUSEWIVES

Models, famously, have many uses. Anthropological models are used in *Before and after gender* to illustrate how gender forms connect disparate aspects of social life—from domestic cooking rituals to the formalities of chieftainship. But these examples also model for us conventions of anthropological analysis and interpretation. The book was written in the era when many formal modeling conventions in anthropology were under dispute: an earlier emphasis on the formal lineage structures of African societies to model kinship and politics was giving way to a new emphasis on ritual, symbol, and performance—accompanied by a new prominence for symbolic anthropology and what came to be known as "the interpretive turn." Strathern was to be instrumental in these changes, in particular through introducing a new emphasis on personhood and self, and drawing on her expertise in Melanesian ethnography to challenge some of the overarching analytic habits of her generation—including an overreliance on the familiar binarisms nature vs. culture, domestic vs. jural, formal vs. informal, and male vs. female. Many of these critiques, her book suggests, were equally relevant to feminist analyses, and to the project of undoing some of its own "stuck" dichotomies of subject vs. object, individual vs. society, freedom vs. oppression, and men vs. women.

The turn to families, homes, and housework in Chapter Three is consequently aimed to demonstrate both that the English model of the housewife is a much more restrictive one than in many other parts of the world, and to explain why this is so (because of the asymmetrical dependency the restriction of the wife to the home enforces). The analysis here is in many ways classically anthropological and reminds us of the strengths of this approach—for example by skillfully showcasing the antinormative uses of crosscultural comparison and its power to disrupt ingrained stereotypical certainties. Usefully, the analysis also explores a contrast within a single British community, namely that of the Bethnal Greeners from London's East End, who were insightfully and influentially studied by

Michael Young and Peter Willmott ([1957] 1962) as part of their innovative community policy program developed over fifteen years from the mid 1950s to the late 1960s. Relationships between men and women changed significantly when the Bethnal Greeners moved out to the suburbs, isolating the house-wives from their communities and increasing women's dependence on the single home. As Strathern shows, both gender and kinship idioms offer crucial structural insights into social tensions that interrelate "private" life with the public sphere—indeed she illustrates how such distinctions dissolve in the context, for example, of an East End wedding at which the aim is to integrate two sides of a family into a new form of alliance and affinity.

Model housewives, then, also model models. And they model roles, or what Strathern calls "the mechanism of role-linkage" to stereotypes and symbols. "There is no doubt that the status of housewife receives a very special loading in English and American society," Strathern notes, continuing:

> Certain stereotypes about women lead to particular roles being stressed in the society (e.g., sexual partner, housewife). This is because the roles pick up culturally relevant feminine characteristics and emphasize them (sexual partnering, house-keeping) and in this emphasis bestow on them certain qualities (e.g., female sexuality is unreliable, female dependency is a sign of weakness)—the roles themselves are stereotyped. In this form, the image of the sex playing the role is then thrown back at society and thus re-played. The particular characteristics which triggered off the association of role and sex to begin with have been enlarged and refocused, by the mechanism of role-linkage. The media words in these sentences are no accident: for the process is almost that of a message being expressed through a medium which returns to the sender a rather special delineation of what he wanted to say. (p. 65)

Building on the substantial feminist critique of the "gross exploitation" of women's unpaid domestic labor, and the underlying mechanisms that ensure the reproduction of this specific form of feminine dependency, Strathern contrasts the lifelong mobility and independence of the West African women portrayed by Esther Goody.

> Divorce in Gonja is easily brought about by either partner, although most frequently initiated by the wife. It appears to be a relatively common occurrence at

all stages of a woman's adult life. While young women do leave their husbands before any children are born, or when they have only one or two small ones, it also happens regularly that more mature women with older children leave one spouse for another. However, as a wife approaches old age it becomes increasingly likely that she will leave her husband to settle with kin. In the early and middle stages of woman's life, marriages tend to be ended by separation which becomes finalized by a subsequent marriage rather than by a legal divorce. When an older woman separates from her husband, however, it is highly unlikely that she will remarry and her status continues that of a "separated" rather than a "divorced" woman. Since separation in old age is so uniformly final it is designated "terminal separation" to distinguish it from the separation which is in fact a transition between one marriage and another. Men, it must be noted, continue to take wives as long as they can persuade women to marry and stay with them. They generally remain married until a more advanced age than women, although elderly men . . . are often single. (Goody 1962: 36)

As Strathern explains, there are several factors that increase women's freedom to choose their own course of action throughout their lives in Gonja, including the separation of childrearing from marriage: leaving her husband does not necessarily mean losing custody of her children, who, like her, enjoy much greater abilities to change households through fostering arrangements that extend across wide kinship networks.

As in other parts of her analysis, Strathern is neither seeking to romanticize extended kin networks and the community resources they make available (as Young and Willmott sometimes did), nor to overgeneralize the housewife's dependency (as some feminist analysts could be accused of doing). As she notes later in the book: "I am not through these examples trying to build up a composite picture of what it is like to be one or other sex on this planet. . . . Nor is the aim to build up an identikit, with scraps of information from here, there, and everywhere." In each of her case studies, the aim is to elucidate the mechanisms that force certain linkages, that frame the message in the medium, tightly sealing the social fate of individuals through perceptions that beget some actions and foreclose others. The image of "a message being expressed through a medium which returns to the sender a rather special delineation of what he wanted to say" restates the housewife's dilemma in different terms from the socialist feminist account of capitalist patriarchy. The housewife idiom in its Euro-American form, Strathern argues, "sends out a blatant message of inequality" because it "emphatically depicts one sex as dependent on the other" and thus devalues women's worth—even in the very sphere (intimate family life) where she is imagined to be most highly valued.

WHO KILLED COCK ROBIN?

We are reminded in her account of the tight junctions between the housewife idiom, stereotype, and role of a basic feature of Strathern's account of gender— namely her insistence on attending to feedback processes that "obscure a sense of direction." There is a cybernetic sensibility in this observation, and its corresponding model of nonlinear, situated, context-specific causality. A crucial challenge for the author, then, is the question of how to handle such observations at the level of written description.

Early on, without any other explanation, Strathern uses as a subtitle the first line of a popular ditty, "Who killed Cock Robin?" This is an ancient verse about a bird killed by another bird, in which other birds play parts in a performance of witnessing, testimonial, and mourning. Both the meaning and the form of the verse are obscure: is it a song, a poem, or a story? Is it a parable, a children's rhyme, or a relic? Its order, like that of idioms, is determined by use rather than by principles of form, order, or design. Technically, it is indecipherable: it is a riddle.

We are reminded of Strathern's choice to allude to this lengthy and obscure piece of verse about a crime (a murder)—which in some ways also resembles a trial—on many occasions throughout the subsequent chapters, especially in the second half of the book, where laws, courts, and legal proceedings increasingly occupy the center ground. Strathern worked on the court systems herself in Mount Hagen and later assisted as an anthropologist in the policy discussions concerning the criminal code and compensation payments for injury—this last a vital dimension of local justice but not one that fitted easily into a judicial system with its roots in European models of property, rights, and individuals.

She has throughout her work been concerned not only with conflict and its representation but also the complicity of representation in the reproduction of injustice. To address this challenge in her own work, she has invented a style that is both extremely precise and yet also frequently opaque. Who killed Cock Robin indeed?

Edwin Ardener, who we will remember from Chapter One describing the men who could not access women's descriptions of social life because they did not even recognize them as such, astutely diagnosed the failure of the anthropologists to account properly for women's lives as a case of male chauvinist modeling. His well-known discussion of the "problem" of women's "inarticulateness" reminds us of the troubling feedback loop inherent in the "who defines the problem" problem—and of the consequent dangers of trying to "articulate" this effect. This is Ardener's (1972) attempt:

> The problem of women has not been solved by social anthropologists. . . . Here is a human group that forms about half of any population. . . . Yet however apparently competently the female population has been studied in any particular society, the results in understanding are surprisingly slight. . . .
>
> At the level of "observation" in fieldwork, the behaviour of women has, of course, like that of men, been exhaustively plotted. . . . When we come to that second "meta" level of fieldwork, the vast body of debate, discussion, question and answer, that social anthropologists really depend upon to give conviction to their interpretations, there is a real imbalance. We are, for practical purposes, in a male world. The study of women is on a level little higher than the study of the ducks and fowls they commonly own—a mere bird-watching indeed. . . . It is the very inarticulateness of women that is the technical part of the problem they present. In most societies the ethnographer shares this problem with its male members. The brave failure . . . of even women anthropologists to surmount it really convincingly . . . suggests an obvious conclusion. Those trained in ethnography evidently have a bias towards the kinds of model that men are ready to provide (or to concur in) rather than towards any that women might provide. If the men appear "articulate" compared with the women, it is a case of like speaking to like. To pursue the logic where it leads us: if ethnographers (male and female) want only what the men can give, I suggest it is because the men consistently tend, when pressed, to give a bounded model of society such as ethnographers are attracted to. (Ardener 1972: 135–39 passim)

Here is a passage in which caricature sits very close beside seriousness: we can't know what the birds are thinking, it would appear, because they are but mute fowl—unable to produce a bounded model (although capable of laying eggs). Ardener sees the absurdity as well as the injustice and irony of this pattern but retains the desire to give a bounded model himself of the situation: in his words there is "an analytical problem" for which he offers an explanation:

> We have, rather, an analytical problem of this sort: if the models of a society made by most ethnographers tend to be models derived from the male portion of that society, how does the symbolic weight of that other mass of persons—half or more of a normal human population, as we have accepted—express itself? . . .
>
> The fact is that no one could come back from an ethnographic study of "the X," having talked only *to* women and *about* men, without professional comment and some self-doubt. The reverse can and does happen constantly. It is not enough to see this merely as another example of "injustice to women." I prefer to suggest that the models of society that women can provide are not of the kind acceptable at first sight to men or to ethnographers, and specifically that, unlike either of these sets of professionals, they do not so readily see society bounded from nature. They lack the metalanguage for its discussion. To put it more simply: they will not necessarily provide a model for society as a unit that will contain both men and themselves. They may indeed provide a model in which women and nature are outside men and society. (Ardener 1972: 135–39 passim)

Ventriloquizing for his underrepresented subjects, Ardener proposes an antithesis—"a model in which women and nature are outside men and society." Politely, Strathern concurs with his general observations but refrains from commenting on his conclusion—delegating the chapter's closing comments to de Beauvoir. Among the latter's suggestions:

> A myth always implies a subject who projects his hopes and his fears towards a sky of transcendence. Women do not set themselves up as Subject and hence have erected no virile myth in which their projects are reflected; they have no religion or poetry of their own: they still dream through the dreams of men. (de Beauvoir 1972: 174)

As the second half of her book moves forward in the depiction of gender as a form, by moving backward to ask how "women" became the "problem" to begin with, we can appreciate why Strathern's modeling strategy deliberately relies on evasion as well as precision, gaps as well as links, silences as well as commentary, and opacity as well as clarity. Birds, we might recall, featured centrally in Strathern's first book, coauthored with her then husband, concerning self-decoration in Mount Hagen. Bird-talk in this context was hardly mute: indeed it was elegant, philosophical, passionate, humorous, and fluent. "Articulation," as both an adjective and a verb, describes a joint or connection. To articulate is not only to pronounce or speak: it describes the formation of a relation. In botany an articulate leaf has branches that connect to central stem. The very idea of a "bounded model" in the context of communication as complex as that of birds themselves appears not only illogical but also naïve. An alternative idiom, of birds speaking to each other in riddles, might appear to some a far more suggestive and respectful model of both social life and its depiction.

GENDERED OBJECTS

The path back to the before of "the woman question" begins in Chapter Four with objections to objects—sex objects, in particular. Had it been published in 1975, this would have made an ideal companion piece to accompany Gayle Rubin's essay on "The traffic in women," which was first published in that year. Whereas Rubin calls for an account of the "exact mechanisms" at work in what she denominated "the sex/gender system," and diagnoses the failure of any existing theoretical system to explain "the set of arrangements by which a society transforms biological sexuality into products of human activity, and in which these transformed needs are satisfied" (1975: 159), Strathern takes a different tack—offering both a different version of the question and a more extensive account of the mechanisms involved. Both Strathern and Rubin, like almost all other feminist anthropologists in the 1970s, critically engaged the "exchange of women" problem and predictably these engagements (which could themselves be the subject of a fascinating synthetic monograph) took a variety of forms. Both Strathern's 1984 review of marriage exchange in Melanesia that critiques universalistic models of this practice, and her later publication *The gender of the gift* (1988), treat gender as a coding mechanism in a system of constant transaction rather than a continuous identity that allows "women" to become "objects." Like the bird feathers that evoke qualities and bodies, human and spirit, "women" are not so much solid things as fluid signs in her model of gender as a means rather than a condition. Her view that "women" do not exist as a fixed class of subjects clearly appears as a primary motivation for Strathern's turn to gender—and this prescient move is now visible and legible as one of the earliest major theoretical models she articulates with both comprehensive and persuasive eloquence.

Chapter Four articulates the female domestic role discussed in the previous chapter with "the world outside"—beginning by emphasizing the importance of a position in the matrilineage to individual freedom of movement and choice as a head of household, a mother, a sister, or even a wife, in the examples drawn from West Africa. This chapter, then, concerns spheres of influence and the mechanisms of their interrelation—a preeminent example of which is the wedding ceremony. The complex calculus of matrimony, kinship, and gender—be it in East London or West Africa—reveals the institution of marriage as, indeed, a site of complex exchanges and transaction between sides, lines, individuals, and families. These negotiations serve the generation of wealth, the accumulation and display of influence, the determination of status, and thus of power. The bride in bridewealth transactions is not simply being bought: she is not simply an object. "In fact, she is the subject of considerable personal attention." At the same time the transactions also affirm gender hierarchies, and men's controlling influence over women—as well as their political dominance more generally.

Part of the riddle of gender, then, are the conflations between identities an institutions and between persons and property that individuals must negotiate both as independent parties and as dependent members of groups. To see gender difference as the "cause" or origin of the way these relations are structured (as many anthropologists as well as feminists often appear to do) is to miss the point that all of sociality is here, in both its fragility and its determinisms. As explicit and nominally binding as the laws or customs of matrimony may be, their fragility and flimsiness is on display as well. Strathern cites Ronald Cohen's (1971) description of Kanuri marriage contracts as leaky containers: "rights in a person cannot be locked away safely like jewellery, or even protected like land-use rights. They exist in an actor who may decide, or be persuaded, to act otherwise. Paradoxically, then, at the core of marriage lies a threat the system will not work" (26).

Even where it might seem the woman's subordination could not be more clearly symbolized and enacted—in the most formal of terms—Strathern is keen to remind her readers of the weaknesses in the argument that women are "nothing but objects" in such exchanges—a point she makes explicit in an unusually directive footnote in Chapter Four.

Returning to Britain again, she cites English Common Law, under which a husband's control of his wife and her property is stated in such extreme terms.

Here, too, as illustrated in a well-chosen set piece from *The woman in white* ([1859–60] 1969) by novelist Wilkie Collins, there is a paradox: it is precisely the extreme legal disenfranchisement of the female family member in marriage that engenders resistance to the institution—within which women could be effectively reconstituted as property owners using the courts. Here again "the world outside" reaches in to the allegedly private domain of the household, and even the intimate relation of conjugality, to extract the woman as an individual—in the name of the family. "In the mid-nineteenth century, among certain classes, a strong force in favor of treating married women as persons in their own right was the notion of the family." The identity of the family, in other words, "had to be expressed through allowing the woman a degree of personal control over the assets." Admittedly, it is a small section of the population who would have had cause or resources to act in such a way. But the point remains that the intersectional nature of marriage settlements—and what Strathern describes as the "device" of recognizing women as individual persons to secure family property—belie simple gender divisions and instead reveal gender, once again, to be a composite, temporal, and shifting quality that attaches more unevenly to "women" than might superficially appear to be the case.

DOMINANT DNA

Having untied the knot between sex and objectification and dissolved the distinction between public and private, the next hiding place for misplaced causality concerning "male-female relations" remains one of the most familiar ones today, namely the argument from biology. In switching topics in Chapter Five, Strathern also changes tactics—here moving away from crosscultural comparison and instead interrogating the uses to which it may be put in the name of universalizing arguments about male dominance and female subordination. At the center of her book, like its watershed, is the dramatic staging of a direct head-to-head comparison between two opposing analysts of patriarchy, namely the British feminist sociologist Ann Oakley and the American evolutionary anthropologist Lionel Tiger.

We begin with Oakley's refutation of the view that the sexual division of labor is an inevitable and natural result of men's and women's physiological differences. In her 1972 account of *Sex, gender and society*, Oakley emphasizes the ample crosscultural evidence of variation in the organization of labor by sex, concluding that "generalisations about how biology inevitably dictates their form and content are not supported by the data" (Oakley 1972: 128). The data she cites come from the ethnographic literature and confirm a "wide range" of possibilities for the differentiation between male and female roles—in some cases, as among the Mbuti described by Colin Turnbull, being "negligible," while in others, such as the Amazonian Mundurucu, manifesting as "extreme" sexual polarity. Strathern concurs with Oakley, adjusting the argument slightly: "The division of labor by sex would seem to be of greatest significance, then, when it becomes an aspect of gender differentiation."

Tiger's view, in contrast, is summarized thus:

> Lionel Tiger has put forward an argument which links patterns of male domi-
> nance to the division of labor on an evolutionary scale. His point, very briefly, is
> this: early man was a hunter, and the exigencies of hunting led to the formation
> of all-male groups which were reinforced by the development of a special bond
> between males as such. Male bonding is written into our heritage. It is this, male
> bonding, which generates the kinds of division of labor between the sexes that
> we see in modern and recent societies. (pp. 136–37)

She quotes him at length. And then adds more. The contrast with Oakley's style is as extreme as the difference in the two arguments. As if caricaturing Ardener's earlier diagnosis of the kinds of models men prefer, Tiger's (1971) overbearing style and grandiose reach seem to perform the same masculine self-aggrandizement he says we now rely on as a species. Both his certainty and his omniscient tone reinforce the uncomfortable sense that he is an apologist for male superiority. But equally striking is the highly speculative nature of his evidence, with which he nonetheless paints in broad strokes. We meet him in the first extract opining about women's employment, noting that although it has expanded greatly, "women work for men." Moreover, "males dominate females in . . . political spheres" and deliberately exclude them from their all male activities because "male dominance and bonding is part of the human 'biogram.'" How does he know this? Because "we may assume," he says, "that hunters were all male." He also assumes they hunted in groups, so that male bonding genes were more successful. And his list of why women could not join the chase is lengthy: they were too slow, moody, emotional, and weak. Also, they couldn't reproduce effectively if they were hunting. And furthermore it is an "underlying species regularity," he claims, "that women leaders to do not inspire 'followership' chiefly because they are women."

Who killed Cock Robin? We are now on to one of the biggest riddles of gender. How can such absurd ideas be taken seriously? "In a sense all the evidence must be impressionistic," argues Tiger, undeterred by this shortcoming. It can only be "inferred" from "broadly Darwinian principles" that any of these claims add up. Still, "male-male bonds are of the same biological order for defensive, food-gathering, and social-order-maintenance purposes as the male-female bond is for reproductive purposes" (Tiger 1971: 42).

By citing him at length it becomes unnecessary to make any critical comment at all, yet still we are waiting for one to arrive—but before we get the Strathern return, there is a new spin. Oakley is back on court, but what is this? She seems to have changed sides! "Since the reproductive distinction between male and female is the one universal, societies use it as a basis for allotting other tasks" (Oakley 1972: 146). But no, it's a feint. Oakley is following a similar tactic to another player on the circuit—Sherry Ortner, who similarly argues that reproduction is just a handy "peg to hang things on." Ultimately, as Oakley, Ortner (1972), Michelle Rosaldo (1974), Nicole-Claude Mathieu (1973), and many other feminists argued during the 1970s, the sexual division of labor is arbitrary.

> The chief importance of biological sex in determining social roles is in providing a universal and obvious division around which other distinctions can be organised. In deciding which activities are to fall on each side of the boundary, the important factor is culture. In early upbringing, in education and in their adult occupations, males and females are pressed by our society into different moulds. At the end of this process it is not surprising that they come to regard their distinctive occupations as predetermined by some general law, despite the fact that in reality the biological differences between the sexes are neither so large nor so invariable as most of us suppose, and despite the way in which other cultures have developed sex roles quite different from our own, which seem just as natural and just as inevitable to them as ours do to us. (Oakley 1972: 156–57)

There are several arguments we might have expected in reply to Tiger's biological reductionism. But Strathern's path lies elsewhere, in pointing out the numerous points of overlap between his argument and Oakley's, since he too argues that the sexual division of labor as it exists today is no longer based on things like physical strength—and that men take certain jobs primarily in order to be with other men. Which job facilitates male bonding is now irrelevant: the men could all be knitting so long as they knit together. The very fact that "Tiger's attention is all on the men" allows Strathern to show how he is proving Oakley right. It is his emphasis on men's need to express their masculinity, she suggests, that helps explain what might seem an unusually high degree of job segregation by sex in some professions. But this overlap reveals something further—namely how the term "division of labor" works to frame the problem in a particular way:

> Tiger has tried to explain how exclusive one-sex (male) associations have developed; Oakley how societies formulate gender and thus make more rigid through cultural and social devices existing distinctions between the sexes. Yet something to which the very words "division of labor" ought also to draw the reader's attention to is the fact that the more these devices stress contrasts between the sexes, the more they must remind the actors that there are indeed two sexes, not one. And any contemplation on the topic must carry the rider that neither can exist by itself. For the fact that tasks are allotted differently to males and females can say two things; it can say that the sexes are differently suited for particular jobs, and it can also say that for all the jobs to be done each sex needs the other. (pp. 141–42)

We can now see where we are headed: the division of labor itself is a symbolic expression—and one whose "direction" may be obscure. It might symbolize cooperation, competition, hierarchy, interdependence, species-specific genetic inheritance patterns, men's fondness for knitting, or women's superior driving skills. Reproduction may be a "prototype" for gender, or an idiom itself. It may offer a "facsimile writ large" of the tendency to create sexual divisions, which in turn, become "devices" used for many other things—some of which have "unexpected results." Or the results may be predictable, for example, when the division of labor reinforces gender stereotypes and these stereotypes in turn become more rigidly determining. Either way, in the language of "devices," "prototypes," "facsimiles," and "mechanisms" we see increasingly a model of gender as a means or instrument. By presenting the sexual division of labor as an example of the tactical, practical, unpredictable, and manipulable qualities of gender and what might be called "engenderments," we can more clearly appreciate that modeling gender is for Strathern the prototype for modeling social life.

Her own performance in this chapter as its author offers further lessons not only in terms of match play but also in the difference actively perceiving and anticipating interdependency, rather than opposition and contrast, can produce (even in tennis!). She devotes the remaining series of examples to readings of extracts from ethnographies that emphasize the different weaves of gender interdependence to be found across the world, even where they might not appear to exist. This optimistic reading strategy does not omit frequent references to conflict, tension, violence, and social disintegration—always key themes for Strathern. The point of these selections is not to overvalue gender complementarity. The point is to avoid foreclosing any options because the oversimplification of gender, it would seem, comes too easily to too many, and with it come costly misperceptions of what the trouble with gender is, exactly.

There is a final point too—a more pointed one, aimed at Tiger, and reserved for a (lengthy) closing footnote. Here, finally, is the long awaited smash of Tiger's lob, pointing out first that so many of his concepts and arguments are unexplained, or lack an "exact mechanism" that tells us how they work. Again eschewing the language of conflict, she patiently returns to the argument that there are "rules which males wish to maintain, boundaries they are anxious to defend, and social devices constructed by them to satisfy needs perceived as important." With a "slight shift" this is a perfectly valid claim, she argues. The problem lies in the search for functional, behavioral—or physiological—causes of this pattern. "Could we not look also for the genesis of symbols, for the source of those mental processes which have produced concepts about gender?" Indeed, is it not the case that "the writing of dominance into male-female relations was . . . a step also in the evolution of the capacity to manipulate symbols"?

The inability to answer this question, she offers, prevents us from understanding basic mechanisms of social life: it substitutes for the complexity of culture a brutal form of male behavior that is imagined to be the origin of society. Or in the words of Strathern: "It is of no less importance that we should understand [the manipulation of symbols] than that we should understand the preconditions for human survival in a physical environment which at once supports people and yet seems to them primarily a resource to be exploited."

BEFORE AND AFTER SUBJECTION

In turning from dogmas of dominance and their discontents to the two longest chapters in her book, Strathern also moves further back in time—extending her prelude to "the woman question" back to the first Women's Rights Convention held in Seneca Falls in 1848. Chapter Six, "Sex and the concept of the person" anticipates many of the regrets expressed much later in *After nature: English kinship in the late twentieth century* (1992)—itself in part a reply to Thatcher's famous claim: "There is no such thing as society. There are individual and men and women and there are families." The problem with the "Rights of Man" is not only its origin in a quasi-legal model of social contract but in particular the transformed relation such a view establishes between persons and the collectivities to which they belong, and on which they depend, which becomes a relation of opposition. As if rereading Lionel Tiger's analysis as the ironic echo to John Stuart Mill's ([1869] 1970) call for the rights of women to resemble the rights of men, Strathern devotes an extended footnote to the Seneca Falls feminists' 1848 resolution to demand "their most sacred right"—to be treated as a free and equal individuals.

> Now, in view of this entire disfranchisement of one-half the people of this country, their social and religious degradation—in view of the unjust laws above mentioned, and because women do feel themselves aggrieved, oppressed, and fraudulently deprived of their most sacred rights, we insist that they have immediate admission to all the rights and privileges which belong to them as citizens of the United States. (cited in O'Neill 1969: 110)

At the time it became such an influential idiom amid the popular pursuit of free citizenship, the notion of "rights" had as its reciprocal part the responsibility of duties: "Rights bestowed upon a person entailed recognition of certain duties," Strathern reminds us. Duty became more and more detached from rights in the context of an increasingly common equation of equality with citizenship, citizenship with freedom, and freedom with individual personhood. The consequences of this abstract model of the individual person have long concerned Strathern, who has repeatedly pointed to the social vortex such a model has increasingly opened up. There are thirty-six subheadings under "individual," "individualism," and "individuality" in the index to *After nature*, and these entries chronicle the emergence of a new era of self-made selves—the deserving and consuming neoliberal subjects, whose ethics are as deliberately chosen as the contents of their supermarket trolleys.

As early as 1973, a concern with this phenomena is evident even in Strathern's choice of an extract from John Mill's *The subjection of women* ([1869] 1970), which is set opposite the adjacent lines of her footnote from Seneca Falls. Here is Mill on what he considers to be modern:

For, what is the peculiar character of the modern world—the difference which chiefly distinguishes modern institutions, modern social ideas, modern life itself, from those of time long past? It is, that human beings are no longer born to their place in life, and chained down by an inexorable bond to the place they are born to, but are free to employ their faculties, and such favourable chances as offer, to achieve the lot which may appear to them most desirable. (Mill [1869] 1970: 142–43)

Here, in Mill's terms, is the argument from Henry Sumner Maine that the world of modernity is defined by the individual "Person." In *Ancient law* (1861), Maine described "the gradual dissolution" of an enforced system of dependence on family and kinship relations that is progressively succeeded by the free individual "as the unit of which civil laws take account." From a situation in which "the relations of Persons are summed up in the relations of Family" emerged a new social order, Maine claimed, "in which all these relations arise from the free agreement of Individuals"—a transformation he codified as the shift "from Status to Contract." "Nor is it difficult to see," Maine further argued, "what is the tie between man and man which replaces by degrees those forms of reciprocity in rights and duties which have their origin in the Family. It is Contract" (Maine 1861: 168–69, emphasis added). This autonomous modern individual, freed from the bondage of kinship, can enter a contract by choice, and exchange his labor for wages in a free-market economy, as opposed to inheriting a familial status with its rigid constraints. Precisely because he has no familial status, he becomes the prototypical modern citizen—the fully enfranchised, rights-bearing, wage-earning worker, and a free individual under civil law. His birth, according to Maine, confirms the dawn of an era defined by the decreasing power and influence of kinship and family ties; freedom is now equated with autonomy.

But as Mill points out, the "tie between man and man" is not a contract women enter into as they are subject to another, namely the contractual ties of matrimony, which Mill compares to slavery. As Strathern notes, Mill's claim that "the social subordination of women thus stands out an isolated fact in modern social institutions; a solitary breach of what has become their fundamental law" (Mill [1869] 1970: 146) suggests, in sum, that women are not full persons. And as Strathern notes, individual freedom has to define the human person:

My contention is that notions about humanity—what a "person" is—has in the European tradition come to be closely bound up with the concept of rights; and this is a particular, not a universal association. A person is seen as a being with a battery of rights and can make demands on the rest of the world as such; failure on the part of others to recognize the rights the person claims is failure to accord that person full human status. (p. 196)

From here we quickly move into what has since become familiar Stathernian terrain, namely how to read cultural forms across each other, and non-European examples against the grain of Eurocentric certainties. It is perfectly possible in many non-European societies to have a notion of individual personhood that does not rest on the principle of individual rights, just as it is possible to have a model of humanity—and even human rights—independently of contract, law, or property. For women and for feminism, Strathern is arguing, the costs of rights-based personhood may not fully have been tallied: it may be that the demand to join the world of contractual ties between man and man, like the possibility of women being granted entry into Lionel Tiger's male bonded imaginary, mistakes half the battle for victory. And there are other costs too, she implies: the equation of inadequate rights with subjection lights a particular path to liberation, and compels redress through the bestowal of greater individual freedom. Not only women are the subjects of such narrow models of emancipation—for rights-based rescue efforts have an ever-wider remit in our ever more modern world.

A careful move halfway through this chapter takes us into the novel by George Gissing that is quoted twice in the Frontispiece to *Before and after gender*, namely *The odd women*, written in 1893—a decade after the first Married Women's Property Act was passed in the 1870s. The novel is quoted at length, as if ethnographically, and as in many other extracts in the book concerning marriage, the nature of the conjugal contract is under discussion between the powerful independent heroine Rhoda Nunn and her persistent suitor Everard.

[Rhoda] "My work and thought are for the women who do not marry—the 'odd women' I call them. They alone interest me. One mustn't undertake too much.". . .

"You are resolved never to marry?" [Asked Everard]

"I never shall," Rhoda replied firmly.

"But suppose marriage in no way interfered with your work?"

"It would interfere hopelessly with the best part of my life. I thought you understood this. What would become of the encouragement I am able to offer our girls?"

"Encouragement to refuse marriage?"

"To scorn the old idea that a woman's life is wasted if she does not marry. My work is to help those women who, by sheer necessity, must live alone—women whom vulgar opinion ridicules. How can I help them so effectually as by living among them, one of them, and showing that my life is anything but weariness and lamentation? I am fitted for this. It gives me a sense of power and usefulness which I enjoy. . . . If I deserted I should despise myself." (Gissing n.d.: 214, 270)

The courtship between the two veers back and forth along a path toward possible marriage: it becomes unclear at what level an objection to the institution or the person intervenes. Everard is at once serious in his commitment to explore a path other than legal marriage, just as Rhoda tries to convince herself to marry. In the end they fail:

"Will you marry me?" he asked, moving a step nearer.

"I think you are 'not quite serious.'"

"I have asked you twice. I ask for the third time."

"I won't marry you with the forms of marriage," Rhoda answered in an abrupt, harsh tone.

"Now it is you who play with a serious matter."

"You said we had both changed. I see now that our 'perfect day' was marred by my weakness at the end. If you wish to go back in imagination to that summer night, restore everything, only let *me* be what I now am."

Everard shook his head.

"Impossible. It must be then or now for both of us."

"Legal marriage," she said, glancing at him, "has acquired some new sanction for you since then?"

"On the whole, perhaps it has."

"Naturally. But I shall never marry, so we will speak no more of it."

As if finally dismissing the subject she walked to the opposite side of the hearth, and there turned towards her companion with a cold smile.

"In other words, then, you have ceased to love me?"

"Yes, I no longer love you."

"Yet, if I had been willing to revive that fantastic idealism—as you thought it—"

She interrupted him sternly.

"What *was* it?"

"Oh, a kind of idealism undoubtedly. I was so bent on making sure that you loved me."

She laughed.

"After all, the perfection of our day was half make-believe. You never loved me with entire sincerity." (Gissing n.d.: 466, original emphasis)

By showcasing the lengthy, complicated choreography played out in a fictional encounter, between two characters who symbolize prominent social issues being debated in their day concerning the legal form of marriage and its institutionalization of female subjugation, Strathern is demonstrating once again the difficulty of separating individual and institutional forms. This is the dilemma through which the characters, forged by the novelist, are cast: for them, too, as for Strathern's readers, it is the form of the dilemma that establishes the tragic plot—for there are no means to resolve the conflict between a true love between equals and the conversion of that bond into matrimony.

Being showcased here as well are Strathern's tactical methods of revealing gender not only as a relation, or as a representation of relations, but as a layering of both and more so we can see how the complex mechanics of gender model social apparatus as a whole, not just as a part. The challenge of depicting gender in this way is enormous, and cannot be undertaken in a manner that offers completeness: this is not a bounded model. It is instead a model that speaks back to that very idea of modeling, repeating the very steps of the fictional characters whose desire for equality cannot take institutional form, and thus dissolves. The argumentation here is performative as well as formal and it speaks through its repetition of form as well as its content: the method of demonstration is strategic, even theatrical, in its gesturing "off stage"—beyond the limits of explicit depiction. The argument runs off the page and out of the frame, it pours out of the book and into its world: the blurring between fiction and ethnography, law courts and love letters, domesticity and politics is highly deliberate and composed. These relations too are gender: that's how complicated but not impossible gender is to describe.

AFTER GENDER

Having begun with the question of how to understand everyday sexual mythologies, Strathern delivers us a model of gender: by the end of the book and in its closing chapter in particular the reader is no longer before but after gender. Readers familiar with the rhythm of Strathern's analytical gait will know the pace picks up and will take giant steps just at the very end of the path. Suddenly the reader is turned around to face the walk they have taken and often will have features of the landscape pointed out that they wouldn't have noticed along the way. And so it is that we reach the obvious and not so obvious conclusions in Chapter Seven, which examines "Sex and the social order," and reveals that we have left a lot behind us. "We are beyond the point when we can say gender is mythological, for men and women have a common humanity, and that is that. Society makes a language out of these differences and similarities, and the very definition of gender contributes to and in return receives impetus from this." And that is that: the riddle of gender not so much of a riddle anymore. Gender is our social grammar, it's our common currency, it's our DNA. Gender is a form of social function, and it is the functionality of social form. "This book has been about uses," Strathern succinctly summarizes. "The woman question is not simply a 'whole people' question. It is much more complicated than that: it is a 'whole society' question." The fact that much of the argument concerning gender invokes a cultural idiom should not be mistaken for imagining it is artificial and dispensable: "You cannot classify an axe as a weapon and hope to ban its use if it is also a work tool." Gender, in all its materiality and ubiquity, makes and remakes worlds: gender is a technology of worldmaking.

In mistaking the "liberation debate" and the "woman question" for the "problem of" sex and the social order, it is necessary to return back along the path we came, noting the careful ethnographic assembly of extracts illustrating how such formulations could have come into being to begin with, and what their form reveals to us about where other problems lie. Repeatedly Strathern points to what she refers to as "cultural subjectivity" or "the cultural subjectivity of our own perceptions." While we have to be conscious of the determining effects these have, it is equally the case that we cannot think without them—and there is no way to "settle" this feedback loop since there is no way out of it. Equally, there is no way to extract the uses made of male-female opposition or interdependence from the work of sociality or its fundamental elements.

Amity and enmity; dependency and autonomy. These are the elements of which societies are made. People distance themselves or become intimate; they observe rank or act as peers of one another. Relations between the sexes provide a model for interaction. Our own concern with relationship and personal freedom is but a reformulation of issues most human societies deal with in one idiom or another. (pp. 279–80)

Oppositional idioms, like axes and digging tools, are favorite subjects of anthropology. It would be in the coedited anthology, *Nature, culture, and gender* (MacCormack and Strathern 1980) that the limiting effect of such polarities on both the human sciences and human societies would be spelled out in much greater detail. In that volume, inspired by the work of Edwin and Shirley Ardener, Sherry Ortner, and Nicole-Claude Mathieu, among others, Carol MacCormack and Marilyn Strathern's contributions confront the dangers to feminism as well as anthropology of "collectivizing idioms" through which the social order is equated with cultural systems, rules with artifacts, and human nature with environment—thus "generating pairs of contrasts related between themselves, and reproducible on paper as opposing columns" (1980: 216). Much of the argument there has its origin in this book.

Many crucial features of *Before and after gender* are articulated through its style, which eschews the oppositional and declarative tone evident in much of the writing about both "male-female relations" and "women's liberation." The book is challenging as well as courteous. It is both generously inclusive of an enormous range of views and examples, and at times seemingly at a remove from its own contents. But what strikes the reader throughout is the sense of a dialogue—for that, above all, is how the book is written and delivered, just as dialogue is itself a central focus of the book. Insofar as gender is a relation, a set of uses, a set of tools, a way of thinking, a social mechanism, a model of society, a worldmaking idiom, a facsimile, an identity, an institution, or a code, it is also a way of asking questions. In its role as a paradigm for social relationships gender is also a means of questioning categories and relations, indeed "that [gender] is used so often [reveals] its potential as a symbol for the idea of relationship as such: the form or structure of relationship." This is gender revealed in a model of elementary relationality that can "deal equally with the definition of boundary and the establishment of communication"—these being the elements of which social relationships are made and undone. Moreover, not only boundaries and connections but also "codes for interaction, rules for communication" and "a basic model of what relationship is about" are the works that gender enables through engenderment.

This is a dialogue that will be reenlivened by the publication of this book— an event that would have had very different consequences forty years ago but is also one for which time is not a particularly helpful measure. The more useful metric will be the book's own primary concerns, namely the making of relations, thoughts about relationality, and means of depicting social life. As a performance in all three categories, the book is itself the model of an exemplary scholarly generosity. It is an outstretched hand, an invitation to embark on a path, and to engage with a question that is impossible to situate in time or place, because it is the question of how people make themselves and their worlds both together and apart.

REFERENCES

Ardener, Edwin. 1972. "Belief and the problem of women." In *The interpretation of ritual*, edited by Jean Sybil La Fontaine, 135–58. London: Tavistock Publications.

Bateson, Gregory. (1936) 1958. *Naven: A survey of the problems suggested by a composite picture of the culture of a New Guinea tribe drawn from three points of view*. Stanford, CA: Stanford University Press.

Cohen, Ronald. 1971. *Dominance and defiance: A study of marital instability in an Islamic African society*. Washington, DC: American Anthropological Association.

Collins, Wilkie. (1859–60) 1969. *The woman in white*. London: J. M. Dent & Sons.

De Beauvoir, Simone. 1972. *The second sex*. Translated by H. M. Parshley. New York: Penguin Books.

Firestone, Shulamith. 1971. *The dialectic of sex*. New York: Bantam Books.

Friedan, Betty. (1963) 1965. *The feminine mystique*. New York: Penguin Books.

Gissing, George. (1893) n.d. *The odd women*. London: Nelson and Sons.

Goody, Esther. 1962. "Separation and divorce among the Gonja." In *Marriage in tribal societies*, edited by Meyer Fortes, 14–54. Cambridge: Cambridge University Press.

Greer, Germaine. 1970. *The female eunuch*. London: MacGibbon & Kee.

MacCormack, Carol, and Marilyn Strathern. 1980. *Nature, culture, and gender*. Cambridge: Cambridge University Press.

Maine, Henry Sumner. 1861. *Ancient law: Its connection with the early history of society, and its relation to modern ideas*. London: J. M Dent and Sons, Ltd.

Mathieu, Nicole-Claude. 1973. "Homme-culture et femme-nature?" *L'Homme* 13 (3): 101–13.

Mead, Margaret. 1935. *Sex and temperament in three primitive societies*. London: George Routledge & Sons, Ltd.

Mill, John Stuart. (1869) 1970. "The subjection of women." In *Essays on sex equality*, edited by Alice S Rossi, 123–242. Chicago: University of Chicago Press.

Millett, Kate. (1969) 1971. *Sexual politics*. London: Rupert Hart-Davis.

O'Neill, William L. 1969. *The woman movement: Feminism in the United States and England*. London: George, Allen and Unwin.

Ortner, Sherry. 1972. "Is female to male as nature is to culture?" *Feminist Studies* 1 (2): 5–31.

Rosaldo, Michelle Z. "Woman, culture and society: A theoretical overview." In *Woman, culture and society*, edited by Michelle Z. Rosaldo and Louise Lamphere, 17–42. Stanford, CA: Stanford University Press.

Oakley, Ann. 1972. *Sex, gender and society*. London: Maurice Temple Smith.

Rubin, Gayle. 1975. "The traffic in women: Notes on the 'political economy' of sex." In *Towards an anthropology of women*, edited by Rayna Reiter, 157–210. New York: Monthly Review Press.

Strathern, Marilyn. 1984. "Marriage exchanges: A Melanesian comment." Annual Review of Anthropology 13: 41–73.

———. 1988. *The gender of the gift: Problems with women and problems with society in Melanesia*. Berkeley: University of California Press.

———. 1992. *After nature: English kinship in the late-twentieth century*. Cambridge: Cambridge University Press.

Tiger, Lionel. 1971. *Men in groups*. London: Panther.

Young, Michael, and Peter Willmott. (1957) 1962. *Family and kinship in East London*. London: Penguin Books.

Concepts in Transition

Concepts and their environments change all the time; perhaps this manuscript captures a particular moment of instability in the way, to choose an antecedent idiom, relations between the sexes were being described. Gender was on the threshold; the idea is here, the term makes a more tentative appearance.

It has been interesting returning to this manuscript, which I cannot have read since the project for which it was intended was abandoned by the publisher. That was a series of books aimed at a general audience, under the editorship of a prominent social anthropologist, which would deal with everyday topics in an anthropological way; I was given the topic "men and women," the initial title of the ensuing manuscript. What was unusual about the project was the textual role to be given to diverse writings: the idea was both to introduce readers to social anthropological thinking and to draw on a wide range of sources. So incorporating other people's texts was part of the exercise. Then the plan was to quote enough to give those unfamiliar with the material sufficient context to understand what was being said; now the lengthy quotations may do the further work of reminding present day readers of times past.

What a past it was, caught up in a debate over "sexual mythologies," "rights," and "sex objects"! And what did people interested in women's liberation do in those days? They wrote. It was by no means their only activity, but certainly that. There was a huge outpouring of pamphlets, books and booklets, articles, and papers, much of it flourishing outside academia before it was drawn within. It seemed obvious to be part of it all, and literature I had accumulated in the 1960s in Britain accompanied me to Australia and Papua New Guinea (where I lived between 1969–76) and grew there too. It was exhilarating. If in this text—written in Port Moresby in 1973–74—several excerpts seem included in order to be criticized, I was taking them seriously; they were a window on present times. For, in the course of going over these materials on "the woman question," what emerged for me then was how many of them seemed to be speaking about society at large, which was my way of resituating a feminist focus.

Other excerpts I seemed to take more at face value. While I hope all are lengthy enough to give breathing space to their own words, there are those I leave as implicit contributions to an argument that is outside them (the argumentative theme that runs through the book), even though others are interrogated. Such excerpts are not interrogated in a literary fashion, as "texts," nor could they simply be treated as "ethnography" to be reanalyzed, although sometimes I use that metaphor; instead from time to time I bring writing to bear on other writing in order to shift the viewpoint. The one deletion I have made throughout is of the countless occasions on which I referred to the inadequacy of the kind of contextualization that I was creating, of not doing justice to the material: too many apologies, hesitations, and authorial doubts. Each voiced hesitation, it seems to me now, gestured rather arrogantly toward an aspiration to do something I could never have properly contemplated: I had no more qualification to write about courtly love than about George Gissing's characters. (My interest in these two—among other areas—had been piqued by my mother, whose role in the book was considerable.) At the same time, to imagine that a "qualification" could even be specified was beside the point. There simply needed to be enough critical counterflow to share with the reader something of the questions I wanted to raise.

The reference to times past applies to the very wordage of this volume. The text is—apart from these deletions, and a little editing that I hope would have been obvious to me then—virtually as it was written. It seems important now to leave the phrasing as it is, if for nothing else than a sign of the changes yet to come. Thus, I unblushingly use conventions long since abandoned, notably the unqualified masculine pronoun as a generic, as well as concepts once prevalent in anthropology such as "role" and "status" (I think "status of women" even creeps in), and I would now avoid speaking of "beliefs" to mean unexamined assumptions. Today's reader will find annoyingly unmoored references to "we" and "us," although I think that at the time this was also part of a deliberate invitation to the then supposed audience—an attempt precisely to imagine the starting point of a nonanthropologist immersed in contemporary vocabulary. If I read myself charitably, the phrase "in her own right," as of persons or individuals, would belong here. Finally, certain terms appear overused. "Stereotype" is one, an index of the rather primitive anthropological vocabulary that was emerging apropos of gender relations. "Symbol" does even more work, largely undefined despite the fact that symbolic or interpretive anthropology was already at that stage well in the making. One might remark that some of the connotations of symbol were obviated by the way that "gender" came to be used, in the sense of a constructed, motivated, and value-pointing analytic for an aspect of what until then had been known through phrases such as "sex roles."

By way of a footnote to what was happening at the time, it is intriguing that certain concepts came with a history of instability already inscribed in them, such as "family," while others—I think of "biology"—were being criticized without the criticism really having taken root. Above all, "nature and culture" was heard on every side and the work is very much of its time here, giving hardly any indication of the future fate of these concepts. But one could play endless games with such a text. And there are, after all, the texts within the text. At the time I was concerned to work "with" the materials that diverse writers had provided, and am just pleased to be with them again.

That would not have happened without the prescience of Sarah Franklin and her inspirational idea for a long forgotten volume, or without Hau's enthusiasm embodied in Giovanni da Col and in Sean Dowdy and his team. Reading Sarah's Introduction and Judith Butler's gracious Afterword has been something of a retrospective illumination. Jean La Fontaine was at the beginning of it all, and I would like to thank her here.

MARILYN STRATHERN
Cambridge, 2016

CHAPTER ONE

The Seductive Symbol

The nature of relations between the sexes has become one of our public preoccupations—it is a topic endlessly discussed and written about. A central discovery to which the debate has led is the existence of "sexual mythologies." We have detailed exposures of some of our current fantasies in Germaine Greer's *The female eunuch* (1970). We have been shown by Kate Millett how myths are manipulated in the cause of political dominance: "The image of women as we know it is an image created by men and fashioned to suit their needs" (Millet 1971: 46). And the discovery itself has assumed the proportions of an ideological tenet among those who feel that the myths should be overthrown or at the least challenged. I quote from an issue of *Shrew* compiled by a branch of the Women's Liberation Workshop (December 1972):

> Women have a capacity for sexuality far in excess of that of men. But thousands of years of patriarchal conditioning has robbed us of our sexual potential and deceived us. . . .

In other words, myths are there to deceive—they can be proved to be untrue.

This book aims at three things. First, it gives an idea of some of the ways in which anthropologists have analyzed relations between the sexes in societies they are familiar with. It suggests that in "discovering" that indeed nearly everywhere male-female relations are *used* in mythical or symbolic ways, one should also understand the many dimensions of this process. Elizabeth Janeway makes the second point:

> [Myths are] to be taken very seriously indeed, because they shape the way we look at the world. The urge to make, spread and believe in myths is as powerful today as it ever was. If we are going to understand the society we live in, we shall have to understand the way mythic forces arise, grow, operate. I do not believe we shall ever get rid of them and, in fact, I do not believe that we could get on without them. (Janeway [1971] 1972: 27)

This leads to the third issue: what makes relations between the sexes so potent as a source of symbolism?

INTERACTION AND ITS REPERCUSSIONS

In the writings of anthropologists there are as many descriptions of the way men and women interact with one another as there are descriptions of societies. And there is no one type of behavior which characterizes male-female relations, no one set of attitudes which human beings have held about sexual relations. These vary, from circumstance to circumstance, from place to place, from time to time. Can one pick out any salient themes? One could follow many of the liberation writers and choose from our own social life a set of circumstances—the subordination of women in public affairs—and trace its existence, or its antecedents, or echoes of it, through other cultures. But I would rather start with a simpler point. Let us just for the moment take the fact that almost everywhere the conditions of maleness and femaleness are used to make statements about various areas of social life—some of which are directly to do with the behavior of men and women toward one another, and others of which have only an indirect bearing on the facts of sex.

Ethnographies—accounts of societies studied by anthropologists—conventionally start with an analysis of men's and women's roles in family life or in economic activity, to be followed by chapters on ritual or belief, which may include beliefs concerning relationships between the sexes. This order I turn on its head. For we must be absolutely clear what we are talking about when we refer to sexual mythologies or to male-female symbolism. To move from descriptions of behavior and actions to a discussion of attitudes and myths might suggest that we have finished when we have analyzed how actual relations are perceived or represented in myth and ritual, or how actual behavior generates certain social attitudes and dogmas. But we have not finished.

Relations between men and women are depicted (symbolized) in certain ways. Women are nothing but children grown up, Wilkie Collins has one of his characters say. This is half of the sexual mythology. The other half is as important. Relations between men and women may stand for (symbolize) other things. A wife must please her husband, said Priest Sylvester, and from his hand she will receive just chastisement, since women's subordination to their spouse was a symbol also of humanity's dependence on God. Both these themes deserve attention: the many ways in which people think about interaction between the sexes, and the many ways this interaction is used to talk about, becomes an idiom for, other things.

We shall be concerned with aspects of *behavior*: this will force us to take into account the various roles and spheres in which men and women act. We shall be looking at relationships such as that between mother and son or husband and wife, and at institutions which provide frameworks for people's behavior such as the household or marriage. But it will be impossible to do this without also coming across various attitudes toward the relations and institutions we want to describe. We shall be forced, in fact, to consider the manner in which people *think*—to take into account how they represent this behavior, how they perceive acts, how the acts are fitted into stereotypes, dogmas, myths.

Looking at the way in which people think also has two parts to it. There are conscious views and opinions, and there are what one could call mental operations—where a person's views of the world are unconsciously shaped by his language, by his experience, by the way the other members of his society portray things. For example, often men and women are depicted as having interests of their own which unite them as one "group" opposed to the other, so that they are talked about as though there were an antithesis between all "men" and all "women." To take another example, in industry there is an antithesis between management and the workers—it is assumed that their interests conflict and that they are in a kind of permanent competition with one another. It seems to many perfectly natural that this should be so. In fact, of course, there are innumerable aspects to relations between men and women and between management and workers. It is the way we think that leads us to stress some aspects more than others, without really being aware of what we are doing. This will become clearer through some concrete instances.

EXAMPLES OF INTERACTION

In the 1930s, when they were studied by Audrey Richards, the Bemba were a tribe living on the northeastern plateau of what was then Northern Rhodesia (Zambia). Bemba attributed their blessings and misfortunes to supernatural agencies which were set in motion either by persons or by impersonal magic forces. Among the latter was the influential combination of sex, blood, and fire.

> *Sex, blood and fire*[1] . . . when brought into wrongful contact with each other, are thought to be highly dangerous to every Bemba, but particularly to babies and young children, . . . and to chiefs, on whom the prosperity of the land is held to depend. . . . Briefly speaking, sex relations according to Bemba dogma make a couple "hot." In this state it is dangerous for them to approach the ancestral spirits in any rite of prayer or sacrifice; and any chief or headman who attempted to perform such a ceremony without purification would run the risk of bringing disaster on his district.
>
> All persons of sex maturity are . . . excluded from a number of rites on the ground that they are "hot," or are likely to be "hot." Such people can pollute the fireplace of a hut by touching it, and then a baby fed with gruel cooked on this fire might sicken and die. Parents who do not purify themselves after intercourse run the risk of killing their children by accidentally touching the family hearth. . . .
>
> To remove the dangers due to sex intercourse a special ceremony is required and this is one which can only be performed by a legally married couple. . . . At marriage each girl is presented by her paternal aunt with a miniature pot about 2½ inches in diameter which must be guarded with the utmost secrecy. With this the purification rite is carried out. It is filled with water and placed on the fire, man and wife each holding the rim. Water from the pot is then poured by the wife on to her husband's hands, and some say on to the wife's as well. New "pure" fire is then relit either by means of fire-sticks, or, as is usual nowadays, with matches. This apparently simple rite is the essential act which removes the condition of hotness from the body of man and wife and renders them free to

---

1.   In this and in subsequent quotations, italics are kept as in original. All footnotes appended to quotations are mine; those in the original are omitted.

touch a hearth with impunity or to approach the ancestral spirits.[2] Some say that it used to be performed after each sex act and others that it was merely done before some ceremony of special undertaking such as harvesting. It is still spoken of with the utmost secrecy. . . . In the ritual life of a chief the pot ceremony is of particular importance.

The ritual links uniting a married couple are thus particularly strong in this society. It is husband and wife who perpetually carry out the dangerous act of sex together, who thereby put themselves in each other's power, and who depend on each other for the ceremonial purification which neither can carry out alone. (Richards 1956: 30–32)

Move from Africa to Papua New Guinea; from the 1930s to the 1950s; and consider this written about the Mae Enga of the Western Highlands of New Guinea.

Men and women generally live in separate houses. The men's house is primarily a secular meeting and sleeping place; it is not the focus of any important ritual activities. Ideally its occupants are males of one patrilineage or one sub-clan, over seven or eight years of age. . . . This residential separation not only provides the anthropologist with an initial insight into the Mae relationship between the sexes; it is also the basis of the local children's introduction to the subject. That is to say, when a boy is about five years old, his father and brothers begin to warn him of the undesirability of being too much in the company of women, and they (and his mother) encourage him to spend more time in the men's house and in herding pigs with older lads. The boy, alarmed by these admonitions, is eager to associate with the men and within a year or so regularly sleeps in their house. In the unusual event of a boy's wanting to remain with his mother, his kinsmen ridicule him and his father beats him and orders him to move.

As the lad grows older, his clansmen give him more explicit reasons for not staying with women. Females, they say, are basically different from males, for their flesh is laid "vertically" along their bones and not "horizontally" across them; thus they mature more quickly than do males and are ready for marriage earlier. Whereas youths are still vulnerable because they are not yet fully adult,

---

2.　The spirits of departed members of the clan have a certain amount of control over the living. They can be prayed to at shrines. Village headmen and chiefs have special means of access to the spirits of ancestors, which gives them power.

adolescent girls have already acquired through the menarche their most dangerous attribute, the ability to pollute males. Young men should therefore employ
magic to hasten their own growth and to protect themselves from the perils of
contamination. Above all, they must recognize the need to avoid unnecessary
encounters with women, including their own mothers and sisters.

Moreover, the lad learns that such pollution implies something more serious than mere uncleanliness. Men regard menstrual blood as truly dangerous.
They believe that contact with it or a menstruating woman will, in the absence
of counter-magic, sicken a man and cause persistent vomiting, turn his blood
black, corrupt his vital juices so that his skin darkens and wrinkles as his flesh
wastes, permanently dull his wits, and eventually lead to a slow decline and
death. . . .

It is understandable that most bachelors believe sexual abstinence to be
the best safeguard against pollution, enervation and deterioration of appearance.
. . . Nevertheless, in everyday life even the most cautious young men must come
into contact with women; consequently, bachelors as a category seek a generalized protection from females. They find this in the intermittent performance of
sanggai, rituals intended not only to cleanse and strengthen the actors but also
to promote their growth and make them comely. Thus, the more effective this
magic is, the more attractive to young women the bachelors become, so that ultimately it procures wives for them and ensures that they will beget children for
the clan. . . .

A young man pays no fee to join the bachelors, but he should scrupulously
observe certain prohibitions. The most important concern copulation and the
taking of food from women's hands, for these are two sure avenues of feminine
contagion. . . . Moreover, a bachelor who breaks the rules also strikes at the welfare of his peers. . . . Consequently, the individual bachelor is morally obliged to
eschew temptation and so secure his comrades' safety, and the senior bachelors
should be ready to apply sanctions to the rare defaulter. . . .

In this way the Mae bachelor protects himself from women until he marries, when he must acquire a stronger defense against pollution. . . . After the
wedding pigs are slaughtered and the marriage is ratified, the groom's father tells
him to give a netbag of pork to a married kinsman whose appearance testifies
to the efficacy of his personal magic. In return, this man spends the next month
teaching him the forms of magic to use before copulating and when his wife
menstruates. (Meggitt 1964: 206–17 passim)

Mae Enga men seem to suffer from precisely the syndrome which affects men in Europe and the United States, or at least in the way that has been analyzed by two women writers considering "The Man's Problem":

> The history and training of the male develops in him a serious deficiency. . . . The deficiency can be termed "weakness," "false consciousness," "stupidity" or "paranoia." There are many terms which indicate that men are debilitated and diseased by their training as men. . . . Many men go insane from the aggressiveness which is trained into them. . . .
>
> Females or black people who are programmed to a similar aggressiveness are as thoroughly diseased and maddened as males in those roles. So neither racial inferiority nor male genes can account for the white man's sickness.
> We must pose the question: "How then does one deal with madness?" Obviously, the person who is the object of aggressive energy, as women are for men, cannot be the therapist. Every action of a woman is a threat to a man. Men are obsessed with their fears of the female—especially femaleness in themselves. Men also have the peculiar problem of dealing with their fears of being tainted with the "blood" of the lower caste, since all males are born of women.
>
> The insane rationale of men's reactions to the slightest objections of women to accept the identities forced upon them (wife, mother, lover, whore, etc.) is the result of their dependence on the inferior role of women for thousands of years. The oppressor is threatened by any hint that women could be regarded equally or even prove superior to him. He responds frantically, fearing the loss of his strength-giving identity. . . .
>
> There are men who do not appear to be the vicious oppressors of women. Yet any man who is not working consciously to change the unequal relationship of men and women is opposing the interests of women. He is just as guilty as the more blatantly violent man and is actually a great deal more insidious. (Dunbar and Leghorn 1970: 314–15 passim)

The revolutionary "solution" to the problem is to do away with myth.

> Feminism is opposed to the masculine ideology. . . . Most women have been programmed from early childhood for a role, maternity, which develops a certain consciousness of care for others, self-reliance, flexibility, non-competitiveness, cooperation, and materialism. . . . If these "maternal" traits, conditioned into women, are desirable traits, they are desirable for everyone, not just women. By

destroying the present society and building a society on feminist principles, men will be forced to live in the human community on terms very different from the present. . . .

Thanks to gains made by our feminist predecessors, . . . we have the confidence to assert feminism as a positive force, rather than asking for equality in the man's world. We can demand that men change. We can consider leading a social revolution, . . . and hope for the justness, benevolence, and change of heart of men. . . . And know that we are a part of a worldwide struggle for human liberation. (Dunbar 1970: 490–92 passim)

In effect this means change in the current identity of the opposite sex. Men on the small island of Wogeo, which lies off the northern coast of New Guinea, admit to similar yearnings.

Men often criticize women for undermining the perfection of male solidarity. If irritated they are apt to say with a sigh what a peaceful place Wogeo would be if there were no females. Women talk too much and carry tales, thereby giving rise to ill feeling between kinsmen. "Look, quarreling between brothers is unknown before marriage but after marriage usual; that's because the wives put evil thoughts into their heads," one villager explained. (Hogbin 1970: 87)

I have not chosen these five examples at random, so it would be a false question to ask what they might have in common. Obviously, they are all about relations between the sexes. The first two describe patterns of behavior (purificatory rituals and sleeping practices), the third is written as an analysis, the fourth and fifth express in the one case and report in the other certain desires.

If you look closely at the descriptions of the Bemba and the Mae Enga you will see that at the same time as telling us about the way Bemba or Mae Enga men and women behave, the writers (both anthropologists) are also telling us about beliefs. Bemba believe that sex relations make people hot and *therefore* a special ceremony has to remove the dangers attendant on intercourse. Saying that sex, fire, and blood when brought into wrongful contact with one another are highly dangerous is how the anthropologist sums up the beliefs and behavior she has learned about. In the course of the description we are also told how Bemba themselves would phrase the matter—a couple who do not purify themselves after intercourse might kill their children should they then touch the family hearth. So there are three kinds of statements here: a description of certain practices (behavior), what the people say about why they carry them out (their beliefs), and the anthropologist's summary.

In the excerpt from Audrey Richards the summary is little more than an abstraction of the events which have been recounted. Note, however, that it is an abstraction which takes into account both the practices and the beliefs of these people. Later in her book these particular purificatory rites are put into the context of other ceremonies, all of which are based

> on an essentially homogenous body of beliefs—that is to say the dogma which links authority with the exercise of supernatural power based on access to ancestral spirits by those who have correctly handled sex and fire. In order to secure blessings in war, for tree-cutting, sowing, first-fruits, the filling of the granaries and for good weather, human fertility, harmonious relations in the village or a successful reign for the paramount chief, those in authority must have ceremonial intercourse with their head wives and then light new fire. The same must be done when a new role is assumed, when, for example, a chief is installed or a girl made nubile, or a couple married. (Richards 1956: 141)

This is straightforward enough. Bemba place such tremendous importance on the purification rites because upon a woman's handling of the hearth depends her husband's strength: his access to his ancestral spirits and, if she is the wife of a chief, blessings for gardens, village life, and warfare.

The writer goes on to ask a question of her material:

> It will be seen that all the major rituals of the Bemba reflect the importance they attach to fertility and the supply of food. . . . It is not easy to account for the tremendous emphasis on fertility and the care of children in Bemba culture. The desire is likely to be strong in all societies where social structure is largely based on descent[3] and groups can only be enlarged by the birth of new children. There are, however, many African tribes with similar social structures in which the emphasis on fertility does not seem to be ritualized in this pronounced way. But it must be remembered that in Bemba culture the lack of any permanent

---

3. That is, membership of the group is determined through a person's ancestors. In the case of the Bemba a man belongs to his mother's clan and is an heir of his mother's brother.

form of possessions[4] makes rights over labour—here rights over the labour of the younger generation—of particular importance. There may also be a correlation between fertility rites and matrilineal descent. . . . Bemba believe that the child is entirely formed from the physical contribution of the mother and not the father, and similar beliefs may hold in the other matrilineal tribes in the area. It is moreover common to find in primitive society that the woman is regarded as solely responsible for the failure of a couple to produce children. Impotence in man is recognized but not sterility. In patrilineal Bantu societies it is common practice for the man's agnatic[5] kinsmen to provide bride wealth for him to secure him a wife. If she proves barren the cattle or other objects are commonly returned or another girl provided from the same lineage group. In a matrilineal society of the Bemba type the situation is rather different. The children of a marriage belong legally to the girl's family and it is to their gain if she produces children. This fact may account for the great care and attention given to fertility rites for girls among such people. . . .

The salient features of Bemba social structure are also reflected in this ritual. The characteristic attitudes to authority in this very hierarchical society are expressed in ceremonies by which chiefs are created and maintained in their supernatural powers, and in those economic and other ceremonies performed by the chiefs themselves. (Richards 1956: 147–48 passim)

Here we have been introduced to three facets of social life which, it is suggested, all have a bearing on the rituals carried out between men and women. There is the fact that people (labor) are highly valued, and ceremonies to do with fertility express some of this value. We are told, however, that this is not enough to explain the particular preoccupation of the Bemba with the topic. We are then informed that the major social groups in Bemba, clans, are composed of men and women who are related through their mothers. A woman and her brother are thus both members of the same clan as their mother; the woman's children will be also, but not the man's children, who will belong to the clan of his wife. Links between people traced in this way are called "matrilineal." The Bemba put

---

4.   Bemba traditionally had no storable wealth—wealth was people, i.e., persons who could work for one.

5.   Agnatic. In this context the same as patrilineal, i.e., members of the clan or lineage group to which the husband and his father belong. "Matrilineal" and "patrilineal" are explained in the text.

great emphasis on the role of the woman, and Bemba girls go through a form of initiation or puberty ceremony which has fertility as a dominant theme. Bemba is one of many Bantu-speaking societies in Central Africa, and in those with similar matrilineal principles of organization we find similar fertility rites for girls; they are absent from many of the societies who reckon group relationships through fathers (patrilineal) instead. But girls' fertility rites practiced elsewhere do not show all of the same features that Bemba ones do—and here a third set of facts are adduced. Bemba have a ritual kingship and a centralized government, and the main religious (priestly) powers are in the hands of chiefs or headmen. Sexual precautions taken by a chief's wife are of significance for the whole community, because its well-being is bound up with the chief's well-being.

What has happened here? We started off with a description of a ceremony which all couples have to perform after intercourse. We end up in the realm of politics and chiefly hierarchies. Let us see, then, where our example from the Mae Enga will take us.

In exactly the same way as was described for the Bemba we learn what practices men and women adopt to escape the dangers of sexual contact, and we learn what the Mae Enga believe would otherwise happen. The anthropologist's summing up is succinct: Mae Enga beliefs and practices reflect "the anxiety of prudes to protect themselves from contamination by women" (Meggitt 1964: 22).

The ritual precautions which men take are but part of a complex of beliefs and behavior, which include a bachelor cult whose members are mainly pubertal boys and young men. This cult at one and the same time makes men attractive so that they will secure wives, and protects them against the actual dangers which close contact with women brings. The author links these facts about Mae Enga with features of other societies in the New Guinea Highlands.

In 1954, Read surveyed the ethnographic evidence from the Highlands of Australian New Guinea and Papua and . . . noted that the people . . . everywhere posses much the same kinds of social organization and material culture. They are sedentary horticulturalists, employing in most cases gardening techniques that support populations dense by Melanesian standards. There is commonly a great emphasis on the acquisition and circulation of valuables such as pigs and shells, whose public distributions enhance the prestige of individuals and of groups. Moreover, the vigorous oratory that accompanies such transactions is a particular expression of the prevailing aggressiveness of the Highlanders. It is not simply that the people are by nature individually quarrelsome or tend to inter-group belligerence; in addition there is in most significant social relationships an unmistakable component of bellicose competitiveness.

Read further asserted that an important and widespread manifestation of this aggressiveness is an antagonism pervading inter-sexual encounters. At one level this is reflected in the pan-Highlands rule of residence which separates men from their wives and takes boys early from the company of women, including their mothers. Often connected with this domiciliary demarcation is some form of male initiation and seclusion intended to strengthen and purify the growing youth, who is regarded as liable to pollution or injury through contact with women. . . .

[Ethnographies available since this date] not only confirm in a general way Read's assertion that relations between men and women in the New Guinea highlands are commonly tense or hostile; they also indicate that there are significant local or regional variations in both the form and the content of the relationship. (Meggitt 1904: 204–6 passim)

Beliefs and practices concerning interaction between men and women are related, then, not to an overt preoccupation with fertility or chiefly authority, as in the Bemba case, but to conflict, aggression, hostility.

Mae Enga clan groups are patrilineal—that is, a boy is normally a member of his father's clan, and marriage rules which prevent members of the same clan from marrying one another imply that women have to be brought in from other clans as wives.

Until recently clans fought constantly over scarce land resources, pig-thefts and failure to meet debts; and in any given clan most of the men lost in battle have been killed by its immediate neighbors. At the same time, because of the rugged mountainous terrain, propinquity has been a significant variable in determining actual marriage choices. . . . The Mae . . . say: "We marry the people we fight."

Typically, then, a man's wife and his mother come from those clans which are perennial enemies of his own clan and which are responsible for most of the deaths of his clansmen. But because the rule of clan exogamy disperses his female agnates at an early age, the only adult women with whom the man is in close regular contact and who exemplify for him the peculiarly feminine characteristics of menstruation and parturition are his own and his "brothers'" wives

and mothers—the women drawn from hostile groups. Here is a possible reason
for the Mae equation of femininity, sexuality and peril. (Meggitt 1964: 218)

Once again we have moved from intimate acts of purification which every couple perform to the world of politics. It is a very different world from Bemba:
the dangers of mishandling sexual relations for a Bemba couple lie in the threat
to their common health—the life of their children and their access to the spirits who will bless the wife with fertility. Moreover the precautions which one
couple takes are similar to and derive significance from the precautions which
someone in political authority must take—a chief or headman—on which depends a community's livelihood. The main dangers to Mae Enga are not to the
spouses or their children[6] but to the husband alone. Although husband and wife
carry out the dangerous act of sex together, it is the woman who is believed to
pollute her husband and the husband whose health is in jeopardy. In Enga, the
community's livelihood depends not on the actions of an office-holder such as
a chief but on the strength of each clan, and thus directly on the strength of
each individual (male) member of it. A wife who threatens her husband is like
an enemy threatening the clan. The idiom in which harm is perceived is not so
much that of supernatural disaster but of interpersonal hostility.

What is common to these two examples is that the anthropologists can only
"make sense" of acts which characterize relations between the sexes by considering many other aspects of the social life of the people as well. In both cases the
sexual precautions people take seem at first sight to be related to topics which are
naturally linked to sex. Bemba men desire fertility in women and hope that the
children they bear will remain healthy. Mae Enga bachelors want to cultivate a
comely appearance and be free from sickness themselves so that they will be able
to marry and have children. But then we realize that these precautions would not
be necessary if contact between sexually potent men and women had not in the
first place been labeled as dangerous. There is nothing natural about this.

For Bemba men and women, as for Mae Enga men and women, sexual
activities are not just private matters; they are not just the concern of individuals. The way in which individuals regulate their contacts with members of the
opposite sex are thought to have repercussions on the well-being of the wider
community. From our two examples we may cite the influence of chiefs or the

---

6.   Though there are circumstances in which a child's life is endangered, this does not
     seem to receive the cultural weighting that the possibility of harm to men does.

solidarity of male clansmen: these can be threatened by incorrect sexual conduct. This is the way Bemba or Mae Enga people would put it. An outsider might put it a bit differently. For this is what we were looking for—a society "using" relations between the sexes to make statements about other areas of social life.

What kind of statements are these? Look at the examples again and you will find that in both the handling of sexual matters is related to power. In the Bemba case, it is bound up with the influence of chiefs and of ancestral spirits; in the Enga case, it is bound up with the personal strength of male clan members. Bemba concentrate on the sexual act itself and on correct conduct between husband and wife, while Mae Enga see possible peril not only here but in all contacts between men and women, even mothers and their sons. Now it is all very well saying that there is a "connection between" the power of chiefs or of clansmen and relations between the sexes, or that the latter "makes statements" about the former. But do we really mean that the one thing symbolizes the other? And are we really dealing with a mythology?

MYTHOLOGIES AND SYMBOLS

We have got as far as suggesting that there can be a connection between the way relations between men and women are perceived and other social activities which have only an indirect bearing on sex. The crucial phrase here is "the way relations are *perceived*." Or, one might put it, the idiom in which relations are expressed. For example, a dominant idiom used to describe relations between Mae Enga men and women is that of antagonism. This is what myths are: ways of expressing things, idioms, dogmas, formulae, parables. But they are more than just images or metaphors or a matter of periphrasis. The word "myth" in anthropological writings is usually reserved for expositions whose purpose is to draw attention to particular characteristics of a subject, implying a process of classification and evaluation. In popular speech, the meaning of myth is dominated by one of its attributes—that it is an indirect statement, often understood as purporting to describe a real state of affairs but in unreal terms. "It is a myth!" has come to mean, "It is unreal or untrue."

Our two examples deal in myth. Mae Enga men believe that women's menstrual blood can kill them; Bemba believe that sexually active people can so pollute a fireplace that children die. To an outsider, these beliefs would qualify as myths in both senses—they are, in the popular sense, untrue and, in the anthropological sense, expressive of certain values. We have already suggested a principal value: that sexual activity is associated with notions of power. Restrictions and rules serve to *demarcate* this.

Myths can be used and manipulated. This how Mae Enga men seem to have used their myths:

> The men have won their battle and have relegated women to an inferior position. . . . A woman remains throughout her life a minor . . . denied any title to valuable property. She rarely participates in public affairs except to provide food for men or to give evidence in court cases. For the rest, she should simply look on passively and keep her opinions to herself. Indeed, men are apt to discourage their wives from attending such gatherings, on the ground that their proper place is in the garden or at home tending the pigs. . . . In short, Mae men expect, and in general receive, deference from their women, even to the extent that the latter should turn aside and lower their eyes whenever they encounter men walking on the same track. (Meggitt 1964: 220–21 passim)

As we shall see later, however, things are not so quite straightforward as they would seem. For the present, let us just remind ourselves that if Mae Enga men do subject their womenfolk to this subservience, they also walk, every day, in mortal fear of their "inferiors."

Myths frequently contain within them symbols. A symbol is an item, often a concrete, material object, which stands for something else, often an abstract notion, a value, an aspect of a relationship. It describes one thing in terms of another. Like myths, symbols make statements which put certain values on the thing being symbolized. They express emotions people have (or should have) toward these things. Whether we call something a myth or a symbol is largely a matter of analysis. Take the dogma of Mae Enga men: "females can harm males." In so far as it purports to be a statement about the physical capacities of females, in which Mae Enga men believe, an outsider could call it a myth. It is a fact Mae Enga men hold about women but one which does not correspond to physical reality. We can dismiss it as a lie; or we can say that Mae Enga men are afraid of something and this is how they express their fear. But supposing the anthropologist suggests that one of the origins of this fear is the fact that the women with whom men most often come into contact come from enemy groups, and enemy men certainly have to be feared because they (in reality) kill men of one's own group. Then we can look on the phrase "females can harm males" as a symbol—it stands for something else. It stands for: "men can be harmed by the groups from which women come." Wives originate in enemy clans, and wives are enemies too.

Mae Enga wives are not only enemies—they mother men's children and they are expected to remain for life with their husband's clan. But they are a constant reminder of the (true) enemies who do exist; they are symbolic enemies.

Some symbols are quite conscious in the minds of the actors. For example, in the bachelor cult which Mae Enga practice, special plants are tended by the cultists. Someone who attacks the principles of the cult by fornicating with girls will cause the plants to deteriorate. The plants symbolize the strength and purity which the bachelors hope to attain through the cult. Mae Enga are probably clear about this in their own minds, and the equation is a conscious one. The plants represent bachelor integrity. They become a focus for all the emotions which the cult members should feel when contemplating their own purified state and the dangers which will beset them in the outside world. However symbols can also be used without such awareness. Here, there is no middle term ("the plants *stand for* strength") but a direct equation ("women *are* harmful"). The emotions which women (as enemies, say) stand for become attached directly to the symbol (all women).

This leads to an important question. When symbols are not being manipulated consciously, how do we know what we are dealing with? The answer is of course that we have moved from the way in which particular people see their society or culture to the way an outsider sees it. In the first place ("the plants stand for strength") we are talking about how Mae Enga perceive their actions; in the second place ("hostile women stand for hostile enemies") we are talking about the kind of equation an anthropologist[7] might make in order to understand the emotions of the people he is studying.

We shall be concerned with both kinds of symbols in this book. The first raises no particular problems. The second raises many. For the first there are culturally correct equations. Cult plants represent strength, purity; they do not represent weakness, pollution. For the second, the outsider can never be quite sure of his equations. He can pick up clues. Why are Mae Enga men so afraid of menstrual blood—what does (if it does) blood symbolize to them? If the symbol is a concrete, material object, its own physical nature may provide him

---

7.   I am taking considerable liberties with the writings of Mervyn Meggitt here.

with clues (e.g., it is something secreted; it is associated with wounds). But if the symbol is *another relationship* he is in very deep water indeed.

A symbol implies some direction, that is, there is a thing X, and Y stands for it: and when natural things are used as symbols, the direction is clear. An eagle "stands for" (symbolizes) the ravenous power of an empire. It would be nonsense to say that the empire "stands for" an eagle. With many man-made things— a flag, the gold of a cigarette carton—the direction is in most situations also unambiguous. But if we suggest that relationships, or aspects of relationships, can be used as symbols we can only surmise at the direction. Let us look again at our example, "females can harm males," and the suggestion that perceiving women in this way is a symbol for "men can be harmed by the groups from which women come." One is suggesting that hostility between men has been transferred to the male-female relationship, and one could imagine reasons for this. For example, it might be the case that it went against other values for men to talk about being afraid of their enemies. Instead of admitting that you are afraid of other men (= your equals, but if you are openly afraid of them then you have acknowledged their superiority), you transfer this fear onto women (= your inferiors anyway, where the attribute of harm just goes to "prove" this further). But we do not really know that it is not the other way round. After all, Mae Enga believe that women do in reality have power to harm men. Suppose we start off with that fact as our baseline. How do they deal with this fact, for it is a fact to them? Men think women are hostile but obviously they cannot retaliate on the women themselves, for they depend on women not only as gardeners but as wives and mothers. So they show antagonism to the groups from which the women come, and kill the women's brothers if they cannot kill the women themselves. Hostility is transferred from the women onto their groups of origin. Relations between political enemies stand for relations between men and women.

Perhaps we should abandon the idea of symbolism in describing the connections between different parts of the culture, and just say there is some kind of parallel between relations between men and women and relations between enemies. However, there was a very good reason for raising the notion of symbolism, namely, that relations between the sexes are *both* natural *and* cultural. This needs expansion.

The physiological properties of men and women or the mechanics of sexual intercourse are "natural things." They can be alterable only within the narrowest limits. The biological characteristics of sex can be used as symbols in the same way as other things of nature can. Isn't this what is happening when Bemba chiefs have ceremonial intercourse with their wives in order to achieve blessings? Isn't the potency of the natural act being used to say something about the powers men hope they will have?

While the use of natural things or material objects as symbols does not present the same problems as the use of relationships as symbols, there is one problematical area. What can make something suitable for use as a symbol are its *perceived* characteristics—the properties which the people concerned attribute to it. The color of gold is used to symbolize wealth and luxury because gold itself is classified as a precious metal and associated with currency. Why should Mae Enga men choose a plant as a central symbol in their bachelor cult? It has innumerable properties—color, size, reproductive system, chromosome count—but the ones that are relevant to its choice as a symbol are ones Mae Enga see in it (perhaps the capacity for growth?). So, in a way we are wrong to draw an absolute contrast between natural and cultural symbols because we are not dealing strictly just with natural things in the first instance—we are dealing with natural things *as they are perceived.*

And this is true of the biology of sex. Everywhere people perceive biological facts in a particular light. Mae Enga men seem to be obsessed by the occurrence of the female menstrual cycle and attribute to the female sex *per se* the capacity to harm males. Bemba believe that a child is formed entirely from the mother's contribution: the husband is necessary to make the woman fertile but the child he procreates is formed of substances from the mother's body and belongs to its mother's clan. Relations between sexual partners, between "men" and "women," between mothers and their sons, are seen in certain ways. As soon as we come down to what a particular society knows or holds about biological facts we are dealing with interpretations of these facts. Writers[8] have suggested that we distinguish between sex and gender. Sex should refer to the biological characteristics of the male and female; gender to the social classifications of people as masculine or feminine, that is, to male and female as they are perceived.

But by way of interpolation it is only right to point out that this form of analysis is itself a cultural construct: that is, a scientific viewpoint teaches us to classify things according to their real, material, empirically demonstrable

---

8.　See, for example, Kate Millett ([1969] 1971); for an excellent exposition of the relationship between sex and gender see Ann Oakley (1972).

properties, and to regard other attributes as metaphysical. The realities of the chemical composition of men and women's bodies, the functions of hormones, the genetic determinants of mental powers, these are endlessly described. We regard these things as basic facts. The emphasis of this sentence should probably be on *we regard* rather than on basic facts. Yet the notion of a "fact" (and especially a scientific fact) is so useful that one cannot get on without it. And before we start getting superior-minded about our ability to distinguish sex and gender, we should remember that creating distinctions of this kind is part of our own cultural apparatus.

David Schneider, in his account of American kinship, makes just this point. He is concerned with the place of sexual intercourse (a "fact of nature") in the thinking of Americans, as a symbol "in terms of which members of the family are defined and differentiated and in terms of which each member of the family's proper mode of conduct is defined" (Schneider 1968: 33). He writes:

> It will be helpful to begin with a few simple distinctions. First, sexual intercourse can be seen as a set of *biological facts*. These are part of the world. They exist, and they have effects.
>
> Second, there are certain cultural notions and constructs *about* biological facts. The example *par excellence* in American culture is the life-sciences—biology, zoology, biochemistry, and so on. This is a cultural system explicitly attuned to those biological facts as such. It discovers them, studies them, organizes what it regards as facts into a system. But it remains a system of cultural constructs which should not be confused with the biological facts themselves. (Schneider 1968: 114)

The line between what is natural and what is cultural is drawn in different places depending on the viewpoint of the observer. An outsider looking at Bemba society would say that the natural aspects of Bemba sexuality are certain biological, genetically determined characteristics of sex. Bemba notions of maternity and paternity, like Bemba notions of clan membership and the sharing of substances, are products of Bemba culture. The Bemba, on the other hand, might well regard their beliefs about procreation as natural facts, and see these as giving rise to social rules (culture), concerning, for example, the recruitment of individuals to clans.

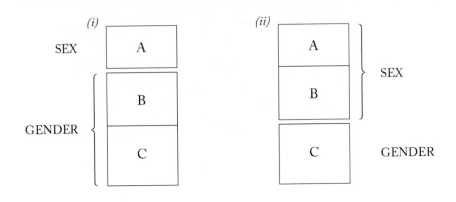

A: biology

B: beliefs about sexuality

C: social rules

Figure 1. "An outsider (i) would draw the line according to his own conventions between A (natural givens) and the rest (B and C).[9] An insider (ii) might make no distinction between A and B (B is his way of thinking about A) but separate these off from the social arrangements (C) to which he sees them as giving rise."

In drawing on relations between the sexes as a source of symbolism, a society may use any of these three areas. It may use biological facts as an outsider would recognize them (A): for example, sexual intercourse is a necessary if not suffi-cient[10] condition for procreation, and it is this fact which Bemba seem to use in stipulating that in order for blessings to fall on the community those in author-ity (who are regarded as responsible for the community's well-being) must have ceremonial intercourse with their wives at the beginning of new ventures. It may use biological facts as they are perceived in the society (B). For the Mae Enga,

---

9.   My A here stands for what a Western observer would regard as the natural, biological facts. This covers both of Schneider's distinctions: for such a person thinks of the reality of the biological facts in terms of the science which describes them. He would say chromosomes really exist—whereas Schneider is pointing out that something does exist, and one system of classification calls these chromosomes.

10.   Whether conception follows after intercourse depends, of course, on other factors (e.g., the fertility of the partners). But intercourse is necessary before this becomes relevant.

relations between men and women can symbolize notions of antagonism, of contrary interests, of hostility, as distinct from the kind of common kinship and solidarity which is found among the male members of a clan—they can do this, because through their menstrual cycle and other attributes women are regarded as "naturally" threatening to males. Finally, other characteristics of relations between men and women (C) may be used in a symbolic way. The subordination of the women to men in public or domestic life ("women are nothing but children grown up") may itself be a source of symbolism: a wife's duty is to attend to her husband in the same way as mankind should render supplication to God.

Let us return to the point raised earlier, that to identify something as a symbol entails a notion of direction, that a symbol is something which "stands for" something else. Now as far as natural properties (A) are concerned, such as anatomy or the behavior of chemical substances, the item chosen as a symbol is in itself not altered by its being used in this way in people's minds. The composition of gold is not affected because people worship it. But when we talk about something that is already in people's minds, such as the way they perceive facts (B) or classify social behavior (C), then using these things as symbols becomes another dimension of the things themselves. Such a feedback process obscures the identification of a single direction. Perhaps sexual intercourse in Bemba is regarded as "hot" and potent partly *because* in some contexts it symbolizes wide-reaching powers fundamental to the total prosperity of the community. In other words, if it were not used as a symbol of power, perhaps Bemba would not stress to quite the same extent the potency of the sex act itself.

One may expect repercussions on behavior, too. Mae Enga regard antipathy between males and females as a natural product of their sexual characteristics. It equally holds that their ascription of gender has become structured around concepts of duality and opposition. If the opposition of masculine and feminine natures can symbolize the conflicting interests of enemy groups, an identity between women and enemies must also affect relations between men and women themselves—not only in the way the other sex in seen but also in encounters which bring them together. Actual enmity between males may make men antagonistic when they interact with women. The response to this antagonism will reinforce the correctness of their classification of women as enemies and thereby the appropriateness of the symbol.

WHO KILLED COCK ROBIN?

Mae Enga remind us of another aspect of sexual mythologies. We can use the phrase to refer to the symbols which depict relations between men and women, and to the use of these relations as symbols themselves. But sexual mythology does not just mean mythologies *about* sex; it can mean also a set of myths *belonging to* one sex (in its attitudes toward the other). Here we could replace "sexual" by "male" or "female." In women's liberation writings the demonstration that we are the dupes of a sexual mythology is the demonstration of the existence of male myth about females.

The previous excerpts on men's problems from Dunbar and Leghorn suggest that the prevalent myth of male superiority actually has the effect of producing an opposite state of affairs—history and training develops in men a serious deficiency, which is in fact weakness. They are weak because they fear the people they oppress. The idiom in which this is expounded is a class or a racist one, and indeed analogies with class and race are made explicitly. What is happening here is that the male myth is being taken at face value. That is, male claims to superiority are treated seriously. They are not just regarded as fanciful but as ideas which have to be destroyed, devils to be exorcised. The authors do this by showing that the myths are wrong (it is not women who are really the weak ones, but men) and in addition do the men no good (they contribute to male paranoia), and could be replaced by attitudes (a conscious desire to change the unequal relations between men and women) which would be myth-free.

For the writers talk of male supremacy as a disease and as a problem which must be dealt with in material and not fantasy terms (Dunbar and Leghorn 1970: 313, 315). That is, male supremacy (i.e., the myth of male supremacy) is an abnormality for which there is a cure, a fantasy which men can be freed from if they will face "the facts." These facts are that (contrary to male beliefs) women are men's equals. Now there are perfectly good reasons for a male myth to be attacked in this way, for this particular myth is seen to uphold and validate a social order which results in actual oppression of women. One way in which to change the social order is to prove that the myths are not valid, and to state that anyone who continues to believe in them is guilty of a crime against nature. I do not here wish to discuss the relationship between male mythology and domination but point out that in women's liberation writings male-constructed mythologies are being dogmatically challenged. And they are often (though not always) challenged in roughly the same idioms, the same terms and phrases, which men themselves use. Sometimes there is even an explicit countermythology, the female version.

Roxanne Dunbar, as we saw above, elaborated on this in a further comment. This started with the premise that feminism is a valid, and in this sense equal, alternative to the masculine ideology. But she goes on further to state that what women want is not equality in the world as men have built it in the present but a place in a world which will have taken into account the true contributions women can make. For women have qualities superior from a human point of view to those men evince at the moment, which if allowed to determine the social order will produce a better society. A woman's version of the world, in short, would be a better place.

Now the articulateness of these criticisms is unusual. Indeed, many present-day writings suggest that there has been only a gradual development of the idea of making a challenge at all, from a time in the past when the myths were unquestionably accepted and when women did not realize they were being oppressed. Needless to say, that one is being oppressed can be "realized" in different ways. What is new nowadays is probably not so much that women are aware of their disadvantages in a male world but that they are speaking about their relations with men in the same way as men used to speak of their relations with women. They are fighting men on their own ground.

In many societies men lay claims to superiority and act as though they were dominant. But the more usual picture is for women to fight (if one may put it like that) not on the same grounds but on different ones. Recall the Wogeo of New Guinea. The world would be a better place, says an American woman, if the men in it were not like men as they are now. The world would be a better place, say Wogeo men, if there were no women (i.e., if the women in it were not like women as they are now). In fact, Ian Hogbin suggests that in spite of contrasts in their economic tasks, allegiances, rights, liabilities, and roles, Wogeo men and women, in a comprehensive view, "are of nearly equal status" (Hogbin 1970: 188). Indeed, unlike Mae Enga, it is not Wogeo men alone who are afraid of too much contact with women—women are equally afraid of too much contact with men. "The established doctrine is that the members of each sex group would be safe and invulnerable, healthy and prosperous, if only they were to keep to themselves and refrain from mixing with members of the other sex group" (Hogbin 1970: 87). We are not told whether these are doctrines which originated first among men or among women; indeed, we could hardly know. We do know that all the Wogeo used to accept them. Nevertheless, the equality here does not prevent men from being the prominent ones in public affairs (in the wider political sphere women are powerless) and claiming that women are subordinate to them.

> Wogeo sexual groups are in balanced opposition. Balanced they are in the sense of being mutually dependent and of nearly equal status, with men having only a slight edge. And they are also in opposition. Men continue to claim authority and to feel that they have the right to be high-handed; and they think that their spouses ought to be faithful. But they also know that troubles tend to arise if they become too domineering, and that few wives, if any, refrain from taking an occasional lover. As for the women themselves, they maintain that their wishes should be respected on account of their importance in the economy and the vital part they play in the social system. But they have to smother their resentments at male pretensions and keep their aggressive impulses concealed, for direct and open retaliation for unfair treatment presents difficulties. They can indulge in adulterous intrigues, but it would be unwise for them to flaunt the liaisons in public. Pollution theories provide a solution. These theories give strong men proof that women are inherently inferior and weak women a means of inflicting punishment on men. (Hogbin 1970: 98–99)

How do Wogeo women react to male pretensions? We have two examples here. One is the surreptitious flouting of the control of individual men (husbands) through taking lovers; the other is acceptance of the theories of pollution which in fact gives them a weapon against males as a sex. Wogeo women also conduct ceremonies for girls, which although less elaborate, parallel boys' initiation rites. Here perhaps we have evidence of a counterculture, a countermythology: that is, women have their own version, composed of some of the same elements which make up the men's version.

Yet there are also situations in Wogeo in which women's reactions to the way men behave are on quite different grounds. They do not in general say that men are wrong in excluding women from participation in public affairs:

> The women's answer is to make fun of the men's self-importance. At a certain stage in a young girl's coming-of-age celebrations . . . the women adjourn to a mountain top and there mock the initiation rite for pubescent lads, something they are supposed to know nothing about. After an interval the men storm the place with sticks and stones and drive them down, but during that evening,

unabashed despite the bruises, they hold a feast of their own and again make references to sacred ceremonies from which they are absolutely excluded. On this occasion the men pay no attention and stolidly go about their business as though not a sound is to be heard. (Hogbin 1970: 87)

What we find then is mockery and derision. Women don't gate-crash male ceremonies: making fun of male superiority during one of their own ceremonies is enough to drive men to fury, to the point of provoking attack.

There are other societies, and Mae Enga is one, in which women do not even hold public ceremonies of their own, and apparently lack anything in the way of an identifiable countermythology, at least one using the same kinds of terms as male myths. For any kind of challenge, we would have to look elsewhere. This leads to a more serious point. Often in anthropologists' descriptions of how a society sees itself we are dealing really with how men see social arrangements. We can put this suspicion more generally and say that the activity of myth-making as such is perhaps something men rather than women are prone to do[11]—and I mean myth here in its widest sense, taking into account the dogmas and values on which men see their social institutions based.

The problem of women has not been solved by social anthropologists. . . . Here is a human group that forms about half of any population. . . . Yet however

---

11. After a close review of current biological information, Corinne Hutt (1972) writes,

We have seen that the male is physically stronger but less resilient, he is more independent, adventurous and aggressive, he is more ambitious and competitive, he has greater spatial, numerical and mechanical ability, he is *more likely to construe the world in terms of objects, ideas and theories.* The female at the outset possesses those sensory capacities which facilitate interpersonal communion; physically and psychologically she matures more rapidly, her verbal skills are precocious and proficient, she is more nurturant, affiliative, more consistent, and is likely to construe the world in personal, moral and aesthetic terms. (Hutt 1972: 132, italics mine)

She goes on to point out that overlying these biological bases are a multitude of social and cultural influences which operate from the moment of birth. Ann Oakley (1972), however, in a survey which covers much of the same ground, questions the causal nature of the relationship between types of perception and biological factors and points to parent-child interaction as exceedingly influential in the formation of an individual's mental apparatus. The debate itself does not concern us. However it arises, it would seem that men, as a category, tend to organize their perception of the world differently from women. The suggestion that this is likely to be the case in many cultures is indeed of interest.

apparently competently the female population has been studied in any particular society, the results in understanding are surprisingly slight. . . .

At the level of "observation" in fieldwork, the behaviour of women has, of course, like that of men, been exhaustively plotted. . . . When we come to that second "meta" level of fieldwork, the vast body of debate, discussion, question and answer, that social anthropologists really depend upon to give conviction to their interpretations, there is a real imbalance. We are, for practical purposes, in a male world. The study of women is on a level little higher than the study of the ducks and fowls they commonly own—a mere bird-watching indeed. . . . It is the very inarticulateness of women that is the technical part of the problem they present. In most societies the ethnographer shares this problem with its male members. The brave failure . . . of even women anthropologists to surmount it really convincingly . . . suggests an obvious conclusion. Those trained in ethnography evidently have a bias towards the kinds of model that men are ready to provide (or to concur in) rather than towards any that women might provide. If the men appear "articulate" compared with the women, it is a case of like speaking to like. To pursue the logic where it leads us: if ethnographers (male and female) want only what the men can give, I suggest it is because the men consistently tend, when pressed, to give a bounded model of society such as ethnographers are attracted to. . . .

Ethnographers report that women cannot be reached so easily as men: they giggle when young, snort when old, reject the question, laugh at the topic, and the like. The male members of a society frequently see the ethnographer's difficulties as simply a caricature of their own daily case. . . . We have here, then, what looked like a technical problem: the difficulty of dealing ethnographically with women. We have, rather, an analytical problem of this sort: if the models of a society made by most ethnographers tend to be models derived from the male portion of that society, how does the symbolic weight of that other mass of persons—half or more of a normal human population, as we have accepted—express itself? . . .

The fact is that no one could come back from an ethnographic study of "the X," having talked only *to* women and *about* men, without professional comment and some self-doubt. The reverse can and does happen constantly. It is not enough to see this merely as another example of "injustice to women." I prefer to suggest that the models of society that women can provide are not of the kind acceptable at first sight to men or to ethnographers, and specifically that, unlike either of these sets of professionals, they do not so readily see society bounded from nature. They lack the metalanguage for its discussion. To put it more simply: they will not necessarily provide a model for society as a unit that will contain both men and themselves. They may indeed provide a model in which women and nature are outside men and society. (Ardener 1972: 135–39 passim)

Edwin Ardener is in effect suggesting that in producing the kinds of descriptions of societies which fit into anthropological theories (especially theories about groups and group boundaries), ethnographers of either sex have themselves a "male" approach (a myth) and respond to the male myths of the people they study.

This would be very hard indeed to disprove. For our own purposes we should note that, in the accounts of societies with which we are dealing, we are likely to find an imbalance in stereotypes. Women (as a category) will seem to be more the attention of explicit social attitudes than men (as a category), because we have better information on men's notions about relations between the sexes than we do on women's notions. We shall inevitably, then, be dealing with a male view of things. In social life men usually have interests far more wide-ranging than women's: they represent *themselves* to themselves many ways. The category "men" is endlessly split up (workers/magnates/priests/hobos/weaklings). When they come to representing interaction between the sexes this can be done through bestowing characteristics onto women as a block, as a whole. The necessity to make such a definition perhaps arises, as Ardener suggests, from men's tendency to create bounded constructs which will include, as well as everything else, their own characteristics as a sex necessarily in contradistinction to the other sex.

Hence we more often find statements of the kind "woman are this or that . . ." than we do "men are this or that . . ." Women are likely to be treated, to be thought about, on the basis of their sex first, other attributes coming second. Simone de Beauvoir said this in 1949:

Humanity is male and man defines woman not in herself, but as relative to him; she is not regarded as an autonomous being. . . . And she is simply what man decrees; thus she is called "the sex," by which is meant that she appears essentially to the male as a sexual being. For him she is sex—absolute sex, no less. She is defined and differentiated with reference to man and not he with reference to her; she is the incidental, the inessential as opposed to the essential. He is the Subject, he is the Absolute—she is the Other.

The category of the *Other* is as primordial as consciousness itself. In the most primitive societies, in the most ancient mythologies, one finds the expression of a duality—that of the Self and the Other. . . . But the very fact that woman is *the Other* tends to cast suspicion upon all the justifications that men have ever been able to provide for it. These have all too evidently been dictated by men's interest. A little known feminist of the seventeenth century, Poulain de la Barre, put it this way: "All that has been written about women by men should be suspect, for the men are at once judge and party to the lawsuit." . . .

A myth always implies a subject who projects his hopes and his fears towards a sky of transcendence. Women do not set themselves up as Subject and hence have erected no virile myth in which their projects are reflected; they have no religion or poetry of their own: they still dream through the dreams of men. (de Beauvoir 1972: 16, 21, 174)

CHAPTER TWO

Stereotypes

Relations between the sexes are a powerful source of symbolism. But for contrasts between "men" and "women" to be useful it must first be possible to define what men are like and what women are like. In addition to the perception of biological differences is the tendency to assign personal and social qualities, characteristics, and capacities to the sexes in a way which distinguishes all men from all women. This process creates two categories or classes: the members of one sex are seen to share a range of characteristics which are different from those typifying the other sex. Such characteristics are essentially sexual stereotypes. These will be stereotypes about what men are "really" like, how women can be expected to react, what is likely to happen in certain situations when men interact with women. They are not rules about how men and women should behave, though rules may come into it, but ways of looking at the behavior of men and women which pick out this trait as typical of one sex, that trait as typical of the other.

The formation of stereotypes is an extremely important step in the building up of a sexual mythology. Stereotypes can be related to men and women in their everyday activities, to the tasks they perform and the way they do them. They are a kind of filter through which the actions of men and women are seen. "Women are capricious" is a stereotype. "Men are strong" is, in many cultures, another one. The acts and behavior of individuals can be fitted into these—"Oh, it is a woman's privilege to change her mind"; or "The least the man about the house can do is mend the fuses." In real life men and women confront each other in myriad situations, in multiple roles. Stereotypes relating to the sexes give a patterning to these. They encourage people to categorize the behavior of others, to make Mrs. R's acts "typical of a woman," or Mr. Z's statements "all you could expect from a man." The most significant effect of this is to keep alive the notion that "men" and "women" can indeed be contrasted in block terms. If this is a crucial step toward the formation of a sexual mythology, it is also a necessary condition for using relations between the sexes as a symbol.

The previous chapter pointed out two different areas of facts which can be drawn upon to provide symbols. There are the sexual functions of men and women—what the society in question considers as the natural or biological properties of the sexes; and the facts of gender—the cultural roles, spheres, and types of behavior assigned to each sex. Stereotypes are the everyday expressions of gender-thinking.

MAKING MEN AND WOMEN

In some societies very explicit attention is given to defining persons as male or female at certain stages of life. The threshold of adulthood is often an occasion for this and ceremonies are held at about the time of a child's puberty, which direct everyone else's attention to the kind of person the adult should be. Although various aspects of the adult's roles may be enunciated, the definition of the person's sex (including here "gender") is often given prominence. For the ascription of sex is a peg on which other things can be hung—"Since he is a man, he will do so-and-so. . ."; "As a woman her jobs are. . . ." More than this, those who go through the ceremonies may be expected to acquire some of the personality characteristics of the gender ascribed to them, so that they become "like men" or "like women" not just through the tasks they perform but more generally by their whole bearing.

Let us go back to Papua New Guinea for a moment, this time to the Sepik River. The Iatmul people live on the middle reaches of the river. This is what their men are like.

From whatever side we approach the culture, whatever institutions we study, we find [a] contrast between the life of the men and that of the women. Broadly, we may say that the men are occupied with the spectacular, dramatic, and violent activities which have their centre in the ceremonial house, while the women are occupied with the useful and necessary routines of food-getting, cooking, and rearing children—activities which centre around the dwelling house and the gardens. . . .

An important man on entering the ceremonial house is conscious that the public eye is upon him and he responds to this stimulus by some sort of over-emphasis. He will enter with a gesture and call attention to his presence with some remark. Sometimes he will tend towards a harsh swagger and over-consciousness of pride, and sometimes he will respond with buffoonery. But in whichever direction he reacts, the reaction is theatrical and superficial. Either pride or clowning is accepted as respectable and normal behaviour. . . .

This self-consciousness is present even at times when there is no specific formal or ritual activity taking place, but it is enormously more marked when the men are assembled in the ceremonial house for some debate or ritual per-formance. . . . The tone of the debates is noisy, angry and, above all, ironical. The speakers work themselves up to a high pitch of superficial excitement, all the time tempering their violence with histrionic gesture and alternating in their tone between harshness and buffoonery. (Bateson [1936] 1958: 123–26 passim)

Initiation ceremonies bring home to the boys what it is to be male.

In the first week of their seclusion, the novices are subjected to a great variety of cruel and harsh tricks . . . and for every trick there is some ritual pretext. And it is still more significant of the ethos of the culture that the bullying of the novices is used as a context in which the different groups of the initiators can make pride points against each other. One [group] of the initiators decided that the novices had been bullied as much as they could stand and were for omitting one of the ritual episodes. The other [group] then began to brag that the lenient ones were afraid of the fine fashion in which *they* would carry out the bullying; and the lenient party hardened their hearts and performed the episode with some extra savagery.

The little boy's introduction into the life of the ceremonial house is con-ducted on such lines as these and it is one which fits him admirably for the irresponsible histrionic pride and buffoonery which is characteristic of that in-stitution. As in other cultures a boy is disciplined so that he may be able to wield authority, so on the Sepik he is subjected to irresponsible bullying and ignominy so that he becomes what we should describe as an over-compensating, harsh man—whom the natives describe as a "hot" man. (Bateson [1936] 1958: 131)

What about the women?

> In the everyday life of the women there is no such emphasis on pride and spectacular appearance. The greater part of their time is spent on the necessary economic labours connected with the dwelling house—food-getting, cooking and attention to babies—and these activities are not carried out publicly and in big groups, but privately and quietly. . . . Compared with the proud men, the women are unostentatious. They are jolly and readily co-operative while the men are so obsessed with points of pride that co-operation is rendered difficult. But it must not be supposed that the women are mere submissive mice. A woman should know her own mind and be prepared to assert herself. . . .
>
> For the most part, the women exhibit a system of emotional attitudes which contrasts sharply with that of the men. While the latter behave almost consistently as though life were a splendid theatrical performance—almost a melodrama—with themselves in the centre of the stage, the women behave most of the time as though life were a cheerful cooperative routine in which the occupations of food-getting and child-rearing are enlivened by the dramatic and exciting activities of the men. (Bateson [1936] 1958: 142–48 passim)

The observer perceives marked contrasts in the reported behavior of men and women. We have seen that Iatmul ceremonies for boys themselves emphasize the stance which men adopt, and it is a stance which men take as a sex in opposition to women. The ceremonial house, such an important institution in the lives of men, is exclusive—it separates men from women. Women are an audience at male initiation ceremonies, passive, not active participants. Simply subjecting them to the ceremonies defines boys as very different beings from girls, who are not treated in at all the same way. Iatmul make a radical distinction between the sexes, then, in terms of the kinds of behavior appropriate to each. As an observer, the anthropologist also notes the different demeanor of men and women he has seen. He can say that in this culture men and women do behave differently. In the case of males he can further point to the way their behavior is eloquently reinforced in the ceremonies which out of boys create men. Iatmul men want to make the boys like themselves, as they see themselves, as "hot" and proud. But women do not go through the same kinds of ceremonies. How are women defined, then?

Part of the answer has already been given: they are defined by default, by their exclusion from the affairs of the ceremonial house, by the mundane tasks they have to do, by the fact that they are not men. However there are other ceremonies in which men publicly and dramatically represent the actions of women. Here we can look for definitions perhaps. What is interesting about these is that elements of behavior which men pick upon to express what it is like to be female are not those which strike the anthropologist as most typical of actual women as they go about their everyday activities. We have been given a picture of Iatmul women as jolly and cooperative, to a degree self-sufficient and pragmatic. They are on the whole cheerful in demeanor and within the household have considerable power and authority. A woman's husband depends on her, for it is she who feeds the pigs and catches the fish from which wealth is derived.

When men imitate women, observe how they depict them. This is a description of one ceremony in which two men dressed themselves up as the "mothers" of a boy whom they tried to find:

> They put on the most filthy old tousled skirts such as only the ugliest and most decrepit widows might wear, and like widows they were smeared with ashes. Considerable ingenuity went into this costuming, and all of it was directed towards creating an effect of utter decrepitude. On their heads they wore tattered old capes which were beginning to unravel and to fall to pieces with age and decay. Their bellies were bound with string like those of pregnant women. In their noses they wore, suspended in place of the little triangles of mother-of-pearl shell which women wear on festive occasions, large triangular lumps of old sago pancakes, the stale orts of a long past meal.
>
> The "mothers" wandered about the village in this way looking for their "child". . . and from time to time in high-pitched, cracked voices they enquired of the by-standers to learn where the young man had gone. "We have a fowl to give to the young man.". . . Actually the [boy] during this performance had either left the village or hidden himself. As soon as he found out that [the two] were going to shame themselves in this way, he went away to avoid seeing the spectacle of their degraded behaviour. (Bateson [1936] 1958: 12–13)

Before we can understand why shame should be involved, we need to know something of the contexts of these ceremonies. We need to know something, too, about Iatmul society. Iatmul men belong to their father's clan. Indeed, a child is stated to be a reincarnation of his grandfather (his father's father) so that the clan is seen as a kind of perpetual physical unit. But Iatmul ideas of conception also show us that the physical contribution of the mother is not ignored.

> It is supposed that the bones of the child are a product of the father's semen, while its flesh and blood (somewhat less important) are provided by the mother's menstrual blood. This idea is carried logically to the conclusion that the afterbirth, lacking bones, is therefore the child of the mother only. (Bateson [1936] 1958: 42)

This theory, about the respective contributions of the parents, does more than just provide an explanation of how babies are made: it is used as a rationale for certain types of behavior among adults. Any offspring of a marriage has links with not only his father's but also his mother's clan, and these are maintained throughout life. A boy can expect that the men of his mother's clan will take an interest in him. And there are standardized situations in which this interest is expressed. For example, whenever a person (of either sex) attains some achievement—kills for the first time, makes a new tool, plays a musical instrument—he is honored for it. The person who honors him is likely to be someone from his mother's clan.[1]

The celebration of the achievement is called *naven* and the two men described earlier who dressed up in tattered old women's clothes were from the clan of a young man's mother. (They called themselves his "mothers.") The young man had made a large canoe for the first time in his life, and they were honoring him. Unable to find the boy the pair had to content themselves with wandering around the village.

> Finally they came to the big canoe which he had made—the achievement which they were celebrating. They then collapsed into the canoe and for a few moments lay in it apparently helpless and exhausted . . . with their legs wide apart in . . . attitudes . . . found . . . amusing. Gradually they recovered and picked up their paddles, and sitting in the canoe in the bow and stern (women sit to paddle a canoe, but men stand), they slowly took it for a short voyage on the lake. When they returned they came ashore and hobbled off. The performance was over and they went away and washed themselves and put on their ordinary garments. [A] fowl was finally given to the [boy] and it became his duty to make a return present of shell valuables to his [uncles] at some later date. (Bateson [1936] 1958: 13–14)

---

1. There are many variations, and the account here is necessarily simplified.

This honoring, then, consisted of men adopting the attire of the opposite sex, with the obvious intent to demean themselves and concluded with a payment from their nephew in return for the food he had been given. Why should the men dress up as women, and why when they do so should they choose to appear disreputable and abase themselves?

The people of someone's father's clan and mother's clan are related to each other through marriage. They are in-laws to one another. Even before children are born to the marriage, the union itself has created a link between the two clans, and it is the woman who is seen as the intermediary. She leaves one clan as a sister to associate with another clan as a wife. Iatmul clans could thus be looked upon as being linked by women. Any privileges or claims which the woman's natal group has on the group of her husband, or which a person's mother's brothers have on their sister's children, arise in a sense because of the relationship created when the woman married. Men of the woman's (the mother's) clan dress up as women to honor their nephew because it is through a woman that they are related to him. By miming the actions of women, by pretending to be "mothers," the men remind the boy of the kinds of ties he has with their clan.

In doing so, they make use of stereotypes. The men do not just dress up in female clothes: they imitate gestures and demeanor. They adopt a waddling, ungainly gait.

> In this disgusting costume and with absolutely grave faces . . . the two "mothers" hobbled about the village each using as a walking stick a short shafted paddle such as women use. Indeed, even with this support, they could hardly walk, so decrepit were they. The children of the village greeted these figures with screams of laughter and thronged around the two "mothers," following wherever they went and bursting into new shrieks whenever the "mothers," in their feebleness, stumbled and fell and, falling, demonstrated their femaleness by assuming on the ground grotesque attitudes with their legs widespread. (Bateson [1936] 1958: 12)

The actors are driving home the point that it is women who link groups: the relationship between mothers and children stands for (symbolizes) social arrangements between clans. And they drive home the point by playing on stereotypes of feminine behavior.

They are doing something else as well, and the element of parody which arises when the stereotypes are put into action gives us a clue. The men are also surely saying something about relations between the sexes as such.[2] They dress up in female clothes and choose filthy ones; they walk around like women, and imitate old, enfeebled widows. It is hard to resist the conclusion that for a man to behave as though he were a woman degrades himself (conversely, if he wants to degrade himself he pretends he is a woman) and women are therefore to be despised. A man cannot adopt a woman's role without also making a disparaging comment on it. Let us look more closely at what this means. In this society it is women who readily give praise: praise-giving is an aspect of a mother's role in particular.

> The attitude [of mothers] is one of humbleness and abnegation of self in pride and joy at the achievement of the offspring. . . . [This] attitude of pride is dramatically combined with modesty and self-abnegation in the *naven* ceremonies when the [uncle] wears filthy female garments, shaming himself to express his pride in his [nephew]. Indeed, . . . we may conclude that a great part of the [uncle's] behaviour in *naven* is an exaggerated statement of this particular aspect of maternity, the mother's self-abnegation combined with pride in the boy. (Bateson [1936] 1958: 76–77)

The men who honor the boy identify with the boy's mother but at the same time express contempt for what the identification forces them to do. They are making a value-statement about women's roles—they are expressing distaste.

This is a society in which transvesticism is on occasion adopted by women as well. What happens when women dress up as men? Their stance is dramatically different.

> The majority of the women, when they put on the garments of men, wear the smartest of male attire. . . . [On one occasion] their faces were painted white with sulphur, as is the privilege of homicides, and in their hands they carried the decorated lime boxes used by men and serrated lime sticks with pendant tassels whose number is a tally of men killed by the owner. This costume was very becoming

2. Within the single *naven* performance we thus find the two facets of sexual mythology: the use of relations between the sexes to say things about other areas of social life (the links between clans related by marriage are symbolized in stereotypes of relations between the sexes, especially between mothers and sons); and the representation of relations between the sexes by other symbols (here, the symbolic use of clothing to make a judgment about what females are like).

to the women and was admired by the men. In it the women were very proud of themselves. They walked about flaunting their feathers and grating their lime sticks in the boxes, producing the loud sound which men use to express anger, pride and assertiveness. Indeed so great was their pleasure in this particular detail of male behaviour that the husband of one of them, when I met him on the day following the performance, complained sorrowfully that his wife had worn away all the serrations on his lime stick so that it would no longer make a sound. (Bateson [1936] 1958: 14–15)

Far from denigrating the fact that they are acting like men, women seem to take enormous pride in their display. Like the men, the women draw on stereotypes of the behavior characteristic of the opposite sex but seem to give it a positive rather than a negative value.

Gregory Bateson, the anthropologist who worked among the Iatmul in the 1930s, has this to say:

Let us consider the contexts in which partial transvesticism occurs, namely, in the case of women who take part in spectacular ceremonies. . . . The normal life of Iatmul women is quiet and unostentatious, while that of the men is noisy and ostentatious. When women take part in spectacular ceremonial they are doing something which is foreign to the norms of their own existence, but which is normal for men—and so we find them adopting for these special occasions bits of the culture of the men, holding themselves like men and wearing ornaments which are normally only worn by men. . . .

We can recognise in the *naven* situation conditions which might influence either sex towards transvesticism. The situation may be summed up by saying that a child has accomplished some notable feat and its relatives are to express, in a public manner, their joy in this event. This situation is one which is foreign to the normal settings of the life of either sex. The men by their unreal spectacular life are perfectly habituated to the "ordeal" of public performance. But they are not accustomed to the free expression of vicarious personal emotion. Anger and scorn they can express with a good deal of over-compensation, and joy and sorrow they can express when it is their own pride which is enhanced or abased; but to express joy in the achievements of another is outside the norms of their behaviour.

In the case of the women the position is reversed. Their co-operative life has made them capable of the easy expression of unselfish joy and sorrow, but it has not taught them to assume a public spectacular role.

Thus the *naven* situation contains two components, the element of public display and the element of vicarious personal emotion; and each sex, when it is placed by culture in this situation, is faced by one component which is easily acceptable, while the other component is embarrassing and smacks rather of situations normal to the life of the opposite sex. This embarrassment we may, I think, regard as a dynamic force which pushes the individual towards transvesticism—and to a transvesticism which the community has been able to accept and which in course of time has become a cultural norm. . . .

Lastly we may consider the adoption of widow's weeds by the [uncle] and the wearing by the women of the best masculine ornaments obtainable. The former is no doubt a buffooning expression of the men's distaste for the women's ethos. . . . In shaming himself he is, incidentally, expressing his contempt for the whole ethos of those who express grief so easily.

The women on the other hand have no discernible contempt for the proud male ethos. It is the ethos appropriate to spectacular display, and in the *naven* they adopt as much of that ethos as possible—and even exaggerate it. (Bateson [1936] 1958: 201–2)

The main point to draw out is that these manipulations obviously depend on a categorization of what men are like / what women are like. Stereotypes about the way males and females behave can be used to such effect because they are so clearly defined. Moreover, the stereotypes do not just describe behavior—they comment on it, evaluate it. So when a Iatmul man dresses up like a woman he makes a caricature, a creature to be despised, not at all like the jolly, actual women with their considerable influence in everyday affairs.

IDEALS AND DEVIANTS

While Bateson was doing his fieldwork among the Iatmul, Margaret Mead was working not far away with another Middle Sepik group, the Tchambuli. Mead's work on the contrasting and variable nature of the ethos by which the sexes are defined (gender) in different societies has become a classic.[3] As far as

---

3. See, primarily, *Sex and temperament in three primitive societies*, first published in 1935; also *Male and female*, first published in 1950.

the Tchambuli were concerned, she found striking contrasts between men's and women's behavior but not ones that were identical with those of the Iatmul. Bateson himself writes: "The ethos of the Tchambuli men was less harsh and more exhibitionistic than that of the Iatmul, while the Tchambuli women were somewhat harder and more business-like than those of Iatmul" (Bateson [1936] 1958: 172).

Every [Tchambuli] man is an artist and most men are skilled not in some one art alone, but in many: in dancing, carving, plaiting, painting, and so on. Each man is chiefly concerned with his role upon the stage of his society, with the elaboration of his costume, the beauty of the masks that he owns, the skill of his own flute-playing, the finish and élan of his ceremonies, and upon other people's recognition and valuation of his performance. . . .

Tchambuli women work in blocks, a dozen of them together, plaiting the great mosquito-bags from the sale of which most of the [shell valuables] are obtained. They cook together for a feast, their clay fireplaces . . . set side by side. Each dwelling-house contains some dozen to two dozen fire-places, so that no woman need cook in a corner alone.

The whole emphasis is upon comradeship, efficient, happy work enlivened by continuous brisk banter and chatter. But in a group of men, there is always strain, watchfulness, a catty remark here, a double *entendre* there: "What did he mean by sitting down on the opposite side of the men's house when he saw you upon this side?" "Did you see Koshalan go by with a flower in his hair? What do you suppose he is up to?" . . .

Although Tchambuli is patrilineal in organization, although there is polygyny and a man pays for his wife . . . it is the women in Tchambuli who have the real position of power in the society. The patrilineal system includes houses and land, residence land and gardening-land, but only an occasional particularly energetic man gardens. For food, the people depend upon the fishing of the women. Men never fish unless a sudden school of fish appears in the lake, when they may leap into canoes in a frolicsome spirit, and spear a few fish. . . . But the real business of fishing is controlled entirely by the women. For traded fish they obtain sago, taro, and areca-nut. And the most important manufacture, the mosquito-bags, two of which will purchase an ordinary canoe, are made entirely by women. The people of the middle Sepik purchase these mosquito-bags, in fact they are so much in demand that purchasers take options on them long before they are finished. And the women control the proceeds in [shell valuables]. It is

true that they permit the men to do the shopping, both for food at the market
and in trading the mosquito-bags. The men make a gala occasion of these latter shopping-trips; when a man has the final negotiations for one of his wives'
mosquito-bags in hand, he goes off resplendent in feathers and shell ornaments
to spend a delightful few days over the transaction. He will hesitate and equivo-
cate, advance here, draw back there, accept . . . reject that . . . insist on changing
half of the purchasing items after they have been spread out, have a very orgy
of choice such as a modern woman with a well-filled purse looks forward to in
a shopping-trip to a big city. But only with his wife's approval can he spend the
[shells] . . . that he brings back from his holiday. He has wheedled a good price
from the purchaser; he has still to wheedle the items of the price from his wife.
From boyhood up, this is the men's attitude towards property. Real property,
which one actually owns, one receives from women, in return for languishing
looks and soft words. Once one has obtained it, it becomes a counter in the
games that men play; it is no longer concerned with the underlying economics
of life, but rather with showing one's appreciation of one's brother-in-law, sooth-
ing someone's wounded feelings, behaving very handsomely when a sister's son
falls down in one's presence. . . . The women's attitude towards the men is one of
kindly tolerance and appreciation. (Mead 1935: 245–55 passim)

Mead raises the question of what happens to the individual who by temperament or personality does not fit easily into the stereotype laid down for his
sex. For like the Iatmul, Tchambuli make very precise contrasts in what they
consider the appropriate behavior for males and females.

While there is reason to believe that not every Tchambuli woman is born with a
dominating, organizing, administrative temperament, actively sexed and willing
to initiate sex-relations, possessive, definite, robust, practical and impersonal in
outlook, still most Tchambuli girls grow up to display these traits. And while
there is definite evidence to show that all Tchambuli men are not, by native endowment, the delicate responsive actors of a play staged for the women's benefit,
still most Tchambuli boys manifest this coquettish play-acting personality most
of the time. . . .

[But they] have selected as the decreed path for all humanity one that is too
special to be congenial to all temperaments. And they have further complicated
the issue by decreeing that men shall feel and act in one way, women feel and act
in quite a different way. This immediately introduces a new educational problem.

If boys and girls are to be adequately adjusted to such contrasting attitudes towards life, it might be expected that their early education would present contrasting features. Yet until the Tchambuli boy and girl reach the age of six or seven the
two are treated exactly alike, and at this age, while the girl is rapidly trained in
handicrafts and absorbed into the sober, responsible life of the women, the boy is
given no such adequate training for his future rôle. He is left about upon the edges
of his society, a little too old for the women, and a little too young for the men. . . .

This period of three, sometimes four, years in the lives of the boys sets up
habits that prevail throughout their lives. A sense of neglect, of exclusion, settles
upon them. When the men or big boys ask them to run an errand, they feel they
are being used, they who are wanted at no other time. . . . So the smaller boys
glower in a resentment that never entirely lifts, and grow up to be typical Tchambuli men, overquick to feel hurt or slight and to burst into hysterical vituperation.
(Mead 1935: 288, 266–68 passim)

In fact, it is the absence of specific training for the Tchambuli boy which creates
the kind of adult he will be. The maladjusted in this society come from among
the men, the more virile youths, violent, possessive and actively sexed, intolerant
of any control, any activity that they themselves have not initiated (Mead 1935:
271). Women who do not fit in have an easier time.

The men are the conspicuous maladjusts, subject to neurasthenia, hysteria, and
maniacal outbursts. The quiet, undominating woman as a rule slips along within
the comfortable confines of the large women's group, overshadowed by a younger
wife, directed by a mother-in-law. Her maladjustment is in no way conspicuous;
if she does not play as conspicuous a rôle as her sex entitles her to, she does not
greatly rebel over her position. (Mead 1935: 275)

In describing the stereotypes which Tchambuli society lays down for each sex,
Mead in fact suggests that these are in a sense ideals: the social personalities of
men and of women should ideally oppose and complement each other. Since we
have seen that these stereotypes demand of persons not only that they should act
like men and women but should in every way behave and think like men or wom-
en, societies such as this must produce "cultural deviants." A deviant is someone

who because of innate disposition or accident of early training, or through the
contradictory influences of a heterogeneous cultural situation, has been culturally

disenfranchised, the individual to whom the major emphases of his society seem nonsensical, unreal, untenable, or downright wrong. . . .

Any society that specializes its personality types by sex, which insists that any trait—love for children, interest in art, bravery in the face of danger, garrulity, lack of interest in personal relations, passiveness in sex-relations; there are hundreds of traits of very different kinds that have been so specialized—is inalienably bound up with sex, paves the way for a kind of maladjustment of a worse order. . . . In addition to, or aside from, the pain of being born into a culture whose acknowledged ends he can never make his own, many a man has now the added misery of being disturbed in his psycho-sexual life. He not only has the wrong feelings but, far worse and more confusing, he has the feelings of a woman. . . .

Thus the existence in a given society of a dichotomy of social personality, of a sex-determined, sex-limited personality, penalizes in greater or less degree every individual born within it. Those whose temperaments are indubitably aberrant fail to adjust themselves to the accepted standards, and by their very presence, by the anomalousness of their responses, confuse those whose temperaments are the expected ones for their sex. So in practically every mind a seed of doubt, of anxiety, is planted, which interferes with the normal course of life. (Mead 1935: 290–306 passim)

This is not all. One can go further and suggest that there may in fact not be a "normal course of life." Stereotypes are by necessity selective. They pick on certain features of behavior, prescribe certain domains of action. And the selection may not be entirely congruent with other aspects of social life. Iatmul men's parody of women is perhaps a desperate attempt to deny the prominence of women's involvement in everyday affairs. In the case of Tchambuli Mead has identified a basic contradiction: ostensibly their society is what she calls patriarchal and women are theoretically under the authority of men, yet in practice females are the dominant ones.

So the Tchambuli boy grows up within two sets of conflicting ideas; he hears that his father bought his mother, he hears how much his father paid for his mother and how much his father will now collect to pay for his son's young wife. . . . At the same time he leads a life that is attuned to the voices of the women, where ceremonies are given for the sake of the women, where the women have the first and the last voice in the economic arrangements. All that he hears of sex stresses the woman's right to initiative. . . . Here is a conflict at the very root of his psycho-sexual adjustment; his society tells him that he rules women, his experience shows him at every turn that women expect to rule him, as they rule his father and brother. (Mead 1935: 270–71)

The position of aberrant men, the temperamental deviants, is made doubly difficult by this.

> The cultural formulation that a man has paid for his wife and can therefore control her continually misleads these aberrant individuals into fresh attempts at such control, and brings them into conflict with all their childhood training to obey and respect women, and their wives' training to expect such respect. Tchambuli institutions and the emphases of their society are, to a certain extent, at odds with one another. . . . These inconsistencies in Tchambuli culture were probably increased by a diminished interest in war and head-hunting and greater interest in the delicate arts of peace. The importance of the women's economic activities may also have increased without any corresponding enhancement of the men's economic rôle. Whatever the historical causes, . . . Tchambuli today presents a striking confusion between institutions and cultural emphases. And it also contains a larger number of neurotic males than I have seen in any other primitive culture. To have one's aberrancy, one's temperamental inability to conform to the prescribed rôle of responsive dancing attendance upon women, apparently confirmed by institutions—this is too much. (Mead 1935: 307–8)

Now in effect what the author has done is to take the differences she has observed in the behavior of men and women (as in the case of the Iatmul where there was a contrast between the histrionic pose of men and the jolly, cooperative getting-on-with-things outlook of women) and suggest that in so far as the sexes are typed and educated to behave differently, these represent ideal standards of behavior. The ideals (the stereotypes) turn out to be at variance with other aspects of the culture. This makes particular problems for the individual whose own personality is at variance with the "ideal."

THE INCONSTANT WOMAN

Yet stereotypes are not always standardized. One cannot always identify these classifications of behavior as contributing to an "ideal type." Or rather, the class of persons which one stereotype supposedly describes may in fact be the subject of several more stereotypes—and there may be little consistency between them. In the societies she was talking about Margaret Mead has suggested that there is a strong tendency for a particular personality type to be favored, which becomes the standard for each sex. If they are to be interpreted as producing an "ideal" then the ascriptions and attributes which make up a stereotype must presumably have some consistency. But there are many contexts in which, far from being able to discern an overall pattern, one is faced instead with blatant contradictions.

When the class of persons to which the stereotypes apply is relatively small—members of a profession, say, or people of a certain physical build—there may not be much room for ambiguity. When the class is as wide as half the society, when stereotypes are applied to men or to women as a sex, it is perhaps not surprising that we should find inconsistencies. Stereotypes are the building blocks of myths, and when the stereotypes contradict one another, the myths seem elusive.

> It is always difficult to describe a myth; it cannot be grasped or encompassed; it haunts the human consciousness without ever appearing before it in fixed form. The myth is so various, so contradictory, that at first its unity is not discerned: Delilah and Judith, Aspasia and Lucretia, Pandora and Athena—woman is at once Eve and the Virgin Mary. She is an idol, a servant, the source of life, a power of darkness; she is the elemental silence of truth, she is artifice, gossip, and falsehood; she is healing presence and sorceress; she is man's prey, his downfall, she is everything that he is not and that he longs for, his negation and his raison d'être. (de Beauvoir 1972: 175)

In Europe during the Middle Ages beliefs about the nature of women crystallized into two quite contrary sets of views. Indeed, almost to the point of preoccupation, the two views were deliberately set against each other in literary debates. A famous thirteenth-century poem, "The Thrush and the Nightingale," has two birds disputing women's characteristics—they play one stereotype against another.

> I heard a wordy battle flow—
> On one side joy, the other woe—
>   Between two birds I knew.
> One praised women for their good.

But shame the sex the other would:
    Their strife I tell to you.

The one was Nightingale by name,
And he would shield them all from shame
    And safe from injury.
The thrush declared that night and day
Women go the Devil's way
    And keep him company . . .

Nightingale: "To censure ladies is a shame,
For they are kind and fair of fame. ...

They cheer the angry, noble or base,
With pleasing pastime and with grace.
    Woman was once created,
As man's companion: how could earth,
Be anything without her birth,
    Or man so sweetly mated?"

Thrush: "No praise of women I report,
For I affirm them false in thought
    And know that they will cheat;
For though they're beautiful, their mind
Is false and faithless, and I find
    Them prone to act deceit." . . .

Nightingale: "Thrush, it seems you're either mad
Or know of nothing else but bad
    To slander women so!
They have true courtliness at heart,
And sweetly use love's secret art,
    Most wonderful to know.

"Man's highest bliss in earthly state
Is when a woman takes her mate
    And twines him in her arms.

To slander ladies is a shame!
I'll banish you for laying blame
    On those who have such charms" . . .

Thrush: "Think of Samson, brave and strong.
To whom his wife did such a wrong;
    For him she took a price.
Jesus said ill-gotten gain
Was worst for one who would attain
    To bliss of paradise."

Then said to him the Nightingale,
Nightingale: "Well, bird, that sounds a likely tale!
    Attend to what I say.
Woman's a flower of lasting grace,
And highest praised in every place,
    And lovely her array." . . .

Thrush: "Nightingale, you are unwise
To put on women such a price;
    Your profit will be lean;
For in a hundred, hardly five
Of all the wives and maids alive
    Continue pure and clean." (Stone 1964: 73–77 passim)

The Nightingale caps the argument, and wins by pointing out that Christ was borne by a woman. It would not have been out of place for the Thrush to retort that Eve was also female, in the same way as he cited Samson's downfall, but he lets the matter be and flies away.

    This is a very clear example of what I am talking about. There are two stereotypes, the saintly female and the evil female. Internally each classification is consistent enough. Taken together they not only contradict one another but also are built up of systematically contrasted opposites. It would be wrong, however, to conclude that we are dealing simply with two classes, the saintly and the evil. For each type is considered as characteristic of another wider class: that of female. The false and faithless exemplify "what all women are like" as much as those who have true courtliness at heart. Indeed, this is exactly what the poem is about. It does not argue that some women are like this and some like that. Not at all. It purports to find out, through the technique of debate, which of the stereotypes is more true, which represents more accurately what women are really like. Should women be classified as the origin of vice or the fount of virtue?

An impression with which a modern reader might be left is that in spite of the formal victory of Nightingale, the poet is in fact telling us that both sets of characteristics are true. Certainly, the demonstration of blatant contradictions between the two views does not lead to a conclusion that perhaps neither applies as they have been formulated; it rather encourages the debaters to stronger argument. The clearest message of the poem is that "women" are indeed a class. They are to be thought of as a single category of persons, even if the precise attributes of the category, their exact nature, is in doubt. This is where we began: one of the effects of stereotypes is to define classes of people. And we can see that not only may more than one set of stereotypes be applied to a class but it does not really matter after all whether they are consistent or not.[4]

In passing we may note that although the stereotype of the virtuous woman may amount to an ideal, it would be hard to use the word to describe the ninety-five females out of a hundred whom the Thrush considers unable to maintain any semblance of purity. The ninety-five, though, are argued to be "typical" of their sex, not the reverse. Types can be nondeviant, then, even if they are not ideal.

The same is true of Iatmul. Perhaps Iatmul men do try to inculcate a desired (ideal) type of behavior into boy initiates. Their definition of what males are like is relatively unambiguous. But there is considerable ambiguity about how female is defined. Women's characteristic bearing as they bustle about the household does not receive the same ceremonial attention that the male penchant for dramatics does. When men carry out initiation rituals, women form an audience and are supposed to be impressed by the displays. Their admiration is sought. Indeed, all male ceremonies have as one of their aims the production of a spectacle at which females will marvel. When women carry out ceremonials of their own (but not including comparable initiation for girls), these are jolly, cooperative affairs, typical of women's other activities. But men do not form an admiring audience. Far from it: they resent the goings-on, and sit apart, sulkily contemptuous. We saw how a Iatmul man cannot put on women's clothes

4.   Further consideration of some Medieval European stereotypes is given in Chapter Seven.

without demeaning himself. It would also seem he cannot abide this open demonstration of what women think they (the women themselves) really are like. A great crowd of women collects together, joking and in the best of humor. The sound of their dancing and excitement carries to the men, who make disparaging criticisms. Far from being an audience, the men are more like an enemy. Indeed, Bateson reports that on these occasions opposition between the sexes comes to a head—spilling over into quarrels between husbands and wives which become very frequent at these times.

The ceremonial behavior of Iatmul women may be standardized, then, and women act out something of how they see themselves. But it would be stretching the point to talk of an ideal, for they are fully aware of men's adverse opinion; and men react as though this kind of behavior represented a threat to society. Women act up to this, ignoring the men during the dance, and retaliating on any obstacles put in their way by discomforted husbands through refusing to cook for them.

If Iatmul men think of themselves as proud and rather grand beings, women play up to this when they admire men's ceremonial displays. They concur in the same stereotype on those occasions when they don men's clothes, for women bear themselves with pride in male regalia. But if women among themselves place value on being cheerful and cooperative, this is not something which would seem to elicit particular admiration from men, and when such behavior is vaunted by a group of women it is greeted with hostility. Indeed, it would seem that a woman with a proud and violent temperament, at odds with the rest of her sex, is the one to be admired by men (for having masculine characteristics). At least in Iatmul men's eyes, then, the "ideal type" is a prerogative of men. When men imitate women they produce a creature who is typical in that all her characteristics are recognizably female, but clearly expresses the nonideal lot of women as a sex.

Here we can see the application of different stereotypes. When the laughter and shouts which accompany women's private ceremonies reach their ears, the men withdraw sulkily; they are typing this as "women's behavior" and it makes them uncomfortable. When they parade, also rather uncomfortably, as "mothers" celebrating some achievement, they do not laugh and joke; they adopt instead a quite different demeanor as "typical of women"—feeble, grotesque, their voices cracked and uncertain. The point is that both kinds of behavior are recognizably feminine. There are (at least) two stereotypes here, and both are seen by men to characterize a single class, the female.

Here, too, is an example of a sexual mythology which belongs to men. The anthropologist openly admits in this case that he is uncertain of what Iatmul women's views would be on ideal behavior. Nevertheless, he provides enough descriptions of Iatmul life to suggest that the major institutions of this society, in which both sexes have roles, are supported by a relatively unambiguous definition of what men are like, and a much more ambiguous depiction of what women are like.

The stereotype of women as ambiguous is a very widespread one. Indeed, imputing inconstancy or caprice to the female as such draws attention to the process of stereotyping itself. Of course women seem capricious, because they are represented as now one thing, now the other. Of course women are prone to change their minds, because conflicting stereotypes make the outcome of their intentions unpredictable. De Beauvoir sees *this* characteristic of women (as ambiguous) as a basic and inevitable product of male mythology.

Woman is defined exclusively in her relation to man. The asymmetry of the categories—male and female—is made manifest in the unilateral form of sexual myths. We sometimes say "the sex" to designate woman; she is the flesh, its delights and dangers. The truth that for woman man is sex and carnality has never been proclaimed because there is no one to proclaim it. Representation of the world, like the world itself, is the work of men; they describe it from their own point of view, which they confuse with absolute truth. . . .

To be a woman, says Kierkegaard in *Stages on the Road of Life*, "is something so strange, so confused, so complicated, that no one predicate comes near expressing it and that the multiple predicates that one would like to use are so contradictory that only a woman could put up with it." This comes from not regarding woman positively, such as she seems to herself to be, but negatively, such as she appears to man. For if woman is not the only *Other*, it remains none the less true that she is always defined as the Other. And her ambiguity is just that of the concept of the Other: it is that of the human situation in so far as it is defined in its relation with the Other. . . . Woman incarnates no stable concept; through her is made unceasingly the passage from hope to frustration, from hate to love, from good to evil, from evil to good. Under whatever aspect we may consider her, it is this ambivalence that strikes us first.

Man seeks in woman the Other as Nature and as his fellow being. But we know what ambivalent feelings Nature inspires in man. He exploits her, but she crushes him, he is born of her and dies in her; she is the source of his being and the realm that he subjugates to his will; Nature is a vein of gross material in which the soul is imprisoned, and she is the supreme reality; she is contingence and Idea, the finite and the whole; she is what opposes the Spirit, and the Spirit itself. Now ally, now enemy, she appears as the dark chaos from whence life wells up, as this life itself, and as the over-yonder towards which life tends. Woman sums up nature as Mother, Wife, and Idea; these forms now mingle and now conflict, and each of them wears a double visage. . . .

Man would fain affirm his individual existence and rest with pride on his "essential difference," but he wishes also to break through the barriers of the ego, to mingle with the water, the night, with Nothingness, with the Whole. Woman condemns man to finitude, but she also enables him to exceed his own limits; and hence comes the equivocal magic with which she is endued. (de Beauvoir 1972: 174–80 passim)

De Beauvoir suggests that this definition of woman is fundamental to men's perception *of themselves*. A woman has to be both more and less of what men are; she has to be both naked and adorned.

But it is not casually given to any woman whatever to serve in this way as intermediary between man and the world; man is not satisfied merely to find in his partner sex organs complementary to his own. She must incarnate the marvellous flowering of life and at the same time conceal its obscure mysteries. Before all things, then, she will be called upon for youth and health. . . . Her body is not perceived as the radiation of a subjective personality, but as a thing sunk deeply in its own immanence; it is not for such a body to have reference to the rest of the world, it must not be the promise of things other than itself: it must end the desire it arouses. The most naive form of this requirement is the Hottentot ideal of the steatopygous Venus, for the buttocks are the part of the body with fewest nerves, where the flesh seems an aimless fact. . . .

Weighted down with fat, or on the contrary so thin as to forbid all effort, paralyzed by inconvenient clothing and by the rules of propriety—then woman's body seems to man to be his property, his thing. Make-up and jewellery also further this petrification of face and body. The function of ornamental attire is very complex; with certain primitives it has a religious significance; but more often its purpose is to accomplish the metamorphosis of woman into idol. Ambiguous idol! Man wishes her to be carnal, her beauty like that of fruits and flowers; but he would also have her smooth, hard, changeless as a pebble. The function of ornament is to make her share more intimately in nature and at the same time to remove her from the natural, it is to lend to palpitating life the rigour of artifice. . . . We come, then, to this strange paradox: man, wishing to find nature in woman, but nature transfigured, dooms woman to artifice. She is not only *physis* but quite as much *anti-physis*: and this not only in the civilization of electrical "perms," of superfluous-hair removal by means of wax, of latex girdles, but also in the land of Negresses with lip disks, in China and indeed all over the world.

Swift denounced this mystification in his famous *Ode to Celia*; he describes with disgust the paraphernalia of the coquette and recalls with disgust the animal necessities of her body. He is twice wrong in his indignation; for man wishes simultaneously that woman be animal and plant and that she be hidden behind an artificial front; he loves her rising from the sea and emerging from a fashionable dressmaker's establishment, naked and dressed, naked under her clothes— such, precisely, as he finds her in the universe of humanity. (de Beauvoir 1972: 189–92 passim)

STRENGTHS AND WEAKNESSES

De Beauvoir has given an analysis of why females as a sex should be so endowed with conflicting attributes that they appear ambiguous. She is concerned to show how these myths about the nature of women define for men a concept of the individual. She is concerned with the limits of personal freedom and identifies women as a primary medium through which men see themselves as acting on the world, on nature. These concerns undoubtedly draw heavily on European tradition, on philosophies which have been preoccupied with notions of individuality, free will, mortality, and such like. It is illuminating in this regard to consider the prominence which sexual intercourse has in her account. It is women's sexuality, she suggests, which allows for so much play on the theme of ambiguity.

Woman . . . is the wished-for intermediary between nature, the stranger to man, and the fellow being who is too closely identical. She opposes him with neither the hostile silence of nature nor the hard requirement of a reciprocal relation; through a unique privilege she is a conscious being and yet it seems possible to possess her in the flesh. . . . And therein lies the wondrous hope that man has often put in woman: he hopes to fulfill himself as a being by carnally possessing a being, but at the same time confirming his sense of freedom through the docility of a free person No man would consent to be a woman, but every man wants women to exist. . . .

When man takes possession of woman through the pleasure he gets from her, he also awakens in her the dubious power of fecundity: the organ he penetrates is the same as that which gives birth to the child. This is why in all societies man is protected by many taboos against the dangers of the female sex. . . . He takes great pride in his sexuality only in so far as it is a means of appropriating the Other—and this dream of possession ends only in frustration. In authentic possession the other is abolished as such, it is consumed and destroyed: only the Sultan in *The Arabian Nights* has the power to cut off each mistress's head when dawn has come to take her from his couch. Woman survives man's embraces, and in that very fact she escapes him; as soon as he loosens his arms, his prey becomes again a stranger to him; there she lies, new, intact, ready to be possessed by a new lover in as ephemeral a manner. . . . A whole literature has expatiated upon this frustration. It is made objective in woman, and she is called inconstant and traitress because her body is such as to dedicate her to man in general and not to one man in particular.

But her treason is more perfidious still: she makes her lover in truth her prey. Only a body can touch another body; the male masters the flesh he longs for only in becoming flesh himself; Eve is given to Adam so that through her he may accomplish his transcendence, and she draws him into the night of immanence. His mistress, in the vertigoes of pleasure, encloses him again in the opaque clay of that dark matrix which the mother fabricated for her son and from which he desires to escape. He wishes to possess her: behold him the possessed himself! Odour, moisture, fatigue, ennui—a library of books has described this gloomy passion of a consciousness made flesh. . . .

Seeking to appropriate the Other, man must remain himself; but in the frustration of impossible possession he tries to become that other with whom he fails to be united; then he is alienated, he is lost, he drinks the philtre that makes him a stranger to himself. . . . The Mother dooms her son to death in giving him life; the loved one lures her lover on to renounce life and abandon himself to the last sleep. . . . Here the alliance between Woman and Death is confirmed; the great harvestress is the inverse aspect of the fecundity that makes the grain thrive. But she appears, too, as the dreadful bride whose skeleton is revealed under her sweet, mendacious flesh.

Thus what man cherishes and detests first of all in woman—loved one or mother—is the fixed image of his animal destiny; it is the life that is necessary to his existence but that condemns him to the finite and to death. From the day of his birth man begins to die: this is the truth incarnated in the Mother. . . . Although he endeavours to distinguish mother and wife, he gets from both a witness to one thing only: his mortal state. (de Beauvoir 1972: 172–98 passim)

We shall come back to the prominence of sexual intercourse as a symbol in Western European culture. For the moment, one might suggest that de Beauvoir is really dealing with the place (and use) of sexuality in Western thought, and not, as she would suggest by some of her examples, human thought in general. Or rather, whereas certain processes which she describes seem to turn up everywhere, the symbols change. It is very common for men to define themselves as a sex through the characteristics they bestow on women, and it also seems to be common that the picture painted of women is blurred, ambiguous, contradictory. Yet while this process is a common one, the content of the symbols does not have to be the same. Carnal knowledge, possession of the flesh, mortality and release of the spirit, boundaries of freedom, domination of the natural world—some of these themes can be traced in European thought back to medieval times and beyond. Sexual intercourse flows through these notions as a symbol of the ultimate ambiguity: it is a means of subduing Nature, and makes Nature yield forth her blessings; it is also the means by which Nature subdues man, for insofar as he is prey to the temptations of the flesh he is not in control of his own destiny. But I am not sure whether sexual intercourse holds quite the same symbolic place in, say, Iatmul thought.

There, too, women seem to be defined somewhat ambiguously. And there, too, the question of who is subduing whom (which sex is dominant) seems to lie at the back of men's confusions. Sexual imagery has a place in this, but there are other images too. There is considerable play, for example, on the ceremonial presentation of the person. The sexes are defined through the emotions it is appropriate for each to display. The themes of publicity and exhibition, the narrow limits within which pride can be expressed, the precise demarcation of public behavior by each sex as underlined in the conventions of transvesticism: the symbols here are those of dramatics. It is not just that it matters desperately how a Iatmul man conducts himself in the ceremonial house or that initiation rituals should be impressive to the audience but that the demeanor of individuals *in public* is seen constantly to have implications for relations between the sexes. For Iatmul obsessions[5] of identity seem to have a lot to do with the way individuals comport themselves in the open, whereas the European use of sexual intercourse as a symbol points to a private domain. The act takes place in private, in seclusion, symbolizing the significance of the individual, on his own, and his struggle with himself. If woman represents nature, and not only Nature in the sense of the outside world but man's own nature, it is appropriate that the kind of the interaction between the sexes which is given symbolic significance is of a most isolated and intimate kind. Man is seen as ultimately having to come to grips with himself. Iatmul preoccupations would suggest a different emphasis.

In both cases, the European and the (New Guinean) Sepik, we are presented with an obsession with self-identity, and it seems to be an obsession most clearly attributed to males. For it is related closely to men's view of themselves as dominant. In both cases, among the processes by which this is achieved is the stereotyping of women in ambiguous terms, as alternately inferior (and already dominated) and competitive (and therefore a target for further domination). But I think we also have a clear example of different emphases being used in this stereotyping, of different facets of the male-female relationship being drawn upon.

This digression should make us alive to one fact: that we are all of our own cultures. Anthropologists coming from England, or America, say, will have to be aware of their own stereotypes. A powerful one, and one that is buttressed by the (culturally appropriate) practices of psychoanalysis in many ways, is that sexuality is the essence of relations between the sexes. This may turn out to be true for many cultures other than our own. But then, again, it may not. We have to be careful, even, how we read the sexual imagery of other societies. The Abelam, who live near to the Iatmul people, and are closely related to them in language and culture, incorporate sexual images in much of their art. The following is an observation by an anthropologist who worked there in the late 1950s and early 1960s.

> Much of the imagery and symbolism of the Abelam, as of many societies, is concerned with sex, but this cannot be helped. As I hope to show, the phallus among the Abelam is not a simple unitary aggressive symbol, although this aspect predominates in the ceremonial house. What I am really trying to establish is what the Abelam are saying about themselves and their culture and society in

---

5. Here, as elsewhere, I am referring to what we may call public (social) obsessions rather than private ones.

their art. Sex may well be all-pervasive in many societies, if not all, but this is all the more reason for not being content with identifying something as a phallic symbol and leaving it at that. The most obvious question to ask next is what does the phallus mean to the Abelam. (Forge 1966: 28)

In other words, we should not assume what is being symbolized in the representation of a sexual organ: in our own culture the penis can stand for male generative powers or (even more strongly) for male sexual dominance. For Abelam, the author goes on to show how in certain contexts the phallus is an organ of nourishment. When represented on carvings of ancestral spirits, it is seen as feeding either a bird, the totem of a particular clan and thus in essence the clan itself, or a pig,[6] creatures who are regarded as in the care of the spirits. In paintings which adorn the ceremonial house there is an artistic equation between the penis and the female breast. For while in some Abelam contexts the penis can symbolize aggression, in others it stands for nutrition. Sexuality is here being given a very particular meaning.

Although she gives emphasis to sexual (erotic) relations, de Beauvoir also comments on the ambiguity of the symbol of the "mother," fecund but giving birth only to mortals. Another writer has taken the mother as the starting point for an analysis of feminine attributes. Elizabeth Janeway looks at myths which deal with women as weak, which say that women should subordinate themselves to men, and should not compete, because they lack strength. She suggests that these statements really cover up fears: that "the myth of female weakness which preaches subordination of woman to man can, it seems, mask its contrary, the myth of female power" (Janeway [1971] 1972: 51).

The dogma that women are really the powerful ones is as much a myth as the dogma that they are weaklings; she is not explaining the one myth (that women are weak) by saying that it copes with reality (that women are strong). Rather, Janeway suggests that both sets of stereotypes are mythical, complementing each other, but used differently. The first becomes an openly expressed rationale in the mouths of men who want to keep women in their place; the second feeds an undercurrent of fear that if women were not kept in the precise place assigned to them, men's dominance would be threatened. In analyzing the origins of this second myth she points to women's procreative powers, but she turns also to a child's early experiences of its female parent.

---

6. The chief domestic animal.

The myth of female power is as much a projection of need and a focus for fears as is its twin. We may find in this connection, however, an answer to an old puzzle: why have women so often and so persistently acquiesced in declaring themselves subordinate to men? . . . There must be some better explanation for women's acquiescence in the myth of female weakness than the response that that's the way they are made. Surely one reason can be found in the myth of female power which lies behind the myth of weakness. . . . The source of the myth of female power lies just where the myth of the Golden Age takes its rise: in the mother-child relationship. . . .

What we are looking at is the effective memory of the mother's power over the child which is *in reality* as complete as the child *imagines* its power over the mother to be. The grown child remembers the mother as slave, as loving nurturer who tends and watches and serves. But the mother is also the master. Having created the child as a living entity (and except for one not-unique act by the father she has created it. I am speaking of psychological, not scientific, truth), she now has the power to create it as a social being, a member of the community; and without her this creation will not take place, whatever ritual initiation the men like to indulge themselves in acting out. The child will not grow into an adult without her care, and the kind of adult it grows into will depend on her. . . .

Meanwhile, the child is in her power, is her toy. She can mold it and shape its habits, play with it, tease it, teach it and frustrate it, push it toward the fulfil-ment of her own desires and mock her husband's hopes, if she wishes to. . . . This is guiltless power too. If she keeps the little creature prisoner, it is for the child's own advantage. Over it she enjoys sovereign rights. . . .

So when women cling to their traditional role, it is not primarily because they find masochistic pleasure in being dominated (though no doubt some do) but because this role offers them power too: private power in return for public submission. This is the regular, orthodox bargain by which men run the world and allow women to rule in their own place. . . . The balance of private power and public submission which women accept touches only the factual aspect of their position. It assumes that power and weakness are separate and opposite things, contraries that contradict and offset each other. But they are not, not in the realm of myth which grows out of the interior world of feeling.

In that inner world, opposites are two sides of the same coin. . . . They are not divided, but are aspects of the same inner emotional tension. In mythic identification of power and weakness, women immolate themselves as a sign of strength. They are the givers; but how can one give if one does not possess riches and substance? The double myth of female weakness and female power is not a contradiction, or a mask over reality, but two streams of feeling which comingle and feed each other. . . .

Both rise in the mother-child relationship. Let us look again at this duality, which is in fact a mutuality. . . . For the child, it represents the Golden Age of apparent omnipotence, when the world seemed to bend to his will simply because he wanted it to and his wishes were answered without any action on his part. For the mother . . . it gives rise to a feeling of superiority. . . . Yet for each participant, the enormous power enjoyed depends on the other's presence, the child to demand and receive, the mother to give and to dominate. Without the other, the power vanishes. Here is the paradox: women are weak because they can be strong only through giving. They are strong because what they give is needed, and the need assures that their dominance will continue. (Janeway [1971] 1972: 51–57 passim, original emphasis)

Janeway's analysis moves away from sexuality as the key to fantasies about female strength and female weakness to consideration of a particular role relationship. This is the relationship between mother and child. The themes of dominance and mastery are there, but in connection with personal coercion, the imposition of will, and an interplay of demands and needs which take place outside the context of sexual intercourse. The way mothers treat children, and the significance this has for the way men think about feminine powers in general, is certainly an aspect of interaction between the sexes. It may well cast a shadow on how men regard sexual encounters. Nonetheless it is based on a power situation which can be considered independently of sex in an exclusively erotic or genital sense.

Particular roles, then, which women play, or are at least capable of playing, such as that of "mother," may be crucial to the whole definition of their gender. Let us look at some family situations, at women interacting with men as mothers, sisters, daughters, and thus in heterosexual relationships which cannot be reduced to being "just about (erotic/genital) sex."

CHAPTER THREE

Families and Housewives

"Family" in English is a contextual term. It can apply to all the relatives (kins-men) one recognizes, sometimes relatives by blood and sometimes relatives by blood and by marriage ("My family goes back a long way," "Our family sticks together"). It can apply to just some of them, others being excluded because the relationship is too remote or they do not mix with the rest ("She's not really a member of the family"). And it can apply to a much smaller unit: a couple and their children—epitomized in phrases which equate "family" with juvenile members ("My wife and family / We have no family yet / He is a family man"). It is the children who "make" the family, a unit here conventionally thought of as comprising a married man and woman supporting their immature offspring. Notions about the family in this last sense provide an illuminating insight into relations between men and women.

It is almost impossible to talk about this kind of family without also talking about a household. The phrase "family life" refers to activities which everyone shares in, and these are activities often based on "the home": cooperation in household tasks, eating together, going away on holiday, and in becoming dependent on others (friends, a hotel) demonstrating their usual self-sufficiency. "Home" and "family" are closely identified. Relations between the sexes within this unit are restricted to those of husband and wife, brother and sister, and opposite sex parent to opposite sex child. These are roles which males and females play in a kinship setting. But in addition there is a very significant allocation of roles which stems from the association of the family with the household. This allocation is structured around the conventional house-keeping arrangement whereby the adult male is responsible for the major financing of the unit, which usually involves him earning a salary or wage at some place of work, and the adult female who, whether or not she also earns, is responsible for "running the home."

A man's obligations to support his wife and children sustain him in his role as worker or wage-earner. But the kind of work he does—whether he is an engineer, a baker's assistant, a company director—also gives him a degree of autonomy. He contributes to the household but his life is not centered on it. A woman's work in the home is much more closely connected to her family responsibilities. The jobs she does are for her children (whose parent she also is) or her husband (whose wife she also is) in a very immediate way. We could put it like this: the position (role) of housewife seems to swallow up other aspects of the woman's status. Indeed, it is the manner in which "housewife" can absorb within itself the conjugal and parental aspects of a woman's family roles which makes it so significant in the formation of stereotypes about the sexes.

> Q: How does the *modern* woman's role contrast to that of her grandmother?
> A: They didn't have modern equipment. Homemaking ideas weren't so pretty then. Men make more now. Couples couldn't afford things. I work half day, have half day to myself. (Lopata 1971: 214, original emphasis)[1]

The question was simply about roles in general; the respondent, a woman, interpreted it in terms of the specific role of housewife. For men, the opposite holds. There is a contrast, not an equation, between occupation and family life. The very phrase, "He is a family man," indicates this. It can be used of someone who not only supports his family (i.e., wife and children) but *in addition* takes more interest in and more part in activities centered on the home than his obligations to his dependents make strictly necessary.

This demonstrates the point that one cannot talk about family roles in the abstract, isolating "mothers" or "husbands" or whomever, because these roles will be shaped by the kind of context in which they are played. They will be shaped

---

1. An interchange at an interview during a study of the attitudes and outlook of Chicago "housewives."

not only by the structure of the family itself, but by other influences as well, such as men and women's occupations. Moreover, we should be aware of emphases, of some roles appearing to be more significant than others. There is no doubt that the status of housewife—as we have just encountered it—receives a very special loading in English and American society. It is the subject of well-developed stereotypes. And these stereotypes define, or contaminate, other roles which women have to play. Parental and conjugal behavior tends be judged by housewife performance.

Roles may contribute to the definition of gender and thus to notions (myths) about masculine and feminine behavior. But it is not just that the sexes are associated with particular roles (men are "fathers," women are "mothers")—it is a matter also of how these roles are perceived. We have had an example of this already. De Beauvoir centered much of her analysis on the fact that women are thought of as sexual objects. In real life this corresponds to a potential *role* as sexual partner. But women are not just sexual partners cooperating in an act which needs two people: they are fantasized as being certain kinds of partners. They are enchantresses who snare men, or pliant beings begging for mastery. It is *these* attributes that become symbols by which the nature of womankind is described.

Attention should be drawn to the feedback process involved here. Certain stereotypes about women lead to particular roles being stressed in the society (e.g., sexual partner, housewife). This is because the roles pick up culturally relevant feminine characteristics and emphasize them (sexual partnering, house-keeping); and in this emphasis bestow on them certain qualities (e.g., female sexuality is unreliable, female dependency is a sign of weakness)—the roles themselves are stereotyped. In this form, the image of the sex playing the role is then thrown back at society and thus replayed. The particular characteristics which triggered off the association of role and sex to begin with have been enlarged and refocused, by the mechanism of role-linkage. The media words in these sentences are no accident: for the process is almost that of a message being expressed through a medium which returns to the sender a rather special delineation of what he wanted to say.

The use of the roles housewife/wage-earner to pattern thinking about male-female relations in English or American society is only a special case of a general phenomenon. But it is an illuminating example of one aspect of male-female interaction blown up large, being used to typify, to symbolize relations between men and women as such. Let us look into the example in more detail.

THE DEPENDENT HOUSEWIFE

Here is some information on households in England and Wales. The analysis is phrased in terms of supporters (mainly the wage-earners) and dependents.

In 1961 there were more than 14 ½ million households in England and Wales. Of these, only seven million, less than half, were composed simply of a married couple and their children (*Census*). . . . "Household," in Census usage, means one or more persons who have exclusive use of at least one room and take their meals on their own; thus bedsitter lodgers who cook their own meals count as separate households. The conventional small modern family of parents and dependent children is only one among a great many types of household structure.

But it matters who is dependent on whom in the household. For social and economic planning the crucial things to know are whether members of a household are physically and/or economically dependent. The physically dependent may be either children below their 'teens, or adults who by reason of infirmity or disability are unable to look after themselves. Physical dependence is the more fundamental since it may entail economic dependence either for the handicapped person or for another person looking after them. . . . Economic independence may be the result of either economic activity (going out to work), or having a pension, receiving a grant, or other income *as of right,* which is sufficient for its possessor to live on without supplementation from either official or private sources (financial independence).

Households can be classified according to the physical and economic independence of their members. It is impracticable to distinguish between the roles of men and those of women in these households; or between those of married women and of single women, or between those of married men and of single men. Eight main types of household structure can be identified. . . .

Types A and B contain only members who are economically and physically independent.

Type A: Married couples where the husband and wife both work; men and women working and sharing a home.

Type B: The man or woman on their own. . . .

Types C to G contain members who are physically dependent. They may contain members who are economically active or financially independent, and they may contain adults who are neither, but who spend their time looking after the members of the household who are physically dependent.

Type C: Both husband and wife are supporting a relative looking after their children. Sisters or brothers are supporting a relative looking after infirm parents. . . .

Type D: The husband (or occasionally the wife) is supporting the wife (or husband) who is looking after the children. One adult, either man or woman, is supporting a relative who is looking after children or perhaps incapacitated parents. In this type a man is usually supporting and a woman doing the looking after and being supported, but both men and women can be found in each role. . . .

Type E: Working adults together both support and look after aged, sick relatives or dependent children: both husband and wife are working and are looking after their own young children. . . .

Type F: The husband is supporting and looking after his incapacitated wife; the widower is supporting and looking after his own children; the unmarried, divorced, separated or widowed mother, her children; the man or woman supporting and looking after incapacitated relatives or parents; the wife is supporting as well as looking after her incapacitated husband.

Type G: The able bodied person is economically dependent and may be supported financially by the dependent, e.g. a daughter looking after aged parents, or by an (inadequate) pension or allowance, e.g. a widowed, separated, divorced or unmarried mother. . . .

There remains the type of household in which there are none who are physically dependent, but in which an able bodied adult is economically dependent.

Type H: The wife continues to stay at home to keep house for her husband and grown-up children. One of a family of unmarried brothers or sisters keeps house for the others. A married woman living with her husband and without children or other dependants keeps house. (Rendel 1968: 32–44, original emphasis)

This particular account was written to draw attention to the wide range of household types, and to inconsistencies in governmental provisions which recognize some household structures as worthy of state assistance and exclude others.

In all these categories, except the second, there can be a variety of civil status relationships between the different members of the household; but within each category, the practical problems and, to some extent, the financial problems of running the household are similar. Most financial arrangements (taxation, national insurance, etc.) and the social attitudes which exist at present, are based on the civil status relationship, rather than on the satisfaction of practical needs.

In type H for example, the first household would benefit from the marriage allowance payable to the husband, but the second household would not; yet their structure is essentially similar. There is no reason why one rather than the other should receive a subsidy from other tax-payers. Nor do financial arrangements take account of the fact that the different functions within a household can be undertaken by either sex. In category F (where one person is supporting others who are physically dependent), a man, but not a woman, may receive a tax allowance towards the cost of a non-resident housekeeper to look after dependent children. (Rendel 1968: 34)

For our purpose, there are two interesting aspects to this analysis. First is what the author intends to do, which is demonstrate what a wide of range of household arrangements exists. In them we find the sexes are actually occupying equivalent positions. Her own argument is that the granting of state benefits is biased by (among other things) conventional attitudes toward men's and women's roles, which discriminate against women but also support stereotypes about men's roles, too. For example, she has a question concerning household type G.

Is there any reason why a widower should not stay at home to look after his children if it is accepted that a widow may? A father's care may be more satisfactory than that of a strange woman employed to look after the children. In the past there have been complaints from widowers that it was virtually impossible for them to look after their own children and in particular that they were refused national assistance, but this attitude now seems to be changing. (Rendel 1968: 33–34)

Even though housekeeping roles can be performed by either sex, she comments that it is the "civil status" relationships between the household members which is recognized in government assistance programs. By civil status here she means such familial relations as those between husband and wife, or ex-husband and ex-wife, or parents and children, which are recognized in law. Government assistance is given only to those who are in certain relationships to others within the household, and the decision of who is fit to receive such aid is influenced by stereotypes about the roles appropriate for each sex. One of the mechanisms by which this is done is to see household roles in family (kinship) terms: the *husband* gets assistance because he supports his family. This contains the hidden assumption that the male partner of a marital pair will be the *household head*.

The second point is of a rather different order. The author is quarrelling with the national assistance program: it is pertinent, therefore, that she classify households according to the respective dependence and independence of their members. That is, members support themselves / other members or are supported by outside agencies. This is undoubtedly an accurate picture of what households in England and Wales are about. I draw attention to the underlying cultural premise that in dealing with households one is dealing with relations of dependency which are so structured that the independent member (the supporter) is the one who makes financial contributions to the household, and all the rest, including those who stay at home and "keep house," are dependent (the supported). This is a precise reflection of the kinds of values which are tied to household roles, and a reflection too of attitudes toward money and money-earning. In association with the conventional allocation of the wage-earning roles to males and house-keeping roles to females, it supports the stereotype of the housewife as a dependent.[2]

The appropriateness of women assuming those household roles which put them in a dependent position is developed in stereotypes about the nature of housewives; and it is only a short step from there to its enlarged and sharpened feedback—how housewives are seen influences judgment of the female sex. These stereotypes contribute, then, to myths about the nature of women. They have many aspects. Two I shall touch on: the isolation of the dependent member (the housewife) and her exploitation.

Helena Lopata traces historical antecedents for the typical characteristics of the American housewife.

> A number of historical factors have combined to create the highly negative stereotypes of American home life and of its women. These include the constriction of the home into a privacy-seeking isolated unit, the acceptance of lower-class definitions of the housewife, and the cultural lag which has prevented women from taking full advantage of the opportunities for multidimensionality offered by the modern urban centers. . . .

---

2. The division of labor between the sexes is being evaluated in such a way as to make one type of contribution typically female, and lower in status than other types. This is found in many places, though it is not always tied to the definition of the household. The men of Hagen in New Guinea, for example, denigrate women's tasks, but in so far as the household is concerned husband and wife are seen to be in a mutually reciprocal relationship.

> In America, the isolation of the home from the rest of the world was reinforced in pioneer years. The farmer built his house in the center of privacy-stressing property, preventing frequent contacts, and often rejecting life outside the narrow belt needed to maintain him within it. . . . The economic and family institutions formed the focus of life; commitment outside the home was certainly not expected of the woman and she was not trained for it. . . .
>
> The upper-class educated woman did not become the ideological model of Americans in the role of housewife, although most middle-class wives and mothers have adopted many patterns of her behavior. It is not her home, run with complexity of interaction and knowledge, which comes to mind when that role is discussed. It is not the person who has opened her home to free movement in and out who is the stereotype of "the housewife." That term connotes all the characteristics of lower-class, uneducated non-involvement: ignorance, passivity in relation to self and to others, hostility or apathy toward neighbors, lack of involvement in the life of the society, and willingness to have the elite run the world. (Lopata 1971: 365–67 passim)

She suggests that the stereotype of the in-turned, isolated housewife stems from the realities of early pioneer settlement, and that it is simply a cultural lag which has prevented new images taking its place. Yet she herself points out that there were always other models (the upper-class woman) for housewife-roles, and does not really suggest why one should have been selected to form the basis of the stereotype rather than another.[3]

Pressures to select the passive, ignorant, dependent image of the housewife must have much more to do with the implicit equation housewife = woman than with specific patterns developed among some households at certain periods in the past. It is primarily a definition of what women are like; and there is always the hidden contrast with what men are like. Sometimes one can actually observe these images being molded in men's hands. Betty Friedan

> sat one night at a meeting of magazine writers, mostly men, who work for all kinds of magazines, including women's magazines. The main speaker was a leader of the desegregation battle. Before he spoke, another man outlined the needs of the large women's magazine he edited:

---

3. Though she does point out that the norms of the pioneer country were reinforced by the lifestyle of immigrants.

"Our readers are housewives, full time. They're not interested in the broad public issues of the day. They are not interested in national or international affairs. They are only interested in the family and the home. They aren't interested in politics, unless it's related to an immediate need in the home, like the price of coffee. Humour? Has to be gentle, they don't get satire. Travel? We have almost completely dropped it. Education? That's a problem. Their own education level is going up. They've generally all had a high-school education and many, college. They're tremendously interested in education for their children—fourth-grade arithmetic. You just can't write about ideas or broad issues of the day for women. That's why we're publishing 90 per cent service now and 10 per cent general interest."

At this point, the writers and editors spent an hour listening to Thurgood Marshall on the inside story of the desegregation battle, and its possible effect on the presidential election. "Too bad I can't run that story," one editor said. "But you just can't link it to woman's world." (Friedan [1963] 1965: 33)

This is a (woman's) picture of men happily secure in a myth of what women want (= what they are capable of wanting). But ever since Friedan wrote her book ("Each woman . . . must unequivocally say 'no' to the housewife image," [1963] 1965: 297) this myth has been under constant battering. One interesting feature of the onslaught has been the attempt to free women from the image of the housewife. Not all women are housewives anyway, and there are functional housewives who are not women (see above). In the strict sense, Friedan is addressing herself to a proportion of and not the total female population (primarily those who keep house for husbands and/or children). But in fact her message that these women should find themselves, should seek their identity beyond the confines of the home, is interpreted as applying to *women as a whole*. It is proof of the success with which characteristics of a particular role (housewife) have been transferred onto the sex (female) whose typical lot it is felt to be.

Further proof of the way this stereotyping and mythicizing process is fundamental to our conceptions of men and women's natures comes from a different quarter. From an Italian perspective, Mariarosa Dalla Costa, in *Women and the subversion of the community*, argues that women's ostensible economic dependence in the household in fact hides gross exploitation. Women should in future resist this ("Hence we must refuse housework as women's work" [Dalla Costa in James 1972: 39]). Her argument rests on the premise, culturally valid for

Western Europe but a premise nonetheless, that the subjugation of the female sex is coincident with the exploitation of the woman-housewife.

These observations are an attempt to define and analyze the "Woman Question," and to locate this question in the entire "female role" as it has been created by the capitalist division of labor.

We place foremost in these pages the housewife as the central figure in this female role. We assume that all women are housewives and even those who work outside the home continue to be housewives. That is, on a world level, it is precisely what is particular to domestic work, not only measured as number of hours and nature of work, but as quality of life and quality of relationships which it generates, that determines a woman's place wherever she is and to whichever class she belongs. . . .

In order to see the housewife as central, it was first of all necessary to analyze briefly how capitalism has created the modern family and the housewife's role in it, by destroying the types of family group or community which previously existed. . . . Now in order to understand the frustrations of women expressing themselves in ever-increasing forms, we must be clear what in the nature of the family under capitalism precipitates a crisis on this scale. The oppression of women, after all, did not begin with capitalism. What began with capitalism was the more intense exploitation of women *as* women and the possibility at last of their liberation. . . .

Capital, destroying the family and the community and production as one whole, on the one hand has concentrated basic social production in the factory and the office, and on the other has detached the man from the family and turned him into a *wage laborer*. It has put on the man's shoulders the burden of financial responsibility for women, children, the old and the ill, in a word, all those who do not receive wages. . . . Since Marx, it has been clear that capital rules and develops through the wage, that is, that the foundation of capitalist society was the wage laborer and his or her direct exploitation. What has been neither clear nor assumed by the organizations of the working class movement is that precisely through the wage has the exploitation of the non-wage laborer been organized. . . . That is, the wage commanded a larger amount of labor than appeared in factory bargaining. *Where women are concerned, their labor appears to be a personal service outside of capital.* . . . Woman . . . has been isolated in the home, forced to carry out work that is considered unskilled, the work of giving birth to, raising, disciplining, and servicing the worker for production. Her role in the cycle of social production remained invisible because only the product of her labor, *the laborer*, was visible there. She herself was thereby trapped within pre-capitalist working conditions and never paid a wage. . . .

With the advent of the capitalist mode of production, then, women were relegated to a condition of isolation, enclosed within the family cell, dependent in every aspect on men. The new autonomy of the free wage slave was denied her, and she remained in a pre-capitalist stage of personal dependence, but this time more brutalized because in contrast to the large-scale highly socialized production which now prevails. Woman's apparent incapacity to do certain things, to understand certain things, originated in her history, which is a history very similar in certain respects to that of "backward" children in special ESN classes. To the extent that women were cut off from direct socialized production and isolated in the home, all possibilities of social life outside the neighborhood were denied them. . . . Thus the isolation from which women have suffered has confirmed to society and to themselves the myth of female incapacity. . . .

It is often asserted that, within the definition of wage labor, women in domestic labor are not productive. In fact precisely the opposite is true if one thinks of the enormous quantity of social services which capitalist organization transforms into privatized activity, putting them on the backs of housewives. Domestic labor is not essentially "feminine work"; a woman does not work less or get less exhausted than a man from washing and cleaning. These are social services inasmuch as they serve the reproduction of labor power. And capital, precisely by instituting its family structure, has "liberated" the man from these functions so that he is completely "free" for *direct* exploitation; so that he is free to "earn" enough for a woman to reproduce him as labor power. . . . In Italy women are still necessary in the home and capital still needs this form of the family. . . . And women are of service not only because they carry out domestic labor *without a wage and without going on strike*, but also because they always receive back into the home all those who are periodically expelled from their jobs by economic crisis. . . .

If we fail to grasp completely that precisely this family is the very pillar of the capitalist organization of work, if we make the mistake of regarding it only as a superstructure, dependent for change only on the stages of the struggle in the factories, then we will be moving in a limping revolution that will always perpetuate and aggravate a *basic contradiction in the class struggle, and a contradiction which is functional to capitalist development*. We would, in other words, be perpetuating the error of considering ourselves as producers of use values only, of considering housewives external to the working class. . . .

We have only attempted to consider female domestic productivity without going into detail about the psychological implications. At least we have located and essentially outlined this female domestic productivity as it passes through the complexities of the role that the woman plays. . . . We pose, then, as foremost the need to break this role that wants women divided from each other, from men and from children, each locked in her family as the chrysalis in the cocoon that imprisons itself by its own work, to die and leave silk for capital. To reject all this means for housewives to recognize themselves also as a section of the class, the most degraded because they are not paid a wage. The housewife's position in the overall struggle of women is crucial, since it undermines the very pillar support-ing the capitalist organization of work, namely the family. (Dalla Costa in James 1972: 19–46 passim, original emphasis)

THE FAMILY'S ENVIRONMENT

We tend to think of the family[4] as to some extent insulated from other areas of social life—goings on among relatives are private matters. Where an identifica-tion is made between the home and the family, a further dimension is added to this through very precise concepts of territorial boundaries.

These may be reflected in the layout of houses, with a prominent front door, and shielded windows. Where concepts of house and home overlap, so do concepts of household and family. It is no accident that the person within the family (the mother/wife) who is most closely identified with the home ("A woman's place is in the home") and the household ("Nothing but a housewife"), should be seen as insulated from the world and defensive of the family's privacy. Women (housewives) "stand for" some of the ideas we have about the nature of the family and family life itself. Men (workers) "stand for" the rest, for the world. But although we think of the family as a discrete, isolated, self-sufficient unit, in fact it is subject to many pressures and influences from the outside. Dalla Costa

---

4. And the following is probably true whether the family is taken as just a nuclear family (spouses and children) or as an extended family, where active ties, including economic ones, are maintained with a variety of relatives. However numerous and varied the members of the family are, perhaps providing its female members with many relationships, one may still look for a boundary between "the family" and "the world."

analyzed its role as an element in the capitalist system. Let us consider other possible kinds of environments.

Michael Young and Peter Willmott's study of what happened to families who moved from a London borough to a suburban housing estate is now famous. The point I wish to pick out is a very obvious one: that the contexts in which families exist influence the way relations are handled within them. This particular move meant that families changed their type of housing, patterns of mobility, leisure time activities, and such like. All these had repercussions on the internal structure of family life. Look at the position of the husband.

> The great triangle of childhood is mother-father-child; in Bethnal Green [the London borough] the great triangle of adult life is Mum-wife-husband. . . . Both mother and husband have claims on the loyalty and affections of the same person, and, if the marriage is to reach stability, they have to adjust these claims by coming to terms with each other.
>
> Some husbands we interviewed were more articulate about it than others. "My wife wants to stay near her mother," said one outspoken husband. "For myself, I've got nothing against my mother-in-law—she's always been very good to me—but I'd like to get as far away from her as I possibly can." Mr Warner said, pointedly, in his wife's presence, "Some people are too close to their mothers, if you ask me. They ought to stand on their own feet a bit more." Mr Marris told us that although he and his wife had moved out to a flat at Enfield when they first married, she insisted on coming back to live with Mum when her first baby was due. "There was a difference of opinion over it," he said, "she wanted to come back to her Mum and I didn't."
>
> The reasons for such an attitude become apparent if one considers the experience of some other marriages. "I know she's your mother," one man told his wife, "but she sometimes forgets I'm your husband." "My sisters are married but they're not really married, if you know what I mean," another informant said. "When they finish work they go straight round to Mum's and don't get home till 9.30 or 10 at night." Mrs Warner, to instance another wife, was so identified with her mother that it turned out that when she said "us" during the interview she meant Mum and her, not her husband and herself: "*We* see so-and-so" meant "I see them at Mum's." Husbands so excluded from the feminine circle can be understood if they feel resentful of Mum's influence. . . .
>
> One man insisted that he never saw his wife's mother: "Do you hear that, Alice?" he shouted to his wife in the next room. "How often do I see your

mother? Ho, ho, that's good, ain't it? I never see her—never. I keep away from her." Mrs Trimble said about her husband's contacts with her mother, "He never goes round her place. When I go round he don't come. He only sees Mum when she comes round here—and that's not very often."

Although, in these families, the husband seeks through "mother-in-law avoidance" to reduce the conflict between himself and his wife's mother, he may avoid conflict in the extended family only to aggravate it in his family of marriage. The wife is determined to keep in close touch with her mother. The husband resents Mum's power but, though he can avoid her direct influence, he cannot avoid the indirect effects of his wife's refusal to follow his example. He can keep away from his mother-in-law, but unless his wife keeps away from her too, the triangle may still be in tension. . . .

Wherever the couple live close to the wife's mother, the husband may find he has hardly any choice but to accept his involvement in her extended family. He is sent round by his wife to borrow some bread when they run out on a Sunday. His wife is not at home when he gets back from work; knowing she will be "round Mum's," off he goes to fetch her. Little Sandra, left at Mum's on a Saturday while her mother goes shopping, is waiting there to be collected by him. In countless ways, if his wife's life is focused on her mother, then so too is his.

The majority of the "in-laws" accept their role with good grace. As far as we could judge, most men are reconciled to their mother-in-law, and their mother-in-law to them. Some actually enjoy her company and speak of her with obvious warmth, like Mr Wilkins, who said, "People complain about their mothers-in-law, but my wife's mother is one of the best in the world." (Young and Willmott [1957] 1962: 62–70 passim)

The physical proximity of the husbands' and wives' families of origin is obviously important here.

However fully he enters his wife's family, the husband does not resign from his own. The men are not drawn right out of their own families into their wives'; they tend to see more of their wives' kin, it is true, but they keep in closer touch with both families than their wives. . . .

In a district in which husbands and wives so often have both parents near, these contacts might perhaps be chance meetings in the street. But this is not so. In the interviews we were struck time and again by the regularity with which men kept in touch with their parents, usually calling at the same time each week. "I go down on my own to see the old lady every Thursday regular." "He goes round there every Friday evening; I don't see her more than three times a year myself.". . . This feeling of obligation was recognized by the wives, who expected their husbands to keep up their regular weekly visits. "He goes round to see her regular," said one woman. "Naturally, she's his mother, isn't she?" Marriage apart, the mother-son bond is recognized in Bethnal Green as being secondary only to that between mother and daughter. (Young and Willmott [1957] 1962: 73–74)

The authors have this to say about their study of families:

If we are to pick out one conclusion, it is the importance of residence. The Bethnal Greeners whom we have been describing did not change their residence just because they got married. They have remained in their district, and consequently in their families, of origin. The wife stays close to her mother because she already shares so many common interests and associations, and since she stays nearby, she keeps them alive and renews them. The wife's relationship most of all with her mother, but also with her other female relatives, is firmer than the husband's relationship with his men relatives, unless indeed he works with them. But the husband, while he may move towards his wife's home, does not usually move far from his own parents; he maintains his connexion with them at the same time as he does in the ordinary way succeed in resolving the tension between himself and his in-laws. . . . All these adjustments . . . are played out within a limited physical space. . . . Where mother and daughter are also neighbours they are almost bound to share with each other the tasks which fall to women, and this despite the many changes in housing, in the child welfare services, in the birth-rate, and, above, all, in the relationship between man and wife.

We have stressed the bearing of residence, in its time dimension, upon family ties and upon the friendliness of unrelated people. But have we not, here . . . perhaps overdone its importance? The best way to test our impressions is to watch what happens when people change their residence. We cannot . . . induce an experimental change and observe the results. We cannot select a sample of people and persuade then to move for the sake of our strange mission. The best we can do is to follow ex-Bethnal Greeners who have recently moved out of the borough to a housing estate. (Young and Willmott [1957] 1962: 117–18)

Some couples moved away from the borough precisely in order to modify the pressure of other relationships.

> Mrs Mann was pulled by conflicting loyalties. She said "I like to see Mum of course," but she was attached to her husband and understood his resentment. . . . Their tiny house has been "condemned by the sanitary man" and is due for early demolition under a slum clearance scheme, so "the Council has been round to see where we want to go." Having talked it over "we put our names down for a house at Greenleigh [the housing estate]. My husband says it will cost more and he'll have the extra journey, but we can make our own life out there." (Young and Willmott [1957] 1962: 67)

It was possibly no accident that the initiative came from the husband. Look now at what has happened to the respective roles of husband and wife as they are played out on the housing estate.

> Mrs Harper, a stout, red-faced woman in her late thirties, had, like her husband, always lived in the same part of Bethnal Green before she went to Greenleigh in 1948. She came from a large family—six girls and two boys—and she grew up amidst brothers and sisters, uncles and aunts and cousins. When she married at eighteen, she went on living with her parents, and her first child was brought up more by her mother than by herself. . . . Their life was still that of the extended family. . . . People were always dropping in on Mrs Harper. "I used to have them all in," she told us, "relations and friends as well." At her confinements, "all my sisters and the neighbours used to help. My sisters used to come in and make a cup of tea and that." . . .
>
> That busy sociable life is now a memory. Shopping in the mornings amidst the chromium and tiles of the Parade is a lonely business compared with the familiar faces and sights of the old street market. The evenings are quieter too: "It's the television most nights and the garden in the summer. . . . "I tried getting friendly with the woman next door but one," she explained, "but it didn't work." It is the loneliness she dislikes most—and the "quietness" which she thinks will in time "send people off their heads." Her husband is of a different mind. "It's not bad here," he says. "Anyway, we've got a decent house with a garden, that's the main thing—and it's made all the difference to the children. I don't let the other people here get me down." He still works in Bethnal Green—there are no jobs for up-holsterers at Greenleigh. This has its drawbacks, especially the fares and

the time spent travelling, but it means he is able to look in on his parents once a week and call about once a month on his wife's father and eldest sister. . . . Mrs Harper herself seldom sees her relatives any more. . . .

Women feel the lack of friends, as of kin, more keenly than their menfolk. Those who do not follow their husbands into the society of the workplace—and loneliness is one of the common reasons for doing so—have to spend their day alone, "looking at ourselves all day," as they say. In one interview the husband was congratulating himself on having a house, a garden, a bathroom, and a TV "the tellie is a bit of a friend down here"—when his wife broke in to say, "It's all right for you. What about all the time I have to spend here on my own?" This difference in their life may cause sharp contention, especially in the early years. "When we first came," said Mrs Haddon, "I'd just had the baby and it was all a misery, not knowing anyone. I sat on the stairs and cried my eyes out. For the first two years we were swaying whether to go back. I wanted to and my husband didn't. We used to have terrible arguments about it. I used to say 'It's all right for you. I have to sit here all day. You do get a break.'" (Young and Willmott [1957] 1962: 132–38, 149–50)

It is the husband—the spouse at most disadvantage in the old situation—who voices approval of the new. Not only is he freed from some of the constraints which beset him in the borough, but the mobility which his occupation forces on him allows him to still maintain links with kinsfolk. But now he is in the position of being able to take the initiative, rather than just having to put up with the pressures of his wife's network.

Young and Willmott emphasize the continuity there was in Mrs. Harper's experience of life among her relatives in Bethnal Green. Change came not when she herself moved from being a daughter to being a mother, or when the children she cared for were her own instead of younger brothers and sisters, but when a geographical shift, a change of location, took her out of the orbit of her extended family. Yet time itself can also be part of the environment: the family and the roles of family members undergo what are sometimes quite drastic changes through time. These changes are not brought about by a sudden, unique upheaval, as was the case for those families who moved to the housing estate. They are a product of the very obvious fact that individuals grow up, mature, marry, and age, and that their relations with other members of their family and the household must alter. These are regular, fairly predictable developments—regular to the point that anthropologists often refer to households (or family groups) as undergoing a "developmental cycle."

Take a case where, as in Bethnal Green, the mother is an important figure in the extended family, but where the social environment of these families is rather different: modern[5] Ashanti society, in Ghana (West Africa). At first sight, Ashanti households seem to present a problem.

> Ashanti to-day is not a stable and homogeneous society. Occupational differentiation; stratification by income, education, and rank; geographical and social mobility; as well as disparate values in religious belief, morality, law, and personal ideals, have produced a diversified and in parts unstable social system. One sign of this is that there *appears* to be no fixed norm, of domestic grouping. The influence of processes of growth correlated with age, sex, social maturation, marriage, economic achievement, and so forth is marked in the structure of the domestic group. (Fortes [1949] 1970: 7, original emphasis)

The anthropologist is struck by the fluidity and diversity of social life, and there seems to be no immediately discernible pattern behind the many different kinds of domestic groups which are found there.

> The Ashanti live in rectangular houses clearly separated from one another. A dwelling-house is occupied by what I shall call a dwelling group. Ashanti domestic organization, nowadays, is very elastic. Not only do dwelling groups vary in composition at a given time, but their membership fluctuates from month to month as people move to and fro for farming or trade. . . .
>
> The most striking feature of Ashanti domestic life appears vividly in one of the common sights in any village or township. As night falls young boys and girls can be seen hurrying in all directions carrying large pots of cooked food. One can often see food being carried out of a house and a few minutes later an almost equal amount of food being carried into it. The food is being taken by the children from the houses in which their mothers reside to those in which their fathers live. Thus one learns that husband and wife often belong to different domestic groups, the children perhaps sleeping in their mothers' houses and eating with their fathers. But inquiry shows that husband, wife, and children sometimes occupy the same dwelling. Frequently, however, the domestic group appears to consist of women only or of a miscellaneous assortment of men, women, and children. . . .

---

5.   The particular study on which the following is based was carried out by Meyer Fortes in 1945–46.

Analysis shows that the position of household head . . . is the key to the most important features of domestic structure. Both men and women occupy this position, and Ashanti maintain that there is complete equality between them in this respect. They say also that the head of a dwelling group is normally the most senior by age, generation, or status of the members. This follows from the rule that seniority carries authority and commands respect. But it is also a basic rule in Ashanti social and political organization that seniority alone does not automatically confer positions of authority. A household head must have the necessary personal qualities to command the respect and adherence of the group and, in particular, he must have the means to maintain his station. . . . Thus a young man may be *de facto* owner of the house, but his mother may live with him and be recognized as titular head. . . .

Ashanti lay great stress on the economic circumstances which enable a person to set up an independent household. Indeed every Ashanti, man or woman, aspires to have his or her own house. But it is only in periods of exceptional prosperity that a man can achieve the means for this before middle age. Though women in theory have the same economic opportunities and legal status as men, in practice their freedom is less. . . . Women occasionally become wealthy and many own more property than their menfolk; but in general the responsibilities of motherhood while the children are young are a handicap to economic achievement. So it is more common for a woman to become the head of a household as a result of her son's building a house for her than by her own efforts. . . .

Among many motives influencing men to set up their own household are Ashanti ideas of dignity. A young man does not mind residing with an older brother or his father or his mother's brother. A man of middle age would regard this as unbecoming. Of course no man of means would be content to live as a dependent member of a brother's or mother's brother's household. He would be expected to take responsibility for young members of his mother's lineage segment, and in particular, to have a house where some or all could live. One of the strongest motives is the desire, among both men and women, for domestic independence. (Fortes [1949] 1970: 10–15 passim)

If we look at these households as changing through time, something of a pattern emerges.

Ashanti domestic structure changes over time in a manner analogous to growth. . . . It may be, for instance, that while her children are young a woman prefers to reside with her husband, but that when they grow up she prefers her own matricentral household. . . .

During the first two or three years of wifehood the great majority of young wives continue to reside with their own kin. Young and inexperienced, they cling to their mothers. As they advance in maturity the pull of conjugal ties increases and reaches its maximum at the peak of the child-bearing years, in the thirties. By this time they have perhaps three children, for whom it is an advantage to be under their father's care. Finally, when their child-bearing years are over and their children are grown up, the desire to establish their own households becomes strong in many women, the more so if they are widowed or divorced. (Fortes [1949] 1970: 24–25)

During the course of his or her life, an Ashanti individual may, then, not only be a member of different households but also experience households with both male and female heads. The fact that either sex may fill this position is important.

In Bethnal Green we saw how a woman's mother and husband were in a sense in constant competition over her loyalties. This affected the degree of support which mothers could expect from their adult daughters and it affected what husbands and wives did with their time together. Young and Willmott speak of the "great triangle of adult life," and in doing so they draw attention to something of significance: that it is three *individuals* who find themselves with some interests in common and some interests in conflict. And the tension is related intimately to these persons—there is no suggestion that relations with other people are constantly brought to bear on the "triangle," that the welfare of the children or solidarity between brothers and sisters could, for example, be crucial factors in the way a woman and her mother and her husband work out their relationships to one another. Other persons may be brought in from to time, but the basis of the triangle is the interest which just these three individuals have in one another.

There is tension in Ashanti families too. But the tension is more than interpersonal. At least three sets of influences affect the life of adults; attachment to their maternal home, the pull of conjugal (husband-wife) ties, and a desire for independence as head of their own household. Now these influences are brought to bear on men and on women alike. They are, moreover, influences which do not arise out of a simple opposition between men and women in certain roles but out of the very important connection which Ashanti nuclear families and Ashanti households have with other institutions.

The most significant institution to consider for our purposes is the matriline-age. Traditional Ashanti villages were divided into wards, each of which was oc-cupied by a group of people who regarded themselves as members of a particular lineage. As in the Bemba case cited in Chapter One, a person traces his ties with other members of the lineage through his mother; brothers and sisters, but not husbands and wives, are thus members of the same lineage group. Although the ties between mother and child are given great social weight from this fact, the father is also regarded as an important figure, and a number of obligations and privileges arise from the father-child relationship. In theory, too, it is an ideal for a man after marriage to have his own home and his wife and children living with him. Here we see a source of some of the tensions which beset Ashanti individuals.

Ashanti discuss the subject interminably, stressing especially the inevitability of conflicting loyalties. For a woman the conflict turns on the difficulties of recon-ciling attachment to her mother with duty to her husband. A man feels it most in relation to his own children and his sister's children. . . .

A man is legally obliged to consider the interests of his sister's children because he is their legal guardian and they are his potential heirs. He is morally impelled to care for them because they ensure the continuation of the lineage segment sprung from his mother. But exceptional importance is also attached to paternity . . . in law, in religion, and in personal relations. It is considered to be a father's duty to bring up and equip his children for life. His love for them and pride in them are often stronger than his legally enjoined responsibility for his sister's children. Ashanti say that the traditional compromise is for a man to have his children living with him till adolescence and then to let them go to their mother's brother. . . . These norms and attitudes have their counterparts in the norms of filial duty (e.g. children have to provide their father's coffin), respect, and affection, the spontaneity of which is often contrasted with the obligatory duty and respect towards the uncle. Christianity and modern changes have ag-gravated but not created these tensions. It is of great significance that there is not a single case . . . of a man and his wife's brother sharing a dwelling. This structural arrangement prevents intolerable conflicts of loyalties. In the domestic environ-ment a child is never confronted with both men of the parental generation who have authority over him. (Fortes [1949] 1970: 23–24)

Here, too, we see a reason for the different types of Ashanti households. Let us look at the internal relations of members of various households. There is a contrast between the composition of domestic groups under male heads and those under female heads. The household of a male head is likely to consist either of his wife (or wives) and children; or in addition, a sister and her children as well. Under a female head a household will consist of the woman's children, and probably a sister and her children as well, and perhaps daughters and their children. Now whereas the household under the male head is often simply a domestic unit, the domestic unit under a female head is invariably something more. It is *also* the core of a matrilineage. It is significant that if there are males living in a household of this second type that they are likely to be sons or sisters' sons or an immediate brother of the household head, but not a husband. It would be contemptible for a man to live at his wife's house, for his ties to his wife are of a personal kind, and this would be tantamount to admitting the woman's personal authority over him. However it is no disgrace for a man to live at his mother's or sister's house, for the household here is a segment of a matrilineage, and the man is acknowledging not the power of an individual woman but the primacy of his lineage.

> The members of the matricentral group, the mother as well as her children, seek to assert its autonomy wherever possible, and to maintain its unity as long as the social relations created within it survive. Full autonomy is reached when the mother, if she lives long enough, or one of the sons, or, less commonly, daughters, becomes head of a household. Inevitably, therefore, a household under a female head must be a matrilineage segment. (Fortes [1949] 1970: 19)

It seems to be the case in Ashanti that mothers and their children feel themselves to be a distinct unit to such a degree that there is this constant tendency for them to assert independence, to become autonomous. It is not just the ambitions of middle-aged women which lead to mothers forming their own households in the later years of marriage, away from their husband, but the fact that their sons are interested in seeing the core of the matrilineage established as a unified and independent group.

MARRIAGE, KINSHIP, AND STATUS

The internal composition of Ashanti households, and the changing patterns which these domestic groups undergo through time, can only be understood in full if we take into account the relationship of these units to much wider group-ings such as the matrilineage. Conflicts between individual husbands and wives or brothers and sisters arise from their lineage backgrounds and the competing demands of lineage and other loyalties. It was also clear that women are able to achieve prominence as household heads because of their status as focal figures for the continuity of the matrilineage. But it must not be imagined that the presence of this form of social structure, matriliny, gives rise to unique conflicts and unique advantages for women in the domestic sphere. The outside world can impinge on domestic life in many ways. Gonja present another example where households tend to undergo radical alteration during the later years of a woman's life, and where again females take the initiative; but matriliny does not come into the picture at all.

The Gonja state lies not far from the old Ashanti kingdom, extending across the breadth of northern Ghana. Gonja do not have the kind of lineage system which influences Ashanti domestic life. Something on which Gonja do put great emphasis is keeping up links between siblings—sets of brothers and sis-ters—even after marriage. Indeed, one's brothers and sisters have to some extent a claim on one's own children, and may ask to foster one of them. The child then goes to live with his aunt or uncle until old enough to marry. They teach him or her domestic or other skills, and in return expect some help. But this is not the chief motive in seeking foster children. Fostering importantly reinforces the ties which exist between brothers and sisters in the senior generation. Something like half the adult population was fostered as children.

What effect does this have on relations between husband and wife? In re-spect of their children their claims are equally balanced: from the wife's side it is usually a brother who will ask for one of the children to go and live with him; on the husband's the request is likely to come from a sister of his. In turn, the couple may foster a nephew or niece from the side of either partner. And a Gonja couple do regard themselves very much as partners—two persons bound by contract to one another, but a contract which can always be broken. In con-trast to the ties of blood which exist between kinsfolk, and are exemplified in the sibling relationship, the marital relationship is looked upon as a transient one. Marriages tend to break up fairly easily.

Divorce in Gonja is easily brought about by either partner, although most fre-quently initiated by the wife. It appears to be a relatively common occurrence at all stages of a woman's adult life. While young women do leave their husbands before any children are born, or when they have only one or two small ones, it also happens regularly that more mature women with older children leave one spouse for another. However, as a wife approaches old age it becomes increasingly likely that she will leave her husband to settle with kin. In the early and middle stages of woman's life, marriages tend to be ended by separation which becomes finalized by a subsequent marriage rather than by a legal divorce. When an older woman separates from her husband, however, it is highly unlikely that she will remarry and her status continues [as] that of a "separated" rather than a "divorced" woman. Since separation in old age is so uniformly final it is designated [by the anthropologist] "terminal separation" to distinguish it from the separation which is in fact a transition between one marriage and another. Men, it must be noted, continue to take wives as long as they can persuade women to marry and stay with them. They generally remain married until a more advanced age than women, although elderly men . . . are often single. (Goody 1962: 36)

So there are two rather separate stages in a woman's life. First, the period when she is attached to a husband, although this may become a succession of husbands through time, and she may have children by each one; and a final period when she turns away from marriage altogether and goes to settle with kin (most likely a brother).

That elderly women tend to live with kin rather than with a husband is an empirical fact. In Buipe, of 19 women over 50, 15 were living with kin while four were living with husbands. . . . All of those with kin had been married. Eight of the 15 had husbands living, while six were widows at the time of the census. . . .

A woman knows that should her husband die first, she will in any case return to her kin in old age. Although her husband's kin have an obligation to support her if she wishes to remain with them as a dependent the majority of widows return to kin. As one woman put it, "If I stayed there they would have expected me to fetch water, carry firewood and cook for them. But here in my brother's house I can sit in the shade of my room and spin thread for my shroud in peace." If she has any kin who are able to do so, a widow will exercise her right to claim support from them. . . . In this situation, for a woman to withdraw from a marriage which she no longer finds rewarding is but to anticipate the inevitable. . . .

Here it must be noted that men do not, as a rule, encourage an ageing wife to leave. Even when she can no longer bear children and has ceased to be interested in sexual relations, a wife is valued as a companion and for the domestic services she renders. . . . The regularity with which men express regret when their older wives desert them leaves no doubt as to their feelings. (Goody 1962: 36–41 passim)

The initiative to move away from the marital home seems to come, then, from the wife. Why does she do it? One factor which makes it easy for elderly women to adopt this course of action is that there is no absolute identification of her children with her marriage. In leaving her husband she is not necessarily leaving her children. Some of them may have spent most of their childhood living elsewhere with foster parents. Moreover, children of previous marriages are likely, if they have not been fostered, to be living with their own father rather than a stepfather (the woman's present husband). So, in going back to her brother she will be residing with someone who may have fostered one of her sons, and if the son is still a boy could be yet living there himself. The children of all her marriages will in any case feel free to visit her at her new home.

A woman does not greatly prejudice her close relationship to her own children and to her grandchildren by leaving her husband in old age to reside with kin. Her [married] daughters will in any case be living in virilocal[6] marriage and will continue to visit her wherever she is. In fact, they will do so more freely and for longer periods if she is living with her kin than would be the case if she were with a step-father. . . . One or more sons may in any case be living with maternal kin. If their mother has remarried, sons too are likely to feel constrained in visiting the house of a step-father, whereas they are welcomed by their mother's kin. . . .

We must . . . consider also the children of siblings. For these are, in a very real sense, felt to be one's own. This was stated and reaffirmed again and again, and is reinforced by the institution of fostering and by the lines of inheritance of property which tends to pass between "siblings,"[7] including first and second cousins, in order of birth. Hence the body of kin for whom wealth is held in trust is composed of siblings and their children. The obligations which are associated with such a kin group include economic support, succour in illness or trouble and contributions to the costs of litigation and funerals. A woman who leaves a husband to reside with a sibling is reasserting her position in this kin

6. That is, will be living at their husband's place.

7. Quotation marks indicate that the relationship is not an immediate one.

group, especially the rights of herself and her children *vis-à-vis* its property and its personnel. Rights in the personnel include the right to a sibling's daughter or granddaughter as a foster child, upon whose help a woman is particularly dependent as her own strength fails. (Goody 1962: 47)

An old woman knows that there will be someone to care for her at her brother's home in her declining years. But this is not everything. The anthropologist, Esther Goody, makes us look at other aspects of kinship relations between men and women, and the kind of status with which women in particular kin roles are endowed.

Those women who most regularly leave their husbands in old age include members of the ruling group. These are descendants of an original band of conquerors, who provide the chiefs and control other political offices. Women as well as men belong to this group by birth, through their fathers. Marriage does not alter a woman's status in this respect, even if she marries a commoner. The implications are clear.

When a woman of the Ruling estate marries out and returns to kin in old age, she is not only maximizing her status by activating her role as sister, but she is associating herself with "brothers" who are likely to hold major chiefships and thus borrowing from their glory. The present paramount chief has moved, as custom demands, from his own Division of Daboya to the capital at Damongo, and his household there includes, in addition to his wives and children, several "sisters" who have chosen to leave not only their husbands but also their natal Division in order to participate in the life at court. There are tangible rewards for so doing. On the occasion of the enrobing of the new chief of Kusawgu Division I met two of the YagbumWura's "sisters" who had been sent to represent him at the ceremony and who were treated throughout with the greatest respect. At the capital each has her own compound and attends her "brother's" audience daily. . . . Terminal separation for those women of the Ruling estate who marry out, serves to maximize status by reassociating them with kin in positions of power. . . . Commoner women who exchange the role of wife for that of sister better their status in the domestic domain but not in the community as a whole.

The status accorded an elderly woman approaches that of a male elder. She possesses the wisdom and ritual knowledge associated with age, and is accorded commensurate respect. The Gonja are very conscious of seniority of age as the basis of respect and deference. . . . By the time a woman reaches late middle age there are apt to be few members left of her parents' generation. Her surviving kin tend to be mostly younger "siblings" and "children," her own and those of her siblings and cousins. She is thus, when living among kin, in a genealogically superior position. In her husband's house, however, she is not only subordinate to him, as is every wife, but she is surrounded by his kin, with whom . . . considerations of birth order are secondary to the constraints of affinity.[8] The role of wife is defined is subordinate, while that of sister is not. (Goody 1962: 42–43 passim)

A woman of the ruling group is thus in a much greater position of power as a sister than as a wife. But even for those who do not belong to this group, the role of sister as such is the more honorable. In moving away to her brother's compound, it is this status as a "sister" which the Gonja woman asserts.

STEREOTYPES AND THE LOCUS OF TENSION

Let us turn back to some of the earlier evidence in this chapter and put these pictures of Ashanti and Gonja women against that of the European housewife.

In all these cases evaluations are put on particular aspects of a woman's roles. Some roles are given more cultural significance than others. We can talk about an Ashanti "housewife," but when an Ashanti woman looks forward to becoming the head of her own household, it is the status of being a founder of a matrilineage which she really covets. She will be thought of as "mother" or "grandmother" before she will be thought of as "housewife." Men have to put up with wives leaving them in old age, because they recognize this aspect of their wife's position. A man's sons belong to his wife's lineage, not his own, and it is his sons who will build her a house, or who will go with her to reside at her brother's place. He himself may have been residing with his own mother. A Gonja woman has not the same status as a "mother," for she docs not found a lineage segment. But Gonja stress the importance of siblings keeping in touch with one another, and throughout her life, and through all her marriages, a woman remembers the fact that she is a "sister." She can look to some males (brothers), if not to others (husbands), to honor her in this role.

There are two things to note here. The first is that the kind of households which Ashanti and Gonja families form change through a person's life-cycle,

---

8.   That is, the deference she has to show to her in-laws (affines).

and one can identify the points in this cycle at which prominence is given to certain roles. It is not just that an Ashanti woman is a wife and a mother but that her status as mother takes primacy when she establishes a household independently of her husband. It is not just that a Gonja woman is a wife and a sister but that she may covet the honor she will receive as a sister so much that it leads to her in the end abandoning her husband and going to live in her brother's compound.

If in domestic life Ashanti and Gonja women are in a sense mothers and sisters first, and everything else second, then the first thing which many an English or American woman must be is a housewife. Here is the second point. In the West African (and to some extent the East London) examples, the role which is stressed to the point of taking precedence over others in certain spheres is a kinship one. "Mother" and "sister" are kin designations. In the other case the comparable role is an occupational one. A "housewife" is someone who does housework. This tells us quite a lot about differences between the societies we have been considering. Does it tell us anything about relations between men and women?

At first sight one might assume that where relations between the sexes within the household are cast primarily in a kinship idiom tensions would be minimized. Men are likely to agree to the actions woman take (and vice versa) because after all one cannot do anything about one's kinship role. Kinship obligations are sanctioned by society. If one has children one cannot help being a "mother" or a "father"; if one is of a family of several brothers and sisters one cannot help being a "brother" or a "sister" oneself. Every man must know that this wife comes from a family where she is also a daughter. Most females pass through the stages of daughter/wife/mother/grandmother, and are related to others who are their father/husband/child/grandchild. And the rights and duties derived from these connections are fairly standard. Hence, one might think that stereotypes which draw on kinship roles reduce conflict between men and women. But in some cases at least the reverse would seem to be true.

There was considerable domestic tension between men and women in Bethnal Green households, so how was this seen? As a product of the triangle, Mum-wife-husband. Look back again at the tensions between Ashanti husbands and wives and the grumblings from Gonja men when their spouses go off. A man can be someone else's son or brother and still want his wife to behave differently from his own kinswomen. There is no inherent harmony in these systems simply because they give primacy to talking about relations in

terms of kinship. Men and women are perceived quite clearly to have conflicting interests.

One can probably go further than this and say that indeed where a kinship
idiom (where stereotypes are formed on the basis of family roles) is predomi-
nant, it can be the case that far from obscuring conflict this actually recognizes
and pinpoints sources of potential tension between men and women. These
roles have an inevitability about them, and conflicts which are also phrased in
terms of conflicts between people in certain kinship positions (roles) are being made to seem equally inevitable. I am not saying that conflict is necessary
everywhere between the sexes. I am saying that in Bethnal Green, Ashanti, and
Gonja households men and women can come into conflict, and that when they
do the reason for this is seen by the people themselves to lie in the fact of kinship. It is seen to lie in the irreducible dilemma of an individual having to cope
with different roles: the same person has to play "daughter" to one person and
"wife" to another.

And, so it would appear to those experiencing the situation, this kind of
conflict is not something that anyone can do anything about. A decision going
one way has to be at the cost of a decision going another. Doing mother's shopping may be at the expense of seeing that husband's tea is on the table when he
gets home from work. Fortes wrote of the Ashanti:

> On the one side are the overwhelming bonds of matrilineal kinship which em-
> brace those arising out of motherhood; on the other, the ties of marriage and
> of paternity. Ashanti are much preoccupied with this problem and constantly
> discuss it. (Fortes 1950: 261)

The conflict of loyalties which the man or woman experiences is felt to be inherent in the kind of social life they lead. And because it is seen this way, in all
relationships lies a reminder of what could happen even to those individuals
who manage to make the best of the situation. It has to do with the social position people find themselves in, and not simply with their personalities or private
opinions. "My mother-in-law isn't a bad old stick," said Mr. White. And then
he went on to add: "But it is not easy. My wife has to side with her Mum every
time there's a difference, and I have to side with my wife" (Young and Willmott
[1957] 1962: 65).

Bethnal Green men appear to cope by looking on the woman as the person
most caught by conflicting demands, and by seeing her as someone who has to

be a wife and a daughter. She has to balance both positions. Primacy is given to neither of these roles. But where the opportunity is offered, the husband may find himself in a position to assert his conjugal claims, as did those men who carried their wives off to the new housing estate. And here we see a transformation. Removed from the kinship triangle, the women do not see themselves as now (at last) just "wives." When it was a matter of reconciling demands made by their mothers and their husbands, it was coping with being both a daughter and a wife. The mother's presence removed, the woman's problems develop a radically new perspective. Being just a wife becomes very quickly overshadowed by a different kind of status—that of housewife.

> The house when the builders leave it is only a shell. . . . The furniture brought from Bethnal Green looks old and forlorn against the bright paint. They need carpets for the lounge, lino for the stairs, and mats for the front door. They need curtains. They need another bed. They need a kitchen table. They need new lamp-shades, pots and pans, grass seed and spades, clothes lines and bath mats . . .—all the paraphernalia of modern life for a house two or three times larger and a hundred times grander than the one they left behind them. With the aid of their belongings, they need somehow to live the kind of life, be the kind of people, that will fit into Forest Close or Cambridge Avenue. . . . "My sister gave me a beautiful Dunkley pram," said Mrs Berry, "because I was going to such a beautiful new house."
>
> In Bethnal Green people . . . belong to a close network of personal relationships. . . . It is true, of course, that people have different incomes, different kinds of jobs, different kinds of houses—in this respect there is much less uniformity than at Greenleigh—even different standards of education. But these attributes are not so important in evaluating others. It is personal characteristics which matter. The first thing they think of about Bert is not that he has a "fridge" and a car. They see him as bad-tempered, or a real good sport, or the man with a way with women, or one of the best boxers. . . . How different is Greenleigh. . . . Where nearly everyone is a stranger, there is no means of uncovering personality. People cannot be judged by their personal characteristics: a person can certainly see that his neighbour works in his back garden in his shirt sleeves and his wife goes down to the shops in a blue coat, with two canvas bags. . . . If people have nothing else to go by, they judge from his appearance, his house, or even his Minimotor. He is evaluated accordingly. Once the accepted standards are few, and mostly to do with wealth, they become the standards by which "status" is judged. . . .

The status is that of the family of marriage much more sharply than it is in Bethnal Green. In Bethnal Green the number of relatives who influence a person's standing is much larger, and they also are varied in their attributes. . . . One connexion confers high status, another low. It is therefore all the more difficult to give a person a single rating. On the other hand, the comparative isolation of the family at Greenleigh encourages the kind of simplified judgment of which we have been speaking. (Young and Willmott [1957] 1962: 156–63 passim)

Beyond the sphere of other kinsfolk, couples cannot be judged in terms of their conjugal roles (or even as parents to their own young children); they are judged in terms of the kind of outward life they live, and for the woman this means the kind of house she keeps.

It will be obvious that I have in turn simplified the account. Nonetheless, I think we can point to a genuine contrast in emphases. In Bethnal Green, when a woman makes household arrangements to suit her husband, against the background of her own family she is asserting her marital relationship. At Greenleigh, things she does for her husband, against the background of a house-keeping neighborhood, contribute to her standing as a housewife. I have suggested that kinship stereotypes may (not always) openly draw attention to the possibility of conflicts. Moreover, if the stereotype gives prominence to one role, as in the case of the Ashanti woman as a mother, the Gonja woman as a sister, it necessarily publicizes the fact that it is in competition with other roles which she could otherwise play concurrently. To stress one kinship position out of the several a person activates can (again, it need not) imply a shedding or diminishing of other commitments. What about the occupational stereotype of "housewife"—what does it do?

It seems to "do" three things. First, rather than draw attention to possible conflict between the sexes it offers a denial. The notion here is that everyone has their own occupation, their own place, so there is no basic contradiction between women being housewives and men being wage-earners (as there is between a married couple also trying to be brother and sister to their own brothers and sisters); indeed, there is the idea that these roles complement each other. Second, the stereotype occurs in a context where occupations are ranked, and where menial tasks come low on the ranking. It would be nonsense to say in Ashanti that "motherhood is all that women are good for"; but it makes very good sense for us to speak in that way of housewives. The occupational stereotype implies a status difference between women who do one kind of job and men who do another. Third, there is this fact of contrast itself. Men and women in Gonja are quite clear about the opposing interests which spouses and siblings have, and most people are both spouses of someone and siblings of someone else. This is a contrast in interests, in the demands and claims one can make on others. In specific domestic situations, as between husband and wife, men and women certainly compete with one another. But if competition is admitted in this way, then power to both sides is also admitted. The kind of contrast which the occupational stereotype suggests is noncompetitive; it is one of fixed allocations and fixed spheres of power. It describes a hierarchical relationship. The rationale for this lies in terms of innate qualifications. In the wage-earning world a central myth is that a person gets the work he deserves. By analogy, women get the work they deserve, and since all women are really only housewives, all women are less capable than all men. It is the women who stop being housewives, or who add other occupations to this one, who compete with men.

In Bethnal Green, females (wives/daughters) rather than males are singled out as being at the center of conflicting loyalties. In Ashanti, although perhaps to a lesser extent in Gonja, men are seen as equally subject to pulls in different directions. They have to reconcile various kinship obligations as much as their womenfolk do. Men, as a category, and women, as a category, are not being contrasted here. They are seen as competing with one another when their interests clash but *both sexes* are regarded as subjected to similar dilemmas. Kinship stereotypes classify the tensions: for both males and females, conflict "is epitomized in the contrast between the mutual trust and loyalty of brother and sister and the notorious hazards of marriage" (Fortes [1949] 1970: 23). All husbands are plagued by the fact that their wives have dual loyalties; all wives have to acknowledge that husbands look on their sister's children as their heirs, and that they cannot automatically expect support from the husband's estate after he is dead. One result is that each sex looks after itself: Ashanti "women prefer to work for themselves as an insurance against the future, rather than to assist their husband" (Fortes 1950: 272).

When members of each sex have an interest in property, or in the proceeds of their labors, they have a choice of where they will live and whom they will support, we have seen that competition can arise. In the West African examples this is most evident between husband and wife. But competition itself implies a kind of equality. Demands are made on and rights asserted by male and female alike. If husband and wife are seen as looking after their separate interests, which may finally take them in different directions, does not this, after all, put them on a kind of parity?

The European housewife / money-earner idiom might appear to do this in stressing the complementarity of men and women's roles in the upkeep of the household. Husband and wife do not compete with each other. They "make a home" together. But this kind of idiom also sends out a blatant message of inequality. For the housewife stereotype emphatically depicts one sex as dependent on the other. And dependence is seen as a weakness. Moreover, in tying each sex to a particular occupation, this kind of role allocation leaves the way right open for society's public evaluation of the respective worth of men's and women's jobs to penetrate what is, paradoxically, thought of as the most intimate and private part of a person's world—family life.

CHAPTER FOUR

The World Outside

If there is a kind of equality between the sexes in Ashanti and Gonja households, how far does this extend? We have seen that households and families do not exist as isolated units but are influenced by their social environment.

This may give the woman particular prestige, as in the case of the Ashanti mother. Much of the value put on her position as a household head comes from her importance to the matrilineage. Similarly, the housewife stereotype receives a particular evaluation because a contrast is being made not only between the husband's and wife's respective household duties but also between the wife's "work" and the husband's "work," and the husband's work takes him into the outside world. So it is in relation to the standards of this world that women's household tasks are judged.

In both these cases the way in which the female domestic role is regarded becomes modified by factors which lie outside the household. At the same time, the household may also be thought of as a domain on its own, an area in which women's prestige or power may be openly expressed; yet whatever status she achieves here, an explicit contrast with men's concerns in more public affairs can put this into strictly relative terms. Frequently the effect is that men and women are seen to act within different spheres. Two sets of arrangements flow from this: the spheres may be regarded as complementary, and the prestige each sex derives from its own particular achievements may be analogous; or the spheres may be ranked, one reckoned to be essentially inferior to the other, so that the kinds of renown accorded to men and to women cannot really be compared.

This second set is common and results in the equations

$$male : female \; [as]$$
$$superior : inferior \; [as]$$
$$public \; affairs : domestic \; life.$$

From the point of view of men participating in public affairs, their evaluation of women's domestic roles is low. While the necessity of women's jobs may be acknowledged, and individual women praised for doing their jobs particularly well, this does not detract from the premise that their sex fits them to a domain inherently less prestigious than men's.

POLITICAL ASPECTS OF KINSHIP

The rigidity of such ranking can vary. It may vary from society to society, and from context to context within a society. For example, the housewife stereotype would seem to separate off men's and women's worlds in a very explicit way and makes the further evaluation that women's work, however necessary, is not quite so important as men's. But this kind of thinking is likely to vary with class or economic difference. Where domestic entertaining is an extremely important adjunct to the *man's* work, the woman's "domestic" jobs acquire some "public" importance; indeed, the more important, the more likely are the menial tasks themselves (cooking and such) to become specialist occupations in the hands of others (servants), and the wife to assimilate herself to her husband's position, becoming a "company wife" or "ambassadress." In households where the total income is low, and the proportion of money passing through the housewife's hands high in relation to this total, the wife's decisions on how the money is to be spent may again blur a boundary between domestic and nondomestic matters. If it is the husband and not the wife who receives a weekly allowance, he is dependent on her management of the funds—not only for the maintenance of the household but for other activities as well. The husband's position may, however, be reinforced by a very positive evaluation of his job as a job of *work* (e.g., coal mining), rather than simply being regarded as a source of income.

What of Gonja and Ashanti? It would be a fallacy to assume that because kinship is so important, and because it is through a kinship role ("sister," "mother") that a woman receives prominence, there is no distinction between domestic and public affairs. In fact, in both societies significant political activities concern men more than women.

We have seen that Gonja recognize a class of rulers, and that a sister of this class who chooses to reside with a brother chief will be honored for her status as such. Actual chiefs, however, are invariably men. These men may be chiefs over particular villages, or they may hold personal titles (an analogy would be the title "minister") and live at the capital. In addition there are a small number of female chiefships. But these are largely nominal positions:

> [Female chiefs] have no formal duties except the preparation of the cooked rice for the annual D . . . ceremony, but they lead the other women of the ruling estate in greeting the divisional chief on important occasions. [They] always appear to live in the divisional capital, usually either in their own compound, or in a section of a brother's compound. . . . The Gonja office carries no responsibility for advising the divisional chief, nor any right to nominate office holders. However a divisional chief tends to appoint older women whose judgment he trusts and he may consult them, especially about domestic ritual and "women's affairs." (Goody 1973: 15)

So even though some Gonja women are chiefs in their own right, they are mainly concerned with "women's affairs," and important political business is in the hands of men.

Esther Goody herself compares the nominal position of Gonja female chiefs with the greater public roles of Ashanti women. Although the main social groupings of Ashanti are formed on a kinship basis (matrilineages), they are not only concerned with family or domestic matters. Matrilineages form political groups and men hold the major offices. Women, however, do participate.

> Every person of free matrilineal descent . . . is by birth . . . a citizen of the chiefdom in which this lineage is legally domiciled. . . . Thus one of the most prized rights of citizenship to-day is the right to occupy and farm virgin forest land freely in the chiefdom to which one's lineage owes allegiance. . . .
>
> Every such politically unitary lineage has a male head who is often *ipso facto* one of the chief's councillors. He is chosen from among all the living

male members . . . irrespective of age or generation, by consensus of the whole body of members of both sexes. . . . It is the duty of the lineage head, with the aid and advice of the older men and women, to watch over the welfare of the whole group. He has the power and the duty to settle private disputes between any of his fellow members so that peace and solidarity can prevail in the group. He is its chief representative in its political and legal relations with other lineages and with the community. He must take the lead in organizing corporate obligations, such as the funeral of a member, and he has to contribute the burial cloth. The crucial payment by the bridegroom by which a daughter of the lineage is legally espoused goes to him and his concurrence is essential for a divorce of any member of the lineage to be valid. Most important of all, both as a sign of his status and as sanction of his authority, is his custody of the male ancestral stools of the lineage. These ancestor shrines comprise the consecrated stools of his predecessors in office and they belong to the lineage as a whole. . . . The heir of a deceased member must be formally approved by the lineage head and his elders, and a widow of any member cannot remarry without their consent. . . .

In all these matters there is a very high degree of equality between male and female members of the lineage. It is common for the head to be assisted by a senior woman . . . informally chosen by him and his elders. This is extended to the State as a whole and to each chiefdom. The senior woman of the royal lineage is the Queen Mother of the chiefdom. Her duty is to watch over the morals of the women and girls, to supervise such feminine matters as girls' puberty ceremonies, which are occasions for joint activities by most of the women of the lineage, and to help to make peace in family quarrels. . . . The female ancestors of a lineage which owns a chiefship are also commemorated and paid ritual homage. The consecrated stools of the queen mothers are preserved in the custody of the ruling queen mother and she performs rites of worship similar to those of her brother the chief. . . . This does not apply to commoner lineages. . . .

Though all political offices, including the kingship, are vested in maximal lineages, ownership of land and other economically useful property is commonly vested in a segment of such a lineage. . . . It is primarily within this segment that the jural authority of the mother's brother is effective. The segment has no appointed head, but one of the experienced senior males is accepted as the leading personality. As in all departments of Ashanti social life, any matter of importance that concerns the segment or one of its members is always dealt with after consulting the senior men and women. But the leading man will have the decisive voice. (Fortes 1950: 254–58 passim)

Kinship in Ashanti, then, involves citizenship rights, the formation of political groups, access to political office. Participation in the public affairs of the lineage concerns women as well as men. And yet it can never concern women to quite the same extent.

> Though women in theory have the same economic opportunities and legal status as men, in practice their freedom is less. Thus their civic status is, in fact, subject to limitations from which men are free. Except for queen mothers, women cannot hold political office. Women have the right to express their views freely in lineage affairs; but they cannot be elected to the headship of a lineage. (Fortes [1949] 1970: 15)

While it is true that in Ashanti women are accorded a particular prominence, and this prominence derives partly from their position within the matrilineage, the allocation of formal offices reflects a basic distinction. Women are most readily accorded status as household heads. This is over the smallest segment of a lineage, and it is a status of domestic rather than public importance. The majority of politically significant positions are held by men.

The fact that ultimate authority is seen to reside with men (it is men who have custody of the ancestral shrines) perhaps throws further light on another attitude. We have seen that a man is unlikely to reside at his wife's place, for this would put him under her (or through her, her brother's) personal authority. Such a disinclination is possibly derived in part from these contrasts in men's and women's roles relating to the outside world. For a moment Ashanti appeared to be offering an example of a society in which the respective spheres of the sexes are regarded as equal (analogous) and their activities as complementary, prestige in matrilineage affairs being open to both men and women. Yet to the extent that Ashanti associate ultimate political importance with men and not with women, and to the extent that a distinction is made between public and domestic life, men have the edge. And this filters into domestic matters as well. A male does not mind living under a female household head where his choice of residence is associated with lineage status; but he would find it almost impossible to submit to the authority of a woman (his wife) on a purely personal basis.

RITUALS OF DOMINATION

The relationship of men and women to one another within the family or house-hold is thus affected by many external factors, including the wider status positions of the sexes in society. The frequent subordination of women outside the domestic sphere may be justified by reference to their innate disqualification for public life. Fitness for such life is seen to be sex-linked (to males). Ashanti say that women are barred from holding office because of the taboos they have to observe when they menstruate. Menstruating women are forbidden contact with sacred objects, and the holding of political office involves religious duties which focus on such objects. It is not just that women because of their child-rearing role do not have time for public activities but that their sex is regarded as an intrinsic barrier to full participation.

These facts are not simply the basis of practical arrangements: they contribute very importantly to how sex is defined, and to how gender is perceived. When particular characteristics are linked to gender they are made to seem supremely "natural." It becomes appropriate that men do this, women do that, because that is the way men's and women's natures are.

The public preeminence which men often claim over women is found expressed over and over again in marriage ceremonies. Although marriage leads to a union which will form the basis of a domestic unit, it is frequently more than that. The tie between husband and wife may have implications for groups beyond the particular "family" which the couple will establish. For their respective kinsfolk also establish new relations through the marriage. Ceremonies often involve all these persons coming together for the first time. In societies where kinship groups also have political interests, or where a marriage means that the woman has to alter her group status, the arrangements are likely to be dominated by men. They appear to be "transferring" the bride from one group to another. Moreover, insofar as the wedding itself is an open affair, and involves public roles such as speech-making, men will tend to take charge. The public stage may be used to enunciate the respective rights and duties of the spouses and the husband's personal authority over his wife. Men's claims to public preeminence over women in general thus emerge in arrangements designed to pair one sex with the other. Marriage ceremonies are often a crucial point at which the statuses of males and females receive symbolic attention.

Let us first consider a situation where kinship groupings do not have much political significance: the groom's and bride's sides must come together, but they do so on a largely personal basis and attention is directed toward individuals getting to know and like one another.

Matrimony is a relationship of social groups as well as individuals, the two principal partners representing the two "sides" from which they come. The twofold division which gives rise to the need for such far-reaching adjustments can be well observed at any wedding in Bethnal Green; and . . . [we describe] one of them, between Sylvia Hanbury and Harry Buxton, she from the Bow end of Bethnal Green and he a docker from Shadwell.

The reception was held at the bride's home. After the wedding in the late afternoon, the bride and groom moved off from the church in their hired Rolls Royce and the wedding guests followed in smaller cars. Once arrived in Mr Hanbury's front room, most of the guests stood about rather stiffly, holding glasses of beer and sniffing the pickled onions. The Buxtons, that is the bridegroom's family, were grouped by the window looking disdainfully at the chipped china dogs on the mantelpiece, the worn linoleum on the floor, and the pictures of country scenes which did not quite conceal the damp patches on the wall-paper. Mrs Alice Buxton, the mother, said, "I don't know whether I'm the bride or not. I'm shaking like a leaf." Mr Hanbury, with a slightly forced joviality, called out for the first toast, and they all turned with raised glasses of beer to the smiling bride and bridegroom, who were standing behind the small table by the fireplace on which towered the tiered wedding cake. "They must have got Mowlems [a building company] to put that up," said one of the Buxtons when the toast was over.

The thirty-two guests squeezed down at the cramped tables for the wedding breakfast of ham and tongue, salad and pickles, trifle and jelly, washed down with ale and Guinness. The heat became greater, the faces more flushed and the talk louder. After an hour, the meal and toasts over, the telegrams read, the trestle tables were cleared and stacked away. Sylvia and Harry concentrated on trying to bring the two families together. They were not to go off to their honeymoon—a three-day stay at [the resort] Clacton—until the next morning. . . . Harry took off his new jacket and carried a tray of drinks around the by now smoky room. Before long he anxiously asked his wife's grandmother, who was sitting close to the fire, "It's going very well, isn't it. Gran? Everybody's mucking in, I mean, you can't tell which side is which, can you?"

At nine o'clock the men decided to go over to the pub, where they all contributed a £1 a head "whip" for the purchase of drinks. Soon the wedding party filled the saloon bar of the City of Paris, where it had been joined by some of Sylvia's and Harry's workmates; not being relatives, they were not invited to the reception, but they dropped in to the pub "to wish you luck."

When the pub closed some of the relatives living in Stepney, Dagenham, or East Ham went home, the others returned to the Hanburys', and many newcomers arrived. Two men could be heard talking about the bride's mother. "She's a funny woman," one of them emphatically declared. "I told her off this afternoon when she said she was tired. "Of course you're tired," I told her straight, "we're all bleeding tired." She didn't take no notice though. Like water off a duck's back. "She *is* a funny woman," the younger man answered seriously. . . .

"To tell you the truth, Frank," the other leaned forward conspiratorially, "I don't think I ever could get on with that woman. Anyway," he added with an air of finality, "you married Ethel, didn't you? You didn't marry her bleeding family." Despite these sentiments, the two of them rejoined the party and soon all of them including the two mothers, were dancing and laughing around the room together, in the early hours of the morning, one family indistinguishable from the other. (Young and Willmott [1957] 1962: 62–64 passim)

New in-laws have to become acquainted with one another in any situation. However consider the very different dynamics of the Gisu of East Africa. Here groups already exist prior to the marriage; it is through lineage membership that a man acquires rights to what he considers the basis of his livelihood, land.

The framework of Gisu social structure is a series of patrilineal localized lineages. . . . Lineage segments are associated with a tract of territory over which they claim exclusive rights of cultivation and settlement. . . . The basic unit in the traditional political system was the village, settled by a minor lineage. The head of the village was the lineage head. . . . Lineage heads were elected by the men of the lineage concerned, meeting in council at the end-of-mourning ceremonies for the previous head. They were chosen for qualities which marked them out as already powerful enough to carry out the duties expected of them. This was essential since the office of lineage head was not endowed with special power or any control of force to implement his orders. The components of a leader's power were prestige, influence and connexions useful to the group. The total of these represented any man's *position* in his village. Prestige accrued to a man who was wealthy, possessed a good reputation, was punctilious in fulfilling his obligations and generous to others less fortunate. I use *prestige* to refer to the characteristics which earn a man the esteem of others and their deference to his opinions and advice. A leader also had *influence*; that is, he was able to prevail on others to accept his decisions by virtue of his relations with them. Influence was usually acquired by economic help: loans or gifts of land or cattle, but it might also be acquired through force of personality and sagacity. Finally, a man whose kinship and affinal ties were of such a kind that they provided his group with a means of conducting their external relations was almost invariably of importance within it. . . . A judicious marriage might provide a man's sons with important and useful maternal kin so that provided the obligations of kinship were generously fulfilled, a man could profit from his father's choice of a wife. (La Fontaine 1962: 89–90, original emphasis)

Membership in a Gisu lineage is obtained through one's father. This holds for women as well as men. But because of the general prominence of men in lineage affairs, because at marriage a woman leaves her natal land to farm her husband's, and because it is through males that lineage mates are connected to each other, women are not considered to be members in the same way as men are.

Gisu often speak as though a lineage were composed only of men, since women are always under the jural authority of some man. (La Fontaine 1962: 91)

This man may be her father (or brother) or her husband. A woman throughout her life is regarded as subordinate to men in general (she does not participate in lineage affairs as they do), and is in addition under the authority of particular males. At marriage her father and the men of her lineage relinquish some of the control they have over her, for she now comes under the authority of her husband. A person cannot marry another member of his minimal lineage, so a marriage always involves two different sets of people. The fact that control over the woman passes from one group to another is marked by ceremonies which involve the transfer of material goods (bridewealth). Not only does the husband acquire personal authority over his wife but his claims to her sexual services and domestic help are seen as being established by these transactions. They are a public affirmation of the husband's legal position.

A Gisu marriage is established by the payment of bridewealth to the woman's father. The amount varies, . . . but certain items are essential. They are: a heifer, a bull (or the equivalent number of goats), a large he-goat, a spear and a hoe.

They symbolize, severally, the rights over the woman which are transferred to her husband. Once the marriage has been legally established by the payment of these articles, the husband has exclusive rights over his wife's domestic and sexual services and her labour. He represents her in any disputes outside his domestic group and is held responsible for her actions. Should she commit adultery, her husband can claim damages against her lover. Her lineage hand over responsibility for her, retaining only the right to see that she is not ill-treated, which includes the right to avenge her if she is killed.

The ceremonies which establish a marriage demonstrate clearly the interest of the two lineages concerned and of the extra-lineage kin of bride and bridegroom. The initial approach is made by the man's kin. Usually his father's brother and sister are sent as messengers to the girl's father. There is a series of visits back and forth, designed to give each party a chance of assessing the circumstances of the family and minimal lineage into which their kinsman or kinswoman is about to marry. If the initial visits satisfy both parties, then a discussion is held at the bridegroom's home to determine the amount of the bridewealth. After some of the items have been paid, preparations are made for the ceremony by which the bride is transferred to her new home. . . . The girl [is] separated from her status as a daughter and transferred to that of married woman, with an intervening period of transition during which she lives in her husband's home as a guest. . . .

Marriage is a contract between men in Gisu society and in speaking of the choice of a spouse we are really talking of the selection of wives on the one hand and of sons-in-law on the other. (La Fontaine 1962: 91–93)

Another factor concerning interpersonal relations should be taken into account. A man's in-laws (affines) are not merely people who have become related to him through his daughter or wife. They are persons to whom he has very specific obligations and on whom he makes demands. A man can enhance his local position according to the kind of marriage he or his female kin make. From the point of view of the father-in-law, the man who marries his daughter is permanently in debt.

Gisu say that the payment of bridewealth in full can never entirely wipe out what is owed to a father-in-law; in exchange for cattle and other objects he has given the means by which a household will be established and a line of sons and grandsons founded to perpetuate his son-in-law's name. Even though the bridewealth represented fairly the "value" of the girl her father is still her husband's

benefactor. A woman's father and brothers are thus in a position to demand favours and help from her husband which he will find it hard to refuse, without the
risk of being labelled an unworthy affine and one who shirks his social obligations. This is a reputation no Gisu wishes to acquire. (La Fontaine 1962: 98–99)

It is not surprising, then, that while

personal characteristics . . . are taken into account in estimating the amount of
bridewealth that is to be demanded for a particular girl, a most important criterion for assessing the value of a woman as wife is what her family connexions are.
The fact that, by acquiring a wife, a man becomes the son-in-law of her father
and the brother-in-law of her brothers is a consideration which carries great
weight with both parties. . . . Many young men, when asked how they would
choose a wife, specified a well-established and influential father or brother as
desirable. Affinal ties create bonds between men that entail not only specific
obligations but a general solidarity that may prove useful in varying spheres of
life. Namondo's father-in-law asked him to bicycle 17 miles to the local town for
nails for the house he was building; Wodero obtained his post as a clerk through
the good offices of a brother-in-law of his father. Musole cultivates a plot of land
in another maximal lineage which has been lent him by a brother-in-law and in
1954 Makanya, a parish chief, settled a dispute between his own village and another village of his parish by appealing to his brother-in-law, the most important
man in the other village and Makanya's direct superior. So useful are affinal ties
that one Christian chief declared that it was virtually impossible for a chief to
live up to the Christian ideal of monogamy: "he should marry several wives, then
he has friends and can rule the people." The more influential a woman's father
and brothers are the more desirable they are as affines. Hence the higher bridewealth that is paid for the daughter of a chief or wealthy man is a recognition of
the value of links with her kin as well as of her higher social standing. Conversely,
a man hopes to acquire a useful son-in-law and values his daughter's suitors according to their economic and social standing. . . .

Gisu bridewealth is paid in installments, and during the period in which
the payments have not been completed, the son-in-law will be subject to requests
for small services, assistance and loans from his wife's fathers and brothers. . . .
We are now in a position to see the objectives of both parties to the marriage
contract. The prospective groom wants a wife who is attractive and who will be a
good worker and mother of his children. He wants influential in-laws who may

be able to help him rise in standing, but he wants them not to be in a position . . . to impose their demands on him continually. The bride's father wishes to increase his wealth by his daughter's marriage, to exploit any assets that she may have, both in her own right and as his daughter, in order to acquire not only the goods he will receive for her but also a son-in-law who will be useful as an ally and able to render him the occasional services he may require. (La Fontaine 1962: 99–101)

The actual amounts which are handed over at a bridewealth involve considerable bargaining; both sides want to appear prestigious while at the same time not giving away too much.

Bridewealth negotiations are carried out by two groups of men, acting on behalf of the parties concerned and representing the interest of their respective lineages. . . . The older [men] lend their skill in discussion to the proceedings and act as the representatives of the minimal lineages concerned, whose care is always to see that members of the lineage do not dissipate their wealth unwisely. Bridewealth is not corporate lineage property as such but members of a minimal lineage are potential heirs to one another and Gisu believe that the prosperity of any member is the good fortune of the whole lineage.

In the normal situation, the bridewealth discussion takes place after a series of visits which have revealed to each group the social standing, reputation and economic resources of the other. They meet with a clear idea of what is likely to be demanded of them. The groom and his agnates[1] are concerned to resist the demands of the bride's agnates and pay as little as possible above the minimum. They will be asked a price that reflects the assessment of the bride's worth reached by her agnates and their estimate of her suitor's capacity to pay. If the groom's party cannot reduce this figure, they will commit him, or his father, to paying a sum which he cannot afford. Payments will not be completed for an unusual length of time and during those years the groom will be in an inferior position, liable to all sorts of demands on his time and resources. . . . For a father-in-law, like any creditor, may, with the permission of his debtor's lineage, seize as security or in lieu of payment, land or cattle belonging to his debtor or his debtor's close agnates. . . . On the other hand, if relations between them are good, the father-in-law may waive some of the later payments, but such a possibility cannot be depended upon.

---

1.   Fellow members of his lineage.

[Yet] the groom's agnates cannot haggle over the payments in such a way as to indicate that they cannot afford to meet them, lest their prestige suffer.... In a situation in which the girl's father is clearly the poorer, the greater equality in standing between the two groups is plain in their demeanour during the bridewealth discussions. If the prospective groom and his supporters show their confidence in being able to meet any demands made on them, they will ensure a position of co-operation on equal terms for the groom in future dealings with his affines. The bridegroom's position as beneficiary of his father-in-law is balanced by his membership of a richer family or lineage. At the outset of a marriage such a situation is rare because the girl's father is careful to investigate the resources of her suitor and phrase his demands accordingly. One can see it though, in the later stages of a marriage, when there are few or no payments outstanding on the bridewealth and the relationship between father- and son-in-law is one of mutual profit. (La Fontaine 1962: 101–4)

It should be clear that what is being bargained over is not just the "value" of the bride; it is the "value" which men on each side, the potential in-laws, put on each other as well. It is not just the husband's rights over a woman which are being "paid for"; he is paying for good relations with his male in-laws. Indeed, these may develop to some extent independently of the marriage which brought them together in the first place.

The son-in-law derives his greatest benefit from his affinal ties if he can weather the [early] period of heavy demands, without depreciating his resources or alienating his affines' good-will. As his father-in-law withdraws from an active part in political life, relations with his son-in-law become more equable. The affinal ties become mutually profitable. In return for having fulfilled his economic obligations, the younger man will be able to ask his father-in-law to use his prestige and influence to help him. The smooth development of a profitable alliance continues after the death of his wife's father. No one of her brothers inherits the father's standing as benefactor and creditor, although they may sue jointly for arrears of bridewealth.... From this point on, if there have been no serious disputes affinal relations become largely independent of domestic harmony between the pair whose marriage gave rise to them. Separation may occur but it does not usually entail divorce, particularly if the woman is past the age of childbearing. She may be living with another man or in a separate household near an adult son, but her brothers and her husband will continue to enjoy as cordial relations as if she were still in her husband's homestead. (La Fontaine 1962: 105–6)

In a society of this kind many social relationships are established, defined, expanded, or terminated, through transactions involving goods, and the tie between husband and wife is only one of many which are created or legalized by property transactions. Men use property to adjust their relations with other men.

Thus in Gisu it is less the bridewealth itself which expresses men's dominance over women than the fact that it is the men who do the transferring. They are the chief actors. Bridewealth transactions are semipublic occasions, involving the defense of lineage interests. The bargaining is not seen to be a sphere in which it would be appropriate for women to participate; the bride has no part in the negotiations themselves. Her role is quite different. A wedding does include ceremonies involving the bride but these have a separate focus: the fact that marriage means for her a change of status, from a child into an adult woman.

> After the conclusion of the bridewealth negotiations, when the agreement between the two groups of agnates concerned indicates that the marriage is to take place, some time elapses while preparations for the ceremonies are made by both sides. The foodstuffs must be assembled and beer brewed for the feasts that accompany the wedding. The bride-to-be is secluded for a period before the wedding. . . .While she is in seclusion she is fed particularly well with large amounts of food and her body is frequently greased with animal fat so that on her wedding day she shall be plump and beautiful, with the shining skin that Gisu admire. On the evening before, her father feasts his agnates and other kin, the men eating separately from the women. Among the women the most important is the girl's father's sister who is the mistress of ceremonies, while the girl's mother plays a subordinate role. . . .
>
> The father's sister's duty at the wedding is primarily to deliver the ritual admonishment to the bride before she leaves her natal homestead, and conduct her to her bridegroom. On the morning of the wedding she "dresses" the bride, that is she supervises her dressing and adornment and when the girl is ready she faces her and formally addresses her. . . . The father's sister speaks of their lineage, of its prestige and achievements; she then tells of the duties of a married woman and how the girl's behaviour in her conjugal home will reflect on her lineage. . . .
>
> The bride then leaves her father's house accompanied by a group of agnates of her own generation under the leadership of her father's sister. They stop at all

the households of the locality and will not move on until a present is given to speed the bride on her way. . . . At a point half-way between the homes of bride and groom the bridal party is met by a group from the groom's lineage, including the groom himself. The party rushes forward as though to attack and the bride's party surrounds the girl and pretends to defend her, refusing to let her go. Their reluctance ends when they are presented with gifts and the whole party then proceeds in procession either to church, if there is to be a Christian wedding or directly to the groom's homestead where there is feasting. The bride is expected to look downcast and sorrowful. She should not speak unless addressed and then should speak only in a low voice. When she is finally conducted into the bridal hut she is expected to show a similar reluctance as her "sisters" prepare her for the night and see that no sorcery has been placed where it will endanger the sleeping mat or bed. Traditionally, the bridegroom was expected to shout out his success when he consummated the marriage by deflowering the bride. . . .

A final ceremony completes the wedding. . . . Accompanied by her new husband, her sisters, and some of her affines, the bride returns home to her parents, bearing gifts with her. There she is lavishly entertained as a guest and presented with gifts to take back to her affines. On her return with her husband she is presented by her mother-in-law with a hoe and shown where to hoe; she then ceremoniously hoes a few paces, and performs the other actions that typify the role of married woman—gathers firewood, lights a fire, and cooks the first meal for her husband. These are practical actions but performed with an air of ceremony so that they symbolize her assumption of the full status of married woman. They confirm and legitimize a change of status which was achieved, both by her physical transfer and by her defloration—the change in her *physical* state which also causes blood to flow. . . . Thus the girl is divested of her role as unmarried daughter. . . . Once the marriage is consummated there is no reversal of the process; an irreversible physical change has taken place. (La Fontaine 1972: 168–72 passim, original emphasis)

The bride is not being treated simply as an "object" because her going from one group to another has involved a payment of goods, though men may sometimes talk about it in this way. In fact, she is the subject of considerable personal attention. The ceremony conducted for the bride is mainly concerned with matters outside the interests of the men in their bridewealth bargaining. Bridal rituals deal with changes in status, progress to maturity, and maternal potential. Yet even here men take a controlling role. A woman's fecundity is seen as something with which the men of one lineage, through her marriage, endow another lineage. Gisu make this quite explicit in that the first defloration by the husband becomes evidence of his access to the female power which will eventually bring him children.

> The virginity of the bride is important because her loss of it is a further step in the development of her female power. It should thus, in Gisu eyes, be controlled by the men of those lineages concerned; that of her father and brothers who transfer this power to others with whom they create new ties, and that of her husband who will benefit from the legitimate children the woman will bear. An important aspect of marriage ceremonies then is the fact that this event occurs in the "right" place and time. It thus testifies to the power of the girl's agnates to exercise control over their female members. In addition, the husband's right to deflower his bride is part of his right to control her powers of reproduction by initiating her reproductive life. . . .
>
> It might be thought that defloration is a necessary physical act merely incidental to marriage. . . . It would seem that for the Gisu it represents male control of the female physical powers of creation, a dogma essential to the maintenance both of male dominance and patriliny, and hence it is the central ritual act of marriage. (La Fontaine 1972: 172–73)

There are two observations to make here. The first is that what closely concerns the groom at marriage are his relations with his future affines, whereas the ceremonies surrounding the bride make these incidental to the implications for her transformed personal status as a married woman. If we look at these in terms of spheres of action, we can say that the groom's sphere is a much more "public" one than the bride's. It is out-going, directed toward transactions with other men; the bride's is inward-looking, directed toward changes within herself. The second is that in what concerns one group (the lineage) communicating with another, men take the chief roles. This is so in the negotiations over bridewealth. It is so also in the extent to which the bridal ceremonies are concerned with the transfer of female power from one lineage to another. Males are seen as controlling the bride's powers and as having the authority to bestow them or rightfully use them. Other stages in a girl's maturation are ritualized (first menstruation and first childbirth), but the greatest ceremony surrounds her marriage, for it is the most public of all these events. It is the event which most directly involves not only men but groups of men (lineages) in confrontation with each other. In short, it is the moment when a woman's domestic status has the greatest implications for political relations between lineages, and it is the stage in her life over which, of all stages, men are anxious to appear in control.

To return briefly to the point, touched upon earlier, that in many societies fitness for public life is sex-linked, in the sense that females by their natures, and by contrast with males, suffer "innate" handicaps. Gisu stress on bridal virginity is associated with a concern for the powers of female blood. It is not just that the groom is the first man to have legitimate intercourse with her but that he must cause her blood to flow. The marriage ceremony demonstrates yet again the peculiarity of women, who bleed when they menstruate and when they bear children. Men also undergo rituals (circumcision) to make them bleed. Male rituals make boys into men, while female bleeding establishes the growing maturity of women.

But there is a crucial difference here. Without the mark of manhood which the circumcision rites confer, young men cannot become full Gisu or full members of their lineage. They are considered unfit to perpetuate their lineage (through proper marriage) or to participate in its affairs. By contrast, for the female, her capacity to bleed is among the very attributes which, far from qualifying, actually disqualify her from important lineage matters.

As in many societies blood has contradictory and powerful qualities for the Gisu. . . . It is associated with wounds and death, particularly in war, but also with life, for blood flows when an infant is born. Blood flowing from the female genitals is powerful in that it is associated with the natural power of women, their inherent physiological qualities which make them capable of child-bearing. It is also dangerous, both to the woman herself and others. A menstruating woman must keep herself from contact with many activities lest she spoil them: she may not brew beer nor pass by the homestead of a potter lest his pots crack during firing; she may not cook for her husband nor sleep with him lest she endanger both his virility and his general health. A menstruating woman endangers the success of rituals by her presence. . . .

Traditionally, the ancestors of lineage segments were the most potent spiritual forces in the Gisu pantheon, . . . the main source of sufferings and blessings, both for lineage segments of varying span and for individuals. [Men's circumcision] ritual emphasized the predominance of men: precedence at ancestral rituals was accorded to those men whose first-begotten child was a son and the blessings these rites bestowed on the participants included, as the most important,

the establishment of a flourishing male progeny. Women, although subject to
the power of the ancestors, were to a large extent excluded from the rituals and
participated only as spectators. (La Fontaine 1972: 162–64 passim)

We could not have a more explicit statement that achievement of manhood
(through circumcision) qualifies the actor for a different sphere of activity than
does the achievement of womanhood (through menstruation, defloration, and
childbirth). For both sexes, a flow of blood is associated with the capacity for
growth. But manhood proves the male's ability to participate fully in lineage
affairs; womanhood demonstrates the female's essential antipathy to such concerns. It is from their physical natures that the contrast is seen to stem.

GUARDIANS AND MINORS

Gisu women as well as men belong to lineage groups, but quite patently they
cannot be "members" in the same way as men because their sex excludes them
from active participation in public affairs. At marriage, a woman passes from
being a daughter to a wife, from being under the authority of her father to
being under the authority of her husband. She remains, in this sense, a minor
throughout her life. The husband's personal domination over his wife is backed
up by her second-class lineage status, which gives males as a whole dominance
over females as a whole. This does not mean that on every single occasion the
husband can override his wife's wishes, or that his powers are unlimited. It
means, rather, that it is seen to be *appropriate* that the male partner in the marriage should have the upper hand because in the larger affairs of society he
belongs to the more significant sex.

Indeed, husbands may find it hard to exert the domestic authority which the
values of their society allow for. Recognition may have to be given to short-term
reversals or modifications of the theory that men have ultimate control. Let us
look for a moment at an Islamic community, the Kanuri of Bornu, in Nigeria.
Here we find a set of values which openly fits husbands and wives into the order
of things.

The most pervasive quality in Kanuri society is that of the sociopolitical hierarchy, and the values that surround this structural mode are the most dominant in
the culture. Such values reflect the value or identity of the society itself and its

long well-known history as a great power of the Sudanic area. In everyday terms, this means that membership in the society is highly valued as is the idea of hierarchy upon which the society is based. Who is senior to whom in a household, a ward, a village, a district, a faction, or an economic organization, defines the manner in which people can interact with one another. To come into a Kanuri village and not greet the chief is a gross insult. Indeed, special modes of greeting are used which reflect whether the people are of similar or different social status. Not to know such things is not to value the nature and history of the Bornu state and its people. . . .

The concept that most clearly incorporates such values is that of . . . "discipline-respect." For the Kanuri, this is the essential quality of all superior-subordinate relationships including such diverse dyads as father-son, patron-client, chief-someone under his jurisdiction, employer-employee, teacher-pupil, *and husband-wife*. The essence of the relationship is loyalty and obedience by the subordinate which is given to the superior in return for political and economic support. . . . The subordinate has faith that he will be supported by the superior, and, conversely, the superior feels that all activities of the subordinate are in the interests of the superior. . . .

The Kanuri are a proud and ancient people whose history has developed for them a culture of hierarchy. The most useful and important relationships in a person's social existence are hierarchical ones and he or she must utilize these superior-subordinate relations to obtain the social, economic, and psychological satisfactions necessary to an ordinary life cycle. . . .

The husband-wife relationship is therefore not simply a sexual one used for subsistence purposes and the raising of children. In Bornu, it is set into the context of the social structure we have discussed. . . . Husbands are superiors and wives are subordinates; in Kanuri terms, this means they can expect a range of obligatory responses from one another as well as a number of tensions and conflicts. Because this is so—that is, because the husband-wife relationship shares many of the fundamental qualities of all Kanuri social relations—we are in effect looking at the entire social system by looking at its most elemental quality, the superior-subordinate dyad as it is exemplified in the husband-wife relationship. This does not mean that there is not more to Kanuri marriage than differences in authority. It does mean that authority is possibly the most important quality of all Kanuri relations and therefore [of] a marriage as well. (R. Cohen 1971: 33–36 passim, original emphasis)

Given Kanuri concern with hierarchy we should not be surprised to find direct symbolic attention given to the superior/inferior relationship between marital partners.

> The day before the actual wedding, a series of ceremonies are performed. By this time, relatives from other villages have arrived and an air of festivity and preparation can be detected in both households. Early in the morning on the pre-wedding day, separately, but at both the boy's house and the girl's . . . the female relatives gather around a large calabash filled with water in which a smaller one is floating. The women beat the smaller calabash with sticks in rhythm while singing songs of praises to the parents. The bride or groom is referred to as a "monkey." . . . The implication here is that the bride and/or groom . . . can only imitate what they see but have not the experience to act in expected ways. At the groom's house, they emphasize his authority and tell him he must be strong and properly control his wife. If not, she will control him and he will not learn how to be a proper husband. If he does learn this, he will be attractive and popular to her and to all women. At the girl's house, her female relatives tell her to be a good obedient wife who, for example, should not eat the meat from her husband's soup while preparing it. She is also told to respect and behave properly to the boy's parents and senior relatives. Thus both ceremonies emphasize the subordination of the wife. Interestingly, the boy's ceremony is performed, or should be, very early—before the one at the bride's compound. It is said that if the ceremony is held first at the bride's house she, and not he, will be the stronger authority in the marriage, and she, rather than he, will become more popular and attractive to the opposite sex.
>
> This piece of lore and others like it always bring a smile to informants when they are asked about it. And stories of henpecked husbands can be gathered in this context. The symbolism here connotes the social reality. Male authority and dominance are expected—their achievement, however, is not an automatic consequence of marriage. . . .
>
> Another advice ceremony takes place at the girl's household. The female relatives of the girl put a small calabash into a large one filled with water (as in the monkey-calling ceremony performed early in the morning). A brass pestle is also placed on the ground. Women beat the calabash and the pestle while singing songs of advice to the bride. These songs repeat over and over again the wife's role of obedience, but emphasize as well that she must not swear on the Koran (take an oath) to her husband because leprosy results if such oaths are broken.

The implication here is that wives very often must lie to their husbands and this practical necessity of the role should be recognized. (R. Cohen 1971: 84–85)

In other words, it is recognized that the ideal image of the authoritative husband and the obedient wife may not be fully realized, but at the same time the proper order of things (the ideal) is reiterated. The subordination of the wife to the husband is only one of many dyadic or pair relationships based on notions of superiority and inferiority, and the general validity of hierarchy as a principle is given expression at these marriage ceremonies. Kanuri women are "minors" in a dramatically defined way:

> The Kanuri have been Muslim for many centuries and their views of men and women are very strongly influenced by Islam and its teachings. In Islam "Men stand superior to women in that God hath preferred the one over the other. . . . Those whose perverseness ye fear, admonish them and remove them into bed-chambers and beat them; but if they submit to you then do not seek a way against them [Koran 4]." In other words, men have greater authority as a caste and if women do not wish to acknowledge their inferior status they should be scolded and beaten. On the other hand, if a woman submits to male authority, her master-male must try to be good to her.
>
> In traditional Islam, a woman has some rights but they are restricted. She is also relegated by law to a separate social existence, and intersection between the male and female realms should be handled with care and circumspection. Thus in matters of inheritance her rights to property are only half those of a male. . . .
>
> In Bornu today, women do not have the vote and their rights to inheritance are limited by Islamic law. . . . They take no part in public or legal affairs. Traditionally, there was a separate women's room beside the law-court and they spoke into the court through a small window. (R. Cohen 1971: 92–93 passim)

Female political rights are modified by the disqualifications that sex brings. This is a further instance of the general proposition that it is very usual to find women excluded from public affairs on a rationale related to some aspect of their innate (and unalterable) nature. Ashanti and Gisu women are affected by the physiological facts of menstruation; Bornu women by their status in Islam, with God's preference for men. In mid-nineteenth century England women were considered essentially unfit to manage or possess property, and this was bound up with their obvious exclusion from political life. The various examples[2] we have been considering in this chapter point in one direction. Marriage specifically brings together persons of the opposite sex. And wedding ceremonies frequently pay attention to relations between men and women in general. The prospective statuses of the sexes are symbolized; and there is often a parallel perceived between the comportment of husband and wife and the overall relationship between males and females. Where property qualifications loom large in the definition of who is fit to enter public life, we should not be surprised to find marriage transactions showing some concern with the respective property-rights of husband and wife.

In the England of the 1850s and 1860s this was so: at marriage a husband not only obtained personal authority over his wife but where she had property he became the legal possessor; franchise, as we know, was limited to those with certain property qualifications. Poor men were excluded from the right to vote; so were women as a category. This is not the point to enter into a full description of women's property rights. I want to draw attention to the symbolic aspects of these qualifications, to the parallels between a husband's control of his wife's property, and the political control of men of wealth over those without wealth, including all women. I also want to draw attention to the obvious enough fact that, however much it may appear so, women can never be just "objects."[3] Such thinking is especially likely to appear on wedding occasions, for these are often both public and in the control of men. But it does not follow that women are nothing but the "acted upon." Ronald Cohen puts it this way for Kanuri:

> In Bornu a woman's sexual activities, her reproductive powers, and some stipulated parts of her economic potentialities are transferable to her husband at

---

2.   Least so in the Bethnal Green wedding. The prominence of the bride's mother, not only formally but in the comments made by some of the men is significant in relation to the triad mother/woman (daughter and wife)/husband which dominates domestic organization. But the emphasis of this style of wedding is above all to bring people together on a personal basis. Attention to relations between men and women in general is possibly to be found in the contrast between the activities at the bride's "home" and the pub to which the men for a while, and in the appraisal of her mother's house with its hidden judgment about what kind of home the bride is going to make for the groom.

3.   Being an "object" may be part of a woman's role, as it may be the part of a man's in certain situations. Nonetheless one would be confusing analysis with stereotype to infer that everywhere women are "nothing but objects" (see Chapter Six).

marriage. . . . The woman herself is not purchased, only these rights. But rights in a person cannot be locked away safely like jewelry, or even protected like land-use rights. They exist in an actor who may decide, or be persuaded, to act otherwise. Paradoxically, then, at the core of marriage lies a threat that the system will not work. . . .

Men as husbands are dominant, but this dominance involves a tension, indeed a contest, in which women do not necessarily comply without trying to maintain their own rights. Not only must men be made to give women what custom says they have a right to ask for, but women may even try to reverse the dominance and take power away from their husbands. The one ceremony the groom goes through as a sign that he has entered the realm of marriage, the . . . ceremony which he can only practice once in his life, is seen as a contest over who is to dominate, and over who will spit out the bitter words rather than accept them—the husband or the wife. . . .

The day after consummation is . . . the favored time for the main portion of the . . . ceremony. In separate parts of the compound, special food is placed in the cupped hands of both the bride and groom. The central act involves throwing this food back into the bowl. Lore has it that the partner who throws the food with greatest force will be the strongest power in the marriage. Again, as in previous rituals, people are aware here of the symbolism. Such ceremonies are not believed to cause marital relations but to symbolize the way in which the sexes interact within marriage. (R. Cohen 1971: 87–93 passim)

Bearing these themes in mind, let us look at a literary description of an English marriage transaction, as described by Wilkie Collins in his novel *The woman in white*, published in 1859–1860. The legal situation would have been recognizable to his readers. The passages concern the engagement of Miss Fairlie to Sir Percival Glyde. Miss Fairlie was an orphan, and her affairs were in the hands of Mr. Gilmore, the family solicitor. By her father's will she had an interest in various pieces of property. This included expectations in an estate then in the hands of her uncle and guardian, a single man; a life-interest in a sum of money which on her death was to go to an aunt of hers, and she had been left £20,000 which was her own entirely when she came of age. For a moment this looks as if she could not have been more propertied! But when her lawyer hears that about three months before she will come of age she is to marry Sir Percival, he is thrown into anguish. Her enjoyment of any benefit from these sources of income will be entirely dependent on what kind of settlement he can draw up for her, on this meeting her guardian's approval and on whether the future husband's lawyers agree to his terms. Without a settlement the wealth would simply become her husband's. The conditions he laid down for the use of the income derived from the estate and the first sum of money were unremarkable, and agreed to by Sir Percival's legal representative. His stipulations as to the £20,000 were another matter. Mr. Gilmore recounts this part of the story:

> My stipulation in regard to the twenty thousand pounds was simply this: The whole amount was to be settled so as to give the income to the lady for her life— afterwards to Sir Percival for his life—and the principal to the children of the marriage. In default of issue, the principal was to be disposed of as the lady might by her will direct, for which purpose I reserved to her the right of making a will. The effect of these conditions may be thus summed up. If Lady Glyde died without leaving children, her half-sister Miss Halcombe, and any other relatives or friends whom she might be anxious to benefit, would, on her husband's death, divide among them such shares of her money as she desired them to have. If, on the other hand, she died leaving children, then their interest, naturally and necessarily, superseded all other interests whatsoever. This was the clause—and no one who reads it can fail, I think, to agree with me that it meted out equal justice to all parties. . . .
>
> We shall see how my proposals were met on the husband's side. . . . After a lapse of two days the document was returned to me, with notes and remarks of the baronet's lawyer. His objections, in general, proved to be of the most trifling and technical kind, until he came to the clause relating to the twenty thousand pounds. Against this there were double lines drawn in red ink, and the following note was appended to them—
>
> "Not admissible. The *principal* to go to Sir Percival Glyde, in the event of his surviving Lady Glyde, and there being no issue."
>
> That is to say, not one farthing of the twenty thousand pounds was to go to Miss Halcombe, or to any other relative or friend of Lady Glyde's. The whole sum, if she left no children, was to slip into the pockets of her husband.
>
> The answer I wrote to this audacious proposal was as short and sharp as I could make it. "My dear sir. Miss Fairlie's settlement. I maintain the clause to which you object, exactly as it stands. Yours truly." The rejoinder came back in a quarter of an hour. "My dear sir. Miss Fairlie's settlement. I maintain the red ink to which you object, exactly as it stands. Yours truly." In the detestable slang of the day, we were now both "at a deadlock," and nothing was left for it but to refer to our clients on either side.

As matters stood, my client—Miss Fairlie not having yet completed her twenty-first year—Mr. Frederick Fairlie, was her guardian. I wrote by that day's post, and put the case before him exactly as it stood, not only urging every argument I could think of to induce him to maintain the clause as I had drawn it, but stating to him plainly the mercenary motive which was at the bottom of the opposition to my settlement of the twenty thousand pounds. The knowledge of Sir Percival's affairs which I had necessarily gained . . . had but too plainly informed me that the debts on his estate were enormous, and that his income, though nominally a large one, was virtually, for a man in his position, next to nothing. The want of ready money was the practical necessity of Sir Percival's existence, and his lawyer's note on the clause in the settlement was nothing but the frankly selfish expression of it.

Mr. Fairlie's answer reached me by return of post, and proved to be wandering and irrelevant in the extreme. Turned into plain English, it practically expressed itself to this effect: "Would dear Gilmore be so very obliging as not to worry his friend and client about such a trifle as a remote contingency? Was it likely that a young woman of twenty-one would die before a man of forty-five, and die without children? On the other hand, in such a miserable world as this, was it possible to over-estimate the value of peace and quietness? If those two heavenly blessings were offered in exchange for such an earthly trifle as a remote chance of twenty thousand pounds, was it not a fair bargain? Surely, yes. Then why not make it?" (Collins [1859–60] 1969: 131–12, original emphasis)

The value to which the guardian's letter refers is his own peace of mind. The letter nevertheless amounts to what have to be accepted as the lawyer's instructions. He is at a serious disadvantage as far as protecting Miss Fairlie goes when he confronts Sir Percival's lawyer, Mr. Merriman.

"You maintain your note on the clause, then, to the letter?" I said.

"Yes—deuce take it! I have no other alternative." He walked to the fireplace and warmed himself, humming the fag end of a tune in a rich convivial bass voice. "What does your side say?" he went on; "now pray tell me—what does your side say?"

I was ashamed to tell him. I attempted to gain time—nay, I did worse. My legal instincts got the better of me, and I even tried to bargain.

"Twenty thousand pounds is rather a large sum to be given up by the lady's friends at two days' notice," I said.

"Very true," replied Mr. Merriman, looking down thoughtfully at his boots. "Properly put, sir—most properly put!"

"A compromise, recognising the interests of the lady's family as well as the interests of the husband, might not perhaps have frightened my client quite so much," I went on. "Come, come! this contingency resolves itself into a matter of bargaining after all. What is the least you will take?"

"The least we will take," said Mr. Merriman, "is nineteen-thousand-nine-hundred-and-ninety-nine-pounds-nineteen-shillings-and-elevenpence-three-farthings. Ha! Ha! Ha! Excuse me, Mr. Gilmore. I must have my little joke."

"Little enough," I remarked. "The joke is just worth the odd farthing it was made for."

Mr. Merriman was delighted. He laughed over my retort till the room rang again. I was not half so good-humoured on my side; I came back to business, and closed the interview.

"This is Friday," I said. "Give us till Tuesday next for our final answer." (Collins [1859–60] 1969: 133–34)

Mr. Gilmore does all he can in the time left to him: he tries to persuade Miss Fairlie's guardian, her uncle, to change his mind and take an active interest in his niece's welfare.

Mr. Fairlie twisted himself round in his chair, polished the magnifying glass with his delicate cambric handkerchief, and indulged himself with a sidelong inspection of the open volume of etchings. It was not easy to keep my temper under these circumstances, but I did keep it.

"I have come here at great personal inconvenience," I said, "to serve the interests of your niece and your family, and I think I have established some slight claim to be favoured with your attention in return."

"Don't bully me!" exclaimed Mr. Fairlie, falling back helplessly in the chair, and closing his eyes. "Please don't bully me. I'm not strong enough.". . .

"My object," I went on, "is to entreat you to reconsider your letter, and not to force me to abandon the just rights of your niece, and of all who belong to her. Let me state the case to you once more, and for the last time."

Mr. Fairlie shook his head and sighed piteously

"This is heartless of you, Gilmore—very heartless," he said. "Never mind, go on."

I put all the points to him carefully—I set the matter before him in every conceivable light. He lay back in the chair the whole time I was speaking with his eyes closed. When I had done he opened them indolently, took his silver smelling-bottle from the table, and sniffed at it with an air of gentle relish.

"Good Gilmore!" he said between the sniffs, "how very nice this is of you! How you reconcile one to human nature!"

"Give me a plain answer to a plain question, Mr. Fairlie. I tell you again, Sir Percival Glyde has no shadow of a claim to expect more than the income of the money. The money itself, if your niece has no children, ought to be under her control, and to return to her family. If you stand firm. Sir Percival must give way—he must give way, I tell you, or he exposes himself to the base imputation of marrying Miss Fairlie entirely from mercenary motives."

Mr. Fairlie shook the silver smelling-bottle at me playfully.

"You dear old Gilmore, how you do hate rank and family, don't you? How you detest Glyde because he happens to be a baronet. What a Radical you are—oh, dear me, what a Radical you are!"

A Radical!!! I could put up with a good deal of provocation, but, after holding the soundest Conservative principles all my life, I could *not* put up with being called a Radical. My blood boiled at it—I started out of my chair—I was speechless with indignation . . .

"You are entirely wrong, sir," I said, "in supposing that I speak from any prejudice against Sir Percival Glyde. I may regret that he has so unreservedly resigned himself in this matter to his lawyer's direction as to make any appeal to himself impossible, but I am not prejudiced against him. What I have said would equally apply to any other man in his situation, high or low. The principle I maintain is a recognised principle. If you were to apply at the nearest town here, to the first respectable solicitor you could find, he would tell you as a stranger what I tell you as a friend. He would inform you that it is against all rule to abandon the lady's money entirely to the man she marries. He would decline, on grounds of common legal caution, to give the husband, under any circumstances whatever, an interest of twenty thousand pounds in his wife's death."

"Would he really, Gilmore?" said Mr. Fairlie. "If he said anything half so horrid, I do assure you I should tinkle my bell for Louis, and have him sent out of the house immediately." (Collins [1859–60] 1969: 138–40, original emphasis)

The lawyer has no choice but to accept his instructions, and he alters the settlement he would have liked to see drawn up. Miss Fairlie herself had indicated to him that she wanted to see her half-sister benefit from her will.

On the Tuesday I sent in the altered settlement, which practically disinherited the very persons whom Miss Fairlie's own lips had informed me she was most anxious to benefit. I had no choice. Another lawyer would have drawn up the deed if I had refused to undertake it. (Collins [1859–60] 1969: 141)

The most obvious point about this fictional set of incidents is the fact that the transactions were entirely in the hands of men. The bride was of course not yet of age, so perhaps this is not remarkable. It was nevertheless customary for men (and not women) to be the prime negotiators over marriage settlements, and the father, not the mother, was the legal guardian of their children. It was his permission which was sought in the marriage of a girl underage.

When she came of age a single woman could own property in her own right. But on marriage her husband acquired possession of all her goods, savings, personal things such as jewels or furniture, income, or whatever.[4] He could deprive her of her assets, and estates she inherited or wages she earned became his. She had few legal claims over her children, and could not be party to a lawsuit. In return, the husband was expected to maintain her, pay her debts (including those contracted before marriage), pay any penalties she incurred, sue on her behalf, and so on. These stipulations amounted to the often repeated formula that husband and wife constituted one person, and that person was the husband.

This was the married woman's situation under English common law, and one justification for these measures was that by their nature females lacked the essential qualities of judgment and rationality which would enable them, among others things, to administer property. It was the husband's duty to apply just such skills of judgment and mature consideration to the maintenance of his wife and the education of his children. More than this, the married woman was at a peculiar disadvantage. The unmarried woman could, as we have seen, once she reached her majority, legally own property. But on marriage, she forfeited this status. Part of this is explicable in terms of the particular cast given to the wife's role. She was her husband's helpmeet. The relationship was an inherently unequal one: she supported him in private, domestically, while he protected her from public life and transactions of hers concerning the outside world were

---

4.   Except her claims to freehold land, although he was entitled to the income she derived from them.

mediated through him.[5] Perhaps, too, it is explicable if we consider other aspects of women's status in comparison with men's. Single women could no more vote than could married women. Men carried the burden of government and all women came under their political domination. Single women did not ordinarily set up establishments, such as households which gave them authority. Women who married did but only to an extent: they entered into a partnership with a man, a partnership which the religious marriage ceremony stressed was one of mutuality. This was interpreted as mutuality of affection, responsibility, duty, and so on; as far as public authority went, one partner asserted dominance. The particular attachment a wife had to a man, and the claims she had on him, could not be held to challenge general male preeminence in the outside world.

We can see how appropriate it was that the assertion of the husband's public responsibility for his spouse should have involved depriving the wife of any rights to hold property in her own name. For those were times when possession of property qualified men for participation in government. The male head of the household was, after all, a kind of governor. That particular individuals might in fact exercise considerable power over their husbands, even to the point of involving themselves in politics, does not affect the category distinction between males and females.

This was the position in common law. A small proportion of the population saw it in their interests to circumvent these provisions. Families of the well-to-do, whose property assets would be of significance, as in the case of Collins' characters, had access to courts of law which could rule that a wife, through a trustee, was able to handle property as though she were still a single woman. A wealthy father (or other guardian) would safeguard his daughter's interests under a marriage settlement. A properly drawn up and legally acceptable settlement could establish provisions for the married woman which would prevent her husband's making unlimited claims over her assets. These provisions might include some rights over her income during her lifetime, and the right at her death to dispose of property through a will of own.

The drama in this part of Collins' story centered on the respective characters of Gilmore, family solicitor, and Fairlie, uncle and guardian. Fairlie was the *legal* guardian, and since the bride was underage his word was absolute. He had complete legal rights to determine what kind of settlement was made. But we

---

5. In legal theory. In practice there were many variations, especially across social classes, in the extent to which women participated in public affairs.

are made to feel that Gilmore was acting as a kind of *moral* guardian—that he had the girl's personal interests at heart, and was trying to secure a transaction which would take into account her wishes as an individual. Much earlier, before there had been no more than a rumor of marriage, Mr. Gilmore had consulted Miss Fairlie. At that time he assumes that the marriage will not take place until she is of age. She wants her half-sister, who has looked after her like a mother, to be a beneficiary. The solicitor replies easily to her request: of course he will make a settlement to incorporate this. In short, when the bride is of age her wishes can be taken directly into account, although a settlement is still necessary to give them legal validity. Otherwise, her rights are those of married women under common law. But because as events turn out she is underage, the terms of the settlement are in the hands of her legal guardian. It is up to him whether he consults with the girl or not. Mr. Gilmore of course suspects a maneuver on the part of Sir Percival, who knows that the guardian would agree to what his future bride might not.

It looks as though there is a paradox here. Common law deprived the married woman of personal possession of any property she owned at the time of marriage, yet to families where this property was of some significance, legal processes were available which could circumvent this. Here we have to look to other aspects of the marriage relationship. Marriages could also be alliances. In the case of propertied families, unions might be created which would bring mutual benefits to both sides. Yet why, as the crux of the drama, should the *wife's* rights be protected? If the alliance is primarily of use to the men on each side, it would seem to be the husband's rights which would be a central issue. Obviously the wife's side might want to protect their claims on her property in the event of the marriage being dissolved through death or divorce. Legal stipulations could be made to cover such a contingency. Through a marriage settlement for example, the wife's separate estates could be made to revert to her family on her death. But there is perhaps more to it than this, which brings us back to the issue concerning women as objects.

Where property was significant it was invariably looked upon as part of a family's identity. The family was its careers, its estates, and its houses. On the marriage of a female member, part of this wealth passed out of the family's direct control. This would be done under specific conditions: for the purposes of making the alliance men would endow the bride with certain assets. It would be a deliberate act on their part, not an automatic consequence of the woman getting married. This endowment could be seen as the woman's contribution to the marriage—her husband acquiring at the same time the duty to keep her for as long as the marriage lasted. It could also be looked on as her share of the inheritance which would otherwise fall to the sons of the family. And, further, in ensuring that the woman maintained some personal control over this endowment, that she could use some portions of it as she pleased, her family was in fact also maintaining its lien on that part of their estate they had given away. This was not a direct lien, for in the normal course of events the property would go subsequently to the children of the marriage, and never revert to the rest of the family's estate. The lien was indirect. The wife's personal control of her family's assets is explicable if we think of the woman as in some way being regarded as her family's *representative*. Marriage does not cut her off from her family, even though she relinquishes its name. She represents her own family in relation to the husband's. Among the devices used to mark out this aspect of her status seems to have been her family's interest in seeing that she was treated to some extent as an individual in her own right. This was made most explicit in relation to the property she brought to the marriage. They were concerned that she should have something for her own free use.

At the same time family interests—rather than simply a desire to give the woman freedom of action—were surely involved. This is shown in the concept of restraint upon anticipation, which operated during the nineteenth century. When a wife's family endowed her with separate use of certain properties, they could also determine in advance when rights to these fell due (e.g., a certain sum yearly). This was to prevent the woman (perhaps under persuasion from her husband) of her own "free will" making all her property over to him at once. Settlements might be made specifically to keep the property out of the husband's hands; and the wife's right to use it could be limited. This seems to have been the case in respect of Miss Fairlie's £20,000. She would on reaching her majority be entitled to this sum in her own right. It would be her own entirely. The sympathetic solicitor tries to draw up a settlement in which Miss Fairlie retains absolute rights over an annual income from this amount but which leaves the principal intact. His motive would be to prevent Sir Percival from forcing his wife to hand over the whole sum to him. (The groom's lawyer accepts this provision as far as the separation of interest and principal go but contrives to deprive Miss Fairlie of any say in the subsequent disposition of the principal.) Even here, then, we find the woman being protected from herself, in the family's interests. Nevertheless—and this is the point to stress—in the event of a marriage and the bride's family's willingness to settle property on her, their identity as a family had to be expressed through allowing the woman a degree of personal control over the assets, whatever the limitations which hedged this. As their representative, she had to be defined as a property-owning person.

It is noteworthy that these concepts are apparently relevant even where the alliance aspects of the union are minimal. Once the uncle Mr. Fairlie died, and she married, their "name" would die out. The author represents Mr. Fairlie as totally caught up in preserving his own peace of mind and comfort of body; the person who cares about "the family" as an entity is the solicitor. Gilmore sees himself as having a particular duty to discharge toward the Fairlie family, and this concern is bound up with his legal responsibility to administer its assets. He takes on the role of champion of Fairlie interests, even though no other men are involved, and even though the chief beneficiary of Miss Fairlie's own disposition is another woman. This is expressed in terms of securing for the bride maximum personal discretion in the disposal of the property. He says to Mr. Fairlie: "Whatever happens in the future, sir, . . . remember that my plain duty of warning you has been performed. *As the faithful friend and servant of your family*, I tell you, at parting, that no daughter of mine should be married to any man alive under such a settlement as you are forcing me to make for Miss Fairlie" (Collins [1859–60] 1969: 140, emphasis mine).

Women could not be treated entirely as objects over whom men decided the disposal of rights. The dramatic narrative suggests that in the mid-nineteenth century, among certain classes, a strong force in favor of treating married women as persons in their own right was the notion of family. This was as much tied up with property as was the common law determination that husbands were their wives' legal representatives. When the right to rule was associated with owning property, it was appropriate that the wife's status as also someone to be ruled should be defined through, symbolized through, her legal inability to hold possessions. But families (of a certain class) were also identified to a large extent with their property holdings. If female members here seem to represent their families, property was an obvious idiom. Hence the marriage settlements and their concern with the wife's property-owning status. It was not just for the woman that her father would try to secure a good settlement; in a symbolic way it was for himself, for his family, as well. And these notions could exist outside self-interest. Wilkie Collins does not make Gilmore one of the Fairlies: his efforts are not for himself, but for "the family" alone.

CHAPTER FIVE

Dependency

A corollary of the frequently found association of females with domestic and males with public (political) matters is the characteristic often observed that women tend to be involved more in individual or personal than in social or communal concerns. Catherine Berndt writes of the Australian Aborigines:

> It was undoubtedly more difficult for women . . . to act together with a common purpose or a common goal—that is, a goal transcending specifically individual interests. There was an appearance of group behaviour on occasions. Women might dance side by side in a combined ceremony. . . . It was perhaps most consistent and most conspicuous in Desert areas, when women and children sat together in a close group visibly separated from men, where men were dancing or singing or emerging from the secret ground, and so on. . . . It is true that, for example in northeastern Arnhem Land, women would act in concert for certain purposes, although on a small scale—in food-collecting groups, for example, or in organizing their contribution to major ritual . . . but although they collaborated in a number of enterprises, this was essentially a competitive situation, whether competition centered on small things like meat and fish and tobacco or on less tangible benefits.
>
> The contact situation has reinforced this domestic-centered orientation, emphasizing either individual interests and welfare or, at best, the well-being of

the nuclear family rather than of the "community" as a whole. And perhaps because women did not have the same corporate commitment to their traditional heritage as men did, they appear to have taken more readily to the new life of mission and government and pastoral stations—and possibly, in general, with fewer regrets. (Berndt [1970] 1986: 70–71)[1]

There is a tautology here. After all, if the major social groupings and the public life associated with them are the concerns of men, if women cannot be members of these groups in the same way as men, if they cannot discharge the same obligations and receive the same benefits, their interests are almost bound to seem antigroup. For while she may be excluded from participation in public life, a woman is held to have interests of her own. And if these cannot be so directly centered as men's on the perpetuation of society's major groups and institutions, they must appear centered on the person, on herself.[2]

The Aboriginal example is telling. Aborigines were never one "society" and it does the material an injustice to talk about them in general terms.[3] Nevertheless, there were certain cultural uniformities throughout the continent, among these being the basic mode of subsistence, which was hunting and gathering. Aborigines did not systematically plant food crops or herd animals: they lived by foraging. Aboriginal societies also placed great emphasis on the religious life. It was elaborate in form and directed toward a fundamental philosophy: "Openly and symbolically Aboriginal religion is concerned with life, all kinds of life, its creation, its maintenance, its paramount importance. To quote Stanner (1965: 217), . . . 'It may not have "magnified goodness," as Bacon said of Christianity, but it did magnify Life'" (White [1970] 1986: 40, emphasis omitted). Much all-male activity is associated with the performance of ritual, and from these women are excluded.

---

1.   [Editor's Footnote] At the publisher's request, the reference is to a later edition than the one available from 1970. This affects other authors from the same collection as well.

2.   This has been said many times, and in many ways. For example, Frances Cobbe writing in 1881: "I have often thought how strange it is that men can at one and the same moment cheerfully consign one sex to lives either of narrowest toil or senseless luxury and vanity, and then sneer at the smallness of our aims, the pettiness of our thoughts, and the puerility of our conversation!"

3.   There is also considerable controversy over the "position" of women (see the collection of essays on woman's role in Gale [1970] 1986).

The previous chapter has considered spheres in which males play key roles. Among Australian Aborigines men are preeminent in the performance of religious ceremonies, ceremonies which are linked explicitly to the continuity of society and of life in general. Insofar as community welfare is bound up with the rites men carry out, we can call them public performances. But women are not totally nonreligious. Although they do not participate in men's rituals, they do have ceremonies, sometimes elaborate ones, of their own. Yet female ceremonies tend to be inward- and not outward-looking, to concentrate on women's personal concerns, whereas male rites are more ostensibly directed toward "society" and toward "life."

The Australian material also leads our attention to another point. There is a pronounced segregation of the sexes in the carrying out of economic enterprises. Men and women do different kinds of jobs. The "division of labor" between them is a marked one. Perhaps there is some connection between the public or ceremonial roles allotted to men and women and their economic roles in everyday affairs. Indeed, what holds for the performance of religious rituals is also true for the division of labor: there is an analogous contrast between wide-ranging (both physically and socially), large-scale activities (men's) and restricted, family-oriented activities (women's).

POLITICS AND THE DIVISION OF LABOR

What prompted the question about the division of labor were Aboriginal women's religious activities.

In many Aboriginal societies women had their own rituals. Phyllis Kaberry has described secret female rites from which men are excluded and which suggest a kind of religious parity between the sexes.

> When we turn to religion, we find that aboriginal woman has a reverence for, and yet a sense of kinship with the totemic ancestors, a reliance on the rites which they have instituted for her needs. She has the same religious beliefs, the same totemic affiliations with the Time Long Past as the men. She has her spiritual heritage, and her exclusion from certain male rituals can neither diminish nor depreciate it. Her conduct is regulated by similar ethical sanctions; she benefits from the increase ceremonies, and as an old woman may perform those for the foods which fall within her particular province. . . . On the other hand, the men

have evolved secret ceremonies . . . designed to further male pursuits. . . . [Various] economic, social, and physiological factors . . . have contributed to their elaborate character as compared with those of the women. The women's rites, however, are important: they for the most part deal with crises when a woman is believed to be particularly vulnerable either because of actual physical dangers, or because of those believed to be inherent in the situation. . . .

Religion . . . in the Kimberley tribes . . . does not set up a rigid division in society, in which the men represent the sacred element and the women the profane element. Both men and women have their spiritual ties with the Time Long Past and the totemic ancestors. Both take part in sacred ceremonies. A ritual differentiation does exist, however, and is expressed in the exclusion of the women from some of the secret rituals of the men; and the exclusion of the men from some of the secret rituals of the women. The nature of these ceremonies is important: they occur at crucial periods in the life of a man or a woman, crucial either in terms of physiological development, or in the acquiring of skill and mastery in those activities which play an important part in existence. For the man, these are circumcision, subincision, and . . . cult totem corroborees, whose function [lies] in endowing him with strength and success in male pursuits. . . . For the woman, there are the menstruation, pre-puberty, introcision, and childbirth rites, black magic and the secret corroborees devoted to love-magic. The individual is secluded temporarily from contact with members of the opposite sex; the supernatural power believed to be engendered by the ceremonies is safeguarded and utilized for specifically male or female purposes as the case may be. The male and female principles in some contexts are mutually dangerous and mutually antagonistic. The women with regard to the men's rituals are profane and uninitiated: the men with regard to the women's ritual are profane and uninitiated. (Kaberry 1939: 273–77 passim)

Women are not totally withdrawn from ceremony and ritual and from knowledge of the spirits; indeed, they have their own body of mythology and lore which is closed to men. But in spite of that we can detect a difference in orientation. Isobel White sums it up.

Women have their own ceremonies, performed at life crises such as puberty, pregnancy, childbirth and sickness, and also as love magic. These have important social and psychological functions for the women, particularly because they are secret from men, and provide women with an escape from male authority. From my personal observation and from the literature I am sure that even the women consider their ceremonies less important to the whole society than the men's. The attitude of both sexes is that women perform ceremonies for purposes that concern women, whereas men's ceremonies concern the whole society. (White [1970] 1986: 40)

Men and women both carry out ceremonies, but men's are directed toward the perpetuation of social life, women's more immediately toward themselves and (in love magic) their individual relationship with men. In Berndt's words:

Aboriginal women were on the whole, and relatively speaking—relative to men—domestic-centered or family-centered. Their "outside" contacts were mainly at an interpersonal level—in trade relations of various kinds, in marriage arrangements, and in reference to particular kin and affines. (Berndt [1970] 1986: 75–76)

She relates this partly to the different occupations and jobs allotted to the sexes.

The relative proportions of men's or women's contributions to the economy varies, of course, according to area and to the nature of local resources—for example, how consistently people can depend on the supply of larger game and fish, turtles, and so on that are conventionally hunted by men. But in this wider economic range, women were relatively independent, relatively self-contained: they did not depend on the economic contributions of men, although they certainly appreciated them. Their focus on their own domestic circle, and their own immediate circle of kin, was reflected in the relative absence of formal obligations to share their personal contributions with others outside it. In this respect, as in a number of others . . . they were family-oriented, focused inward on their own families rather than outward toward the "community" in general. (Berndt [1970] 1986: 70)[4]

---

4.   From Kaberry's description: "The husband must from time to time give kangaroo to his wife's parents and brothers; besides this he always distributes a little among his blood relatives. Most of what the woman has obtained is consumed by herself, husband, and children; if she has a little extra she takes some to her mother, sister, mother's mother, father, in fact to any close relative. She on another occasion receives similar offerings from them, and also meat from her male relatives, which she shares with her husband and children. These gifts are not compulsory as are her husband's to her people" (Kaberry 1939: 33).

Betty Hiatt gives a generalized account of the division of labor between the sexes in a hunting and gathering community:

> In these societies men hunt and women gather. . . . Women gather such foods as vegetables, shellfish, small animals and eggs while men hunt large land and sea animals and catch fish. Women, though bearers and rearers of children, are able to perform gathering activities most successfully. Few such activities are violent by nature, nor do they require absolute physical freedom or sudden outbursts of energy and strength as do many hunting pursuits. Most foods that can be gathered, vegetables and shellfish in particular, occur in predictable areas and can be harvested simply by travelling to those places. Thus, women and children are able to spend gentle days collecting food, with perhaps, occasionally the added excitement of a mini-chase for a small reptile or mammal. The essential characteristic of the women's contribution to the diet is that it is reliable. It is unlikely that they will return from a day of gathering empty-handed. Usually they will have eaten some food themselves during the day and yet have collected enough to bring some back to the camp for those members of the community who were less successful in their quest.
>
> Most hunting activities require a thorough knowledge of the habits of the desired prey as well as efficient equipment, freedom from physical hindrances and reserves of great strength and endurance that can be summoned when necessary. If for no other reason then, men suit these activities better than women, because they do not produce children and because they are not responsible for looking after them. The characteristic feature of the men's contribution to the diet is that it is highly prized. It is also, however, unpredictable and unreliable. Men who have spent a day hunting or fishing may return with nothing to show for their efforts. (B. Hiatt [1970] 1986: 5)

The impression we have here is that tasks are allocated according to the natural physiological capabilities of the sexes—women have to care for children, which they can combine with gathering roots and small animals, while men are physically adapted to hunting. In actuality this is probably more a matter of gender (what males and females are perceived to be capable of doing) than of sex (their biological capacities).

Australian material suggests it is not simply that men hunt and women gather, they also do different things with the food they get. Both contribute to the diet but their contributions are not necessarily treated in the same way. The meat men catch is likely to be elaborately divided up, parceled out, and sent to others as gifts. Women's vegetables and such, on the other hand, are kept almost entirely for the family. Now this has nothing to do with physiological capacities: it has to do with the way men's and women's contributions are valued, with expectations about men's and women's concerns. Most of a woman's catch is used to feed herself and her family (including the menfolk) and is the basis for day-to-day subsistence. Men are much more likely to share their bag with a wider range of people, to send select portions to this or that person, to make *gifts* out of what they hunt. Gifts establish or maintain relationships with others. To whatever extent this is a product of the contrasting nature of the foodstuffs (a regular if small supply of root crops, the sporadic windfalls of large amounts of animal protein), it nevertheless holds true that one result is that men's economic activities are more clearly than women's related to the enlargement and development of social contacts.

Ann Oakley (1972) argues cogently against interpreting a division of labor between the sexes as an inevitable and natural result of men's and women's physiological differences.

> Every society does have rules about which activities are suitable for males and which for females; but these rules vary a great deal from one society to another, and generalisations about how biology inevitably dictates their form and content are not supported by the data. (Oakley 1972: 128)

She ranges across the world to cite examples of women performing tasks that require strenuous exertion, of arrangements made by them so that work patterns are not disrupted through pregnancy or childbirth to any great degree, of cases where females have been hunters and fighters. She quotes comments on the Australian Aborigines which point out that women's work here is harder and heavier than men's. She also documents the great variation that exists in the extent to which sex is made a basis for the division of labor.

> The degree of differentiation between male and female roles varies within a wide range. Sometimes the rules are merely preferential, and very little anxiety is shown by either sex over temporary reversals of the rule. Cora du Bois reports that in Alor, although there are distinctions between the economic roles of the sexes, it is not thought unhealthy for anyone to take on the other sex's work— rather they are admired for possessing a supplementary skill. The women control

the subsistence economy and the men occupy themselves with financial deals . . .
but many men are passionate horticulturalists and many women have financial
skills. In some cultures, on the other hand, where horticulture is defined as a
female pursuit, a proclivity for it in a man is regarded as proof of sexual deviation. . . .

The Mbuti pygmies described by Colin Turnbull in "Wayward Servants"
have a social structure in which the role of biological sex as a determinant of
social role and status seems to be negligible. Hunting and gathering are the main
activities on which they depend for survival, and both sexes take part. They also
share political decisions and have the same social status. There is very little division of labour by sex; men often care for even the youngest children. Pregnancy
is no bar to hunting . . . Where other societies, in their rituals, emphasize the
distinctions between the sexes, Mbuti rituals emphasize the lack of them, and
this does not seem to give rise to any anxiety about sex roles.

The Mbuti represent one extreme. At the other are those societies which
impose rigid sex roles, and in which this may give rise to great anxiety. The Mundurucu Indians of central Brazil are an example of a society in which the polari-
sation of sex roles and sex groupings has become a primary structural element.
The physical and social separation of the sexes is virtually complete: men and
boys live in men's houses separate from all females. Each sex group (with the
exception of small children) interacts only within itself, and antagonism between
the two is shown on many ritual and other occasions. The sexual polarity per-
vades not only economic tasks and social roles, but the area of personality as well,
where it takes the form of a concern with dominance and submission. Anxiety about people's ability to stay within the prescribed sex roles and personality
types, and about the real or imaginary desire to transcend them, is expressed in
many pieces of folklore and ritual. (Oakley 1972: 147–50)

The division of labor by sex would seem to be of greatest significance, then,
when it becomes an aspect of gender differentiation. Taking human societies
as a whole, it is more usual than not to find some allocation of jobs on a sexual
basis.

The examples which Oakley cites are, of necessity, recent ones. Lionel Tiger
has put forward an argument which links patterns of male dominance to the
division of labor on an evolutionary scale. His point, very briefly, is this: early
man was a hunter, and the exigencies of hunting led to the formation of all-male
groups which were reinforced by the development of a special bond between

males as such. Male bonding is written into our heritage. It is this, male bonding, which generates the kinds of division of labor between the sexes that we see
in modern and recent societies. It is also bound up with patterns of dominance.

In many countries, women's employment has expanded considerably, and a wider
range of possible posts is open to a greater number. But it remains the overall
pattern that women work for men. Even though women may formally control
business through equities, their disposition of wealth and control is through the
agency of male advisers. And that work which females typically do is generally
awarded lower status than work men do.

Males dominate females in occupational and political spheres. This is a
species-specific pattern and is associated with my other proposition: that males
bond in a variety of situations involving power, force, crucial or dangerous work,
and relations with their gods. They consciously and emotionally *exclude* females
from these bonds. The significant notion here is that these broad patterns are
biologically based, and that those variously different expressions of male dominance and male bonding in different communities are what one would expect
from a species highly adaptable to its physical and social environments, and
where learning is a crucial adaptive process. . . . Male dominance and bonding
are features of the human "biogram." New archaeological data underlie the claim
that hunting is at least 14 million years old and that man separated from other
primates possibly 20 million years ago. . . .

We may assume . . . that hunters were all-male, and that to the extent that
co-operative rather than solitary hunting predominated, a significant genetic
factor in selection was the *group* of hunters as well as the individuals compos-
ing the group. In the reproductive situation, the genetic package was the male-
plus-female, a unit which ensured the existential continuity of the species. So, in
the hunting situation, it was the hunting group—male-plus-male-plus-male—a
group which ensured the survival of the entire reproductive community. Thus
was the male-male bond as important for hunting purposes as the male-female
bond was for reproductive purposes, and this is the basis of the division of labour
by sex. I have already noted some of the reasons for this. Those who hunted alone
would be less likely to kill large animals and thus less likely to reproduce. Secondly, those males who took females on the hunt might be (1) distracted from
hunting by sexual blandishment, (2) certainly slowed down on a chase, because
females are slower than males, and not specialized for effective bursts of high-
energy-using activity, which males are; (3) they might also be affected by the

varying behaviour and mood of females in the various phases of their menstrual cycle as well as by what may be a greater female propensity to express particular perhaps ill-adapted emotions in states of crisis; (4) females would be less able and willing to engage in physical struggle with prey animals, and less able to defend the group from predators and possibly human opponents.

In other words, there would be a definite genetic advantage to those males who insisted on hunting in all-male groups. There would be clear disadvantages to those communities who permitted females to join the hunt.... Those females who hunted with males could not reproduce as numerously as non-hunting females; the female hunting "propensity" would not be maintained or augmented in the genetic pool. (Tiger 1971: 98–112 passim, original emphasis; changed sequence)

How does this link up with men's prominence in public affairs?

It is true that females may have much power in some types of family structure and undoubtedly exert decisive influence over socialization of the young. Females may also participate fully in economic activity (though here again it is significant that lower status typically attaches to female work) and in many communities may play political, religious, intellectual, etc., and certainly "expressive" roles of consequence. But it may be incorrect to belittle the importance of "access to a public forum" in symbolizing the actual power relationships between the sexes in a community. When a community deals with its most vital problems, when statements of internal and external importance are made, when—particularly in warfare—decisive actions must be taken, at these times females do not participate. The public forum is a male forum....

Of course, many of the reasons for female non-participation in higher politics arise out of a variety of straightforward social situations, such as the complexities of the role of child-rearing, the legal propertylessness of females in some communities which must inhibit their freedom of political action, the fact that often they may not easily enter professions such as law which may be a typical prelude to political careers, and the simple fact that females are generally less well educated and have fewer broad opportunities for political experience than males.

But I have been stressing that there are other underlying species-regularities involved. First, that women leaders do not inspire "followership" chiefly because they are women and not only because of the consequences of those factors noted above; secondly, even if they want to, women cannot become political leaders because males are strongly predisposed to form and maintain all-male groups, particularly when matters of moment for the community are involved. The suggestion is that a combination of these two factors has been the basis for the hostility and difficulty those females have faced who have aspired to political leadership. This has been the basis of the tradition of female non-involvement in high politics, and not the tradition itself. (Tiger 1971: 57, 74–75)

Tiger argues, then, that in their evolutionary past the hunting activities of males and the essential child-rearing tasks of females did indeed lead directly to a situation where great value was put on men maintaining solidarity among themselves. This principle of male bonding evolved from certain economic circumstances. But it is this principle (rather than the persistence of similar economic circumstances) which in modern societies[5] accounts for the dominance of men in public affairs and a division of labor which allocates different tasks to the sexes.

In a sense all the evidence must be impressionistic—impressionistic in the way we infer from how selection works in community life that broadly Darwinian principles of sexual selection apply in some measure to humans. Against this background I want to treat the following propositions: (1) that, when they can, males choose their work-mates in processes analogous to sexual selection; (2) that the bond established generates considerable emotion; (3) that males derive important satisfactions from male bonds and male interactions which they cannot derive from male-female bonds and interactions; and (4) that the sexual division of labour is a *consequence* of males' wishes to preserve their unisexual bonds and not simply a result of physical and temperamental differences with females in any culture. (Tiger 1971: 100, original emphasis)

A modern hunting and gathering society may (as in some Aboriginal societies) or may not (as in some of the examples Oakley cites) show patterns similar to the prototype division of labor which generated the principle of male bonding. But such bonding invariably seems to give rise to a sexual division of labor of some sort.

---

5.   By this phrase, I mean all those in existence today.

ACROSS THE DIVISION

Tiger compares the principle of male bonding to that of female-male bonding. Each has been necessary for the species. He postulates

> that male-male bonds are of the same biological order for defensive, food-gathering, and social-order-maintenance purposes as the male-female bond is for reproductive purposes. (Tiger 1971: 42)

He stresses the attraction which all-male working groups have for males. That women get lowly jobs to do is presumably a by-product of the high value which men put on their own occupations. Tiger's attention is all on the men—who, so he suggests, seek job specialization because this will reinforce the male bonds. On his own argument, current forms of labor divisions between the sexes are a product of this bonding rather than a direct carry over of those primeval circumstances which put men and women at certain advantages or disadvantages for particular jobs. We would therefore be justified, if we went along with Tiger, in regarding contemporary occupational arrangements as arbitrary as Oakley would have us believe.

> Since the reproductive distinction between male and female is the one universal, societies use it as a basis for allotting other tasks. The biological specialisation suggests other specialisations, but the actual pattern of male and female activities will be devised by each society according to its beliefs about the reproductive functions of men and women, and these beliefs are culturally determined. . . .
>
> Despite the differences, then, in the ways different societies allocate work between the sexes, the use of sex as a criterion seems to be a feature of most, if not all, societies. The anthropologist Claude Lévi-Strauss considers that some form of the sexual division . . . of labour is a device which establishes the mutual dependency of the sexes upon one another. . . .
>
> The chief importance of biological sex in determining social roles is in providing a universal and obvious division around which other distinctions can be organised. In deciding which activities are to fall on each side of the boundary, the important factor is culture. In early upbringing, in education and in their adult occupations, males and females are pressed by our society into different moulds. At the end of this process it is not surprising that they come to regard their distinctive occupations as predetermined by some general law, despite the

fact that in reality the biological differences between the sexes are neither so large nor so invariable as most of us suppose, and despite the way in which other cultures have developed sex roles quite different from our own, which seem just as natural and just as inevitable to them as ours do to us. (Oakley 1972: 146–57 passim)

Like Tiger, Oakley has pointed to the fact that almost everywhere a sexual division of labor exists. She suggests that the actual way tasks are divided between the sexes is a cultural matter—that is, different societies do things differently—and there is no necessary relationship between the sex of the worker and the job he or she does. Except in one sphere: males and females have different roles to play in the reproductive process (and postnatal care of babies). She argues that this is the prime biological distinction between the sexes upon which societies build in constructing their models of what the sexes are like (i.e., in creating gender). Her interest is just this—the way in which gender is formulated in different contexts—and she points to the contrasting roles of men's and women's reproductive functions as the prototype for specialization. *Why* there should be a need for specialization in occupation (beyond the reproductive process) is partly answered by Tiger: men have to be able to express the fact that they are men (i.e., put into operation the principle of male bonding).

In present-day societies there is often more to the division of labor than this. We can turn Oakley's statement on its head, and it will still make good sense. Biological differences (for the purposes of reproduction), she suggests, may be used as the basic model for the social differences which are attached to each sex. Equally, we may say that the process of social differentiation ("men carry spears; women carry digging sticks") calls attention to perceived differences in biology.

Now both Tiger and Oakley have been concentrating on the generation of *differences* between the sexes. Tiger has tried to explain how exclusive one-sex (male) associations have developed; Oakley, how societies formulate gender and thus make more rigid through cultural and social devices existing distinctions between the sexes. Yet something to which the very words "division of labor" ought also to draw the reader's attention[6] is the fact that the more these devices stress contrasts between the sexes, the more they must remind the actors that there are indeed two sexes, not one. And any contemplation on the topic must carry the rider that neither can exist by itself. For the fact that tasks are allotted

---

6.   And which Oakley notes only in passing in the reference to Lévi-Strauss.

differently to males and females can say two things; it can say that the sexes are differently suited for particular jobs, and it can also say that for all the jobs to be done each sex needs the other. Iatmul men, as we saw in Chapter Two, *had* to have an audience of women to play to. Insofar as a division of labor is artificial, it states that neither sex can get along alone.

Descriptions of the work done by men and women among the Australian Aborigines give us an insight here. For observers of societies such as these can stress various things. They may stress the relative independence of the contribution which each sex makes to the household. Jane Goodale writes of Tiwi Aboriginals:

> Personal achievement appears to be the dominant value for which Tiwi males and females strive during their existence in the world of the living. Economic independence and achievement is encouraged at an early age for both. Children are taught that only when they are very young or when they become old may they expect someone else to feed them. (Goodale 1971: 337)

Or they may point to what appears to be a fundamental dependence on the woman who provides the more steady food supply. In the same paragraph Goodale goes on to say:

> It is significant, I believe, that Tiwi women not only provide the majority of the daily food supplies but also the daily protein. Males residing in a group of which they are not the dominant members . . . are expected to contribute fairly frequently to the larder. . . . But the Tiwi consider food provision to be a woman's work, with only the exotic foods of the deep sea and the air to be in the male domain, and women can gain considerable renown by excelling in food supply, particularly in those aspects requiring knowledge and skill in hunting small game. (Goodale 1971: 337)

Or the writer's emphasis may be on the basic cooperation which underlines this apportionment of jobs. Kaberry argues:

> There is . . . the point that there is no real co-operation, since the women contribute the greater portion of the food-supply. It seems to me that there is a danger in such a statement of confusing the qualitative with the quantitative. A woman would bring in . . . five or eight yams, perhaps a dozen fish and lily-roots. Her

husband may have brought in a kangaroo which, if he has meat or is in debt to some affinal relative, he gives away without keeping any for himself. But very often he cooks it, sending portions of the animal—head, tail, or shoulder—to different relatives, retaining the rest for family use and possibly distributing a little more the next day.

In actual quantity, the woman probably provides more over a fixed period than the man, since hunting is not always successful. She always manages to bring in something, and hence the family is dependent on her efforts to a greater extent than on those of her husband. Without the constant foraging for smaller foods, something like a state of starvation would ensue if the small quantities of meat were the sole means of subsistence. If a woman is lazy then her husband grumbles, and if he has had a tiring day himself he quarrels, and perhaps attempts to beat her. . . .

On the other hand, whatever may be the argument of dieticians and vegetarians as to the necessity for meat, there is no doubt about the native attitude. Meat is regarded as an essential element of diet, and it is just as incumbent on the man to contribute this whenever possible, as it is for the women to go out for roots and tubers. It is not left to caprice, inclination, and the stimulation provided by sport to drive him forth; he does not loll in the shade waiting to be fed by his devoted wife. He goes out day after day and generally returns with something if only an iguana, a frill lizard, a wild cat, or some larger fish obtained by spearing. . . .

The possibility of ill-luck in the chase was admitted, but on the few occasions when a man was consistently unfortunate or lazy, his wife berated him, and if particularly exasperated attacked him with both tongue and tomahawk. In fact, effort on his part was as compulsory as it was for the woman. . . . In short, the only conclusion that can be deduced from this . . . is that there is a very real co-operation between man and wife, and that it is an expected and recognized feature of marital life. (Kaberry 1939: 24–27 passim)

It seems that we have here, in the sketches of these anthropologists, a facsimile of an image writ large across the world: that the same social conventions which separate the sexes recognize the mutual necessity of both. Indeed, many societies set up rules which allocate tasks between men and women in such a way that the daily provisioning of needs *cannot* be done by one alone. Nor need this division be restricted to economic activity; for example, men may see themselves as responsible for the spiritual well-being of society, while women look after the more mundane concerns of day-to-day living. Many Aboriginal communities believe that women have the sole power to create bodily life, while men have the power to create spiritual life. Sexual intercourse[7] does not have a prominent place in their beliefs about procreation; the contrast maintained is that between the physical endowment a woman gives her child and spiritual endowment, which either comes from the particular father or from men's ritual activity on behalf of society in general. There is a contrast here—but also quite obviously a notion of complementarity.

The previous chapter emphasized the extent to which such divisions lead to a ranking process, so that the jobs of one sex appear more or less "important" than the jobs of the other. As regular food providers Aboriginal women are more important than men; but for ensuring the fundamental continuity of society, for the performance of those religious ceremonies on which "life" depends, men are in the ascendant. Such notions provide models in terms of which people think about the respective statuses of each sex. In a division between the political and the domestic life, between the socially significant and the trivial, between the spiritual and the corporeal, between the rulers and the ruled, we can also see a kind of further division. If males see themselves as protectors, governors, patrons, representatives, and keepers of life, they must have someone to protect, govern, patronize, represent, and give life to.

The economic division of labor between men and women, which allocates to each the work for which they are fit, symbolizes two things. It draws attention to mutual need as well as mutual differentiation. It can emphasize disparity and interdependence in nature, in the biological make-up of the sexes. And it can reinforce, and indeed is also part of, disparity and interdependence in society in all those other spheres where the sexes maintain contrasting but complementary roles. When men take it on themselves to perform the rituals which will ensure the clan's fertility and ensure that their wives will give successful birth; when they plead in the law courts on behalf of a sister or daughter; when they sacrifice to the ancestral spirits for their mother's health—they are saying "women need

---

7. A recognition of the importance of sexual intercourse in procreation would give both males and females some physical equality, whereas ignoring the father's role allows the equation to be made between male and spiritual matters, female and corporeal matters. This is a dramatic instance of a rigid contrast between the sexes underlining their interdependence. A child cannot be produced by one sex alone: Aboriginal dogma represents this in terms of life being the product of both physical and spiritual animation.

men." And despite appearances to the contrary, this can have only one corollary: "men need women."[8]

SYMBOLS OF INTERDEPENDENCE

A division of labor between the sexes potentially draws attention to the essential interdependency of males and females, as well as to disparity between them. Indeed, there are societies in which work is so apportioned between men and women that neither can subsist alone. Each sex is very explicitly dependent on the contribution of the other, whatever the judgments made about the respective worth of these contributions. It is not just a case of its being convenient for work to be shared but of specific rules restricting activities, so that neither can do the work of the opposite sex.

The nomadic Fulani herd cattle in West Africa. A group of them who live in the same province (Bornu) as the Kanuri, described in the previous chapter, were studied by Derrick Stenning in the 1950s. Men and women have very different roles to play in the keeping of cattle, and a viable domestic unit must contain members of both sexes.

> The family [is] the basic economic unit of [Fulani] social organization. . . . In the homestead of the male herd-owner live his household; normally a simple family composed of himself, one wife, and her children, or a compound family composed of himself, his several wives, and their children. In circumstances in which cattle are the sole basis of subsistence for such a household, meat does not form a regular or staple diet and animals are not often sold, since this represents a withdrawal from the capital stock of the herd. Killings are confined to male beasts or, where possible, sick or maimed animals. . . . Sales take place only when there is an over-riding need for cash, for example, to buy corn in a bad dry season or to raise tax. In these circumstances the family lives on milk, for . . . Fulani do not drink cattle blood or make blood foods. Either milk or milk products must be drunk or eaten *ad nauseam* or milk must be sold or exchanged for other foods.

---

8. Dependency does not have to be two-way. In the care of the young or the very old, it is usually one-way. But it is a sleight of hand to represent two-way dependency (between adult males and females) as though it were only one-way (e.g., "women are like children"). Any division of labor enlarges the area of two-way dependency.

Thus the limiting factor in the dependence of a given family group upon its herd lies in the milk output. If the milk output falls temporarily below a certain minimum, cattle will have to be sold to pay for food, thus potentially reducing still further the fecundity of the herd. Humans share milk with calves; if they make too great a demand upon the milk of the herd, the well-being or even the lives of the calves, and therefore the future fecundity of the herd, is prejudiced. . . .

We have here been considering the herd as supporting the human family dependent upon it; we have taken the family as "given" and examined the general properties of the herd associated with it. But there is a sense in which the human family supports the herd. Fulani cattle are not natural groups of wild animals followed and exploited intermittently by humans. Fulani herds are domesticated in a particular way, and this domestication entails a degree of special organization in the families dependent upon them. Desirable pastures have to be sought and cattle led to them. Water supplies have to be arranged and cattle watered regularly. Diseases and accidents of many kinds have to be avoided, or their results treated. . . . The supply of milk available to calves and humans has to be controlled by careful milking. Among the [Fulani] the division of these tasks between the sexes is clear-cut. Men have to do with cattle, their seasonal movements, daily pasturing and watering, and veterinary care. Women have to do with milk and its marketing, in addition to their domestic tasks of food preparation and the care of the homestead both at rest and on the move. Adult men are herd-owners and managers, male children and adolescents are herdsmen. Adult women are dairywomen and purveyors of milk, female children and adolescents are dairymaids. The [Fulani] family is a herd-owning and milk-selling enterprise.

Given this strict division of labour, and a herd of a certain size, a herd-owner's family must attain a size commensurate with its responsibilities towards its herd. It must also maintain a balance of the sexes, so that these responsibilities may be efficiently carried out by appropriate members of the family. A [Fulani] herd-owner must have at least one wife. Man and wife must reproduce at a certain minimum rate and in a certain proportion of potential milkmaids and herdsmen. (Stenning 1959: 101–3 passim)

Each sex does, in a sense, exercise exclusive rights toward particular aspects of cattle herding. The jobs are not interchangeable. This is made explicit in the layout of the homestead's camp, and the rules which prevent men and women from trespassing in each other's areas. The orientation and arrangement of the

[Fulani] homestead symbolize the crucial relationships within the family and also that of the family to its herd.

Compared with the clusters of circular thatched mud huts which in some form or another constitute the hamlets and villages of most of the sedentary populations of the Western Sudan, the homesteads and camps . . . seem haphazard and rudimentary. In the wet season even a large camp blends with the bush, and in the dry season it is possible to pass within a few yards of a homestead without realizing it is there. Household equipment is limited to the amount which may be carried on the head or on pack-oxen, and shelters must be made of whatever tree foliage the district has to offer. . . .

Homesteads and camps always face west. . . . In all but overnight camps a curved back-fence of branches cut from nearby trees . . . is put up to ensure a measure of privacy, keep out hyena, and deflect the course of stampeding cattle frightened by their nightly visits in the wet season. Immediately in front of the back fence are set the beds of the household. . . . Alongside or in front of these bed-shelters there may be other ancillary shelters put up for specific purposes. . . . These shelters do not always contain a bed made with poles and stakes, but usually a rough couch made of bundled grass and bark-fibre mats. In front of the bed-shelters there are domestic hearths, . . . which consist simply of three stones or parts of white-ant nests, forming a support for a cooking pot, supplemented perhaps by an iron tripod bought in the market. . . .

In front of this group of shelters is staked down a long two-stranded leather rope . . . to which the calves of the household herd are tethered when the herd is in its corral. In front again of the calf-rope is the cattle corral. . . . This is often merely a circular patch of earth trampled by the beasts' hooves. . . . Round the corral under convenient bushes or trees there may be rough beds of the type found in the ancillary huts. In the centre of the cattle corral is a smudge fire round which the cattle gather in the early morning and in the evening when they return from pasture. . . .

There is a clear division in the homestead between the male and female spheres of action. Between the back fence and the calf-rope is the female area. It is normally the wife's duty to fell suitable trees, or collect them, for her part of the back fence, although she may be helped in this by her sons. The main shelters in this part of the homestead are the [domestic areas] of the household head's wives, and the essentials of these shelters—the domestic utensils and the bed—are regarded as the wives' own property. . . . The ancillary shelters in this part of the homestead are also to do with women. [They shelter] the aged mother of the household head, [or] the household head's daughter in her first pregnancy. The only males who sleep in this part of the homestead are the household head and his infant sons. The household head has no hut or bed of his own, but sleeps in the [domestic areas] of his wives in rotation; the wife with whom he sleeps cooks an evening meal for him.

No males, other than infant boys, eat in this part of the homestead. Although a household head's horse may be tethered there, it is looked after by the infants of the household, who feed it with grass cut by one of the lads of the household and water fetched by one of the unmarried daughters. . . . Apart from the help given by the sons of the household in erecting the back fence and the sheep or goat folds when camp is pitched, or lifting household equipment on to pack animals when camp is struck, males do not work in [a woman's domestic] area. It is not considered seemly for any male of cattle-herding age—that is, above the age of about ten—to go into this area unless asked to do so for some specific purpose by a woman of the household. . . .

The [domestic] area is given over exclusively to the day-to-day execution of women's tasks. A wife maintains all her own equipment. She makes coiled basketry mats for calabash covers and for sale in the market; bark-fibre mats which are used as blankets, roofing, and as part of the harness of the pack-oxen. She scours, sews, and decorates calabashes, stains and polishes her bed-poles, lashes and refurbishes the ceremonial items of her household equipment. A wife plans the subsistence of the household. She milks cows and prepares butter and milk for market and for home consumption. . . . Infants of both sexes, her own unmarried daughters and daughters of her husband's former wives, and the wives of her sons eat with her at her own hearth, and no female ever eats outside. . . .

West of the calf-rope is the male area of the homestead, where the cattle, the main interest and preoccupation of the men, are kept. Women are allowed into the cattle corral only in special circumstances. A household head's wife, or a daughter deputed by her, may milk her allotted cows at milking times, but not if she is more than about seven months pregnant. When, during the day, a cattle corral is vacated, women do not cross it and children do not play in it. . . . When not herding or absent from the camp on business or pleasure . . . men sit under the shade of a tree to the west of the cattle corral. Here they receive visitors and exchange news, mend clothes, and make cowhide sandals. . . . Women rarely come near the men's shade tree in the daytime, and men rarely go into the homesteads. A man's instructions to his womenfolk are called across the intervening cattle corral, and infants may find employment carrying this and that between the women's shelters and the men's shade tree. (Stenning 1959: 104–11 passim)

These rules very clearly delimit the spheres of the sexes. They also make it quite obvious that each needs the other. The crucial social relationship is that of husband and wife as herder and milker, and marriages are contracted with the division of labor between the spouses giving rise to clear expectations.

The marital contract . . . was one in which the husband required of his wife that she should bear children, particularly boys, the future inheritors of the herd; the wife's expectations were that the husband should maintain sufficient cattle for the maintenance of herself and her children. (Stenning 1959: 181)

The picture would seem to be of a stable, well-regulated form of domestic economy, in which almost equal weight is given to men's and women's contributions. But the very explicitness of these arrangements leads also to an estimation of the personal worth of individuals which brings unexpected results. These I describe in the next section.

THE SUBVERSION GAME

At this point I alter the focus a little. An outsider can perhaps "see" that if the division of labor makes certain jobs the exclusive concern of one sex, then the two sexes are necessarily dependent on one another. But this may or may not be openly recognized. We have already noted (Chapter Three) how our own folk-ideology tends to regard the housewife in English society as the dependent partner, in spite of beliefs that house-keeping jobs are the appropriate province of women and not men, and men *need* women to house-keep for them. So notions about the appropriateness of a division of labor do not have to lead to conscious assertions of mutuality. Indeed, they may form the basis for judging the affairs of one sex as less important than the other. If we take into account the contrast between public and domestic spheres of action, things are more complicated still. It is all very well for an outsider to say that the governors need people to govern but the mainstream values of the society may emphasis the obverse: people need to be governed. This is what we find again and again in male-female relations. That women depend on men is frequently much more explicit than its rider, men depend on women.

Moreover, it is highly unusual in human societies to find interdependence between the sexes as an explicit value governing all aspects of social life. Even if it is acknowledged in economic terms (and it need not be) it may be denied in those political or religious dogmas which give the male ultimate dominance. This means, however, that those areas in which interdependence is recognized put ammunition into the hands of the dominated. I do not imply that everywhere there is a "sex war." The notion of a sex war involves a very particular evaluation of the structure of society, which pitches one sex against the other as opposed interest groups ("classes"). If indeed it is very common for men to be concerned with "society" and women with "themselves," one would not really expect to find constructs which ranged the sexes against one another like two sides in a battle. What one might expect would be situations in which individual women asserted their own interests, and perhaps got away with it, in spite of their formally coming under male control.

Let us go back to the Fulani. I described the family, and the fact that explicit recognition was given to the husband-wife unit as the basic combination of male and female essential for economic viability.

> The crucial symbol in this complex is the calf-tether, which at once separates and connects the male and female elements. . . . As we have seen, the calf-rope dividing the corral from the domestic hearths also divides men and women in their everyday life. But it is at the calf-rope that the only routine co-operative work of man and wife is done. When the herd does not require examination or treatment, husbands frequently join their wives at milking time to help release the calves from the rope and return them to it when they have been suckled. . . . The only time a man crosses the calf-rope is when he lies with his wife, and the only time a wife crosses the calf-rope into the corral is in order to obtain milk. . . . The marital contract appears to be one in which calves, the increase of the herd, are identified with children, the increase of the family. . . . The marital duty of a husband is to keep the herd at such a size as to be able to provide for his dependents; the wife's duty is to bear children who become the labour force of the family. A wife expects from her husband milk; a husband expects from his wife children. The whole stability of . . . marriage, and the economic efficiency of the family of which it is the origin, is bound up with the fulfillment of these expectations. (Stenning 1959: 122–24 passim)

But where expectations are so clear cut, failure to realize them may have drastic results.

> If this is indeed the essence of the marital contract, it follows that the rupture of this contract by divorce should occur primarily when these expectations are not realized. Men may therefore be expected to divorce their wives when they do not bear children, women to divorce their husbands when insufficient cattle are provided for them to milk. (Stenning 1959: 181–82)

In fact, Fulani divorce is easy and frequent and is resorted to by both sexes.

> The most common grounds for the divorce of a woman mentioned by men were: real or assumed barrenness; incompatibility with her co-wives; insubordination to her husband; acts which brought him into public disrepute, such as thieving in the market or habitual lying; adultery with a kinsman *in flagrante delicto*. Those mentioned by women were: a husband's incontinent sales of cattle to buy luxuries or curry favour with chiefs or officials; long absences on unnecessary visits; inconsiderate choices of camp-sites at long distances from water supplies or markets; obviously favouring a co-wife; and meanness, in failing to provide the women and girls of his household with clothes for feasts. (Stenning 1959: 172)

The lists are interesting. Although barrenness is among the reasons men state for divorce, and Stenning notes that the fate of a barren woman is one of perpetual insecurity, men also divorce women for compromising their public image. Women in turn seem to resent men's involvement in outside affairs. A man with a small herd may find it difficult to keep his wife—and not just because he cannot provide enough milk to feed her children. Women also want milk to sell at market. And they dislike the husband dissipating cattle for his political advancement.

> A herd may prove or promise to be insufficient for a wife's needs in two ways, each of which may occasion the wife's recrimination and make divorce on these grounds more likely. Firstly, the herd itself or its milk output may be reduced; secondly, the household dependent upon it may be increased so that a wife has at her disposal relatively less milk. . . . Women, rather than men, nowadays encourage side ventures in small stock such as sheep and goats, which can be sold when cash is needed without depleting the herd from which their main subsistence

derives. Conversely, women do not approve the efforts of their husbands to better themselves politically when these involve presents of cattle to chiefs in whose gift a desired title may lie, or sales of stock to purchase a horse, saddlery, a sword, and gowns, which are necessary if a man is to make his mark in this way. Women will also disapprove of sudden migrations made for political motives, and the occurrence of such a migration is accompanied, in marital histories and genealogies, by a number of divorces of men by their wives. But normally, so long as they have access to markets and domestic water supplies…wives support the seasonal deployments of cattle, although sometimes with reservations. . . .

In seeking divorce . . . women may not merely desire to escape from a domestic situation that they regard as intolerable, but may also seek one which represents an advancement for them in terms of the number of cattle they have at their disposal for milking. They say: "A Fulani woman marries where she can get milk." (Stenning 1959: 185–88 passim)

Women desire to be near markets, so that they can earn the wherewithal to buy things for themselves and their families. It is also contact with the outside world. When it comes, however, to their husbands' contact with the outside world—with the purchases he has to make to become an important figure—we can almost discern a note of jealousy. Women's marketing and their other activities are concentrated in the first place on themselves; men's activities belong to a political world in which women have no real part to play. A husband's self-advancement may be at the expense of what a wife feels is her due. In a sense, husband and wife are in competition over the cattle which they both look after. Situations arise where each would like to see the beasts and the dairy products disposed of in ways which bettered their own position.

Consider another situation where a strict division of labor also exists but one which does not quite so openly make both husband and wife mutually responsible for the basis of wealth and livelihood. Among the sedentary neighbors of the Fulani in Bornu live the Kanuri (see Chapter Four).

Men and women live essentially segregated lives . . . Men control political jobs, religious functions, and almost all gainful employment. There are a few occupations that are strictly feminine, such as female hairdressing, pottery, and the retail selling of cooked foodstuffs. Women's main work is seen as cooking, maintaining a clean household, fetching water, and the raising of young children. . . . The only major overlap between men's and women's work is in farming. To a variable degree, rural women help on the farm. . . . Across the entire gamut of tasks necessary for the maintenance of social life, Kanuri culture ordains that there be as strict a segregation of the sexes as possible.

This segregation also involves evaluation. The entire set of possible tasks and activities to be carried out in life are then divided into two realms by their association with a particular sex. By definition, woman's work is unmanly, undignified, and lower in status than man's work. Overtly, at least, both sexes accept these cultural norms. In everyday life it affects job evaluation. Thus when discussing the possibility of a food processing plant with Kanuri friends, I quickly ran up against the idea that it might be hard to enlist a male labor force because as one informant noted "It is woman's work." . . .

Variations in segregation are simple at a gross level of description. All wealthy men in either the rural or urban setting do not allow their wives to help on the farm or go outside the household for water. These tasks are accomplished through laborers and by having a water source inside the compound. . . . City women and wives of wealthy husbands, especially the latter, are the most segregated from their men folk in the conduct of daily tasks. . . . Purdah varies along with these same qualities. In a sense, the exclusion of wives from society is the ideological end-point of sexual segregation, since the woman is segregated from all men except her husband and her kin. . . . Then woman and her tasks become scarce values to control and hide from other men who also seek control.

But conditions vary. Rural peasants need help on their farms; water must be obtained from wells, often at some distance from the household. Even among the poor of the city, women must go out of the compound for water. Therefore, the poor cannot so easily keep women totally out of participation in overlapping activities and interactive areas in which they contact the man's world. (R. Cohen 1971: 98–99)

In this society, with its pronounced dogmas of male superiority, men come to be afraid of their wives' insubordination. We should note one particular element of these ideas. It is not simply that Kanuri women are minors and inevitably under the authority of a male. The particular tie between husband and wife is seen to be analogous to other ties between people (patron-client and so on) which are based on notions of personal bonds. The pair is bound one to another through trust or loyalty. The one gives obedience, the other gives protection or support. But because this is so, the whole question of the adequacy of what each gives to the other may lead to tension within the couple. This shows itself in conflicts over household arrangements, the one area where husband and wife come into regular interaction; it also shows itself in men's fears about female sexuality. The jobs which Kanuri wives do are of much less economic importance than those of Fulani women. Men justify this in terms of Muslim doctrine. But the same doctrine also admits that husband and wife have mutual sexual interests in each other, and the husband's chief job is to guard and control his wife's sexuality. If they are deprived of all else, Kanuri wives are regarded as potent sexual beings.

Kanuri society provides, then, an example of a culture where the interdependency aspects of men and women, in the roles of husband and wife, are played down to the minimum. A woman depends on her husband for almost all her contact with the outside world, and for basic economic support; apart from raising children, he depends on her for jobs associated with the household only and jobs which a rich man may have servants and clients perform.[9] The only unambiguous area of interdependency is in reproductive and sexual matters. And it is over his wife's sexual behavior that a Kanuri husband most fears he will lose control.

In spite of the fact that women are relegated to the house and in the main to tasks associated with the household, there is nevertheless a degree of mutual expectation between husband and wife based on their respective marital duties and, as in the Fulani case, there

> is also tension between husbands and wives over the limits of proper expectation. . . . In Bornu . . . agreements on what each spouse may expect of one another are really rather vague. The wife knows roughly how much purdah any particular man expects and he knows roughly what freedom she considers essential, but there is much room for argument since these guidelines do not ever fit every case. Possibly the best examples of such tension points are situations involving cooking for extra people or the visiting of kin by the wife. The wife may know something of her cooking responsibilities before she enters the marriage, but the husband may be using this new marriage to expand his social network. Thus he may invite people to eat on sudden notice and demand that food be brought for him and his friends. When it is not forthcoming, or comes and is poorly done or skimpy, the man may feel he is being shamed before people he is trying to

---

9.   There are differences between urban and rural Kanuri, and between the rich and the poor. Poor farmers depend more on their wives' labor than other men do.

impress with his largesse and hospitality. The wife feels she has been shamed and dealt with unfairly, since no warning was given of the need for such extra work, and the result is an undeserved demonstration of incompetence. Such occasions produce tensions and arguments. The wife may tell the husband to warn her in the future so they may both be better prepared—that way lies reconciliation and cooperation if the husband agrees. He may instead tell her she must be ready at all times because he never knows when extra people will be offered his hospitality. She may agree and cook more from then on or she may disagree and say that she did not realize this marriage involved so much extra work—implying that had she known she would not have entered into such an agreement and possibly it might be better to end the relationship.

No matter how strict the seclusion of a Kanuri wife, she has a jural right and obligation to return to her own kinsfolk for important occasions such as *rites de passage* or when someone is sick. Again, although these rules are quite clear, husbands and wives may disagree on the exact way in which such obligations are to be carried out. He may feel that she should wait a few days before going, or stay for a shorter period, and she may not agree. The structural rules governing her rights of return run counter to the ideology of dominance, since this is one area of the wife's life over which the husband does not have control, and this conflict can create tensions, especially if other factors are already contributing to mistrust and conflict. Thus one man in a rural village was extremely agitated over his wife returning to her village several miles away. He already had reason to suspect her fidelity and knew that she would be traveling through the village of a former husband. . . . His suspicions were almost intolerable and yet he could not prevent her from going. This marriage ended in divorce a few months later. (R. Cohen 1971: 110–11)

We have seen that a division of labor points at once to the essential differences between the sexes, as defined in particular societies by the radically separate tasks for which they are considered fit, and to the obvious result that through a division in this way each sex has to depend on the other (a fact of social reality, which may or may not be consciously formulated in statements about interdependence). Where the division of labor goes with an evaluation which makes male jobs the superior ones and thus appears to be a mechanism which *supports* male dominance, any area in which men are acknowledged to be dependent on women can become one in which they suffer challenges to their superiority. Cohen cites two illuminating Kanuri incidents.

A chief quality of the husband's role is that of provider. But the expectation is not very explicit about minimal standards. In rural areas, all husbands try to provide their wives with some new clothes after the sale of the cash crop in winter. But some crops fail, others go untended, and still others may be sold (illegally) as future to pay off debts. . . . Similarly with market money. Some husbands are quite generous, others give very little while still others do the marketing themselves and do not give their wives regular money for food purchases. . . .

The possibilities of tension over the husband's provider functions can be exacerbated by the jural rule which maintains husbands and wives as separate economic property-owning individuals. In effect this means that a husband must share his capital because of the expectation of being a provider, while there is no essential need or expectation for the wife to do so. . . . Although the ideology calls for male dominance, the wife may maintain areas of economic *independence* over which he has no legitimate control. . . .

Ideally, a wife should be obedient, compliant, and modest (i.e., self-restrained), no matter what are the circumstances of her marriage. In practice, such compliance to cultural expectations are very rare. Instead, the actual interaction is governed by the socio-economic status of the husband, his degree of dependency upon his wife, her attitudes to the ideology of female submissiveness, and a number of other factors. Two examples representing extremes of variation will clarify some of these relationships. In one case, a middle-aged rural farmer and low status supporter of a political leader had finally, after a number of years, managed to find a wife. His status as a slave had meant that few women wished to enter into marriage with him. . . . Up until this marriage, he was eating at the compounds of other men and had developed several of these relations socially, which obligated him to the compound heads who fed him. He now felt free from such encumbrances and indeed could invite others, including myself, to come and eat with him, thus reversing his subordinate status as a food receiver to that of potential leader through his ability to provide cooked meals for others.

His wife helped him on his farm, cooked his meals, and was personally quite a handsome women with a rather gay witty way about her that often spilled over the bounds of modesty into rather raucous and bawdy conversation.

On one occasion . . . at about 5:00 p.m. his wife came out of her sleeping hut and started out of the compound. He turned to her quickly and asked where she was going. "Walking" she answered tartly. Not to indicate a destination or a proper excuse was extremely provocative, since she was in fact proclaiming independence over a matter customarily and jurally under a husband's authority.

The husband answered sharply "Stay!" and she simply said "I go," again defying him. This interchange was repeated several times until finally the wife said "I am going, and if you like I won't come back." At which point the husband fell silent. After she left, the now terribly embarrassed man complained bitterly to me about how wicked Kanuri women are today. . . .

Everyone remarks on [this story]. . . . The husband has very low status and needs the wife. The wife, they say, sounds like an extremely nasty and immodest women. The height of her immodesty is in her retort that she is simply going for a walk, which means she is suggesting the possibility of meeting other men as if she were an unmarried woman. Almost all informants remark that such a woman should be gotten rid of, but they sympathize (rather contemptuously) with the plight of the husband whose dependence on his wife's functions has allowed her to play such a free role as his spouse.

At the other extreme is the case of Mallam. He is an extremely well thought of and respected number of his community. His regular monthly salary from his civil service post puts him at the bottom rung of the upper classes, while his older full brother's position as a senior member of the emirate civil service solidifies this upper class membership. His two wives, he says, are in strict [purdah]. Recently, one of his wives came out of the front door of their city household to buy some cosmetics from a street vendor. Mallam was sitting under the shade of a tree across the street with friends and neighbors and he observed her purchase.

Quietly and with his usual dignity, he arose, went over to this wife and divorced her, telling her to pack her things and leave his house that evening. Explaining his action, he said that her disobedience was unforgivable. Had he not told her many times that she could always send a small child, or ask him, or a client servant living in the household, to make any purchases she required? Did she not know that in his household [purdah] was strictly enforced and his wives left only on necessary visits to their own kinfolk or other absolutely essential business, discussed first with him so that he could grant his permission? Certainly she knew that. Therefore, Mallam theorized, the only possible reason this wife could break such rules was because she was going "to start trouble in the compound." Better, then, to scotch it before it began.

When I suggested alternative hypotheses such as her desire to make her own purchases and therefore choices among the varieties of merchandise, or her boredom at being within the household all the time (she was seventeen years old), Mallam rejected such explorations. To him, such ideas were irrelevant even if true because his authority and its implied abrogation by her actions were too important as issues to look for rationalizations or excuses. And, for *me* to think of *her* welfare, rather than *his* authority, he said, showed that I was not a Kanuri! The conversation then turned to stories of how Europeans find it difficult to control their wives. (R. Cohen 1971: 103–5, original emphasis)

The early evening, when the first incident happened, is the time when the wife should start preparing her husband's supper. She should see that water and food is ready. It was a provocative time for a woman to leave the house: a husband expects his wife to perform various personal services for him at the end of the day. Mallam's problem was a different one. Although some women do take part in marketing, a husband may look on his role as provider as eliminating even this from a woman's proper range of jobs. His wife was challenging this role; she was disregarding the division of labor between them.

A factor which runs through Kanuri life is the institution of purdah. It is not just that female tasks confine women to the household but also that specific dogmas demand they be kept in seclusion. As we have seen, the extent to which husbands insist on the full observance of the purdah rules varies, and is most likely to be strictest in the households of richer men. Here the husband can afford servants to do the menial tasks which take the wives of poorer men outside. Husbands who enforce strict purdah forbid their wives to leave the house except on certain occasions, and have them sleep in special quarters which are often walled off from the rest of the compound, and which other men rarely enter. Now among the dogmas which uphold the necessity of such arrangements is the doctrine that women are sexually unreliable.

> There is a widespread belief that women, at least most of them, can be seduced with very little difficulty. As one woman informant said to me, "If the right things are done, then it is possible [for a man] to have nearly any woman in Bornu." . . . In Bornu [this] is not thought to be due to an innate and uncontrollable sexuality on the part of women, but to the material and social gains she can obtain through the granting of her favors. . . .
>
> In both the Islamic world in general and Bornu in particular, the most obvious correlates of these images of women as inferior, different, and sexually untrustworthy, are the ideas of purdah and of the "code of modesty." If a woman cannot adequately operate in the man's world outside the home, then she should be confined within the household where she can do those things (food preparation, reproduction, and care of children) for which she is ordained. Furthermore,

if she is kept in the household and if all interactions between men and women are governed by rules of strict control in which any sexual content is severely limited, then possibly some of the opportunities for insubordination and sexual misconduct can be avoided. . . .

Kanuri follow the general Islamic belief that men are dominant, and that men should by reason of traditional Islamic dogma take precedence over women in society. Women are weak, and in this ancient view they are easily seduced because of their innate lack of control over the more basic physical passions. Men, being more rational, are therefore more in control of themselves and can rule others, especially women. (R. Cohen 1971: 93, 97)

In other words, a woman who bestows her favors on men other than her husband is in the most direct possible way challenging not only his rights in her sexuality, not only the affection which should exist between them, but his dominance over her. She can do this because in drawing attention to an area of interdependence, she exposes his dominance as less than absolute. For the husband expects sexual attention from his wife, and it is significant that in this culture care of the husband's person is one of the wife's duties. She may fan her husband while he rests, and invariably in the evening will prepare his bed and then massage and oil him. This is also the time of day when the couple discusses matters concerning them both.

When the massage is completed, the husband may, if he wishes, invite her into his bed. . . . Besides intercourse, this time in the husband's sleeping quarters is used for general discussions of household affairs, money matters, cooking, cleaning, the management of children, etc. If the couple is intimate, more confidential matters can also be discussed at this time: rivalries, ambitions, competition with others, and even more secret activities such as profits gained in trade or by other means. This is the one time during the entire day when husband and wife are fully alone and neither is required to be engaged in his or her economic or other social responsibilities. (R. Cohen 1971: 100)

It is hard to resist the conclusion that acknowledgment of mutual dependency between Kanuri spouses is closely tied up with sexual reciprocity. It is no wonder that husbands whose wives defy them are perturbed most by the imputation that the woman is going to seek liaisons with others. Kanuri interpret female defiance in terms of sexual immodesty.

SEGREGATION, SUPERIORITY, AND DOMINANCE

Kanuri culture gives weight to the sexual bonds between husbands and wives; Fulani to their economic interests in the herd which is the family's base. In both cases husbands are most sensitive to the possibilities of insubordination when the wife's activities seem to exploit her prominence in these matters. She takes more than she is given. To put it simply, the Kanuri wife is valued sexually, and she is thought to express her independence through seeking affairs with other men; the Fulani wife is valued economically, and she is suspected of putting her ambitions in marketing before the joint needs of the family in the products of their stock. Conversely, the Kanuri husband must provide his wife with all she needs from the outside world, and failure to do so may lead to her behaving immodestly; the Fulani husband must see that the herd's resources maintain his wives and children and not squander them entirely on political advancement, or his wife leaves him. Yet a division of labor between the sexes may seem an inevitable extension of gender stereotypes. Males and females are allotted different tasks because their natures suit them to contrasting styles of life. In turn, the division of labor enlarges on the stereotypes, becomes itself an extension of gender.

As Berndt writes of Australian Aborigines:

> A spear is a symbol of maleness. One symbol of femaleness is a dilly bag or basket or a wooden food-carrying dish. But a digging stick, although less sharply distinctive in form, is also a female symbol—indicating the main economic activity that is the prerogative and virtual monopoly of women, the sphere of food-collecting. A digging stick is a domestic tool. A spear can be a domestic tool too, but more aggressively so, in hunting and fishing and even, occasionally, in digging: its wounding and killing functions (in regard to game, meat and fish) are paralleled in the fighting spear. Although in some situations a woman's digging stick can serve double duty as a fighting stick, normally this is for use against other women, not against men, whereas a man's spear is not limited to victims of one sex. Some women made this distinction explicit in pointing to differences in their roles as against men's, and the boundaries of tolerated behaviour for women as contrasted with men. "We carry digging sticks, not spears. We are not men!" (Berndt [1970] 1986: 72)

We again encounter the possibility that the same division of labor which points up contrasts between the sexes, can also imply their mutual interdependence.

In the food quest, the digging stick and the spear complement and supplement each other in the conventionally accepted division of labour. Either could stand alone. A man could manage by himself, over a period, as far as food-getting went, just as a woman could, although his efforts were fraught with rather more uncertainty than hers. But pooling their resources, combining their efforts, was a matter of mutual advantage. If woman was the main "bread-winner" (i.e., responsible for vegetable goods and shellfish and smaller creatures, occasionally larger ones) and man the main "meat-winner" (responsible for larger animals and birds and larger sea creatures), sharing ensured a more satisfying diet for both. (Berndt [1970] 1986: 72)

The areas in which this interdependence is admitted varies from society to society. When the division of tasks is tied very explicitly into notions about male superiority (superior because of the jobs men do), I have suggested that the very idea of interdependency may be largely suppressed. Indeed, from an analytical point of view we could almost see the segregation between public (male) and domestic (female) spheres of activities as itself a "division of labor," but because generally this kind of separation is bound up with assertions of male dominance its interdependency aspects are likely to find little explicit expression. Men stress the need for women to be controlled rather than female acquiescence in being ruled. Otherwise put, if we were to take these divisions between men and women as a simple reflection of their natural capacities, there should be no cause for conflict between them on this score; yet time and again, it is through the performance of their respective tasks that men and women are able to challenge one another. Why should they, and why should the division of labor be such an effective area in which to do so?

It is significant, I think, that when we talk of the division of labor between the sexes, the social relationships to which we most commonly refer are those between husband and wife. And these are not euphemisms for any couple that mate, for any kind of sexual bond, casual or not. It is in the specific relationship of spouses to one another that we find the clearest statements enunciating the tasks appropriate for each sex. For this, as the last chapter commented, is of course a relationship which usually brings males and females together in the full light of social attention. Husband and wife are bound to each other by multitudinous social rules: theirs is a legal as well as a moral and emotional relationship. And although they are persons who are linked in the first place through social ties, these ties invariably emphasize the essential biological necessity of male-female interaction. It is husbands and wives—and not lovers as such—who are almost everywhere charged with the function of reproduction. (Indeed some societies place very definite sanctions on this relationship, extramarital sexual relations being held to impair a couple's fertility or the health of children.) They are persons, then, bound to each other in the sexual (reproductive) sphere. And their bonds are socially emphasized. The division of economic tasks between them enlarges on these facts of dependency; it makes them dependent on one another *beyond* the purposes of reproduction. Look at the Fulani family: basic economic viability is seen to rest directly on cooperation between husband and wife. If dependency could in reality be denied, it would not matter a jot how husband and wife behaved toward one another. In fact, it often matters desperately.

Both Kanuri and Fulani men are dependent on women for basic social prestige. A Kanuri man needs someone who will cook for him so that he can entertain; a Fulani man needs a woman who will milk his cows so that he may establish a herd of his own. A wifeless male is no one. At the root of a man's ambitions, then, lies reliance on a woman's cooperation. How the wife comports herself is important for the husband because he cannot escape the facts of his dependency on her. Yet we have seen that a division of tasks into those fit for women and those fit for men can also substantiate male claims to superiority over women. In Chapter Four it was suggested that where strong assertions are made about the respective superiority and inferiority of males and females, as categories, it often seems important that these should be reiterated in the marital relationship. Marriage is the test as it were: a man and a woman enter into a relationship founded in the first place on their sexual differences. Marital relations differ here from other ties between the sexes, such as mother and son, or female oracle and male supplicant; or whatever. Sexual differences may be relevant to the situation but are modified by other aspects of the relationship, such as parenthood or ritual expertise.

Most marriage ceremonies explicitly unite the bride and groom in a way which leaves no ambiguity about their respective statuses. For the first prerequisite for a marriage is that the partners should be of opposite sex,[10] and the sexual identity of each must be in no doubt. Thus it is not uncommon to find puberty

---

10. There are some notable exceptions to this, especially in societies which do not operate a strict equation of legal and genetic parenthood, and cultural situations which separate reproduction from sexual intercourse.

ceremonies for children—and especially girls—coinciding with or culminating in marital rites. But as earlier chapters have also reminded us sexual identity (gender) is not just a matter of sex (biology). It is bound up with all those other characteristics which make a man male and a woman female. These may include assumptions to the effect that the male is the more socially significant partner.

By now it should be obvious that a division of labor between husband and wife very neatly confounds a complex situation. On the one hand, it enlarges the extent to which spouses are seen to depend on one another: it is not just for reproductive purposes alone that they establish a union. And it reminds others that for certain essential purposes men and women are necessary to one another.[11] On the other hand, it is also very common for the division of labor to support just those dogmas which put a different evaluation on men's and women's contributions to society. And sexual identity (gender) is closely dependent on such dogmas.

Where sexual identity is tied up with doctrines of superiority and inferiority, and where the division of labor upholds these doctrines, marriage must also become a vehicle through which this aspect of identity is validated. Obedience as well as cooperation is demanded from the wife. A wife's failure to perform her allotted tasks is a direct threat not just to their personal happiness, not just to the family purse, but also (when these conditions hold) to the husband's domination as a male. Hence we can see now why the division of labor is such a subtle area, one in which the subordinate sex can offer challenge: for a woman failing in her tasks draws attention at one and the same time to the fact her husband is dependent on her in reality, and that there are loopholes in his assertions of superiority. However we may switch the pronouns too. Women become openly dependent on men when they marry. A Fulani woman needs a herder to keep her supplied with milk; a Kanuri wife wants someone to buy her the things she needs. And social arrangements are invariably such that the men on whom women can make these demands most effectively are those cast in the role of husband. Among the rights a woman frequently acquires at marriage is the right to economic support. The exclusiveness of the marital relationship is defined just so: if she acquires these rights in a husband she cannot demand them from

11. And this is true even if doctrines of physiology do not make the partners equal in this sphere. As in subsistence, a woman's role in reproduction may be rated lower than the man's role ("she is an empty vessel to be filled"); but the necessity of her cooperation cannot be denied.

other men. Only those males defined as husbands are under strict obligation
to provide such support. In the same way many cultures lay down rules which
make it certain that a man can expect, to the point of being able to demand it, a
meal and a bed only in his wife's house.

At the same time, whereas it seems quite common for husbands to use their
wives' dependency on them as yet further validation of women's inferiority to
men as a whole, the reverse does not hold to the same degree. From one point of
view a woman is reciprocally in a position of strength too. Yet social conventions
often mean that women cannot use this position of potential strength to claim
general superiority themselves, for men have already preempted that claim. In
the case of men it is bulwarked by their ostentatious concern with the affairs
of the outside world and with society in general. And this brings us back to
another strand in the arguments of this chapter. If men have preempted interest
in the maintenance of social (public, political) life, there is an alternative sphere
for women which possibly gives them some complementary gratification: interest in themselves.

In sum, then, a division of labor often stresses the particular complementarity of and disparity between husband and wife, a relationship affected by
gender stereotypes in general since it is one which throws primary emphasis
on sexual difference. When the interests of spouses diverge—and they do not
have to—there will be a tendency for the husband to seek support for his position from the public values which males uphold in the outside world (so that
"women" can be seen to threaten "society"). And there will be a tendency for
the wife's interests to be expressed for herself, or her children, in personal and
essentially private terms.

Consider the two citations from George Gissing's novel, *The odd women* (see
Frontispiece). One enunciates the gender stereotyping which equates male and
female natures with the jobs they do:

> "I don't think, Edmund, there's much real difference between men and women.
> That is, there wouldn't be, if women had fair treatment."
>
>   "Not much difference? Oh, come; you are talking nonsense. There's as
> much difference between their minds as between their bodies. They are made for
> entirely different duties!" (Gissing 1893: 241)

The second is a clear statement (from a woman) of how women stand in the way
of men, how they disrupt male ambitions. Such ambitions must be by definition

public, outward-facing, turned toward the world, rather than inward-facing, to-ward the family, if it is the man's marital partner who is regarded as standing in his way. (Otherwise they would be directed in part toward her as well!)

> "I have heard him speak bitterly, and very indiscreetly, of early marriages; his wife was dead then, but every one knew what he meant. Rhoda, when one thinks how often a woman is a clog upon a man's ambition, no wonder they regard us as they do."
>
> "Of course, women are always retarding one thing or another. But men are intensely stupid not to have remedied that long ago." (Gissing 1893: 126)

If this is a catastrophe, it is clear that a strict division of roles between the sexes as husband and wife has not provided much remedy for those West African societies we have been looking at. For it is founded on a contradiction, and a contradiction which, if we are to believe Tiger, has an ancient ancestry. Male bonding may be a primary source for all-male groups and the maintenance of these with dogmas of domination; it thus comes to be part of our human heritage. But so is male-female bonding. Men who set up exclusive single-sex groupings, which come to depend on category equations of the kind "male = the dominant sex," find themselves creating problems in the very areas they seek to master: those situations where men and women interact as individuals. The marital relationship is a prime example; and for reasons of sexual (gender) identity, puts the male partner into a painfully vulnerable position. How right Wogeo men were to wish (see Chapter One) there were no women in the world, and how significant that the women whose presence they most regretted were those cast into the role of wives.

From a certain perspective the division of labor seems an incredibly clever device. It at one and the same time expresses the needs of men for male-male bonding, and disposes of the "problem" of male-female bonding in those cul-tures which associate the jobs men do with their inherent superiority. Women are necessary but inferior. And yet so much hangs on the concept of necessity. Interdependence is the other word I have been using for it. Interdependence need have nothing to do with equality, nor with ranking men's and women's contributions as comparable or as mutually prestigious (though some cultures may make these equations). Admitting interdependence need not detract from other assertions which men make about their superiority. Dominance, however, is not the same as superiority. Superiority in this or that characteristic can be used to justify domination, but the two do not have to go hand in hand. It need not involve a contradiction to say men are superior to women even if they are dependent on them (for some things). This is the obverse of women being necessary but inferior. When it comes to relations of domination, interdependence becomes another issue altogether.

For what it does modify is the *power* situation between men and women; what it can contradict is the male attempt to assert that the particular patterns of social dominance to which male-male bonding gives rise are equally applicable to relationships dependent on male-female bonding. We should not be surprised that in those societies which most firmly associate the jobs men do with their ultimate superiority over the second sex, and further make the division of labor between males and females an inherent component of male domination, men run into difficulties in coping with the incontrovertible facts of sexual interdependence.

FOOTNOTE TO CHAPTER FIVE: A TENTATIVE COMMENT ON "DOMINANCE"

The reader who looks closely at the quotations I have given from Tiger's book, *Men in groups*, and my own paraphrasing of his argument, will find that the exact mechanism by which patterns of domination are evolutionarily associated with a division of labor between the sexes is left undefined. I hint at this gap in the last section, by contrasting superiority and dominance. For notions of superiority are inherently cultural constructs, whereas many zoologists, ethologists, physical anthropologists, and others see a tendency toward forming dominance hierarchies as a fundamental human endowment. Dominance and submission behavior can be observed among nonhuman primates and in other animal species, whereas patently notions about superiority must rest largely on what the actors say about themselves. If we suggest that any particular sexual division of labor in a contemporary society upholds or confounds the claims of one sex to superiority over the other, we can handle the proposition in much the same terms as any proposition which points to connections between the various aspects of social life. Even if we move away from notions about rank to people's ideas about power relations and say that the same division also upholds/confounds claims to dominance, one sex being or regarding itself as in a situation of control over the behavior and freedoms of the other, we are still in essentially the same field. However Tiger's propositions, if I understand them aright, would give a much greater weighting to the concept of dominance.

He is not talking just about people's ideas about power, illusory or realistic; he is not talking just about social arrangements which result in unequal power relations. He is referring to a biotypical tendency which is "programmed" into the species. During the time when proto-man was a hunter, male bonding and the formation of dominant/subordinate relationships was crucial to the success of the species. But it seems to me a flaw in Tiger's presentation that he slips from discussing intramale dominance patterns to male over female dominance without making exactly clear what mechanisms are involved.

It is quite uncontroversial to state that in many (not all) present-day societies males regard themselves as dominant over (both superior to and more powerful than) females, and that a variety of social arrangements are seen to uphold their position. Among these are the division of labor and men's prominence in the public life. The urge to express dominance is undoubtedly of ancient ancestry, and an equation of females with subdominant males is a device which appears to enlarge the area over which successful males can exert domination. Yet it is also arguable that extending power inequalities into the male-female relationship per se ultimately runs up against other pressures of a comparably respectable antiquity.[12] In short, expressions of male domination over females may be *an extension* of (and also symbols of), rather than an inherent component of, those dominance patterns which have apparently contributed so much toward our survival as a species. At least there is nothing in Tiger's presentation to suggest the contrary: only the evidence that he slips from talking about one thing (patterns of dominance within all-male groups) to another (dominance patterns between males and females) without a blush. Let us see how he does it; and remember that his basic proposition is that male-male bonding originated as being biologically of the same order as male-female bonding. For he begins with the suggestion that bonds between males may have been as important as male-female bonds for survival, and ends up with this somehow also being proof of the essential dominance of males over females.

---

12. The evolution of the particular characteristics of pair bonding between human males and females. Males and females also interact outside this bond, but that is another matter.

First: the development of all-male bonds and dominance ordering.

My proposition is that specialization for hunting widened the gap between the *behaviour* of males and females. It favoured those "genetic packages" which arranged matters so that males hunted co-operatively in groups while females engaged in maternal and some gathering activity. Not only were there organic changes in perception, brain size, posture, hand formation, locomotion, etc., but there were also social structural changes. The male-female link for reproductive purposes and the female-offspring link for nutritive and socialization purposes became "programmed" into the life-cycles of the creatures. It is suggested here that the male-male link for hunting purposes also became "programmed" to ensure equal non-randomness in the conduct of social relationships in this matter as in reproductive ones. . . .

If sex differences are perforce related to male bonding, and if male bonding is related to breeding advantage, . . . what sociological processes would have led to breeding advantage for those males who entered into effective male bonds and for those females who were receptive to such males and who tended to reject non-bonded males? One of the most striking analogical suggestions arises from the primate data. These data confirm that in all but two species, lemurs and hamadryas, male bonds exist between dominant members of a troop or community of primates, and that it is the members of the dominant bonds who have sexual access to estrous females. . . .

If dominance behaviour can be regarded as biologically based, . . . and if dominance behaviour itself directly relates to bonding—an apparent precondition of reproductive success—then we may see how male bonding might have become programmed into the brains of the descendants or inheritors of the process of bonding-cum-dominance I have described. The transition to hunting-based social organization would augment and reinforce the tendency for successful breeding males to be members of close, co-operating, aggressive groups, and it would more sharply mark the division of labour on socio-sexual grounds. . . .

I have suggested, then, that the relationship between male bonding, political organization, and sexual difference is possibly a function of human brain development which was based upon a particular breeding and ecological system and which culminated in *Homo sapiens*. This system was characterized by the genetic advantage of those males who could dominate, who were willing and able to bond to dominate and hunt, and who could none the less maintain "affectionate" if undemocratic relationships with females and young. If this is so, we may have partly interpreted the strong emotion which accompanies bonding, political, and hunting and hunting-type behaviour, and explained the marked sexual differences in participation in these activities. . . .

Given the argument I have been making, one would predict that there will be far fewer female organizations than male ones. Where they do exist, the relative obscurity of the female organizations and their apparent unimportance for the macro-life of the community is striking and provocative. I am not saying females do not aggregate . . . for some purposes, such as childcare, gathering, and farming, or for simple gregariousness. But those female organizations which do exist bear much less direct relationship than do men's organizations to the political structure of their communities and the establishment of the dominance hierarchy. (Tiger 1971: 44–52, 72 passim, original emphasis)

So far, so good. The same evolutionary pressures which resulted in the formation of male bonds also encouraged those males with dominance tendencies, so that the growth of male bonding and dominance orders *among males* went hand in hand. Both these facts produced situations congenial to the emergence of social groupings wider than the reproductive unit, and it tends to be males who are interested in "the macro-life of the community."

Since women are unimportant in this "macro-life," community affairs are likely to be essentially about what interests males in their relationships *to other males*. According to Tiger's own wording,

That females only rarely dominate authority structures may reflect females' underlying inability—at the ethological level of "pattern-releasing" behaviour—to affect the behaviour of subordinates. . . .

The upshot of all this is the contention that *male dominance* coupled with sexual dimorphism occurs cross-culturally; it may be a phenomenon rooted in the nature of *Homo sapiens*. Accepting the first half of the statement does not require accepting the second. Simply, a view of the close links between politics and socio-sexual role may provide a picture of political activity with a useful emphasis on the factor of maleness in determining the participants in and forms of politics. . . . If it is true as I have been proposing that human males characteristically form all-male groups which tend to have political or quasi-political functions, and that they seek to exclude females from these groups, then this is one explanation for the male near-monopoly of high political office. It supplements the explanation which is based upon the possibility that *male political dominance* is a reflection both of human evolution and contemporary traditions and socio-economic constants. . . .

Sexual selection occurs in terms of culturally mediated cues of status and desirability. These cues are based on a biologically founded propensity to respond to members of the opposite sex within a certain range of possibility. Does political response occur in the same or a similar way? In the most general case of sexual response, erotic and reproductive propensities are satisfied by contacts with the opposite sex. The hypothesis here is that in the most general political case, defense and needs for social order are satisfied most effectively by soliciting subordinate or co-operative relationships with adult males. Thus, females of all ages and pre-adult males will seek subordinate relationships with adult males who will protect them when the group is attacked and who will enforce social order when internal disturbance occurs. Adult males will either themselves undertake direction of the response to a specific difficulty or will attach themselves as co-operative followers to those individuals who apparently possess some plan of action and the legitimacy to carry out these plans.

The hypothesis contains the proposition that the defenders and policemen must be males. Females will not suffice, except to perform subsidiary and supporting functions. This is because females cannot act as "releasers" for the behaviours appropriate to managing interferences to social order. This is the suggested reason for female non-success in politics, for female subordination in matters of war, police, and . . . defence of the immediate environment. The subdominant status of females arises, then, from phenomena amenable to ethological study, as well as to cultural study.

The connection between unisexual aggregation, and the relation of emotional display to "biological importance" of a behaviour pattern, is (1) that defence and maintaining the social order are clearly crucial to the persistence of human social systems; (2) that these behaviours are typically undertaken by males, usually without female full colleagues. Therefore we can predict (3) that on all *occasions defined by a community* as vitally important and during which strong emotion is experienced by community members aware of the overall situation a male or males will assume the most significant roles. (Tiger 1971: 74–86 passim, my emphasis)

What has happened here? First there is the unexceptional statement that females are rarely members of groups dominated by males. These groups are usually those which take on themselves the discharge of public (political) functions.

We then come on to the ambiguous phrases of "male dominance" and "male political dominance." These could refer simply to the fact that politics is a male domain, in which case "dominance" is a curiously emotive word to use. It could refer back to the earlier argument that within male political structures it is common to find dominance orders among the men who participate. But this is not what is meant. I think Tiger is saying that male involvement in politics (public life in general) gives them dominance over those who are not so involved, that is, over the nonmales. This is expanded in the following sections in which he suggests that leadership roles must be male, and we have an equation of the subdominant male with the female.

Now leadership roles became necessary for survival, "for defence and maintaining the social order." And he gives himself away in the words "occasions defined by a community" as vitally important. For what *is* this social order, who is the vocal community who can define their priorities, who is it who attacks? Essentially men and men's affairs. On Tiger's own admittance, macro-life (and what else is defense and social order?) is a male prerogative. We are talking about rules which men wish to maintain, boundaries they are anxious to defend, and social devices constructed by them to satisfy needs perceived as important.

In order to talk about "male dominance" and mean "dominance of males over females," a few intervening steps have to be taken. First there has to be an equation of all males = dominant males.

> Male bonding I see as the spinal column of a community, in this sense: from a hierarchical linkage of significant males, communities derive their intra-dependence, their structure, their social coherence, and in good part their continuity through the past to the future. (Tiger 1971: 60)

A community has a spinal cord of males; this is internally differentiated from top to bottom (dominance order within males) but provides the essential structure which contrasts males with nonmales. In this sense all males are dominant over all females. Next there has to be an equation of males = society, which is also made neatly in the spinal cord analogy. Male structures provide the basic *social* structures—hence all the argument about politics being men's domain and such. And finally, and this is what we have learned from Ardener (see Chapter One), there has to be a *contradictory* equation which brings women into society. Men can only see themselves as dominant over women if they apply their intramale dominance order to male-female relationships, and this involves also acknowledging that females are members of the same society. Hence, too, all the problems of how far women really are "social beings."[13]

So we come to statements of the following kind:

> I have discussed male dominance in political, defensive, and aggressive organizations and argued that in these areas male dominance is species-specific. Closely connected with male dominance in power-aggression structures is a pattern of male bonding which is a co-determinant and/or reinforcement of male dominance. . . . Of course, it is possible to claim that male dominance of organizations results chiefly from the fact that males are stronger and bigger, and that the notion of male bonding is unnecessary and misleading. But I do not accept that the concepts of bonding and dominance can be separated in this way. Politics is by definition an intensely social process which must be seen as a group not an individual phenomenon; in which, therefore, the importance of bonding is paramount. Since it is males who dominate politics, it is male bonding which is crucial. (Tiger 1971: 91–92)

The slide from one position to another is smooth. "Male dominance" in political, defensive, and aggressive organizations cannot just mean "the patterns of dominance" we find in matters which concern men. If it did, size and strength would be irrelevant as a sex-characteristic. For the female sex is the hidden comparison

---

13. See Callan (1970: 144, 149): "I should like to suggest, roughly, that one structural feature common to a good deal of human and animal social life is that the males are the conspicuous participators, the upholders of the contours and corners of the social map, and that the position of the female is characteristically more subtle or even equivocal with respect to this map. This may come about in evolution for quite simple reasons connected with the relative degrees of 'biological expendability' of male and female, particularly in species where the young are slow to develop and/or child-rearing is predominantly the concern of the female. The male is then released for the activity of maintaining a social structure, and presumably the advantages of having such a structure are sufficient to justify subjecting the male (once his essential function of fertilization is accomplished) to the increased hazard of conspicuous appearance or behaviour associated with social competition. . . .

  "The concept of 'dominance,' looked at in one way, breaks down into systems whereby individuals acquire and possess differential 'rights' and 'obligations' in respect of resources such as food or space. . . . One peculiarity about females may be that as well as being potential possessors they are also potential objects of these 'rights.' . . . I suggest in addition that certain loosenesses in the position of females . . . could represent one group of possibilities for resolving a problem primitively 'given' in the nature of systems based on 'conspicuous participation' among males."

here, and Tiger means males' dominance over females in political matters (read: social life in general).

It is highly significant, I think, that the question of general male domination in social life does not emerge in Tiger's account until he is way past describing the early days of hunter-gatherer life, when male-male bonding was put forward as a simple alternative force to male-female bonding. He makes it no necessity at this early stage to suggest that female subordination is an essential component of male-female bonding. Now I am aware that rituals of submission may involve quasi-sexual behavior; also that cooperation and/or bonding may take place between superior and inferior, or other individuals of unequal status (such as parent and child); also, finally, that relations may exist between males and females outside those who are pair bonded to one another. But without competence to judge the zoological and ethological writings on the topic, I must address my questions to Tiger's argument alone.

> I have outlined the ways in which males dominate females in a variety of important social sub-systems—particularly politics and economics—and I have indicated ways in which we can see this dominance as part of a species-specific patterned propensity. Intrinsic to the notion of male dominance are, I have suggested, those bonds formed among the males, and I have presented some evidence for the claim that male bonding is, again, a patterned feature of the human behavioural repertoire. (Tiger 1971: 124)

This is a plausible hypothesis—if, that is, one is allowed a slight shift of perspective.

For what we have been given here is an excellent account how *dogmas* of male domination could have arisen, of how the male-female relationship could have been used to buttress notions about dominance relations, about how females have indeed come to be equated with subdominant males. Men talk about their "own" social arrangements (primarily concerning males and male affairs) in terms (symbols) which embrace also their relations with women. Unsuccessful men are just like those who never even entered the stakes—the non-men. And the corollary: male-female relations are depicted in idioms drawn from other areas of life. Women are to be controlled just as powerful men control the lives of weaker ones.

Tiger's material suggests the possible conclusion that antecedents for constructs such as these go back a long way. When men fight what is it about but their own dominance orders (among men)? If women are made the objects of competition, if it looks as though women need men's "protection," this is already because men are manipulating their relations with women to score off other men. It is probably true that dominance and submission have been written into male-female relationships for a very long time. I am sure, too, that this is related to male bonding and the emergence of all-male dominance orders, and indeed to the concept of "society" as such. But there is no reason to assume that we must look for the genesis of this solely in terms of behavioral necessities (females were dependent on males for protection from predators full stop). Could we not look also for the genesis of symbols, for the source of those mental processes which have produced concepts about gender? Doubtless there were situations in which females were dependent on male strength: but doubtless too males exploited such a contingency. And the purpose of these maneuvers would be a sharper definition of what male-ness meant, a sharper definition of what dominance was about. The writing of dominance into male-female ties was more than a step in the evolution of power relations—it was a step also in the evolution of the capacity to manipulate symbols.

Let us look at Tiger's account in this way, then. We are not dealing with the entailments of behavior alone. We are in addition dealing with the development of mental constructs (symbols) about dominance, in which those most anxious to define themselves, men, have to do something (intellectually) about their relations with non-men. If male bonding was of such paramount importance, it is not surprising that men's dogmas of dominance should have been developed to encompass women as well. And they attempt to encompass women not only as a category (nonpolitical and inferior beings) but also as individuals, in those relationships where males and females interact on a pair basis (notably husband and wife). The great variability we find in these systems of dominance today perhaps is a hint that such constructs have never been totally successful.[14] Situations arise in which women seem to be in competition with men, in which a sex war appears to rage, in which females subvert male concerns, in which *women* are against *society*. Perhaps the real competition is to be located not between men and women but between the old program notes for male-female bonding and the massive thesis men have tried to make out of all-male bonding.

---

14. Dominance ordering among men is not necessarily stable.

CHAPTER SIX

Sex and the Concept of the Person

We have come back to the place of sexuality in relations between men and women. Certain cultures stress it more than others. For a moment this looks like a nonsensical statement: sexual relations must bind some men and women everywhere. But only some. No society allows or guarantees unrestricted sexual access of every female to every male. This proposition would be ludicrous in demographic terms alone but we also find social arrangements which define certain categories of people as suitable sex partners and others as not, and stereotypes which classify men and women on attributes other than potential sex partnership. Men and women can have relations with each other that have nothing to do with sex in the sense of erotic or genital contact. Earlier chapters have given examples of the way some cultures mold these. Women may exploit their status as mothers or as sisters, or be regarded as essentially housewives or the milkers of cattle. They may be seen as persons swayed by passions which male rationality must control, or as members of a lower order fit only to be governed by their superiors. So too should we probably relegate the idea that all women are potential sexual objects and that (erotic/coital) sex is the essence of relations between men and women.

Let me put this another way. All societies have to take into account the fact that some men and some women will engage in sexual intercourse. But interaction between the sexes must also inevitably take place outside this very specific kind of bond. The significant point is that societies make different symbolic use of the facts of coitus. Recall the two very first examples: the Bemba of East Africa and the Mae Enga of Papua New Guinea. Bemba use sexuality as a powerful symbol of fertility and community prosperity, and when a couple engage in sexual relations precautions have to be taken to ensure that benefit and not disaster results. Mae Enga characterize relations between the sexes as antagonistic and their beliefs about the hazards of sexual intercourse contribute to this general formulation. Relations between men and women are essentially hostile, and female sexuality is a very specific locus of danger for men.

For both societies it would be fair to suggest that sexuality *as such* is not regarded as the primal basis of male-female interaction; in those contexts in which coitus takes place certain controls are necessary because sexual interdependence must not jeopardize other aspects of male-female relations. Bemba convert the act into one which draws attention to the importance of women as child-bearers; it is the survival of children which is in danger if the rules are not observed, a belief which goes hand in hand with other beliefs about the preconditions necessary for receiving blessings from the ancestral spirits. We have seen that a couple, after intercourse, must purify themselves lest their children are killed by accidentally touching the family hearth. Richards says that a baby's food is often cooked on a separate fire: "The art of Bemba motherhood in fact consists very largely in guarding children from danger from fire" (Richards 1956: 30). There is an antithesis between the cooperation a couple engage in to raise a family and sexual relations as such. In this matrilineally organized society one might suspect that this is the domestic analogue of male-female relations outside the marital relationship. For men depend on women other than their wives to produce children for the matrilineage. Women with whom they specifically do not engage in sexual intercourse (their sisters) bear the offspring (sister's sons) who will succeed to their position in society. The formula that women are "just sexual objects" is nonsense in a situation like this. Mae Enga provide a neat contrast. It is not the essential cooperation between spouses or between the men and women (their sisters) of the lineage which has to be protected against sexual intercourse. The dependency of men on certain women for their sex needs runs counter to the generalized antagonism which characterizes their opposition as discrete social categories. It is hostility between the sexes which has to be protected from sexual intercourse. This is done by making the act itself one of the areas in which danger lurks. Too much intimacy between husband and wife is considered to be at the cost of other, more valuable things:

proper growth, male strength, clan solidarity. Again, to say that women are "just sexual objects" is nonsense. As wives, women are (clan) enemies, and sexual or erotic involvement has to be accommodated to this fact.

Sexuality in these situations is subordinated to other aspects of male-female interaction. The symbols which men and women use to typify significant aspects of their interrelations include sex as only one among others. Clearly, remarks such as this are a matter of emphasis, of "the degree to which" such and such a value or situation is stressed. These simplifications are made for the sake of underlining what conversely seems to be a distinctive feature of many European and American cultures: the use of sexuality, and primarily coitus itself, as a central symbol for male-female relations.[1]

This state of affairs is not dissimilar to that of the Kanuri. The total dominance of men over all women in matters of significance is justified by (symbolized by) the doctrine that women's sexual impulses must be controlled. Kanuri beliefs are a variant on the Islamic dogma that "women are innately inferior to men in the psychological qualities necessary for successful activity in public life. . . . For, as one writer (Antoun 1968: 690–91) has recently suggested, Islamic thought conceives of women as being driven by 'inordinate sexuality. They are animalistic in their behaviour.' . . . Men, on the other hand, although they can experience lust, can exercise restraint through superior powers of reasoning which is theirs by virtue of Allah's will" (R. Cohen 1971: 93). In other words, a basic metaphor to describe relations between men and women is that of their respective sexual impulses, a contrast being made between animal instinct (female) and cortical control (male). It is a metaphor which is applied not simply to those particular men and women who form sexual unions but also to males and females as categories. Male and female sexuality is being used as a symbol for the *general* relationship between men and women.

This chapter considers the place of sex, in the sense of sexuality, as a symbol of male-female relations in our own culture. In particular I shall comment on the significance of the female epithet "sex object," and shall argue that this is

---

1.   But, if this is so, it unfortunately makes verification of my assertions extremely hard. A Western observer might indeed say that sex is at the root of all these other manifestations; that the procreative aspects of sex were the origin of Bemba concern with children, that hostility in the sex act overflowed into other Mae Enga relations between men and women. Given my opinion that observations of this kind are the product of a certain cultural premise, their truth or falsity would be almost impossible to prove.

essentially a cultural construct of the European tradition, rather than a description of the universal lot of women. Male attempts to dominate women may be
more or less worldwide; the perception of women's resultant status in terms of
(a) sexuality and (b) an object is, however, another matter. We shall be dealing
with a particular way in which male-female relations are looked upon.

The chapter also returns to another strand in my account of sexual mythologies: to the proposition that male-female interaction is also used to symbolize
areas of social life which essentially concern activities to do with other things.
If such relations are used to symbolize the character of affairs between men (for
example, domination of men over women is a way of talking about dominance
hierarchies among men), then the particular qualities which a society attributes
to male-female interaction will form the basis of the symbolic process. And
where it is true that sexuality is a symbol applied to relations between men and
women, as such there ought to be some carryover in the way male-female interaction is used to symbolize these other areas of social life. It will be something of
a test if we can show not just that male-female relations are used to make statements about relationships between men or between people in general but also
that a particular source of the (European) symbolism lies in that sexual-erotic
component which stereotypes these male-female relations.

SEX, TRADE, AND FREEDOM

Prostitution is often regarded as an epitomizing focus on females as "sex objects." A prostitute may be contrasted with a married woman, or she may be
compared to one, as de Beauvoir does. We should remember that de Beauvoir
sees women's role in all intersexual encounters as that of "other": the prostitute
is the ultimate exemplar of this.

> Marro says: "The only difference between women who sell themselves in prosti-
> tution and those who sell themselves in marriage is in the price and the length
> of time the contract runs." For both the sexual act is service; the one is hired for
> life by one man; the other has several clients who pay her by the piece. The one
> is protected by one male against all others; the other is defended by all against
> the exclusive tyranny of each. In any case the benefits received in return for the
> giving of their bodies are limited by existing competition; the husband knows
> that he could have secured a different wife; the performing of "conjugal duties"

is not a personal favour, it is the fulfilling of a contract. In prostitution, male desire can be satisfied on no matter what body, such desire being specific but not individualized as to object. Neither wife nor hetaira succeeds in exploiting a man unless she achieves an individual ascendancy over him. The great difference between them is that the legal wife, oppressed as a married woman, is respected as a human being; this respect is beginning definitely to check the oppression. So long as the prostitute is denied the rights of a person, she sums up all the forms of feminine slavery at once. (de Beauvoir 1972: 569)

As a background to understanding what the (European) phrase "sex object" means and indeed to understanding de Beauvoir's concern with "the rights of a person," let us look at a case where prostitution is regarded in a very different light.

The homeland of the Hausa is northern Nigeria, the same region inhabited by the Fulani and the Kanuri described in Chapter Five. Many of them have migrated southward, forming town communities in other parts of Nigeria but maintaining links between themselves which they utilize most successfully for trade purposes. Like Kanuri they subscribe to Islam. Abner Cohen studied one such group of Hausa migrants in the Western Region of Nigeria (1962–63). Most migrants are male, and many are only transient dwellers in the quarter of the city, known as Sabo, where Cohen worked. A man who marries is more likely than a bachelor to settle in the town.

A man shows a high degree of commitment to living in the Quarter if his wife, or wives, and his children live with him in the Quarter.

This criterion, however, is not by itself as significant as it is in many other migratory situations in Africa. Hausa marriage, both in the North and in Sabo is highly unstable. In Sabo it is easy for a man to find a wife and it is also easy for a woman to find a husband. . . . In both the North and in Sabo, housewives conduct a trade in their own right and nearly always have some capital, as well as an income, of their own. Children are no handicap to mobility of either parent. . . .

It is nevertheless the case that a married man who has his wife, or wives, and children with him in the Quarter is more committed to settlement than if he had his family staying in the North. His degree of settlement will be highest if his wife was born in . . . and if her parents live in the Quarter. This is because Hausa wives are attached to their parents, particularly their mothers. A Sabo housewife will always press her husband to let her go to visit her kin in the North for many weeks. In many cases which I recorded the wife had extended her visit and even stayed indefinitely, sometimes insisting that the husband should move back to the North. Sometimes the wife contracted a lover and finally divorced the husband. In a number of instances which occurred during my field work period or shortly before, a young husband would go to the North to bring back his wife and would decide or be prevailed upon to stay there indefinitely. (A. Cohen 1969: 35–36)

Moreover, marriage enhances the migrant's status, and may enlarge the contact network on which his trade ventures depend.

Marriage in Sabo always entails the acquisition of relatively permanent housing arrangements, as no man can marry without giving his wife at least one separate room of her own. Marriage is also crucial in that the man becomes more creditworthy and hence he has a chance to pass on to a more responsible, more profitable, and more stable occupational role. Soon his wife will set up some trade from within her seclusion inside the house and will in many ways indirectly connect him with more people. More contacts will be made when children are born. As his wife becomes settled in her trade she will foster one or more children from her or his relatives. In short, marriage will push up the position of a man on all scales of settlement. (A. Cohen 1969: 40)

Among migrants, then, although marriage confers certain benefits, most men are bachelors and not in a position to marry, and form a transient population. Cohen distinguishes between two classes of Hausa women: the prostitutes who move continually with mobile migrants within the network of Hausa communities, and housewives who become attached to settled men. The prostitute is regarded as a free, floating person; the housewife is subjected to purdah and the rules of seclusion which follow from this.

The main division of the women into housewives and prostitutes is in keeping with local usage and ideology and represents one of the most important organizational features of Sabo society.

All the prostitutes are former housewives who have either divorced their husbands, been divorced by them, or run away from them. As [has been asserted] of the Hausa in Northern Nigeria, every adult woman is or has been married.

Womanhood is a social status and a female acquires it only on marriage. Marriage is thus the rite of passage from childhood to womanhood. If, after divorce a woman remains single, she will be called . . . a prostitute. . . . A divorced woman who does not . . . marry within a short time and . . . begins to go out of the house in daylight . . . becomes known as prostitute.

In Sabo society, prostitution does not carry the same stigma which it does in Western or in some other societies. The Hausa [prostitute] is idealized in the culture as a woman of strong character, intelligent, and highly entertaining. . . . No great shame is inflicted on the parents or other relatives of the prostitute, though it is nearly always the case that women leave their natal settlements when they become prostitutes. . . . It is not shameful for a man to visit a prostitute. . . .

In Sabo, the prostitutes are coveted and admired by men and are always sought after in marriage. Male informants in the Quarter say that the prostitutes make ideal housewives in many respects. They are entertaining companions, they excel in the arts of lovemaking and, when they are in love with a man, they are most devoted and sincere to him. Informants emphasize, however, that to marry a prostitute a man must have a strong character himself, as, because of her love of freedom and of independence she needs to be tamed and kept under constant control. . . . Prostitutes are very selective in the choice of both lovers and future husbands and there is always a great deal of demand for them. Informants are agreed that if all the prostitutes of the Quarter decide to get married immediately they will all find husbands on the same day without much difficulty. . . .

The important point to be emphasized here is that prostitutes frequently marry and slip into the anonymity of wifehood, and wives frequently divorce and emerge into the freedom and independence of prostitution. In men's thinking these two roles represent two aspects of womanhood. Some women move from one status to another a number of times in their career. Thus every woman is a potential prostitute.

In Sabo belief, as in that of Hausa society in the North, prostitution is closely associated with the bori cult which, according to the prevailing attitude in the Quarter, is the work of Satan. . . . In effect every woman is a potential bori initiate and hence a disciple of Satan. This belief is mixed, in men's minds, with the Islamic attitude towards ritual purity and pollution. A man who performs the ritual ablution in preparation for prayer will have to perform the ablution once again if he even in the meantime talks with his wife, let alone comes into physical contact with her. Similarly, when a man is about to have sexual intercourse with his wife he utters the formula: "I seek refuge in Allah from the wickedness of Satan," and he has to have a bath after intercourse in order to purify himself. Thus in Sabo it is indirectly regarded as the religious duty of every man to be on his guard against the potential mystical dangers and machinations of women and to keep women constantly under tight control. (A. Cohen 1969: 55–59 passim)

The prostitute is seen as exercising personal freedom, and this is exemplified in her bestowing her sexual services on whomever she likes. A prostitute who becomes a housewife, on the other hand, finds her station radically altered, and submits to purdah.

> In Sabo, all the housewives, with the exception of the very old among them, are strictly secluded from public life and from contact with men. . . . Seclusion is a public, and not only an individual, concern. Men are under constant communal pressure to isolate their wives from public life. In July 1963, while I was still in the field, a public meeting was held in the central school building of the Quarter and was attended by the Chief, nearly all the business landlords, the leading malams, and a number of men from the permanent core of the population. The meeting decided unanimously to accept the instructions of the malams that the seclusion of the married women of the Quarter should be tightened further by prohibiting the women from attending weddings, even at night, where they were likely to encounter men. Thus the seclusion of the married women became almost total for at least those who are under fifty. Seclusion is so well established that when a housewife is seen in public in the street people immediately conclude that she has been divorced. (A. Cohen 1969: 59–60)

A housewife is in no position, then, to express personal freedom in the terms a prostitute does. But she enlarges her status in another direction.

> While it has been important for the development and functioning of the Hausa network of communities [abroad] . . . to have a population of women, in the persons of the prostitutes, regularly circulating in the various communities, following the men, it has been equally important for the functioning of the same network of communities that women should be completely settled in order to perform the many domestic, economic and biological roles without which a community will not continue to exist.
>
> The housewives bear children, run the households and ensure domestic stability for men who are often on the move. Apart from this, however, housewives

play an important role in the economy of the Quarter. This is the business which they run, from their seclusion, as traders in their own right. It is one of the most significant paradoxes in the position of women in Sabo society that they can engage in business and amass wealth for themselves when they are in the bondage of seclusion and wifehood, but cannot do so when they are free as prostitutes.

Apart from the few very young and very old, all the housewives are engaged in business from behind their seclusion. About a third of them dominate the business of retailing the local sale of such popular items as kola, oranges, and plantain, while the remaining two-thirds dominate the cooking industry of the Quarter. . . .

The housewives do all the purchasing of their merchandise and raw materials and, then, all the selling, from behind the purdah, without going out of the house. It is here that children, mainly girls between 7 and 14, perform their most important contribution to Sabo economy. Without child labour a housewife is completely cut-off from business and from the outside world.

A housewife can mobilize child, female, labour in three main ways. By bearing and raising up her own children, by fostering children from her brothers, sisters, sons or daughters, and, failing these, by hiring . . . girls [from elsewhere]. . . . Generally, if she has no children, or if her children are too small to be of any help, she resorts to fostering. . . .

It is not necessary here to go into details about the institution of fostering in Sabo, but it is sufficient to emphasize in brief only two relevant aspects of it. Firstly, the institution helps housewives to have a more or less regular service of child labour. Many women foster a child, or children, twice in their business career; early in their married life when by custom they can foster their brothers' or sisters' children and, much later, as their fostered and their own children mature and leave, when they can foster their grandchildren.

The second aspect is that a prostitute cannot foster children. In fact almost all the prostitutes who have children of their own see to it that those children are fostered by some kin, if they are not already in the custody of their legal father . . . A prostitute thus can give children to be fostered but she is not given children for fostering. For some obvious reasons, rearing children and prostitution do not go together. The prostitutes are often on the move and sometimes two or more prostitutes have to share the same room and it is therefore very difficult for them to keep children

For these and some other reasons a prostitute cannot engage in business in the Quarter. This means that they have no income other than that which they get from soliciting. The prostitutes lead an exciting, free, and independent life but they are not well-off, and the majority possess only a number of glossy gaudy dresses, and very little, simple furniture. . . .

The prostitute is free to participate in public life but cannot acquire much wealth. The housewife, in comparison, can accumulate a great deal of wealth. Unlike the prostitute, she pays no rent. She and her children are fed and clothed by her husband, and, being settled and leading a respectable stable life, she is worthy of credit and she has a steady clientele. She also enjoys a steady source of capital from the "cut" which she takes from the household money and from the productivity of her children. Thus her possibilities for acquiring wealth are great, but because of her seclusion, she cannot invest this wealth in expanding her business by entering into competition with men.

A few women own houses bequeathed to them by their deceased parents or husbands and a number of them are said to possess large sums of money in cash allegedly hidden in some secret place. Some of them also have a great deal of jewellery. But the particular craze among nearly all the housewives in recent years has been to sink all their profits in acquiring ever increasing numbers of Czechoslovak-made, brightly-coloured, enamelled bowls. Within the world of Sabo housewives, these bowls have become the most important status symbol and women are ranked in status in proportion to the number of bowls they possess. Some housewives in the Quarter have managed to accumulate hundreds of them, which they meticulously arrange in ceiling-high columns in their small dark, rooms. . . . Space is scarce in Sabo and husbands are greatly annoyed by the mountains of bowls. A current, sardonic, complaint among the married men of the Quarter is that, because of the bowls, a man cannot nowadays find space in his wife's room for even his morning prayers. (A. Cohen 1969: 64–68 passim)

Prostitution and the occupation of housewife are alternative lifestyles open to the women of Hausa migrants. And they are alternatives; there is no suggestion by the author that the one activity diminishes the woman's status as a person any more than the other. The manner in which prostitution is institutionalized and its relationship to Islamic notions about female sexuality also carry certain cultural implications. The housewife puts herself in a position where her sexuality must be controlled; the prostitute seemingly indulges her sexual impulses. And the conclusion Hausa men seem to draw from this is not that the latter is letting herself be exploited by men but that these are the terms through which she expresses personal freedom.

DOMINATION AND STATUS

These Hausa migrants seem to have made a very clear distinction between the areas in which men exercise authority over a woman's freedoms and the areas in which feminine independence is allowed expression. This is done through recognizing two quite different categories of female: the secluded if wealthy housewife, and the free if poor prostitute. Where such categorical distinctions do not exist, and it is the same woman who is both under male authority and who tries to exercise personal freedom, male-female relationships (and particularly husband-wife ones) may erupt in tension, as can be judged from examples in the last chapter. Cohen himself contrasts the Hausa situation with that of Nupe and Yoruba, other Nigerian peoples.

> Sabo men are saved from the kind of tragic fate of some Nupe men. Among the Nupe . . . married women are traders who travel widely in the course of their trade, who use contraceptives to avoid pregnancy, who engage in adulterous liaisons with other men, who frequently work on the side as part-time prostitutes, and who often lend money to their poor husbands who are thus enslaved to the wives for life. The only reaction which Nupe men seem to offer to this fate is to escape into the fantasy of witchcraft beliefs, in which women figure as evil witches and men as benevolent wizards. Sabo husbands have also escaped the lot of many Yoruba men whose trading, un-secluded wives frequently sue for divorce in order to marry new lovers whom they have contacted in the course of their business, and who usually pay the expenses of the divorce proceedings.
>
> In Sabo, in comparison, the wealth which the housewives might have used in economic competition with men is, because of enforced seclusion, mostly directed to harmless, conspicuous expenditure. Moreover, this wealth serves to stabilize marriage, as women can steadily increase it, by continuing in marriage. . . .
>
> Hausa men in Sabo thus uphold two organizational principles governing the position of women in their society. The first is the ideal of the prostitute as a woman freed from the ties of her natal community who is thus rendered mobile and capable of following male migrants to their new settlements. The second is that of the settled housewife who maintains the household, bears children, and renders important services within the economy of Sabo. (A. Cohen 1969: 68–70 passim)

Hausa prostitutes are "necessary" to men; this is a very different statement from saying that they are in their individual encounters with the opposite sex exploited and abused as "sexual objects." They do not have to relinquish their rights as "a person" when they trade their sex: indeed, there is evidence that Hausa look upon it quite the other way around.

Marriage, on the other hand, in which the authority of the husband is at issue, is perceived to do just this: restrict a woman's personal freedom. She relinquishes the right to govern her own activities, and in submitting to purdah is also admitting the Islamic doctrine that females are beings who must be controlled by males. If we equate lack of freedom with diminished status as a person,[2] then perhaps after all we do have an example of the woman in her role as wife being something a little less than a person. Whether Hausa make such equations is another matter. Certainly they contrast men's and women's affairs in terms of their relative social freedoms, and compare the public mobility of prostitutes and housewives.

But suppose in the Hausa housewife we do have a case of women being considered as objects, to be kept hidden from the eyes of the world, and in so far as they are objects being less than full persons. It would seem that diminution of the woman's personal standing is a direct correlate of the kinds of institutionalized authority men have over her. The more general case might be that male domination results in some deprivation, for the female, of full "human" or "personal" status. (This recalls Tiger's argument, and the identification of male = social being, with its corollary female = not the same kind of social being. In male terms, women do not have the same freedoms as men because they are not men. They appear to be diminished persons, namely diminished men [where persons = men].) When male domination is symbolized in erotic relations, as possibly in Europe, any sexual encounter may confirm the subordination of women, and the more casual the encounter, the more nakedly this is expressed. Hence prostitution in Europe is the ultimate slavery. But where male domination, as in Hausa, is expressed through conjugal control of female sexuality, another matter altogether, the sex act on a casual basis with nonwives (prostitutes) may not carry the same implications for female subordination.

We have already encountered other situations in which domination by men seemingly makes of female persons something less then male persons. Women can be at a disadvantage in public life: in Ashanti and Gonja, the Ghanaian societies described in Chapters Three and Four, women cannot hold the same

---

2.   That is, if we make the (ethnocentric) definition of a person someone who can exercise rights and must have freedom to do so.

political offices as men; in mid-nineteenth-century England, wives' ownership of property was modified by the fact that they came under the control of their husbands. Under such circumstances, then, females are not the same kind of legal or political entities as males. Adult married women are jural "minors," in the sense that they are not considered fit to govern themselves; their relations with the outside world must be mediated through men who will represent their interests and shield them from contact with others; it may also be the case that feminine sexuality must be guarded and controlled. Yet before considering yet another African example, this time from Liberia, I must make one thing clear.

I am not through these examples trying to build up a composite picture of what it is like to be of one or other sex on this planet. At the outset we started with the proposition that relations between the sexes differ considerably from society to society. It is true that we can discern similarities, but it is not true that the particular points made about men or women in this or that society hold universally. Nor is the aim to build up an identikit, with scraps of information from here, there, and everywhere. Rather, I am interested in the fact that male-female relations cannot be treated as isolates, and that they are a product not simply of economic or biological factors but in addition of the way society perceives itself. Relations between the sexes are connected with politics, with dominance ordering between men, with the definition of social groups—as well as with themselves. We must understand this first, before we can understand what "sex" is about, in our own society or anywhere. Moreover, my choice of examples that derive from similar geographical and cultural regions has been quite deliberate. It was in order to bring out the subtleties of the interplay between male and female stereotypes that I compared the New Guinean Iatmul and Tchambuli in Chapter Two; the contrasts in roles between first the Ashanti and then their near neighbors in Ghana, the Gonja, in Chapter Three; and the relationship between the division of labor, interdependence, and subversion of authority for the Kanuri, Fulani, and Hausa, drawn from the same broad area in northern Nigeria. The opposition between "men" and "women" seems such a simple one that there is a danger of treating it crudely. The results and the implications of the opposition are of the most complicated kind. It is of no less importance that we should understand this than that we should understand the preconditions for human survival in a physical environment which at once supports people and yet seems to them primarily a resource to be exploited. This analogy too is deliberate: for in European societies there is a strong relationship between the treatment of "Nature" by "Man" and intersexual relations.

The Kpelle of Liberia do not completely exclude females from participation in public life: they are able, for example, to act as principals in court hearings. Indeed, many Kpelle courts and moots concern women; the majority of these are initiated by men who accuse other men of having designs on their wives, but it is also possible for a woman to take the initiative. James Gibbs describes a case in which a woman sued for divorce from her husband. The observation to be extracted from this material is that in some respects the plaintiff (the wife) was treated as a "person": the paramount chief before whom the case was heard gave consideration to her evidence and ostensibly conducted the court in much the same way as he would have done had the litigants all been male. But in other respects she was not treated as a man would have been, for the outcome of the court was a foregone conclusion *because she was a woman*. Her judicial position was affected by other aspects of relations between men and women in Kpelle society. She was not being treated entirely as a person but also as a female.

The Case of the Sojourning Wife. In this case, heard before a paramount chief, Nyema (the plaintiff) sued her mother, Gopuu, requesting that the old lady return the bridewealth that had been paid for her because she no longer wished to live with her husband. This was therefore a suit for divorce and the "real" defendant was Nyema's husband, Kwi Kwili.

When Nyema was asked why her mother . . . should return her bridewealth, she replied in the manner customary for Kpelle wives seeking divorce; "I do not want my husband's home anymore." To substantiate her charge, she recounted the history of her marriage as first wife to Kwi Kwili, . . . Kwi Kwili, in turn, gave his chronicle of their marriage. A crucial element in the dissension between them was the fact that after their marriage Kwi Kwili inherited some additional wives. . . . There was jealousy between Nyema and the new wives. Quite some time after that, Nyema's father had died in another chiefdom and she went to the funeral and stayed, remaining away from her husband for a year and a half. She came back to institute suit for divorce.

Nyema made her allegations against Kwi Kwili in the following order:

1. A child of hers had died because of her husband's mother's witchcraft.

2. Her husband had not supported her because he failed to clear a rice farm for her.

3. He had disrespected her by not going to offer condolences whenever any of her relatives died.

4. He had not shown appreciation for special wifely acts: (a) treating his illnesses, (b) helping him to acquire money to offer the chief . . . (c) showing more concern and consideration than her co-wives.

5. Her husband "overlooked" her, did not treat her with kindness or gratitude. The key allegations seemed to be the witchcraft charge and the nonsupport charge, because each was repeated. But when questioned by her husband at the beginning of his testimony, Nyema indicated that she was not leaving him because of the child's death but because of the nonsupport.

Kwi Kwili made the following allegations of his own:

1. Nyema was guilty of promiscuous behavior, notably the taking of frequent lovers.

2. She objected to his inheriting additional wives.

3. When he did accept his inheritance of plural wives, Nyema, as the headwife, treated the co-wives badly . . .

4. By staying away so long, she had deserted him.

Finally, Kwi Kwili countered his wife's primary allegation by referring to two of his own. He stated that the reason why he had not cleared a farm for her was that she was [both] living elsewhere and forming liaisons with another man or men.

At the beginning of the case the chief established that Nyema wanted to leave Kwi Kwili "because of his ways." He then questioned her.

Chief: All right! Nyema, it reaches you. What did this person [the husband] do to you?

Nyema: The thing he did to me . . . when a person is in a home her child should live. And when a person is in a home, someone should work for her.

Thus a veiled accusation of a child's death by alleged witchcraft opened her allegations, which continued for many minutes. She catalogued the additional complaints noted above. Finally the chief, a bit exasperated and weary, turned to her and spoke:

Chief: The thing that you are saying, say it to the point. What are you saying? Say it to the point.

Nyema: This person they gave me to—when I have a child, his mother eats it. [She has restated—more baldly—the witchcraft accusation with which she opened her allegations.]

Chief: Who is that who eats human beings?[3]

Nyema: This person's [indicates her husband, Kwi Kwili] mother. . . .

---

3.   That is, whom are you accusing of witchcraft (of "eating" your child)?

Chief (to spectator): Man, you who are sitting like that. . . . What did you come to look for?

Man: . . . I just came to sit and listen to the case for a while.

Chief: You are sitting in a bad place. . . . [Turning to Nyema] Are you through?

Nyema: There [in all I have said] is why I say: I don't want him. . . . [It is] because I took him from death[4] and he overlooks me. He is just behaving like that to me.

Even though Nyema ranked nonsupport as her major allegation, it was clear that the child's death was also a great concern to her. It is equally clear that the chief was not anxious to probe into the matter and found a subtle way to avoid it by distracting Nyema, who was prone to ramble in testifying. We cannot be certain of whether or not the chief's gambit was conscious or unconscious. The effect was the same in either case.

The paramount chief granted the divorce, holding Nyema at fault, and he ordered Nyema and her mother to return Kwi Kwili's bridewealth and to pay damages. This is the usual pattern in Kpelle divorce actions. The person who brings suit for divorce is felt to be at fault, and the plaintiff in divorce cases is almost always a woman. (Gibbs 1969: 197–98)

Gibbs comments on the way in which the chief conducted his investigations to "prove" that the wife was indeed at fault.

The only allegation of Nyema's investigated by the chief was that of nonsupport. In finding her at fault he accepted Kwi Kwili's counter allegation that he had not farmed with her because she had deserted him. The chief did not delve into Nyema's plea that she waited in vain at her deceased father's house, expecting Kwi Kwili to send for her. . . . There was no attempt to see whether she could substantiate any of her other reasons for holding her husband at fault—even the fairly serious charge of witchcraft. Even in delving into the nonsupport charge, the chief questioned Nyema in such a way that it was all but impossible for her to win her point. At a point early in Kwi Kwili's testimony, . . . the chief interrupts him to question Nyema. . . .

Chief: Nyema, during the *whole time* you were in this man's hand, didn't he make any rice farm for you? [Emphasis added.]

---

4.   That is, looked after him in illness.

Nyema: When we were at Zowa, his mother and I used to make rice farms. . . .

Chief (to Nyema): . . . did you say this person has not made *any* farms for you. [Emphasis added]

Nyema: I said that he used to make farms for me. But since we crossed the river,[5] he has not made farms for me nor built a house for me.

Chief: And since you two came here?

Nyema: It was just recently that they told him that if he didn't come back across the river, his women will no longer be his. This is why he came here.

Chief: Since he came here, has he made any farm for you?

Nyema: I told you that I was at our home.

Chief: Go and sit down. That is just what they said about you.

By rephrasing Nyema's question to make it seem that she was holding that Kwi Kwili had *never* made a rice farm for her, it made it easy for Kwi Kwili to disprove her allegation simply by showing that he had farmed with her at some point in their marriage. Moreover, the chief led Nyema to the point of repeating that she had lived at her father's home for a long period of time, thereby setting the stage for Kwi Kwili's subsequent allegations of promiscuity and desertion. Thus the chief used his investigatory initiative to act somewhat as a prosecutor. (Gibbs 1969: 199, original emphasis)

The chief's conduct of the case is explicable in terms of certain general aspects of male-female relations. Among the salient features of Kpelle "ethnic character," Gibbs (1969: 185) indicates a preference for indirect forms for expressing aggression and male feelings of inadequacy vis-à-vis women. The large number of adultery cases which the courts have to deal with are in part a result of the first. "The adulterous acts Kpelle men direct at other men's wives suggest a need for power over women, for power over other men, and for directing hostility against other men." (195)[6] The handling of divorce cases is related to the second.

---

5.   That is, went to live somewhere else

6.   An example of men using male-female relations to "say something" about their feelings toward other men. "Kpelle men use actions toward women not only as a means of asserting power over women, but also as a way of communicating their negative feelings and power needs toward their fellow males" (Gibbs 1969: 194).

The incomplete investigation of the wife's allegations can be explained in two ways. The first is a judicial explanation. A Kpelle woman sues for divorce because she no longer wishes to stay with her husband. The chief hearing the case has only to determine that this is indeed so and to find a single basis for allocating fault. Having done so, he need proceed no further, . . . Kpelle divorce cases take on something of the cut-and-dried flavor of Monday morning drunkenness cases in American municipal courts. . . .

However, there is a second, psychological, interpretation, based on the fact that the incompleteness of investigation operates to the woman's disadvantage. The chief, seeking out a single ground for allocating fault, usually airs the one most likely to show the woman at fault, not the one or two that have contributed most to the bad feelings between the litigants. This selective manner of focusing on allegations is a way in which Kpelle chiefs not only handle divorce cases with dispatch, but also express male control and dominance. Although chiefs can see fault on both sides in the divorce cases they hear, Kpelle conventions with regard to the handling of divorce cases require a unilateral ascription of blame. Thus, regardless of his actions toward his wife, the husband is almost always declared the winner and to his wife is ascribed the fault. The divorce court is one arena in which a Kpelle man—either litigant or spectator—can find counterbalance for feelings of inadequacy vis-à-vis women. . . .

Kpelle men . . . owe much of their status to women; thus they have a not-too-latent envy of women as powerful figures and, correspondingly, some uncertainty about their identity as males. . . . The androcentric bias in the investigation of allegations and assignment of fault serves to alleviate Kpelle men's feelings of inadequacy vis-à-vis women. Thus we see the law functioning, not only to settle disputes, but also to gratify the personality needs of litigants. (Gibbs 1969: 196, 200)

The woman plaintiff is handicapped, as it were, by being female. Her judicial status is not identical to a man's: she is not the same kind of "judicial person" as he is. This puts her at a power disadvantage in public forums, such as courts are, for these are arenas in which men are concerned to show their strengths. In public a woman cannot expect to be accorded the formal rights which the structure of a court hearing leads her to suppose are the common rights of litigants. (Nyema answers the chief, gives a series of allegations, and in fact plays the judicial game even though her own experience of previous court cases must have informed her how the decision would run.)

I have used the term "person" in this context in order to underline what seems to me a significant point about intersexual relations in European cultures. It may or may not be relevant to Kpelle ideas about humanity. But they were enacting on the public stage a set of ideas Europeans often find themselves confronted with behind-stage: as sexual mates women are both partners, invited to engage in a joint enterprise, and things, objects to be manipulated. These latter concerns are intimately bound up for *us* with (European) notions about what a person is.

PRELUDE TO THE WOMAN QUESTION: THE IDEA OF RIGHTS

English and American[7] debates which, at the turn of the nineteenth and twentieth centuries, raged over the respective statuses of males and females were known as this: "the woman question." That it was the position of *women* (one of the sexes and not the other) which was seen as crucial to clarify is related not just to women's position as the obviously underprivileged, the category whose lot was in need of amelioration, but to developments in the concept of the person. Legislative act after legislative act throughout the late eighteenth and nineteenth centuries had made the formal admission that slaves were people, that Roman Catholics and Jews were people, that the unpropertied poor were people, yet there remained that nub: were women people?

I am not being facetious. This was the era of written constitutions, the time when the kind of person someone was became defined explicitly in terms of the *rights* accruing to him. These rights might be enshrined in governmental laws; or they might be stated to belong to the individual through natural laws which gave every human being a right to this or that kind of treatment. The rights might be defined as natural or legal ("socially natural")—but the idea of "rights" was an important cultural idiom through which entitlements to full citizenship were expressed.[8] The notion of rights contributed also to the stereotype

---

7. I subsequently use the term "European" to encompass common cultural traditions here.

8. An idiom developed at a time when considerable weight was also given to its reciprocal, the notion of duty. Rights bestowed upon a person entailed recognition of certain duties also incumbent upon his status. It is significant that the idea of duty has today such a diminished popularity that the concept of "rights" has developed into an aggressive assertion of individuality. This point is expanded later.

in terms of which humanity and the individual were perceived. "The rights of man" was a rallying cry. The common humanity of people, what it meant to be a person, was framed in quasi-legislative terms, a notion itself no doubt derived from ideas about society as a "social contract."[9] And if common humanity was

---

9. Consider, for example, the "Declaration of Sentiments" and "Resolutions" adopted by the Seneca Falls convention in America, 1848. This was the first Woman's Rights Convention to be held.

When, in the course of human events, it becomes necessary for one portion of the family of man to assume among the people of the earth a position different from that which they have hitherto occupied, but one to which the laws of nature and of nature's God entitle them, a decent respect to the opinions of mankind requires that they should declare the causes that impel them to such a course.

We hold these truths to be self-evident: that all men and women are created equal; that they are endowed by their Creator with certain inalienable rights; that among these are life, liberty, and the pursuit of happiness; that to secure these rights governments are instituted, deriving their just powers from the consent of the governed. Whenever any form of government becomes destructive of these ends, it is the right of those who suffer from it to refuse allegiance to it, and to insist upon the institution of a new government, laying its foundation on such principles, and organizing its powers in such form, as to them shall seem most likely to effect their safety and happiness. . . . Such has been the patient sufferance of the women under this government, and such is now the necessity which constrains them to demand the equal station to which they are entitled.

The history of mankind is a history of repeated injuries and usurpations on the part of man toward woman, having in direct object the establishment of an absolute tyranny over her. . . .

Now, in view of this entire disfranchisement of one-half the people of this country, their social and religious degradation—in view of the unjust laws above mentioned, and because women do feel themselves aggrieved, oppressed, and fraudulently deprived of their most sacred rights, we insist that they have immediate admission to all the rights and privileges which belong to them as citizens of the United States. . . .

The following resolutions were discussed . . . and were adopted:

WHEREAS, The great precept of nature is conceded to be, that "man shall pursue his own true and substantial happiness." Blackstone in his Commentaries remarks, that this law of Nature being coeval with mankind, and dictated by God himself, is of course superior in obligation to any other. It is binding over all the globe, in all countries and at all times; no human laws are of any validity if contrary to this . . . therefore; *Resolved*, That such laws as conflict, in any way, with the true and substantial happiness of woman, are contrary to the great precept of nature and of no validity, for this is "superior in obligation to any other." *Resolved*, That all laws which prevent woman from occupying such a station in society as her conscience shall dictate, or which place her in a position inferior to that of man, are contrary to the great precept

to be defined in terms of rights which made everyone equal, the presence of the second sex, against whom there was so much legislative discrimination, clearly posed a problem. (Were all human beings people?) This could be got away with as long as that other dogma existed: that there were people of different orders. But the injection of the further idea of equality into the definition of humanity made this position untenable.

One of John Stuart Mill's chief arguments in his essay, *The subjection of women* ([1869] 1970), was that modern society had in almost every sphere, except that of relations between the sexes, recognized that persons must be given freedom of individual choice.

> For, what is the peculiar character of the modern world—the difference which chiefly distinguishes modern institutions, modern social ideas, modern life itself, from those of time long past? It is, that human beings are no longer born to their place in life, and chained down by an inexorable bond to the place they are born to, but are free to employ their faculties, and such favourable chances as offer, to achieve the lot which may appear to them most desirable.... The modern conviction, the fruit of a thousand years of experience, is, that things in which the individual is the person directly interested, never go right but as they are left to his own discretion; and that any regulation of them by authority, except to protect the rights of others, is sure to be mischievous. (Mill in Rossi 1970: 142–44 passim)

Women are the only ones who do not come under the new dispensation: "the social subordination of women thus stands out an isolated fact in modern social institutions; a solitary breach of what has become their fundamental law" (Mill in Rossi 1970: 146).

We might argue that in any society the kinds of rights someone has defines the kind of person she or he is. A very clear example is the case of Muslim wives and the demands they make on their husbands for support. They have a "right" to expect support, and divorce may be the outcome of the husband's failing in his obligations. At the same time there are many restrictions on personal freedom, which an outsider might also consider as defining the "kind of person" the woman is. Whether or not Muslim women themselves regard these rules as impinging

---

of nature, and therefore of no force or authority. *Resolved*, That woman is man's equal.... *Resolved*, That it is the duty of the women of this country to secure to themselves their sacred right to the elective franchise. (O'Neill 1969: 108–11)

on their rights is another matter. The case cited previously (pp. 156–58) certainly represented a wife exploiting her husband's fears about loose behavior. Violating the rules of propriety became a weapon in her hands; but it was a provocation against the husband, rather than a rebellion against the unjust restrictions themselves. On the other hand, a wife's insistence that she be given proper clothes, jewelry, and the minute household attention she expects might well be looked upon by her as very much to do with her "rights." Exactly where rights and duties fall in a relationship, then, is a cultural matter. Thus, some areas of a relationship, as that between husband and wife, may be propped up in terms of the rights each can expect from the other, while in others the question of rights may not arise.

In addition, it is probably true that cultures everywhere have something analogous to a concept of humanity. That is, it is recognized that every "human being" or every "person" shares with all others certain common characteristics, whatever the particular roles, statuses, and so on which differentiate them in social terms. Sometimes the concept of "human being" stops at the society's boundaries—the rest are strangers or foreigners of a subhuman status. Sometimes human beings turn into something less than human—as may happen if a person is identified as a witch; or human affairs may be under the control of nonhumans, when they are guarded by spirits or ghosts. A person can behave in a way which goes against all norms of "humanity," and attempts are made to make him see that he has crossed a boundary.

It should not come as any surprise that cultures identify humanity through different characteristics. My contention is that notions about humanity—what a "person" is—has in the European tradition come to be closely bound up with the concept of rights; and this is a particular, not a universal, association. A person is seen as a being with a battery of rights and can make demands on the rest of the world as such; failure on the part of others to recognize the rights the person claims is failure to accord that person full human status. Now this is a kind of political or constitutional model of what a "human being" is. It makes out of every category of persons an interest group.[10] It has, I think, profoundly affected the way the woman question has been tackled.[11]

---

10. English use of the word class is illuminating here. We may use it as a synonym for either a category or an interest group. One can switch between these usages with great ease.

11. For example, an address to a conference held in 1967 on "women in a changing world": "the social development of the last hundred years had resulted in bringing half the human race into political and legal citizenship in turning married women

These points will become clearer as we proceed. In order to underline this particular way of looking at people, let me cite for the last time an African situation. It brings us back to our very first example, the East African Bemba, although it concerns Bemba who have left their rural occupations to seek a livelihood in towns. Bill Epstein recounts a dispute between a Bemba husband and wife heard in an urban court.

> The matter involved a husband and wife, both Bemba, and had been referred to the court by the location authorities. The gist of the wife's complaint was that she had been assaulted by her husband, once on a public path returning from a beer drink, and a second time when he had seized her violently and bitten off a piece of her ear and swallowed it. The husband's reply . . . was . . . that his wife had an excessive love of fornication. In L. she had committed adultery twice, and in N. twice again. Once . . . he found his wife naked in the path fighting with a man. . . . On the second occasion they were again drunk, and he had bitten her ear because she refused to listen to what he said: she behaved like a goat, and could not resist adultery when he was away for a short time. The statement of the parties concluded, they were questioned at length by the court. . .
>
> The defendant had earlier agreed that there were no witnesses who could speak on his behalf. His wife, however, was accompanied by her brother, who was invited to make a statement before the court. He confirmed the husband's testimony, saying that his sister seemed to think only of drinking and running after other men. . . . The fact that his sister had had her ear bitten off was her own affair entirely since she always refused to listen to what he told her. At last the court passed judgment:
>
> As to all this, you [the husband], we find that you have a case for "breaking" your wife's ear and swallowing it.[12] Therefore the court finds that you should pay £5. You will take £3 and give it to your wife, the remainder will be paid to the court. Furthermore, we feel that you ought to divorce her otherwise you will kill her one day with your beatings. As for you, girl, we see that you have no child. This is because you love only fornication. So that the fact that you had your ear bitten off is your own fault entirely. You must cease this habit of committing adultery as though you were a dog which knows nothing of respect. (Epstein 1967: 378–79)

---

from chattels into formally equal heads of their households, and in the family progressing from a despotic to a democratic institution" (Fawcett Society 1967: 5).

12. That is, we will charge you on this act.

The author goes on to comment on some unusual facets of this judgment.

> The facts in issue in this case were never really in dispute. The husband admitted the main charges against him, and he agreed in the end that what he had done was wrong. Yet the court devoted a good deal of time to the hearing, and it is clear from the whole line of questioning, as well as from the judgment, that it considered the husband had suffered considerable aggravation. In a sense the woman got what she deserved. But if this is so, why should she have been made an award of a fairly substantial sum of money? In many matrimonial disputes the court will often award a small sum—10 shillings or a chicken—to the aggrieved party. Such awards are best regarded not as compensation, but as an earnest of good-will opening the way to full reconciliation. In the present case, however, far from seeking to reconcile the parties, the court actually advised a divorce. The award to the woman has to be seen therefore as compensation for damages received. Does it follow then that assaulting one's wife is an offence for which the husband is always liable irrespective of the blame that may attach to the wife's prior conduct? Clearly not, for a husband's beating of his wife is recognized as an appropriate way of asserting his authority in the household. . . . If, on the other hand, liability derives from the gravity of the damages sustained, why did the court not simply treat the matter as a penal offence and just impose a fine? I want to suggest that the court members here were not being inconsistent in their thinking, but that their finding flowed from certain assumptions about the nature of the human person which derive from tribal culture and philosophy.
>
> A clue to the nature of these assumptions is contained in the court's reprimand to the woman that she should cease behaving like a dog that knows nothing of [respect]. The phrasing of course is designed to emphasize the repugnance of her behavior in the eyes of the court, but the contradistinction of humans and animals recurs so frequently in judgment as to suggest that something more fundamental is involved than mere rhetoric. . . One is entitled to expect of one's fellow-men that their behaviour will conform to certain standards: man enjoys the gift of intelligence, and knows therefore that in his behavior he must display proper manners and respect; in so far as one does not measure up to these expectations one's humanity (*ubuntu*) is diminished. But there is also a further attribute of the person which is involved here. This is conveyed in the Bemba word, *-tuntulu. -Tuntulu* is an adjective meaning whole, complete, in good health, etc., but it also has overtones of wider import. Thus one may ask "Is the animal dead . . . ?" and receive the answer, "No, it is still alive (*iyo ituntulu*)."

. . . The life-principle is a sacred value which finds its highest embodiment in the whole human person, which ought not therefore to be diminished, save in special circumstances. It is this basic postulate, I believe, which accounts for the overriding concern that the courts display in regard to physical violence to the person, and leads to the principle that one is liable in damages for any act which has as a direct consequence the diminishing of another's person, even though the act itself may have been prompted by that other's prior wrong. (Epstein 1967: 379–80)

The dispute did not simply revolve, then, around the husband and wife's respective rights in relation to one another. The court had identified acts which were inhuman, an assault on humanity, and was concerned to react in such a way as to condemn them. Further, the particular Bemba notions about what was inhuman in the man's behavior cannot be encompassed by simple reference to an individual's "rights." Let us look further into this concept.

Offending acts, like the act of homicide itself [can] lead to consequences which are irreversible. Under tribal conditions, at least, a person who has lost his ears or his teeth can never be made whole again. . . . Indeed, wholeness as an attribute of the person was given quite explicit expression: like life itself it is a gift of God. The clear lesson . . . is that he who resorts to violence, even in defense of his legitimate interests, does so at his peril, since the consequence of his act may well be the maiming, or most heinous of all, the complete physical destruction of another person.

[In] the tribes with which we are concerned . . . there was usually some degree of central administration, and the exercise of power and authority was controlled institutionally, often through an elaborate system of political offices. In such systems the application of physical violence becomes a monopoly of the state: not only does the state deny to the individual the right to take the law into his own hands, but it also arrogates to itself the right to inflict physical punishment for certain classes of offence. It is clear therefore why men who resort to violence should do so at their peril. But this still leaves unanswered certain questions. . . . Why, for example, was compensation awarded where the imposition of a fine or some other penalty would seem sufficient for the court to make its point? Africans in Zambia, however, do not see the matter in quite this way. For them the award of compensation for damages suffered to the person is one of the most basic and distinctive principles of their customary law. . . . The judges should be as much concerned with the nature of the damage sustained as with wrongful acts as such, and this I suggest has its roots in assumptions about the human person as a whole being. I suggest further that this view of the problem also helps to account for a number of other features of legal doctrine and practice amongst the Bemba and certain other tribes of the region. Thus where a man has sustained physical injuries there is a reluctance to hear this case until the wounds have fully healed: once a case has been settled it cannot be re-opened if the injury turns out to be more serious than was at first suspected. . . .

A good instance of this is rape. . . . African judges tend to treat such matters relatively lightly; the offence is classified as . . . adultery or illicit fornication, and it is the infringement of the husband's marital rights rather than the affront to the woman herself which is the basis of the action. The assumption here is that women in general are complaisant in sexual matters: if the offence occurs within earshot of a place of habitation and she does not cry out or make report immediately afterwards it is presumed that she consented to the act which carries no threat to her integrity as a person. On the other hand, if the offence took place in the bush it was viewed quite differently. The woman was no longer a person in a position to give or withhold her consent freely, since she had no protection against the threats of a man who, it was said, might kill her if she refused him. Such an offence was indeed a thing of mystical ill omen . . . which defiled the country. . . . [And] if it were not reported but was subsequently discovered, both parties were severely punished.

This reference to mystical notions also serves as a reminder that in traditional African thought the gravest threat to life and limb was not always provided by physical violence alone. . . . Take the following example: amongst ourselves a man who preferred to have sexual intercourse with his wife while she was asleep might simply be regarded as having curious tastes in such matters. I was told that European District Officers to whom such complaints by African women were occasionally referred would dismiss them as a matter for the individual parties concerned. But to the African court members who have to judge such cases the practice has quite a different connotation. It is an abhorrent and unwholesome act which no "reasonable man" would contemplate because it is tantamount to using a woman as a corpse. By his act the husband violates the integrity of his wife as a person: he has deprived her of part of her life-substance which he can then put to use magically in order to grow wealthy and powerful. The whole thing smacks of witchcraft and is believed to carry a serious threat to the woman's life. . . .

A man who has intercourse with his wife while she is asleep, . . . forfeits his
claim to be a full human being. . . . His offence is much more serious than that of
a physical assault: it is in the Biblical sense an abomination and carries the most
heinous threat of all to the integrity of the person—death by witchcraft. (Epstein
1967: 381–83)

The idea of a "person" and "personal integrity" is there; so is the idea of
"humanity." Someone can suffer an attack on his or her integrity as a person
through the acts of others. Yet the *idioms* in terms of which these ideas are
defined do not seem to be those of rights and duties. It is not a woman's "rights
as a person" which are assaulted when she is raped in the bush, but her "wholeness as a person." There seem to be two dimensions to the Bemba concepts here.
First, someone who violates the common norms of humanity is behaving like
an animal—hence the human/animal contrast. Second, the assault suffered by
the victim is seen as an assault on his or her bodily entirety and anything which
illegitimately diminishes that entirety—mutilation or failure to recognize consciousness—is an inhuman act. Now in his account the anthropologist draws
attention to the overall structure of Bemba society, the centralized control of
violence, and so on. In a sense these notions of humanity are making an equation between the human body and society as a whole. An assault on the body
is animal-like, the behavior of creatures outside society; the injury suffered is
an injury to the person's sustaining life-principle and, furthermore, may defile
the country. We have already seen how Bemba notions of sexual conduct are
bound up with the prosperity of the community (Chapter One). Saying that the
community suffers when a person's bodily wholeness is violated is very close to
saying that the physical integrity of a body and the integrity of society are one
and the same. Indeed, the place which the idea of *wholeness* has in Bemba concepts of the person perhaps makes sense if we relate this to the way the society
perceives itself. Each "person" (= each social being) is a part of the wider society. Rules regulating sexual conduct have implications for the community's well
being, and the preservation of an individual's physical wholeness does too. So
Bemba possibly see their society as a "body," dependent on the paramount chief
and other rulers who bestow mystical as well as physical blessings on its members. Mutilation of an individual's body does not simply challenge the ruler's
right to inflict punishment; it also challenges his responsibilities to the spiritual
welfare of those under him.

Bemba certainly have the idea of an "individual's rights." The husband's marital rights are infringed when his wife commits adultery. But the notion of rights of this kind does not contribute centrally to notions about "the person" or "humanity" in the way that it seems to in European societies.

In the past European societies have also used the body analogy to describe society: "the body politic," the term "corporation" for a legal entity, and so on. But if the body is seen to be made up of separate individuals who enter into a social contract with one another for their mutual benefit, we are in a very different world from Bemba. There it is not the legal or constitutional relationships *between* members of the society which are emphasized rather the wholeness of the society in its physical and spiritual entirety.

A European "person" thus comes to be an entity which has what we could almost call a political character: within society persons are defined by the rights they can claim against others. We make an equation between "a person in his own right" and "human being." And humanity is seen in terms of rights which are "basic," and which override social and intersociety differences, but which are nevertheless rights. They may also override distinctions between the sexes. The call that females should be treated as persons appeals to just this. The rights women have are not the same as those of men: but men and women are both human. To claim those rights by which all persons should be defined, turns attention to the unequal distribution of rights between the sexes as they stand at present. "We should not be given these rights (as females) but those rights (as human beings)."[13] Moreover, a "person" defined in terms of rights accruing to him is more than just a political entity. He is a political entity of a particular kind.

There seems to be a strong undercurrent of ideas in our thinking about "humanity" and "persons" which makes the "human being" an underprivileged person. Look at the vocabulary. People have to contend for their rights. Women have to fight to be treated as equal human beings with men. This is how the struggle is thought of. The idea is that the world is divided up into competing elements to such an extent that there is a perpetual conflict over whether "basic human rights" are going to be accorded or not. Some classes of persons deprive others of their rights. This or that category of people can draw attention to

---

13. In some contexts to be male or female is seen to be less than human: "Children should be given *human* models to emulate, not just male and female models. We must each have the courage to fight to live our own beliefs in undifferentiated sex roles" (from the Congress to Unite Women, quoted in Tanner 1970: 31, original emphasis).

their deprived status by claiming for themselves rights which others will not automatically cede to them. In other words, it is assumed that people do *not* everywhere agree on what basic human rights are; or if they do, do not allow all people to be classed as human. The very specific nature of European ideas about the person is the product of this cultural milieu. And it considerably modifies the manner in which men and women have regarded one another in the last couple of centuries, which has seen in almost every sphere an effort to first identify and then liberate the underprivileged of the world.

PRELUDE TO THE WOMAN QUESTION: SUBJECT AND OBJECT

In Chapters One and Two, the excerpts cited from de Beauvoir's *The second sex* provided a potent analysis of what it is like to be a woman who is not only dominated by men but in every encounter becomes an object for men's self-definition. The man is the subject; the woman is the object. It is common to find that in constructing their universe, in creating social systems and systems of values, males do indeed define their relations toward females in terms of what females are like. Through feminine exclusion from public affairs or from matters of importance, men further think of women as different kinds of persons from themselves.

For a moment it perhaps looks as though all the statements in the previous paragraph are of the same kind—that de Beauvoir's formulation simply pinpoints in rather concrete terms some very general propositions about the relations of men and women toward one another. What should be done, if it is possible, and I think it is possible in any case to only a limited degree, is to separate out those which have a modicum of general validity from those which belong rather specially to our own culture. Ways of looking must always be rooted in culture. This is what culture is about: the words, the concepts, the descriptive phrases, the stereotypes, the myths, which are used to build up a picture of how the world seems. No one can be free of these concepts; one can only use the language at one's disposal. Someone can be personally subjective in his statements, that is, color what he says by his own outlook and opinions. And he can also be culturally subjective, that is, say these things in the words and phrases, with the ideas, which his culture furnishes him with. All one can hope is to be aware of at least some of the areas of cultural subjectivity in an analysis.

It is probably true of many human societies that the sex which most actively constructs theories about how society and the world are composed, including what the other sex is like, tends to give itself the place of prominence. This prominence may be described in many idioms. It may involve concepts of domination, of hostility between the sexes, of unequal apportionment of skills and talent, of contrasting personality types, of occupations of different worth, of men and women not being the same kind of persons, and so on. It is only a tendency: there are societies which do not place great importance on male-female contrasts; these may be ones where social differentiation in general is not greatly emphasized. Alternatively, societies of this latter kind may make of the male-female dichotomy a major axis of differentiation where little else exists.

There is a further point. We could say that everywhere, since people more often than not live in a social world devised largely by males, females are necessarily—like everything else—the "objects" of male concepts. That is, in incorporating women into their universe, men (subject) think about women (object) in particular ways. Now while one may use subject and object in what one hopes is a purely *analytical* way, the terms themselves also carry a heavy *cultural* overload for Europeans. As I have hinted at several places, this is bound up with the way we think of "persons." De Beauvoir's statements are an excellent illustration. A person, in the European tradition, is as we have seen, a unit endowed with certain rights. In order to exercise these rights there must also be an exercise of free will. However the grammatical formulation of subject and object means that only the subject can act; an object is acted upon. Therefore an object cannot "do," it only "is": an object cannot exercise free will. An object cannot be a person.[14]

It is an interesting fact that not a few anthropologists have been concerned at one time or another to point out that in this or that society, despite appearances to the contrary, females are not really being treated as "objects." The reader will find an example in the discussion of Gisu bridewealth (Chapter Four). The evidence suggests it usually has something to do with the kind of person which the woman is in that society. Thus in situations where certain rights to women's services or to the children they bear are indicated by bridewealth payments

---

14. De Beauvoir's more general contrast is between man as Subject and woman as Other (rather than object). The relationship is one between actor and acted upon, but the acted upon can, on occasion, be seen also as a being endowed with free will, whose possession thus becomes the more piquant. In explicit reference to sexuality, she uses the term "object," e.g., "Woman . . . is even required by society to make herself an erotic object" (de Beauvoir 1972: 543).

between the kinsfolk of the bride and the groom, it may look as though the woman is simply the "object" of a transaction. The anthropologist may be at pains to comment that this does not mean that females are nothing but chattels over whom men have rights of disposal. In some cultures, indeed, men them-selves may formulate it like this; the anthropologist then tries to distinguish what the men *say* about the way they "possess" and "dispose of" women and the realities of social life, in which women do indeed have to be treated to some ex-tent as free agents. Consider the quotation from Ronald Cohen in Chapter Four (pp. 118–19). Equivocations of this kind stem, I think, from the basic European equation of "a person = a nonobject." The anthropologist is faced with a situation in which women are treated as one kind of person in one situation (as having no say over marriage arrangements) and as another kind of person in other con-texts (as influential in household affairs). It is his own culture which leads him to formulate the first situation as one in which the woman is being treated as an object; and the second where she is awarded rights as a person. But suppose the men of the society publicly say the same thing, "women are just chattels, objects to be exchanged for valuables in marriage," yet then belie these apparent assertions by listening to what their wives say to them in the privacy of their homesteads. The anthropologist squirms with the tortured conclusion, "In this society women are not *really* treated as objects." Probably what he should say is, "In this society, people do not make an equation between objects and nonper-sons. A woman can be the object of a transaction and still remain a person (even though a different kind of person from a man)."

The point is that the concatenation of European ideas about free will, the relationship between actor and acted upon, the person as someone who has and who exercises rights, gives rise to an equation: just as a subject = a person, an object = a nonperson. And this affects anthropologists' analyses as much as the prejudices of anyone else.

De Beauvoir herself adds a dimension to these concepts in her constant references to nature. Possession and manipulation of women is analogous to the exploitation of the natural world. She also points to the paradox that man also feels himself prey to the natural world, to be devoured in the end by mortality. "Woman . . . is the privileged object through which he subdues Nature. . . . As subject, he poses the world, and remaining outside this posed universe, he makes himself ruler of it; if he views himself as flesh, as sex, he is no longer an independent consciousness, a clear, free being: he is involved with the world, he is a limited and perishable object" (de Beauvoir 1972: 188, 194). In her account, times and places are run together to provide a general picture of the feminine condition. However, we can in fact discern shifts in the emphases Europeans have given these aspects of male-female interaction.

It is arguable, for example, that in the Middle Ages, when there was a greater preoccupation with mortality than exists now, there was also a greater preoccupation with free will as an instrument to control animal nature. Man was indeed seen as subject to Nature, and as one of Nature's prey. This might be in the guise of death himself, who destroyed flesh; or it might be in guise of the devil who through women and the delights of the flesh destroyed the spirit. With the subordination of disease and the sterilization of death, we hear much less about the temptations of the body (Nature's mastery over man) and much more about the struggle with the environment (man's mastery over Nature). There are not many spheres in which it is assumed that human ingenuity will not in the end prevail: Nature is an object on which man exercises his freely-taken decisions. Indeed, the theme of exploitation, of subject acting upon object, is so explicit in our thinking that the environment has become another area of agitation for reform—ecological liberation, if you like. It is highly significant that with increasing domination of the environment, which is interpreted in terms of subject (rational economic man) acting upon object (the given resources of the world), women have lost much of their malevolence as temptresses who entice man away from the path of life, and have come to be seen more instrumentally, as tools for male self-expression. The idioms have changed.[15]

The Islamic position mentioned earlier in the chapter supposes a contrast between animality (female) and rationality (male), and a concern with subduing sexual impulses. On the part of the man this is done through internal mental (spiritual) control; on the part of the woman through the authority of her husband over her. These contrasts in the expressions of male and female sexuality, I suggested, become symbols for relationships in general between the sexes. European emphasis has been on the respective roles of sexual partners as actor and acted upon. In the nineteenth century, among certain classes, this was associated with ideas about different kinds of sexuality, where it was the actor, the one taking the sexual initiative, who had to express his impulses, while the acted upon might be enjoined to passivity. This particular dimension has since been largely dropped; the opposition between subject and object remains.

---

15. For a discussion of the place of "nature" in American kinship thinking, see Schneider (1968).

As to the inflammatory phrase, "sex object," that women are thought of as "nothing but" sex objects is the strongest and most provocative smear with which campaigners for women's rights attempt to bring down the male stronghold. The demand that women should be treated as human beings, as persons, to be given certain rights as such, goes hand in hand with the denunciation of any male institution which makes sex objects out of women. It is not just that women being treated as objects is at odds with their being accorded full status as persons in their own right but also that their exploitation is a sexual one.

THE WOMAN QUESTION: IDIOMS OF SEX AND FREEDOM

I have supposed that sexual, in the sense of erotic/coital relations between the sexes, has for a long time in European cultures been a central symbol in terms of which the male-female relationship as such is thought about. Kate Millett directly responds to this tradition when she opens her book on sexual politics (essentially about male power structures which have oppressed females) with descriptions of specifically coital encounters (Millett [1969] 1971). Germaine Greer's chapter on the feminine stereotype is concerned almost entirely with the blandishments with which women hope to attract men to erotic interaction. "The stereotype is the Eternal Feminine. She is the Sexual Object sought by all men, and by all women. She is of neither sex, for she has herself no sex. Her value is solely attested by the demand she excites in others" (Greer 1970: 50). Yet European culture has been undergoing change, and it would be curious not also to find changes in the attributes of sexuality. Some indication has been given in gross terms of shifting contrasts in the relationship actor / acted upon and man/nature. A subtler shift is found in various novels written in English at the latter part of the nineteenth century, of which three are chosen here.

They are works concerned rather directly with the status of women. The narratives turn on social arrangements, on problems which men and women encounter in everyday live, and on the definition of females as persons in their own right. And this concern is directed, in two of the novels quite explicitly, to the question of emancipation. At the same time they use different idioms, symbols, to approach this question. They trace an overall shift from concern with women's conjugal status and their freedom as persons in relation to the men they marry, to concern with women's erotic status and their freedom as persons in relation to the men with whom they engage in sexual partnerships.

This seems concomitant with developments in the notions of those "rights," referred to earlier (pp. 193–94): what we might call a shift from a political, in the sense of constitutional, notion of rights (rights involve responsibilities and are defined in a social context in which each partner to the contract agrees on the freedoms and limits of their activities) to a political, in the sense of interest group, notion of rights (minority or underprivileged interest groups claim identity through the right they can force the world to cede, as an expression of individuality rather than relationship).

Putting it like this possibly affords some insight into the passionate concern with which earlier feminists campaigned for female suffrage. Political reform was seen as a major instrument for the modification of society—either through revolution which would change the character of government ("The rights of man") or through legislative reform (universal suffrage: "the right to vote"). The politicization of the masses—the underprivileged working classes or the female sex—would *alter* their condition, because the rights they could claim and the responsibilities they could bear would become redefined.[16] This is what I would

---

16. The aims of the protagonists of female emancipation in the nineteenth century were almost millennial in scope. Women in politics would improve not only their lot but also the lot of men, and the public good. To be chaste, temperate, truthful, brave, free is an ideal of personal virtue applicable to men as well as women, wrote Frances Cobbe, first in 1881. This is not so dissimilar from Dunbar's cry (see Chapter One) that by building a society on feminist principles the human community will be transformed. Her piece is entitled, "Female liberation as the basis for social revolution" (Dunbar 1970). But the differences are also significant. Dunbar writes of women as oppressed, to be liberated, one of the instruments of male domination being the family. The family must be destroyed and the jobs associated with child-raising must be differently apportioned. Old roles must go: men must learn maternal skills as well. Personal liberation is only possible if the instruments of domination of one human being over another are abolished, and this includes the institution of the family. Like any other institution which gives people power over others, it is to be abhorred. Cobbe ([1881] 1894), on the other hand, considers what should be the correct social and personal duties of women: the new freedom, and she was referring specifically to the then recent property acts (see below), would develop in women a new sense of responsibility. As the conditions of freedom were secured, marriage would become a blessed thing to man and women alike. The family was regarded as a kind of nation-state in miniature. It was a new constitutional framework for the spouses that Cobbe was seeking. This is not the place to debate how far either of these two views were representative of the thought of their times (I do not pretend to a historical analysis). In any case, ideas which have only become widely popular in the latter part of the twentieth century had already been given isolated expression earlier. Dunbar quotes Engels' 1884 identification of the family as the basic unit of

call a constitutional model. Possibly one reason why female suffrage has not brought the social transformations its proponents hoped for lies in the changes there have been in our concept of the person—in the move from a constitutional to an interest-group model. Obviously these are not comprehensive changes. There is much lingering of old ideas and overlap with the new. But I think we can discern shifts in emphases. We are no longer in a world of the apportionment of rights and duties between citizens within society but a world which puts more emphasis on individual autonomy, which recognizes that the person is a person to the extent that he or she can do his or her "own thing," where individual freedom of action has become a right.

This leads to a state of competition, not only between individuals but also between those who have certain characteristics in common (as a category), because in defending the right to possess those characteristics they too are an interest group. The emphasis is not so much on alteration of social status as on forcing others to cede rights which will *validate* the status the interest group already identifies itself as having. Any category, including children, who can claim some area of dependency or oppression, becomes an interest group which seeks to free itself. Dependency itself may be identified as a crime against humanity ("Teachers should discuss with us not lecture us!"). It is not just that political reform does not necessarily lead to social reform, or that women have failed to take advantage of the opportunities legislation now allows them: it is also perhaps that women (as an interest group) have come to perceive other areas of injustice which no amount of constitutional juggling can modify—because the new definitions of freedom, of the person, of the full human being, are no longer about this. They are not about rights in the old sense. But let us return first to that former world.

Collins, whose mid-nineteenth-century novel provided insight into English marriage transactions of the period (Chapter Four), has been described as a radical feminist. In drawing attention to the indignities which Miss Fairlie (who became Lady Glyde) suffered, he was drawing attention to injustices in real life.

There is a good deal of social criticism implicit in *The woman in white*. . . . Much of this stems from Collins' own predilections; he was a radical feminist. The

capitalist society and of female oppression. The modern individual family, he wrote, is founded on the domestic slavery of the wife: she is the proletariat in relation to her husband, the bourgeois. This is a text in current use by many feminists.

framework of the story happens to be founded on fact. The elaborate method whereby Lady Glyde is parted from her inheritance was taken from the Douhault case, a famous French conspiracy that Collins read about in Méjan's *Recueil des causes célèbres*, which he picked up at a bookstall during one of his jaunts to Paris with Dickens and in which he found several of his best plots. The Douhault case provided him with not only the machinery . . . but also with all the principal rôles in the story. (Richardson 1969: vi–vii)

If you recall, one of the salient points which the author makes, through the words of the family solicitor, is that the marriage settlement fails to take into account the bride's own wishes. It is not the fact of settlement itself which is criticized so much as the way in which the men who designed it abused their position of trust. They disregarded the woman as one who had a minimal right to give expression to her own wishes. The undisguised contempt which the author makes the solicitor hold toward the selfish uncle, who wants nothing but peace of mind, is repeated in words he puts in the mouth of one of the villains of the plot. The villain is an ally of Sir Percival Glyde, and both are to benefit from the settlement, which will bring them financial gain. And it is this scoundrel whom Wilkie Collins has say that men must manage women, and women "are nothing but children grown up" (see Frontispiece).[17] The author is, in so many words, pointing to a connection between men's self-interest and their view of women as nothing but objects to be managed. To treat her as a person, Miss Fairlie's wishes would have been consulted.

The whole arrangement of the marriage, about which the bride is unhappy and from which she is eventually rescued by the man who loves her, derived from transactions between men. It was a sense of duty to her father's deathbed wish that made Miss Fairlie accept no other course than continue the engagement to Glyde, which had begun when her father was alive. Her sister refers to it as "an engagement of honour, not of love" (Collins [1859–60] 1969: 60). At the end of the novel, the bride eventually finds freedom in accomplishing those two things closest to her heart: her sister continues to live with her, which also presumably means that there is no further obstacle to the sister's potential enjoyment of her property; and she marries the man for whom she had already conceived a love before she was espoused to Sir Percival Glyde. Her freedom

---

17. An apparently common formulation, and one uttered by Lord Chesterfield among others.

lies not in disavowing marriage, not in rejecting the responsibilities of a house-wife, but in escaping from the clutches of unscrupulous men who use her status on the marriage market for their own material gains. One of the themes of the book (and one highlighted in the excerpts quoted earlier) is the position of women in relation to property. It is her wishes in respect of the disposal of estates which the solicitor so takes to heart. The heroine's property status holds the key to her freedom as an individual. Highly illuminating is the very last scene, which is set in her ancestral home on the death of the selfish uncle. The position of the two sisters as women with property interests is vindicated, even though it is a vicarious one, for the book ends with their revealing to the true (loved) husband what his child has now become.

> Some dim perception of a great change dawned on my mind. Laura spoke before I had quite realised it.[18] She stole close to me to enjoy the surprise which was still expressed in my face. . . .
> Marian . . . rose and held up the child kicking and crowing in her arms. "Do you know who this is, Walter?" she asked, with bright tears of happiness gathering in her eyes.
> "Even *my* bewilderment has its limits," I replied. "I think I can still answer for knowing my own child."
> "Child!" she exclaimed, with all her easy gaiety of old times. "Do you talk in that familiar manner of one of the landed gentry of England? Are you aware, when I present this illustrious baby to your notice, in whose presence you stand? Evidently not! Let me make two eminent personages known to one another: Mr. Walter Hartright—*the Heir of Limmeridge*." (Collins [1859–60] 1969: 569, original emphasis)

Collins' definition of the wife's freedoms (her status as a person) was thus closely bound up with the control she had over the disposal of property. (He specifically sets the story among the landed gentry.) It is significant that re-form of married women's property status was much in the air at the time.[19] The first Married Woman's Property Act was passed in the 1870s; in its final form

---

18. Laura: ex-Miss Fairlie; Marian: her sister; Walter Hartwright: the true husband. This part of the narrative is recounted by the latter.

19. A Married woman's Property Bill was introduced in 1857 but failed. *The woman in white* was published first in serial form over 1859–60.

it was of limited reach but nevertheless allowed that a wife in some respects could own wealth for her separate use. The Married Woman's Property Act of 1882 provided that any woman with property marrying, or any married woman acquiring property, should be entitled to retain such assets as her own. A married woman also became capable of acquiring, holding, and disposing (including by will) any separate property as though she were unmarried and without having to submit to a trustee to intervene in her interests. Wives might still be subject to the authority of their husbands; but in the sphere of property they could act, as far as the provisions of the law went, as legal persons in their own right.

It is clear that such a step modified the nature of female dependency in marriage. But dependency still existed, and the question of women's personal freedoms took a fresh turn. Let us look now at a novel written in 1893, nearly a decade after this momentous Act.[20]

In the 1880s agencies were set up in London to provide training for women who wanted to seek work as clerks, commercial artists, and such. George Gissing's novel, *The odd women*, takes one of these as its chief setting. It is a small concern, run by Miss Barfoot. She is introduced to us thus:

> Of society in the common sense Miss Barfoot saw very little; she had no time to sacrifice in the pursuit of idle ceremonies. . . . Her studies had always been of a very positive nature; her abilities were of a kind uncommon in women, or at all events very rarely developed in one of her sex. She could have managed a large and complicated business, could have filled a place on a board of directors, have taken an active part in municipal government—nay, perchance in national. And this turn of intellect consisted with many traits of character so strongly feminine that people who knew her best thought of her with as much tenderness as admiration. She did not seek to become known as the leader of a "movement," yet her quiet work was probably more effectual than the public career of women who propagandize for female emancipation. Her aim was to draw from the overstocked profession of teaching as many capable young women as she could lay

---

20. One may discern a development of ideas through time, in the extent to which they spread or become popular, even though the initial manifestations of these notions are out of chronology. The reader should not lay too great emphasis on the historical framework given to these comments. (I subsequently give an example of a book published in the 1880s which seems to me to anticipate twentieth-century rather than reflect nineteenth-century preoccupations.)

hands on, and to fit them for certain of the pursuits nowadays thrown open to their sex. She held the conviction that whatever man could do, woman could do equally well—those tasks only excepted which demand great physical strength. At her instance, and with help from her purse, two girls were preparing themselves to be pharmaceutical chemists; two others had been aided by her to open a bookseller's shop; and several who had clerkships in view received an admirable training at her school in Great Portland Street. . . .

In one of the offices, typewriting and occasionally other kinds of work that demanded intelligence were carried on by three or four young women regularly employed. To superintend this department was Miss Nunn's chief duty, together with business correspondence under the principal's direction. In the second room Miss Barfoot instructed her pupils, never more than three being with her at a time. A bookcase full of works on the Woman Question and allied topics served as a circulating library; volumes were lent without charge to the members of this little society. Once a month Miss Barfoot or Miss Nunn, by turns, gave a brief address on some set subject; the hour was four o'clock, and about a dozen hearers generally assembled. (Gissing n.d.: 80–81)

Rhoda Nunn is the heroine of the story, though she would probably not relish the title. From her girlhood, circumstances make it necessary that she will have to earn her living, and her position is contrasted with those of the Madden sisters with whom she used to stay.

Partly at home, and partly in local schools, the young ladies had received instruction suitable to their breeding, and the elder ones were disposed to better this education by private study. The atmosphere of the house was intellectual; books, especially the poets, lay in every room. But it never occurred to Dr. Madden that his daughters would do well to study with a professional object. . . . The thought . . . of his girls having to work for money was so utterly repulsive to him that he could never seriously dwell upon it. A vague piety supported his courage. Providence would not deal harshly with him and his dear ones. . . . The one duty clearly before him was to set an example of righteous life, and to develop the girls' minds—in every proper direction. For, as to training them for any path save those trodden by English ladies of the familiar type, he could not have dreamt of any such thing. Dr. Madden's hopes for the race were inseparable from a maintenance of morals and conventions such as the average man assumes in his estimate of woman. . . .

[By contrast] with a frankness peculiar to her, indicative of pride, Miss Nunn let it be known that she would have to earn her living, probably as a school teacher; study for examinations occupied most of her day, and her hours of leisure were frequently spent either at the Maddens or with a family named Smithson . . . Mr. Smithson was . . . secretly much disliked by Dr. Madden because of his aggressive radicalism. (Gissing n.d.: 6–7)

When Dr. Madden dies the three surviving sisters find themselves in a world in which they have no place. The two elder women, now in their thirties, are dogged by ill-health, partly the result of a poor diet, having supported themselves as a nursery-governess and lady's companion for some years, but with all their hopes pinned on the marriage prospects of their youngest sister, Monica. They are victims of their upbringing, and Miss Barfoot's school has as one of its aims the prevention of such social mutilation. Rhoda Nunn suggests that Monica become a pupil at the school; as to the other sisters,

"Poor things! Poor things!" sighed Miss Barfoot, when she was alone with her friend. "What can we possibly do for the older ones?"

"They are excellent creatures," said Rhoda; "kind, innocent women; but useful for nothing except what they have done all their lives. The eldest can't teach seriously, but she can keep young children out of mischief and give them a nice way of speaking. Her health is breaking down, you can see."

"Poor woman! One of the saddest types."

"Decidedly. Virginia isn't quite so depressing—but how childish!"

"They all strike me as childish. Monica is a dear little girl; it seemed a great absurdity to talk to her about business. Of course she must find a husband."

"I suppose so,"

Rhoda's tone of slighting concession amused her companion.

"My dear, after all we don't desire the end of the race."

"No, I suppose not," Rhoda admitted with a laugh.

"A word of caution. Your zeal is eating you up. At this rate, you will hinder our purpose. We have no mission to prevent girls from marrying suitably—only to see that those who can't shall have a means of living with some satisfaction." (Gissing n.d.: 75–76)

Rhoda Nunn sets up an opposition in her mind between marriage and the advancement of women. It is not that marriage per se is disastrous, but that most girls rush into matrimony like blind things, and most marriages are disasters. The hidden contrast here is between the ordinary sort of marriage which is the lot of most and "true" marriage based on love and the meeting of minds. Only the latter does not debase the female partner. As we shall see, these distinctions become crucial to the plot. Early on Rhoda makes her views plain to Miss Barfoot, when referring to a former pupil who left the school to live as the mistress of a married man.

> "If every novelist could be strangled and thrown into the sea we should have some chance to reforming women. The girl's nature was corrupted with sentimentality, like that of all but every woman who is intelligent enough to read what is called the best fiction, but not intelligent enough to understand its vice. Love - love - love; a sickening sameness of vulgarity. What is more vulgar than the ideal of novelists? They won't represent the actual world; it would be too dull for their readers. In real life, how many men and women *fall in love*? Not one in every ten thousand, I am convinced. Not one married pair in ten thousand, have felt for each other as two or three couples do in every novel. There is the sexual instinct, of course, but that is quite a different thing; the novelists daren't talk about that. The paltry creatures daren't tell the one truth that would be profitable. The result is that women imagine themselves noble and glorious when they are most near the animals. . . . It is your work to train and encourage girls in a path as far as possible from that of the husband-hunter. Let them marry later, if they must; but at all events you will have cleared their views on the subject of marriage, and put them in a position to judge the man who offers himself. You will have taught them that marriage is an alliance of intellects—not a means of support, or something more ignoble still." (Gissing n.d.: 86–87, original italics)

In due course Rhoda meets Everard, Miss Barfoot's cousin, who is represented as intelligent, though with no devotion to the kinds of large causes which concern the two women. In a number of conversations Everard and Rhoda discuss the implications of matrimony.

> "I would have no girl, however wealthy her parents, grow up without a profession. There should be no such thing as a class of females vulgarized by the necessity of finding daily amusement." [Said Miss Barfoot]
>   "Nor of males either, of course," put in Everard, stroking his beard.
>   "Nor of males either, cousin Everard."

"You thoroughly approve all this, Miss Nunn?"

"Oh yes. But I go further. I would have girls taught that marriage is a thing to be avoided rather than hoped for. I would teach them that for the majority of women marriage means disgrace."

"Ah! Now do let me understand you. Why does it mean disgrace?"

"Because the majority of men are without sense of honour. To be bound to them in wedlock is shame and misery."

Everard's eyelids drooped, and he did not speak for a moment.

"And you seriously think, Miss Nunn, that by persuading as many women as possible to abstain from marriage you will improve the character of men?"

"I have no hope of sudden results, Mr. Barfoot. I should like to save as many as possible of the women now living from a life of dishonour; but the spirit of our work looks to the future. When *all* women, high and low alike, are trained to self-respect, then men will regard them in a different light, and marriage may be honourable to both."

Again Everard was silent, and seemingly impressed.

. . .

Everard [returned to] what was practically a resumption of their last talk.

"Have you a formal society, with rules and so on?"

"Oh no; nothing of the kind."

"But you of course select the girls whom you instruct or employ?"

"Very carefully."

"How I should like to see them all!—I mean," he added, with a laugh," it would be so very interesting. The truth is, my sympathies are strongly with you in much of what you said the other day about women and marriage. We regard the matter from different points of view, but our ends are the same."

Rhoda moved her eyebrows, and asked calmly, —

"Are you serious?"

"Perfectly. You are absorbed in your present work, that of strengthening women's minds and character; for the final issue of this you can't care much. But to me that is the practical interest. In my mind, you are working for the happiness of men."

"Indeed?" escaped Rhoda's lips, which had curled in irony.

"Don't misunderstand me. I am not speaking cynically or trivially. The gain of women is also the gain of men. You are bitter against the average man for his low morality; but that fault, on the whole, is directly traceable to the ignobleness of women. Think, and you will grant me this."

"I see what you mean. Men have themselves to thank for it."

"Assuredly they have. I say that I am on your side. Our civilization in this point has always been absurdly defective. Men have kept women at a barbarous stage of development, and then complain that they are barbarous.

. . .

"There's something in your way of putting it that I don't like," she said, with much frankness; "but of course I agree with you in the facts. I am convinced that most marriages are hateful, from every point of view. But there will be no improvement until women have revolted against marriage, from a reasonable conviction of its hatefulness."

"I wish you all success—most sincerely I do."

He paused, looked about the room, and stroked his ear. Then, in a grave tone, —

"My own ideal of marriage involves perfect freedom on both sides. Of course it could only be realized where conditions are favourable; poverty and other wretched things force us so often to sin against our best beliefs. But there are plenty of people who might marry on these ideal terms. Perfect freedom, sanctioned by the sense of intelligent society, would abolish most of the evils we have in mind. But women must first be civilized; you are quite right in that."
(Gissing n.d.: 147–48, 151–54 passim, original emphasis)

Everard is presented as now serious, now frivolous. It nevertheless becomes clear that the pair "fall in love." As we should expect, much turns on Rhoda's self-questioning of what quality this "love" has. Much turns, too, on the question of marriage. In the first place Rhoda fears that she would be betraying the women she trains by herself marrying.

"My work and thought are for the women who do not marry—the 'odd women' I call them. They alone interest me. One mustn't undertake too much.". . .

No man had ever made love to her; no man, to her knowledge, had ever been tempted to do so. In certain moods she derived satisfaction from this thought, using it to strengthen her life's purpose; having passed her thirtieth year, she might take it as a settled thing that she would never be sought in marriage, and so could shut the doors on every instinct tending to trouble her intellectual decisions. But these instincts sometimes refused to be thus treated. . . . An hour of lassitude filled her with despondency, none the less real because she was ashamed of it. If only she had once been loved, like other women—if she had listened to an offer of devotion, and rejected it—her heart would be more securely at peace. So she thought. Secretly she deemed it a hard thing never to have known that common triumph of her sex. And, moreover, it took away from the merit of her position as a leader and encourager of women living independently. There might be some who said, or thought, that she made a virtue of necessity.

   . . .

"You are resolved never to marry?" [Asked Everard]

    "I never shall," Rhoda replied firmly.

    "But suppose marriage in no way interfered with your work?"

    "It would interfere hopelessly with the best part of my life. I thought you understood this. What would become of the encouragement I am able to offer our girls?"

    "Encouragement to refuse marriage?"

    "To scorn the old idea that a woman's life is wasted if she does not marry. My work is to help those women who, by sheer necessity, must live alone—women whom vulgar opinion ridicules. How can I help them so effectually as by living among them, one of them, and showing that my life is anything but weariness and lamentation? I am fitted for this. It gives me a sense of power and usefulness which I enjoy. Your cousin is doing the same work admirably. If I deserted I should despise myself." (Gissing n.d.: 214–16 passim, 270)

There is another issue too, related intimately to the estimation of Everard Barfoot's sincerity, and it is on this that the plot finally turns. When Everard first declares his love for Rhoda he also states that he could not consider matrimony: "If I marry now, it will be a woman of character and brains. Marry in the legal sense I never shall. My companion must be as independent of forms as I am myself" (Gissing n.d.: 212–13). Rhoda, who at that stage does not think of herself as reciprocating his sentiments, suspects that he is simply indulging her—pretending to comply with her own mood of independence. She argues to herself that any proposal for a union of free love must be frivolous and that if he truly loves her then he will in the end propose legal marriage. But legal marriage is what she will deny herself. In other words, her own definition of herself as a person is of one who will scorn conjugal union, in order to better work for the "odd women," and it is *she* who cannot take the idea of free love seriously. Indeed, at one stage she wishes to bring him to the point of proposal so that she will have the enjoyment of refusal. What she desires to refuse is matrimony, not a sexual liaison as such.

The culmination comes in two contrasting scenes between Everard and Rhoda. At the first Everard makes it again clear to her that he would make her his wife in anything but legal form. This would overcome her scruples to matrimony, if she could but take him seriously. For a moment she does, and she admits to herself that it would be easier to declare to her friends that she had formed a union of this kind than to say she had married. But she refuses to answer him at once, though he is desperate for affirmation.

> The one word of assent would have satisfied him. This he obstinately required. He believed that it would confirm his love beyond any other satisfaction she could render him. He must be able to regard her as magnanimous, a woman who had proved herself worth living or dying for. And he must have the joy of subduing her to his will.
>
> "No," said Rhoda firmly. "I can't answer you tonight. I can't decide so suddenly."
>
> This was disingenuous, and she felt humiliated by her subterfuge. . . .
>
> "I can't—until I am sure of myself—of my readiness—"
>
> Her broken words betrayed the passion with which she was struggling. Everard felt her tremble against his side.
>
> "Give me your hand," he whispered. "The left hand."
>
> Before she could guess his purpose he had slipped a ring upon her finger, a marriage ring. Rhoda started away from him, and at once drew off the perilous symbol.
>
> "No—that proves to me I can't! What should we gain? You see, you dare not be quite consistent. It's only deceiving the people who don't know us."
>
> "But I have explained to you. The consistency is in ourselves, our own minds—"
>
> "Take it back. Custom is too strong for us. We should only play at defying it." (Gissing n.d.: 386–88)

Then with a curious volte-face Rhoda suddenly throws all away and says that she will agree to a formal marriage. They make arrangements for obtaining a license.

> "Isn't it better?" Rhoda asked, as they walked back in the darkness. "Won't it make our life so much simpler and happier?"
>
> "Perhaps."

"You know it will." She laughed joyously, trying to meet his look. . . .

"Why, you may laugh as well."

"But you have spoilt my life, you know. Such a grand life it might have been. Why did you come and interfere with me? And you have been so terribly obstinate."

"Of course; that's my nature. But after all I have been weak."

"Yielding in one point that didn't matter to you at all? It was the only way of making me sure that you loved me."

Barfoot laughed slightingly.

"And what if I needed the other proof that you loved *me*?"

. . .

And neither was content.

Barfoot, over his cigar and glass of whisky at the hotel, fell into a mood of chagrin. The woman he loved would be his . . . but his temper disturbed him. After all, he had not triumphed. As usual the woman had her way. She played upon his senses, and made him her obedient, slave. To prolong the conflict would have availed nothing; Rhoda, doubtless, was in part actuated by the desire to conquer, and she knew her power over him. So it was a mere repetition of the old story—a marriage like any other. And how would it result?

She had great qualities; but was there not much in her that he must subdue, reform, if they were really to spend their lives together? Her energy of domination perhaps excelled his. Such a woman might be unable to concede him the liberty in marriage which theoretically she granted to be just. Perhaps she would torment him with restless jealousies, suspecting on every trivial occasion an infringement of her right. From that point of view it would have been far wiser to persist in rejecting legal marriage, that her dependence upon him might be more complete. . . .

Free as he boasted himself from lover's silliness, he had magnified Rhoda's image. She was not the glorious rebel he had pictured. Like any other woman, she mistrusted her love without the sanction of society. Well, that was something relinquished, lost. Marriage would after all be a compromise. He had not found his ideal. . . .

And Rhoda, sitting late in the little lodging-house parlour, visited her soul with questionings no less troublesome. Everard was not satisfied with her. He had yielded, perhaps more than half contemptuously, to what he thought a feminine weakness. In going with her to the registrar's office he would feel himself to be acting an ignoble part. Was it not a bad beginning to rule him against his conscience?

She had triumphed splendidly. In the world's eye this marriage of hers was far better than any she could reasonably have hoped, and her heart approved it with rapture. . . . But must not Everard's conception of her have suffered? . . .

Why was she not more politic? Would it not have been possible to gratify him, and yet to gain his consent to legal marriage? By first of all complying she would have seemed to confirm all he believed of her; and then, his ardour at height, how simple to point out to him—without entreaty, without show of much concern—that by neglecting formalities they gained absolutely nothing. . . .

What was her life to be? At first they would travel together; but before long it might be necessary to have a settled home, and what then would be her social position, her duties and pleasures? Housekeeping, mere domesticities, could never occupy her for more than the smallest possible part of each day. Having lost one purpose in life, dignified, absorbing, likely to extend its sphere as time went on, what other could she hope to substitute for it?

Love of husband—perhaps of child. There must be more than that. Rhoda did not deceive herself as to the requirements of her nature. Practical activity in some intellectual undertaking; a share—nay, leadership—in some "movement"; contact with the revolutionary life of her time—the impulses of her heart once satisfied, these things would again claim her. But how if Everard resisted such tendencies? Was he in truth capable of respecting her individuality? Or would his strong instinct of lordship urge him to direct his wife as a dependent, to impose upon her his own view of things? She doubted whether he had much genuine sympathy with woman's emancipation as she understood it. Yet in no particular had her convictions changed; nor would they change. . . . No longer an example of perfect female independence, and unable therefore to use the same language as before, she might illustrate woman's claim of equality in marriage.—If her experience proved no obstacle. (Gissing n.d.: 388–93 passim, original italics)

Various twists and turns of events lead to the pair becoming estranged. When they finally come together, Everard without hesitation this time, asks her directly to marry him. But Rhoda refuses. She accuses him of being "not quite serious": it was she and not he who had earlier spoken of marriage. She now declares that she will never marry him:

"Will you marry me?" he asked, moving a step nearer.

"I think you are 'not quite serious.'"

"I have asked you twice. I ask for the third time."

"I won't marry you with the forms of marriage," Rhoda answered in an abrupt, harsh tone.

"Now it is you who play with a serious matter."

"You said we had both changed. I see now that our 'perfect day' was marred by my weakness at the end. If you wish to go back in imagination to that summer night, restore everything, only let *me* be what I now am."

Everard shook his head.

"Impossible. It must be then or now for both of us."

"Legal marriage," she said, glancing at him, "has acquired some new sanction for you since then?"

"On the whole, perhaps it has."

"Naturally. But I shall never marry, so we will speak no more of it."

As if finally dismissing the subject she walked to the opposite side of the hearth, and there turned towards her companion with a cold smile

"In other words, then, you have ceased to love me?"

"Yes, I no longer love you."

"Yet, if I had been willing to revive that fantastic idealism—as you thought it—"

She interrupted him sternly.

"What *was* it?"

"Oh, a kind of idealism undoubtedly. I was so bent on making sure that you loved me."

She laughed.

"After all, the perfection of our day was half make-believe. You never loved me with entire sincerity." (Gissing n.d.: 466, original emphasis)

They part finally, and Everard marries someone else.

The chief interest of the story for our purpose is the centrality of marriage as an institution. The two are represented as playing with the idea of free love but only to test one another out. On Rhoda's part the test is of Everard's sincerity. Does he mean what he says, or is he but pandering to her idealism? On his part, it is a test of the extent to which he can dominate her, and force on her what his definition of the perfect union would be. He is willing to offer free love, if the initiative can be his. He is willing later to accede to the compromise she apparently wanted (a legal marriage) if he can still appear to dominate her: he *demands* her agreement to his proposal. It is domination she will not accept and she rejects the proposal. He sees his love for her as likely to survive only through the reforms he hopes to introduce if they are to live together; and the revelation of what she takes to be Everard's frivolity kills Rhoda's love. She must be allowed to remain as she is.

The suggestions of marriage and free love are counters in the game of domination. First Everard and then Rhoda take up one position and then another. The inconsistencies in their stand arise from a basic conflict between the ideals of equality and the fact that a conjugal partnership must be unequal. It is for those signs of inequality, of dominance, of the refusal to give or the taking of too much, that both of them strain—and test one another out in the wary suggestions of how their union shall begin. Theirs is a battle of wills.[21] Sexuality is not the central issue (it is made clear that each desires the other). What is crucial is the kind of partnership they will form when they decide to live together. The concern of the novelist is with domesticity in the *conjugal* relationship as such, rather than the erotic ties which may or may not go along with this. He is exploring the implications of a couple setting up a life-long establishment. And the most crucial issue in such a domestic relationship is the nature of the partnership, with its necessary limitations on personal freedom, its incitement to now one party and now the other to jockey for a position of power.

It seems that the novel's central antithesis is not between legal and illegal union—for Everard and Rhoda would contemplate setting up a domestic establishment in either case—but between domesticity and personal freedom. (A similar theme is pursued in a subsequent novel, *In the year of Jubilee*, where a secretly-wed couple live apart, perpetuating some of the freedoms of their premarriage days, although this arrangement is not presented as ideal either.) Marriage brings domestic imprisonment for the husband as well as the wife. Commentators on Gissing's works have pointed out the unhappy circumstances of his own domestic life, and have suggested that the themes and scenes of his books show us some of his private anguish. But it is in the way he perceives and presents the problems that we can perhaps discern parallels with a widespread preoccupation of his time.

This is a preoccupation with what should be the ideal relationship between a man and a woman who commit themselves to one another within the *institution*

---

21. When contemplating union with Everard (union of any kind), Rhoda says to herself she would demand of him "a flawless faith." Everard, reciprocally, in his own musings would require Rhoda manifest "an absolute confidence" in him.

of a domestic and conjugal partnership. The institution itself brings certain limits to their personal freedoms: however "equal" and independent the partners start off by being this equality cannot survive in a household situation based on a premise of dependency. Both the formal legality of the union and sexuality itself are side issues. In *The odd women* there is the suggestion that one chance for the survival of personal freedom lies in both parties accepting the equality of the other on every front—and the point on which Rhoda judges Everard to have fallen down is that his commitment to their partnership does not match hers. She thinks he is less serious. The other important area in which this equality must be proved is in intellectual matters: the couple must be matched in their mental outlook. Everard says at one point, "But a free union presupposes equality of position. No honest man would propose it, for instance, to a woman incapable of understanding all it involved." (Gissing n.d.: 213)

In seeking out the extent of the other party's commitment, each tests the degree to which "love" exists between them. At the end, love is lost. But an equality of passion was another of the signs by which the couple judged their positions. There is no suggestion that dependency in a sexual partnership as such touches also on the question of personal freedom. Rather, Gissing makes it clear that at one stage Rhoda's and Everard's love were equally matched. To prove that "true love" existed would be one proof that the partnership could at least start on a premise of equality.[22] All the problems come in contemplating the conversion of a sexual union into a domestic, conjugal institution.

Olive Schreiner's *The story of an African farm* treats sex in an entirely different way. The book was first published in 1883,[23] but in the way it handles male-female relations, to my mind belongs to the twentieth rather than the nineteenth century. Gissing brings together equality and independence: a partnership can only admit the independence of each side, the man's and the woman's personal freedom, if they enter into it as equals. A free union presupposes equality; conversely, their equality will be some guarantee of personal liberty. Schreiner, on the other hand, argues that there is a disjunction between equality

---

22. A theme not unfamiliar in other works of about this period, such as H. G. Wells' *Ann Veronica* (1909). A couple demonstrates their equality in love by living with each other before marrying: they are equals first, symbolized in the equality of their love. Whatever happens to the marriage they have proved this to themselves. Rhoda quite explicitly demands of Everard a matched sexual enthrallment as a sign of the equality between them.

23. Under a male pseudonym.

and independence or freedom. She denies that love, however equally expressed, can allow the partners to remain at liberty. And this has nothing to do with institutions: it has to do directly with the nature of the sexual relationship itself. The question of domesticity is irrelevant; the conflict is between personal freedom and commitment as such. However equal the commitment on both sides, the fact of commitment itself, the fact of *relationship*, impinges on the individual.

Gissing was working out the question of dependency and autonomy but using a context where the parameters of dependency were defined through certain institutions; the husband and wife become each other's domestic prisoners. Schreiner has moved a step further. Admitting any tie at all, admitting that any relationship involves dependency, inhibits the individual and his freedom of action. Lovers imprison each other.

The setting of Schreiner's novel is an isolated South African homestead. Three children—two girls and a boy—are looked after by an old Boer woman. Lyndall manages to go away to school: unlike her girl cousin she has no prospects of inheritance.

> "There is nothing helps in this world," said the child [Lyndall] slowly, "but to be very wise, and to know everything—to be clever."
>
> "But I should not like to go to school!" persisted the small, freckled face [of her cousin].
>
> "And you do not need to. When you are seventeen this Boer-woman will go; you will have this farm and everything that is upon if for your own; but I," said Lyndall, "will have nothing. I must learn."
>
> "Oh, Lyndall! *I* will give you some of my sheep," said Em, with a sudden burst of pitying generosity.
>
> "I do not want your sheep," said the girl slowly; "I want things of my own. When I am grown up," she added, the flush on her delicate features deepening at every word, "there will be nothing that I do not know. I shall be rich, very rich; and I shall wear not only for best, but every day, a pure white silk, and little rose-buds, like the lady in Tant' Sannie's bedroom, and my petticoats will be embroidered, not only at the bottom, but all through."
>
> The lady in Tant' Sannie's bedroom was a gorgeous creature from a fashion-sheet, which the Boer-woman, somewhere obtaining, had pasted up at the foot of her bed, to be profoundly admired by the children. (Schreiner [1883] 1971: 45–46, original emphasis)

When she returns to the farm as a young woman she gives an account of the world outside to Waldo, the boy.

"Have you learnt much?" he asked her simply, remembering how she had once said, "When I come back again I shall know everything that a human being can."

She laughed.

"Are you thinking of my old boast? Yes; I have learnt something, though hardly what I expected, and not *quite* so much. . . . I have discovered that of all cursed places under the sun, where the hungriest soul can hardly pick up a few grains of knowledge, a girls' boarding-school is the worst. They are called finishing schools, and the name tells accurately what they are. They finish everything but imbecility and weakness, and that they cultivate. They are nicely adapted machines for experimenting on the question, "Into how little space a human soul can be crushed?" I have seen some souls so compressed that they would have fitted into a small thimble, and found room to move there—wide room. A woman who has been for many years at one of those places carries the mark of the beast on her till she dies, though she may expand a little afterwards, when she breathes in the free world.

. . .

"Can you form an idea, Waldo, of what it must be to be shut up with cackling old women, who are without knowledge of life, without love of the beautiful, without strength, to have your soul cultured by them? It is suffocation only to breathe the air they breathe; but I made them give me a room. I told them I should leave, and they knew I came there on my own account; so they gave me a bedroom without the companionship of one of those things that were having their brains slowly diluted and squeezed out of them. I did not learn music, because I have no talent; and when the drove made cushions, and hideous flowers that the roses laugh at, and a footstool in six weeks that a machine would have made better in five minutes, I went to my room. With the money saved from such work I bought books and newspapers, and at night I sat up. I read, and epitomized what I read; and I found time to write some plays, and find out how hard it is to make your thoughts look anything but imbecile fools when you paint them with ink on paper. In the holidays I learnt a great deal more. I made acquaintances, saw a few places, and many people, and some different ways of living, which is more than any books can show one. On the whole, I am not dissatisfied with my four years. I have not learnt what I expected; but I have learnt something else. . . . Do you take an interest in the position of women, Waldo?"

"No."

"I thought not. No one does, unless they are in need of a subject upon which to show their wit. . . . But we are cursed, Waldo, born cursed from the time our mothers bring us into the world till the shrouds are put on us. Do not look at me as though I were talking nonsense. Everything has two sides—the outside that is ridiculous, and the inside that is solemn."

"I am not laughing," said the boy sedately enough; "but what curses you?"

He thought she would not reply to him, she waited so long.

"It is not what is done to us, but what is made of us," she said at last, "that wrongs us. . . . the world tells us what we are to be, and shapes us by the ends it sets before us. To you it says—*Work!* and to us it says—*Seem!* . . . And so the world makes men and women. Look at this little chin of mine, Waldo, with the dimple in it. It is but a small part of my person; but though I had a knowledge of all things under the sun, and the wisdom to use it, and the deep loving heart of an angel, it would not stead me through life like this little chin. I can win money with it, I can win love; I can win power with it, I can win fame. What would knowledge help me? The less a woman has in her head the lighter she is for climbing. I once heard an old man say, that he never saw intellect help a woman so much as a pretty ankle; and it was the truth. They begin to shape us to our cursed end," she said, with her lips drawn in to look as though they smiled, "when we are tiny things in shoes and socks. We sit with our little feet drawn up under us in the window, and look out at the boys in their happy play. We want to go. Then a loving hand is laid on us: 'Little one, you cannot go,' they say; 'your face will burn, and your nice white dress be spoiled.' . . . Afterwards we go and thread blue beads, and make a string for our neck; and we go and stand before the glass. We see the complexion we were not to spoil, and the white frock, and we look into our own great eyes. Then the curse begins to act on us. It finishes its work when we are grown women, who no more look out wistfully at a more healthy life; we are contented."

. . .

"I see in your great eyes what you are thinking," she said, glancing at him. . . . "How is this woman who makes such a fuss worse off than I? I will show you by a very little example. We stand here at this gate this morning both poor, both young, both friendless; there is not much to choose between us. Let us turn away just as we are, to make our way in life. This evening you will come to a farmer's house. The farmer, albeit you come alone and on foot, will give you a pipe of tobacco and a cup of coffee and a bed. If he has no dam to build and no child to teach, tomorrow you can go on your way with a friendly greeting of the hand. I, if I come to the same place tonight, will have strange questions asked me, strange glances cast on me. The Boer-wife will shake her head and give me food to eat with the Kaffirs, and a light to sleep with the dogs. . . . We were equals once when we lay newborn babes on our nurse's knees. We will be equals again when they tie up our jaws for the last sleep."

Waldo looked in wonder at the little quivering face; it was a glimpse into the world of passion and feeling wholly new to him.

"Mark you," she said, "we have always this advantage over you—we can at any time step into ease and competence, where you must labour patiently for it. A little weeping, a little wheedling, a little self-degradation, a little careful use of our advantages, and then some man will say—'Come, be my wife!' With good looks and youth marriage is easy to attain. There are men enough; but a woman who has sold herself, ever for a ring and a new name, need hold her skirt aside for no creature in the street. They both earn their bread in one way. Marriage for love is the beautifullest external symbol of the union of souls; marriage without it is the uncleanliest traffic that defiles the world. . . ."

"But some women," said Waldo, speaking as though the words forced themselves from him at that moment, "some women have power."

She lifted her beautiful eyes to his face.

"Power! Did you ever hear of men being asked whether other souls should have power or not? It is born in them. . . . Yes, we have power; and since we are not to expend it in tunnelling mountains, nor healing diseases, nor making laws, nor money, nor on any extraneous object, we expend it on *you*. You are our goods, our merchandise, our material for operating on; we buy you, we sell you, we make fools of you, we act the wily old Jew with you, we keep six of you crawling to our little feet, and praying only for a touch of our little hand; and they say truly, there was never an ache or a pain or a broken heart but a woman was at the bottom of it. We are not to study law, nor science, nor art; so we study you. There is never a nerve or fibre in your man's nature but we know it.

. . .

"They bring weighty arguments against us when we ask for the perfect freedom of woman," she said; "but, when you come to the objections, they are like pumpkin devils with candles inside; hollow, and can't bite. They say that women do not wish for the sphere and freedom we ask for them and would not use it!

"If the bird *does* like its cage, and *does* like its sugar, and will not leave it, why keep the door so very carefully shut? Why not open it, only a little? Do they know there is many a bird will not break its wings against the bars, but would fly if the doors were open." She knit her forehead, and leaned further over the bars. (Schreiner [1883] 1971 185–93 passim, original emphasis)

Lyndall finds herself pursued by the farm manager, Gregory, who had been intending to marry her cousin. When Gregory declares his love she takes him at his word:

"You are the one being that I love!" said Gregory, quivering; "I thought I loved before, but I know now! Do not be angry with me. I know you could never like me; but if I might but always be near you to serve you, I would be utterly, utterly happy. I would ask nothing in return! If you could only take everything I have and use it; I want nothing but to be of use to you."

She looked at him for a few moments.

"How do you know," she said slowly, "that you could not do something to serve me? You could serve me by giving me your name."

He started, and turned his burning face to her.

"You are very cruel; you are ridiculing me," he said.

"No, I am not, Gregory. What I am saying is plain, matter-of-fact business. If you are willing to give me your name within three weeks' time, I am willing to marry you; if not, well. I want nothing more than your name. That is a clear proposal, is it not? . . ."

"Do you really mean it?" he whispered.

"Yes. You wish to serve me, and to have nothing in return!—you shall have what you wish."

She held out her fingers for Doss to lick—"Do you see this dog? He licks my hand because I love him; and I allow him to. Where I do not love I do not allow it. I believe you love me; I too could love so, that to lie under the foot of the thing I loved would be more heaven than to lie in the breast of another. . . .

"Would you not take my arm, the path is very rough?"

She rested her fingers lightly on it.

"I may yet change my mind about marrying you before the time comes. It is very likely. Mark you!" she said, turning round on him; "I remember your words:—*You will give everything, and expect nothing.* The knowledge that you are serving me is to be your reward; and you will have that. You will serve me, and greatly. The reasons I have for marrying you I need not inform you of now; you will probably discover some of them before long." (Schreiner [1883] 1971: 231–32, original emphasis)

Lyndall at this stage manipulates Gregory. She has had a letter from a man she knew and loved while she was away from the farm, hinting at the possibility of marriage. She wrote back to say she had to decline because she was to be married to another in three weeks' time (Gregory). This brings her former lover, who is never named, to the farm. But Lyndall tells him that he only loves her because he wants to be master, and only came because she had provoked him by refusing his proposal.

She interrupted him.

"You got my short letter?"

"Yes; that is why I came. You sent a very foolish reply, you must take it back. Who is this fellow you talk of marrying?"

"A young farmer. . . ."

"What kind of a fellow is he?"

"A fool."

"And you would rather marry him than me?"

"Yes; because you are not one."

"That is a novel reason for refusing to marry a man," he said, leaning his elbow on the table, and watching her keenly.

"It is a wise one," she said shortly. "If I marry him I shall shake him off my hand when it suits me. If I remained with him for twelve months he would never have dared to kiss my hand. As far as I wish he should come, he comes, and no further. Would you ask me what you might and what you might not do?"

Her companion raised the moustache with a caressing movement from his lip and smiled. It was not a question that stood in need of any answer. . . .

"Why not marry me?"

"Because if once you have me you would hold me fast. I shall never be free again." She drew a long low breath.

"What have you done with the ring I gave you?" he said.

"Sometimes I wear it; then I take it off and wish to throw it into the fire; the next day I put it on again, and sometimes I kiss it."

"So you do love me a little?"

"If you were not something more to me than any other man in the world, do you think—" she paused. "I love you when I see you; but when you are away from me I hate you. . . ."

"If you do love me," he asked her, "Why will you not marry me?"

"Because, if I had been married to you for a year, I should have come to my senses, and seen that your hands and your voice are like the hands and the voice of any other man. I cannot quite see that now. But it is all madness. You call into activity one part of my nature; there is a higher part that you know nothing of, that you never touch. If I married you, afterwards it would arise and assert itself, and I should hate you always, as I do now sometimes." (Schreiner [1883] 1971: 236–37)

For a moment it looks as though Lyndall is simply concerned with the question of domesticity too, that an established life would erode freedom. But there is more to it.

He smiled.

"Well, since you will not marry me, may I inquire what your intentions are, the plan you wrote of. You asked me to come and hear it, and I have come."

"I said, 'Come if you wish.' —If you agree to it, well; if not, I marry on Monday."

"Well?"

She was still looking beyond him at the fire.

"I cannot marry you," she said slowly, "because I cannot be tied; but, if you wish, you may take me away with you, and take care of me; then when we do not love any more we can say good-bye. . . ."

"Oh, my darling," he said, bending tenderly, and holding his hand out to her, "why will you not give yourself entirely to me? One day you will desert me and go to another."

She shook her head without looking at him.

"No, life is too long. But I will go with you." (Schreiner [1883] 1971: 238–39)

Lyndall says she cannot marry her lover because that would tie her. Her marriage to Gregory, on the other hand, would not tie her at all. She would be master of the relationship—Gregory would do what she wanted, and no more. Her feelings were not engaged with him; there was no problem of commitment to Gregory: she would take his name but give nothing. Her autonomy would be untouched. With her lover the position is radically different. It is *because* she is emotionally bound to him, because she would let him do what he wanted, because she is already to that extent unfree, that a formal commitment would deprive her of all freedom. Whether they love each other equally or not is quite irrelevant. And it is not simply that as a woman Lyndall would find herself dominated by her man-husband, although this issue is also pertinent to her decision. It is that her own commitment would lessen her individuality. When this unnamed man, with whom she does go away but from whom she later parts, implores her once more to be his wife, she writes back,

> I cannot marry you. I will always love you. . . . I must know and see [the world], I cannot be bound to one whom I love as I love you. I am not afraid of the world—I will fight the world. One day—perhaps it may be far off—I shall find what I have wanted all my life; something nobler, stronger than I, before which I can kneel down. (Schreiner [1883] 1971: 279)

Whatever it is she wants, it is not to be found in a relationship of that kind, where her sense of self will be confined by emotions over which she has no control.

It is finally worth noting that while the heroine of Gissing's novel admits to passion, she does not consider a purely sexual (erotic) relationship as an end in itself. Rhoda resists both sex and marriage because of the fundamental inequality between herself and Everard. Lyndall, on the other hand, does not resist her lover sexually (indeed she has a child by him). She resists marriage because this would transform the relationship between them both. Her personal freedom would be entirely lost if she were to add to the sexual ties the further bonds of marriage: she rejects the very idea of total commitment for which Rhoda strove so hard.

Both novels are concerned with the woman question, with the relationship between being female and being a free person. But the essentials of the terms in which one should be treated as an individual in one's own right are different. The former stresses equality, and the sad rarity with which two human beings can in fact ever be matched. The latter stresses independence, and the sad impossibility of retaining freedom within a relationship.

THE WOMAN QUESTION: SEX OBJECTS

The aim of this chapter has been to underline one part of the process of sexual mythology, that part which casts male-female relationships into certain molds, certain stereotypes. The molds are forged by other customs and institutions, sometimes in an obvious way, sometimes less obvious. Even the terms within which we hope to analyze a situation belong, after all, to culture as well.

An example of a rather obvious stereotype of male-female relations in European societies is that which plays on the contrast between woman-house-wife and man-worker. Another, more prevalent perhaps in the previous century than today, is that of woman-child and man-adult. Such stereotypes refer to the economic system (people's occupations) and to kinship (the parent-child bond). These institutions impinge on relations between men and women, but they do not encompass the totality of all that constitutes male-female interaction. To this extent the stereotypes are identifiable. They are aspects of the male-female relationship; and we are probably far enough removed from them to realize they are only aspects. An example of a stereotype which is less obvious is the labeling of women as sex objects.

This looks paradoxical. Many times has the demand, or the plea, been published that women should *not* be treated as sex objects but as persons, a demand or plea, in short, which identifies and exposes the stereotype. What I think is *not* obvious is that the acknowledged stereotype (women are sex objects) and the presumed "reality" (women are persons and should be treated as such) both spring from a common source. Constructing a contrast between an object, who is, and a person, who does, belongs to a rather specific tradition of thought. In other words, relations between men and women are symbolized through the same images by which we build up our concepts of the natural, physical world, "reality," and mankind's place in it. Subject and object: the actor and the acted upon. For I intend no derogatory dismissal of these mental constructs in suggesting that we are dealing in the first place with stereotypes—I simply want to point to the cultural subjectivity of our own perceptions. It is a perfectly respectable activity to pursue these perceptions and analyze situations outside our own culture in terms of them. This is the basic premise of science: to build up an internally consistent system of ideas which makes sense of the natural world to those observing it. We can analyze the condition of maleness and femaleness through the concepts of doing and being, subject and object, as de Beauvoir does, regardless of the culture under scrutiny. But we are missing something if we do not realize why we should have come to the point of thinking in just these terms.

Our preoccupation with the roles of actor and acted upon is related to the way we view the works of nature and the works of mankind; it is related also to our view of politics, of rulers and the ruled, of capitalist and proletarian, of the powerful and the exploited. Man exploits nature; industrialists exploit workers; males exploit females. When the exploitation is identified as obnoxious, it follows that an attempt is made to turn the subject : object equation on its head. Man cannot just use nature, for he is also dependent on it; workers should be regarded as human beings, and women also: persons with the right to exercise their free will. For human beings are identified as free agents, as actors who must interact with others as actors. Along this train of thought, any evidence of limitation to freedom becomes classified as limitation to the person, a constraint on liberty, and thus on full human status. Indeed, the European concept of freedom to act as the essential quality of being human can be extended to the point that dependency of any kind on others becomes classified as a covert form of subordination and of submission to oppression.

When we talk about the liberation of male-female relations, and cry that one sex should acknowledge the other as free, of equal human potential, and such, we are employing concepts of the person which belong in a very particular way to our own intellectual traditions. This is not to say that they are not the best and the most important ones we have; but it is to say that they are our possessions in a special sense.

We also accord sex a rather special place in our thinking. This seems to be associated with a preoccupation with things. Some other cultures also express male dominance through the apparent submission of women in coitus. Much of our own terminology uses the specific idiom of ownership, of taking, of having, of possessing. And the grammatical subject of these acts must be an animate actor. The subject : object contrast in turn becomes emotionalized by reference to the concrete and apparently natural roles of the sexes in intercourse. Men are crude: women are frigid; men are lustful: women are alluring; men hunt: women deceive. Men force themselves on the world, play out ambitions, seek to better their position; women are isolated, they can only insinuate their way into situations, capriciously pursue their own ends. And so forth. The roles of the sexes in erotic encounters provide metaphors and analogies for talking about relations between men and women as such.

Indeed, the dominance of males is identified by many modern female writers as primarily sexual dominance: sex is the chief instrument of their mastery. Thus "sexual politics" is both male subjugation of females in society, and the use of sexuality to further this.[24] Females are eunuchs because they have been

---

24. Millett is aware of the processes of symbolism at work: "Coitus . . . among other things . . . may serve as a model of sexual politics on an individual or personal plane" (Millett 1971: 23). Right at the end of *The second sex* de Beauvoir says,

de-sexualized, in effect castrated, by males. A deprived status in the world at large and mutilation of their sexual energy are one and the same thing.

Sexual (coital) subordination of females has become a central symbol for relations of dominance and subordination between men and women. Liberation of the dominated, *in these idioms*, necessitates some transformation in the implications of sexual intercourse. Sex is separated from the notion of needs and dependency and may be separated from the idea of relationship. A curious write-up ("A liberated woman despite beauty, chic and success") of Gloria Steinem by *Newsweek* (August 16, 1971) contains this description:

> But even [a] "series of little marriages," as Steinem calls them, were carried forth with her usual independence. "She is your ideal liberated woman," says Jane O'Reilly, "I don't think she believes in everlasting love for one person; she concludes love affairs and then carries on the friendship. . . . She tells her grieving girl friends to stop pretending they are madly in love and just be friends—very simple, good advice,"
>
> Marriage for Steinem is a dubiety, "I may get married some day, but not in the conventional sense I used to think of it," she said last week. "Marriage makes you legally half a person, and what man wants to live with half a person?"

In a review of Greer's work, Les Hiatt points succinctly to the particularity of our view as women as sexually dominated.

> Germaine Greer, like Kate Millett and most other feminists, is a cultural determinist. But the thing that distinguishes *The female eunuch* and gives it a flavour of its own is the explanatory rôle assigned by the author to an alleged suppression of

---

Sexuality has never seemed to us to define a destiny, to furnish in itself the key to human behaviour, but to *express* the totality of a situation that it only helps to define. The battle of the sexes is not implicit in the anatomy of man and woman. The truth is that when one evokes it, one takes for granted that in the timeless realm of Ideas a battle is being waged between those vague essences the Eternal Feminine and the Eternal Masculine. (de Beauvoir 1972: 726, emphasis mine)

To emancipate woman is to refuse to confine her to the relations she bears to man, not to deny them to her; let her have her independent existence and she will continue none the less to exist for him *also*: mutually recognizing each other as subject, each will yet remain for the other an *other*. (de Beauvoir 1972: 740, original emphasis)

female sexuality, Greer maintains that the socialization of females aims to neutral-ize their sexual energy, thus rendering them submissive and pliant. In so far as it succeeds, the process eliminates the woman as a competitor for male goals and leaves her no alternative but to accept the rôles of mother and passive wife. The bitterness engendered in women by this outcome makes family life a scene of con-stant bickering, resentment, and misery. To make matters worse, the ideology of male dominance rules out the possibility of an equalitarian sexual relationship. So things are bad for women at work, at home, and in bed. If they wish to free them-selves from the domination of men and compete on equal terms, women must first regain their sexual energy. All other measures are palliatives or compromises. . . .

As is widely known, Freud postulated a causal connection between sexual suppression and cultural achievement through the mediation of sublimated libi-do. On this view, presumably, the particularly heavy suppression of female libido might have to be seen as a sufficient condition for outstanding success, rather than as a cause of chronic failure. Greer argues, however, that whereas male sexu-al energy is diverted outwards in the form of aggressiveness and competitiveness, female energy is turned inward upon the self, because women are deprived of scope and contacts with external reality upon which to exercise themselves.

Supposing we could reverse the internalization, would Greer favour continuing the suppression of female sexuality so that women could become outwardly as aggressive and competitive as men? One way out of this dilemma would be to abandon the Freudian energy model. The notions that human en-ergy is fundamentally sexual and that aggression is transmuted sexuality seem dubious. . . . In essence, sex requires co-operation, aggression signifies opposition.

It seems to me that there is a much less devious way than Greer's of ex-plaining why women are underdogs: their dominance strivings are suppressed. Their sexuality is also held down, which is sad but not especially relevant to the question why they have an uphill battle to do as well as men in non-sexual arenas. Looking at the matter as an anthropologist, I would guess that in most cultures the special target of suppression in females is not their sexuality but their aggres-sivity. I could certainly name numerous societies where female sexuality is nur-tured and relished but where women are nevertheless expected to be subordinate to men in all important decision-making. (L. R. Hiatt 1971: 66–70 passim)

In this chapter I have made two apparently contradictory assertions; one, that sexuality has traditionally been a prominent symbol in the representation of male-female relations in Europe; two, that changes in European notion of "the

person" and "the human being" have produced the twentieth-century stereotypes of the oppressed female sex-object and the liberated-female sex-subject.
In a way both propositions are true. Sexuality has been a prominent symbol but
what it stands for has undergone change. One such shift has been from coitus as
a symbol of mutual commitment to a symbol of domination/submission.

Voiced concern with male-female dominance became widespread in the latter part of the nineteenth century. The chief locus of male domination was seen
to reside in those legal and constitutional arrangements which made it impossible for women to act as "free individuals." The disabilities suffered by married
women in particular were very real, and the attack on men treating women as
chattels and slaves centered on attempts to remove the legal provisions which put
a wife completely into the hands of her husband. One aspect of this was agitation
for reform of women's property rights. In a context like this, with blatant legal
inequalities between husband and wife well in the foreground, sexuality ("true
love") could be a gentler symbol[25]: in *The woman in white*, the love Walter had for
Laura was a guarantee that he would cherish her person. It could also be an indication of the possible mutuality which partners could find in one another, and
to which they should be true despite the social pressures of marriage as an institution.[26] It stood for that fundamental equality which was held to exist among

---

25. I am not claiming that this was the only symbolic role of sex. It was also extremely
    important in the nineteenth century for the contrast between passion and reason,
    which had a central place in the way people judged the public and private behavior
    of themselves and others. (Sexual restraint = "reason" controlling the lower
    "primitive" instincts.) It is interesting in this regard to find a separation of female
    sexual roles similar to that of the urban Hausa, between housewife and prostitute.
    It was perhaps the association of sexual control (rationality) not just with conjugal
    partnership but with public demeanor which meant that prostitution had, by
    definition, to belong underground. There was a strong association between molding
    oneself (one's own passions) and molding the world. Marital chastity was perhaps
    an extremely powerful representation of the colonial/reformist drive.

26. Mill writes of the "natural attraction between opposite sexes." He was concerned
    mainly with pointing out the legal injustices under which women labored in the
    1860s but he also spoke of sexual submission: "However brutal a tyrant [a wife]
    may unfortunately be chained to . . . [the husband] can claim from her and enforce
    the lowest degradation of a human being, that of being made the instrument of
    an animal function contrary to her inclinations" (Mill in Rossi 1970: 160). He
    identifies their legal insecurity as the main cause for distress rather than the sex act
    itself; for women had few legal sanctions they could bring to bear on their husbands
    and few means of serving a relationship with a hated spouse. It was the social and
    political power of the husband which was Mill's main target.

all human beings, and of which reform of the marriage laws among others would allow expression. Many novels of the time dealt with the question of formal marriage and free love, and the kind of equality spouses could find in one another.

With the partial amelioration of the status of married women, new problems emerge. Gissing's work depicts not so much the subjection of women through unequal status in marriage as the enslavement of both spouses to domesticity, a dull, inhibiting interaction which will wear away the freedom and independence of perhaps one or perhaps both partners. Men's need for dominance is seen as a direct challenge to either party being able to enter a union on an equal footing. Sex itself, however, it not the instrument of domination. It becomes, at least in *The odd women*, a symbol of free commitment. If the partners can show that their love is commensurate, then at least a declaration of basic equality has been made. But were one to remove domesticity as an inevitable consequence of union, the focus must shift onto the sexual component of the relationship. The problem of male domination is still there: now it must reside in the very fact that commitment itself challenges the freedom of the individual. Conventions can be circumvented but one cannot circumvent the tyranny of a relationship. Lyndall, in *The story of an African farm*, recognizes her attachment to her lover as diminishing her status as a person.

In each of the three novels from which I have quoted, the contemplated union (Miss Fairlie and Glyde; then Rhoda, and Everard; and finally Lyndall and her unnamed lover) leads to questions about what it will mean for the woman as an individual. Sexuality has a different role in each case. The differences are related to what is identified as the chief locus of female oppression: property rights, domesticity, the very fact of relationship. Concomitant with these shifts is a denigration of dependency. When dependency was equated with the childlike status which married women endured, the attainment of legal adulthood and personal equality resulted in independence. Independence of sexual partners and not their mutual need becomes the dilemma in which Lyndall found herself.[27] In the anatomical idioms of our day, the sex act itself, rather than the

---

27. See de Beauvoir: "Even in mutual love there is a fundamental difference in the feeling of the lovers, which the woman tries to hide. The man must certainly be capable of justifying himself without her, since she hopes to be justified through him. If he is necessary to her, it means that she is evading her liberty; but if he accepts his liberty, without which he would neither be a hero nor even a man, no person or thing can be necessary to him. The dependence accepted by woman comes from her weakness; how, therefore, could she find a reciprocal dependence in the man she loves in his strength?

love or passion surrounding it, has become the focus of attention. Where oppression is still identified, it represents male domination; where independence
is sought, it represents the exclusive claims of each partner. Equality of endowment ("Women are not really castrated men but sexual beings in their own
right") and of the aims of intercourse ("Both partners have a right to reach
climax") is the new symbol of emancipation. In putting much emphasis on apparently natural functions, on the "scientific realities" of the act, the problem of
what one does with relationships can be shelved.[28]

Although I have cast this discussion of sex as a symbol of male-female relations into a quasi-historical mode, chronology is not necessary to my argument.
At any one time people may perceive the question of dominance in relations between men and women in different ways. Legal disabilities and the constraints
of domesticity are still with us. One may also expect that particular individuals,
according to their viewpoints, will put their own symbolic values on sexuality. Varying ideas and symbols can coexist. This is demonstrated when people
deploy systems of ideas as the starting point for politicization. On some issues
there is unity; on others, division. The simple conclusion is that Europeans regard sexuality as bound up with the domination of males over females, and the
particular ways in which the symbol of sex is and has been used can be related
to ideas about the "person" or "human being."

Sexual relations have not been our only model for male-female relationships. Adult-child and worker-housewife have been noted. Nor is sex as a symbol restricted to depicting interaction between men and women. Schneider has
argued that (for Americans) sexual intercourse is a central symbol of kinship.
His account is worth quoting at length.

> A married couple without children does not quite make a family. Neither do a
> married woman and her children without a husband nor a married man and his
> children without a wife. . . . And of course one may say of an older couple, "Their
> family has all grown up and is married; each has a family of his own now."
>
> This last example makes clear another condition which is part of the defi-
> nition of the family in American kinship. The family, to be a family, must live

---

"It is a different matter if the woman has found her independence in marriage;
then love between husband and wife can be a free exchange by two beings who are
each self-sufficient" (1972: 670–71).

28. A problem explored minutely in Doris Lessing's writings.

together. So for parents whose children are grown up and married, the saying is that those children "have families of their own," implying that one's family is where one lives and that it is not possible to be a member of two families (in this sense) at one time. . . . The family is a unit which lives together; if it does not, it is not a family in this particular meaning of the term. . . .

The state of a family's well-being is described in terms of living together, too. If husband and wife have been having marital difficulties, the critical question may be whether or not they are still living together. If they are, the outlook may not be considered so grave as if they are no longer living together. Living together can also be used as a euphemism for sexual intercourse, for it implies an intimacy between a man and woman that precludes any other interpretation.

Informants describe the family as consisting of husband, wife, and their children who live together as a natural unit. The family is formed according to the laws of nature and it lives by rules which are regarded by Americans as self-evidently natural. . . . The family, in American kinship, is defined as a natural unit based on the facts of nature. In American culture, this means that only certain of the facts of nature are selected, that they are altered, and that they are built upon or added to. This selection, alteration, and addition all come about through the application of human reason to the state of nature.

The fact of nature on which the cultural construct of the family is based is . . . that of sexual intercourse. This figure provides all of the central symbols of American kinship. . . . There are two kinds of love in American kinship, which, although not explicitly named, are clearly defined and distinguished. One I will call *conjugal* love. It is erotic, having the sexual act as its concrete embodiment. This is the relationship between husband and wife. The other kind of love I will call *cognatic*. The blood relationship, the identity of natural substance and heredity which obtains for parent and child is its symbolic expression. . . .

The conjugal love of husband and wife is the opposite of the cognatic love of parent, child, and sibling. One is the union of opposites, the other is the unity which identities have, the sharing of biogenetic substance. The mother's identity with her child is further reiterated by the fact that the child is born of her body and that it is nurtured and nourished there before it is born, as well as being nourished from it after the child is born. This restates again and again that the two are of a common substance.

It is the symbol of love which links conjugal and cognatic love together and relates them both to and through the symbol of sexual intercourse. Love in the sense of sexual intercourse is a natural act with natural consequences according to its cultural definition. And love in the sense of sexual intercourse at the same time stands for unity. . . . Both love and sexual intercourse turn on two distinct elements. One is the unification of opposites. The other is the separation of unities.

Male and female, the opposites, are united in sexual intercourse as husband and wife. Their different biogenetic substances are united in the child conceived of that union and their relationship to each other is reaffirmed not only as husband and wife to each other, but as parents of their child, father and mother to the same offspring.

But what was one must become two. The child is born of its parents and is separated from them physically through its birth. It is this which differentiates parent from child, father and mother from son and daughter. The separation which begins with the act of birth continues until the child grows up and leaves its family to marry and found its own family. . . .

Sexual intercourse also is, and stands for love. The definitions of American culture state that love is spiritual and enduring and is not aimed at specific narrow material ends. Love is a relation between persons, not between things. It means unity, not difference, It means who you are, not how well you perform. It means trust, faith, affection, support, loyalty, help when it is needed, and the kind of help that is needed. . . . One can speak of the family as "the loved ones." Love can be translated freely as *enduring diffuse solidarity*. The end to which family relations are conducted is the well-being of the family as a whole and of each of its members.

Yet certain specific acts which are part of the cluster of symbols that define kinship and family also have the value of signs for other symbols of that defining cluster. Sexual intercourse between husband and wife is not only an act which specifically defines the conjugal relationship, but it is also an act which is a sign of love. . . . The members of the family are defined in terms of sexual intercourse as a reproductive act, stressing the sexual relationship between husband and wife and the biological identity between parent and child, and between siblings. . . .

The child does not live without the milk of human kindness, both as nourishment and as protection. Nor does the child come into being except by the fertilized egg which, except for those rare cases of artificial insemination, is the outcome of sexual intercourse. These are biological facts. They are facts of life and facts of nature.

There is also a system of constructs in American culture about those biological facts. That system exists in an adjusted and adjustable relationship with the biological facts.

But these same cultural constructs which depict these biological facts have another quality. They have as one of their aspects a symbolic quality, which means that they represent something other than what they are, over and above and in addition to their existence as biological facts. . . . What, then, do the cultural constructs depicting the facts of sexual intercourse symbolize?

They symbolize diffuse, enduring solidarity. They symbolize those kinds of interpersonal relations which human beings as biological beings *must* have if they are to be born and grow up. They symbolize trust, but a special kind of trust which is not contingent and which does not depend on reciprocity. They stand for the fact that birth survives death, and that solidarity *is* enduring. And they stand for the fact that man can create, by his own act and as an act of will, and is not simply an object of nature's mindless mercy.

In just the same way that reproduction is a set of biological facts that is prerequisite to the continuity of a society as a body of people, so too, diffuse, enduring solidarity is a social and psychobiological prerequisite to the continuity of both the society and its culture.

But how can this be expressed? How can it be said? . . . What better model than sexual intercourse and its attendant psychobiological elements? These biological facts are transformed by the attribution of meaning into cultural constructs and they then constitute a model for *commitment*, for the passionate attachment which is one side of trust, and for the unreasoning and unreasonable set of conditions which alone make "solidarity" really solidary, and make it both enduring and diffuse. (Schneider 1968: 33–52, 116–17 passim, original emphasis)

Schneider takes sexual intercourse as ultimately providing a model for commitment. This is one of the uses to which I have argued it has been put in respect of male-female relations. But there it may also stand for the opposite: for exploitation, not solidarity; for independence, not mutuality. Males dominate women through sex; sex between two persons may be incompatible with an enduring relationship. Thus, not only can sexuality symbolize different relationships (kinship, male-female), it can symbolize contrary ideas (commitment, oppression).

There is more here than vagaries in conjugal arrangements. Over the last hundred years, a very explicit equation has been made between female bondage and (first) woman's deprived marital status, and (then) her mutilated sexuality. And more than this: sex is an extremely powerful source of symbolism. It arouses emotions. And it is so powerful that it can symbolize quite contrary notions and still lend weight to each. Part of its power must lie, as Schneider has pointed out, in its relationship to nature and, in this thinking, in the place of mating in the biological programming of male-female bonding. A further source of power comes from the energy released by the feedback effect of deploying relations between the sexes as symbols for other things.

Sexuality itself may symbolize areas of social life which are not directly or only about men and women. Schneider has given us the example of kinship. Sexual liberation can also be a symbol of human liberation.

Revolution must relate to both the means and nature of [any] breakthrough. There must be the acceleration of collective demystification accompanied by the conscious dismantling of the external framework, there must be the connection with the experience of the other oppressed groups, there must be a political alternative, a way out which relates to all the groups. Object-consciousness cannot be shattered by individual rationality, it cannot be simply eliminated by external change. . . . It demands social revolution and it demands it whole. It demands release from the inner and the outer bondages. It is not to be fobbed off with an either/or. Which brings us all back again to marxism and the whole people question.

Well here we all are then—millions of us—our situation demanding a fundamental redistribution of wealth, a profound social transformation in the ways people relate to each other and an end to alienation. Communism is the necessary condition of our freedom. A communist society means having babies in a state of social freedom. It means you don't starve when you're helpless to fend for yourself or have to be a dependent. It means the possibility of such communication that human beings share the pains of labour and the ecstasy of creation. Real comradeship involves the end of subjugation and domination, the explosion of sado-masochism and the climax of love. . . .

The woman question is not comprehensible except in terms of the total process of a complete series of repressive structures. Thus the particular form of domination changes but the process operates in both pre-capitalist and post-capitalist society. The function of revolutionary theory is to keep track of this moving shape of these subordinations. . . .

The revolutionary struggle is thus extended and sustained in a multi-structural, multi-dimensional way. As well as the macro-theory, which is about systems at war, about a mass movement for political power, marxism has to explore the way human beings relate to one another. This means noticing all the little unimportant things which revolutionary theory tends to regard as not worthy of attention. Like how we live with one another and how we feel and regard each other, how we communicate with each other. We are contained within the inner and the outer bondages and unless we create a revolutionary theory of the microcosm as well as the macrocosm we shall be incapable of preventing our personal practice becoming unconnected to our economic and institutional transformation. We will consequently continually lose ourselves in the new structures we have created. . . . It also means some forms of action will be directed specifically towards transforming people's perception and comprehension of themselves and the world as well as being concerned with material change. The so-called women's question is thus a whole people question, not only because our liberation is inextricably bound up with the revolt of all those who are oppressed, but because their liberation is not realisable fully unless our subordination is ended. (Rowbotham 1971: 28–30 passim)

The abolition of sexual discrimination is a necessary condition for the full realization of human potential. Sheila Rowbotham is talking about the realities of existing bondage, about the solution to oppression in social life. Men and women are interest-groups in this process, as are other categories of people. She is using symbols as well. No human being can be liberated until women are liberated; real comradeship involves the climax of love.

CHAPTER SEVEN

Sex and the Social Order

One of the guises under which sexuality appears is love. Love can mean much more but it can also be used as a direct marker of a sexual relationship. An interesting illustration of this is the way the notion of romantic or courtly "love" developed in Medieval Europe. It is first found in poems and songs ("romances") which appeared with some suddenness at the end of the eleventh century in the Provence region of France and spread over much of Europe. This Love takes the form of a passion which attaches a man to a woman in a singular way. The man sees himself in service to the woman and this service dominates his code of conduct, whether in the end he receives reward from her hands or not. The object of his love is elevated, elusive; the male lover must prove himself worthy of the passion he would have the female bestow upon him.

Many scholars still profess themselves at a loss to explain why these ideas should have emerged at this time.[1] For they do present a "problem" to be accounted for insofar as such an image of male-female relations runs counter to all else that is known about men and women of that period. Commentators have wondered just what historical event or atmosphere could have inspired this novel expression, this new kind of a relationship between the sexes.

---

1. For example, "The origin of these extraordinary ideas is not known" (Stone 1964). Much of the factual evidence on which I base my subsequent comments is derived from C. S. Lewis' *The allegory of love* (1936), although I do not give specific references in the text.

Perhaps part of the answer lies in what is so self-evident. The contrast between women's status "in real life" including what is known of life at court, which is the chief setting of these romances, and the representation of women as objects of unselfish love does not have to be explained away if we admit that there was indeed a disjunction. Once that has been done, the door is open for a quite different interpretation. We do not have to relate the love-lyrics' image of male-female relations simply to its real life counterpart because that is not what they were primarily about. It is more plausible to argue that they were also about something else. The love these songs celebrated, therefore, did not necessarily correspond to new feelings and changes in the relationship between the sexes. I shall suggest that it was not relations between men and women that were their principal focus but relations between men.

THE RELEVANCE OF LOVE: BODY AND SPIRIT

First I must declare naivety. The following interpretations are based on what can only be a cursory reading—not just because I am ethnographically unfamiliar with the Middle Ages but because I do not have a historian's equipment. These remarks will be exploratory in every sense; they are intended to indicate a particular perspective, and nothing more.

The argument is roughly this. If we treat medieval literature as a kind of commentary on life and society, we ought to be alert to certain ways of representing things. If our interest is male-female relations, we should by now be well on our guard and able to separate out quite different kinds of treatment in the poems or songs or doctrines which attempt to talk about men and women. We may expect to find some or all of the following:

1.) works which deal directly with contemporary social or personal aspects of relations between men and women;
2.) works which reinforce or devise stereotypes about the natures of the sexes;
3.) works which use these stereotypes as symbols to represent values or attitudes in social life not directly to do with male-female relations at all.

These elements do not have to be mutually exclusive; there may be various combinations in any one piece of writing.

Literature of the first category is to be found in treatises written for the edification of wives or daughters, which expound the rules of proper conduct and consist basically of advice (from men) on how women should comport themselves. Poems which would also fall into this category, of a somewhat later date (fourteenth and fifteenth centuries), are to be found among those works of such writers as Chaucer or Dunbar which deal directly with the question of domination. Chaucer's *Wife of Bath* recounts a tale in which a knight is sent out to find the answer to the question: what is it that women most desire? The answer is unambiguous: a woman wants power, over both her husband and her lover. Dunbar's Scottish poem, "The treatise of the two married women and the widow," depicts three ladies who describe their marital histories to one another. They desire not reform in the male-female relationship but a reversal of formal dominance. "They wish to have the mastery in the fullest sense, to rule the male sex, to use them for their own ends, discard them when they are no longer of any use, and if possible to humiliate them as well in order to demonstrate the omnipotence of female power" (Hope 1970: 200).[2] The inversion of the formally acknowledged ideal, man's mastery over woman, is no doubt a sardonic comment on men's rather than women's position. But I think it would be legitimate to take it as a critique of male-female relations per se. There were many situations in which women of the time enjoyed considerable independence—for example, in the management of estates, in access to trades and occupations, in the ownership of property and in being able to plead and sue in court—and the degree to which expressions of this independence were compatible with or derived from the status of a wife was an aspect of male-female interaction. The question of authority in the marital relationship is described with much realism and had at least some bearing, we might surmise, on real conflicts. Aspects of the nineteenth-century novels considered in the last chapter were concerned with contemporary legal and social problems between husbands and wives (though this was not all they were about). In medieval writing, too, we find direct attention sometimes paid to the ambiguities and ambitions arising from the inequalities of everyday life. The prominent theme is not downfall and redemption, or service and reward, but power.

Questions about conjugal domination may also be related to the second category of works, those dealing with stereotypes. The definition of the husband as master and head was a stereotype, derived both from legal and economic

---

2. Hope also gives Chaucer's example, cited above.

circumstances and from church doctrine as well. Dunbar's ladies are deriding a stereotype when they seek male-like omnipotence. "Women were to be kept in their place and that place was an inferior one as custom, church and law all agreed," writes Alec Hope (1970: 199); yet in fact, in the words of an envoy to the court of James IV, the women of Scotland at least were "absolute mistresses of their houses, and even of their husbands, in all things concerning the administration of their property, income as well as expenditure" (201). It is male pretensions to dominance, supposedly upheld by the natural order and the will of God, which Dunbar's ladies bitingly deride in their conjugal autobiographies:

> Afterwards I married a merchant, well-provided with goods. / He was a middle-aged man and of low stature. / But we were not a match either in kinship or class / . . . I kept it always fresh in his mind that I took him only as an act of grace / and so that he should realise his position I courteously taught him. / He dared not sit down unless I told him to, for he was always ready to run / before I repeated an order, so terrified was he of my reproach. / But my will was always being worsted by my womanly nature; / the more he abased himself for my love the less I thought of him. / . . . He was a man with much money and rich in goods / [so] I let him be my broker to discharge all my business / and he was glad to accept that fine position from me / and expected to win my favours by his frequent gifts. / He clothed me in gay silk and choice raiment / . . . But I very cunningly put aside that courtly clothing / until the death of that drone who was useless in the bedchamber. / . . . I banished from my bounds all his brothers / and his relations I always held in hatred as my enemies, / by which you may believe I had no love for the man himself, / for I never liked any person who belonged to his blood. / And yet there are wise men who believe all women / are known to be bad managers and can be recognised by this. (Hope 1970: 287–91 passim; translation of part of Dunbar's poem, "The treatise of the two married women and the widow")

The object of attack is those male stereotypes which make of husbands dominant, aggressive, masterful, and omnipotent managers of their wives.

We may also hear in the clash between husband and wife an echo of a larger struggle between male and female. Much medieval writing is concerned with the identification of women and sin.

> The conviction rapidly . . . became entrenched in the early Church, that coitus is not only in some sense unclean and defiling, but also intrinsically evil or sinful. . . .

Closely connected with . . . this negative view of the venereal was the sexual asceticism which has always controlled and dominated the Church's conception of sanctity, the good life, and the pursuit of perfection. . . . It encouraged a dualistic idea of human nature in which the body was opposed to the mind or soul, and sexuality was associated with the "flesh" as something carnal which must be subjugated to the rule of the spirit. . . .

Although the Church proclaimed the spiritual equality of the sexes, it nevertheless perpetuated the Aristotelian view that the male is the norm of humanity and the female a deviation therefrom. . . .

Woman's utility (in the venereal sense) was conceived as of two kinds. She was useful to man in the work of generation in which, as the "seed-producer," he was regarded as playing the principal role . . . and she was useful as a "remedy". . . whereby his imperious venereal impulses could be directed creatively, or at least expended harmlessly. . . .

Not only was woman to be used, however, she was also to be feared, for in her (it was thought) sex and sin were peculiarly associated. Primitive Christian teaching endorsed the Jewish belief that she was the original transgressor, and the author of all human ills [including death]. . . . Certain misogynists among the Fathers not only assigned to every woman individually a share in the guilt for Eve's fall, but actually regarded each member of the feminine sex as herself in some sense another Eve—a temptress by nature, always seeking to ensnare man by her wiles and to destroy them. (Bailey 1959: 233–36)

Augustine . . . distrusts the sexual relationship, even within marriage, as the most obvious symbol of fallen Man's inability to control passion by reason, though he was ready to allow the unedifying activity as indispensable for the procreation of children.[3] The argument that women were to be reprehended because their ancestress Eve had been the direct cause of the Fall of Man was frequently used. . . . This concept of woman as the great seductress crops up again and again, in varying degrees of hysteria, throughout much of medieval literature, though it was sometimes trumped by St Augustine's reminder that the Incarnation also had occurred through a feminine medium. . . . St Paul's conception of

---

3.   De Beauvoir (1972: 199) quotes St. Thomas' dictum that original sin is afresh transmitted to each newborn because he is the outcome of a sexual union. She recounts some of the obscenities through which the church fathers gave voice to their horror of the female body.

the male-female relationship as an analogy of the relationship between Christ and the Church . . . certainly dignified woman's position, [but] still it left her in a subordinate status. . . .

A permanent sexual relationship with its usual sequel of domestic responsibilities was incompatible with a life of devotion to philosophical or theological study because of its absorption of time and diversion of attention. (Morrall 1970: 117–18)

Here is an equation of woman with sexuality. All women are Eve: man's first mate. Relations between men and women are depicted as based on that primary relationship which was a sexual (coital) one. Sexuality itself is also evil, as was the first act which brought carnal knowledge into existence. The debate between the thrush and the nightingale (see Chapter Two) directly considered this aspect of woman as sin-bearing, and you will recall that the thrush's argument is based chiefly on female perfidy being identified in sexual encounters (she deceives, betrays, and so on). In short, the images on which is built the equation of woman with sin rest in their turn on an equation of woman with carnal temptation.

These are stereotypes about the nature of females (females are to be guarded against because they are sexual beings). Once this stereotyping has occurred the way is now open for representations of the third category: interaction between men and women can stand for other encounters. In struggling with his own sexual desires which women arouse in him a man witnesses battle between body and soul. The carnal union of husband and wife challenges the spiritual union of soul and God. This is conceivable only because the latter *relationship* is identified as being of the same type as the former; otherwise there would be no challenge.

Sexual intercourse stands for (symbolizes) both man's traffickings with the flesh and his communion with spirit. Encounters with human women may symbolize contest with the devil; devotion to a quasi-human woman (Mary, the mother), redemption. The erotic overtones of poems addressed to Our Lady have often been noted. To some extent the same duality held also for all women. Not that men as such were equated with sin, but indulgence in the demands of the body were contrasted with the delights of service to Christ, the bridegroom, who could save them from themselves. A thirteenth-century Franciscan poem reassures a young girl novice that to have a lover in Christ is to experience a permanent union no earthly relationship could match. For her part she must guard her maidenhood. Unblemished, she will attain paradise. Either Christ or

Mary could be the object of such love-passion. The male-female relationship, then, and specifically in its sexual/erotic aspect, was a central symbol of Christian teaching. It embodied the basic contrast between flesh and spirit, between body and soul, between this world and the other world. Sexual indulgence in this life could mean damnation in the next, whereas asceticism in human relations enabled that other marriage to take place, and a spiritual consummation with divinity.

As one would expect, there was also a feedback process. Sexual union could symbolize both damnation and redemption, and mortal marriages were contrasted with eternal ones. But it was also possible to contrast some types of human sexual unions with others. So it was also possible to see in the sanctified conjugal relationship a reflection of the divine union.

> With Augustine . . . Christian monogamy was pre-eminently sacramental since it exemplified not only "the unity of us all made subject to God, which shall be hereafter in one Heavenly City," but also (and supremely) the mysteries of the Incarnation and of the union between Christ and the Church. . . .
>
> His argument is not that the bond of matrimony is . . . indestructible . . . but that matrimony is declared by St Paul to be a *magnum sacramentum* in which Christ and the Church is signified—therefore the nuptial bond, once it has been established between Christians, ought not to be severed, with the result that the symbol of the supernatural union is destroyed. (Bailey 1959: 93)

It would seem that this interpretation of male-female interaction had an uphill struggle against the weight of the more powerful symbol of human women as inherently sinful.[4]

---

4. To some extent resolved in the spiritual subordination of the female conjugal partner to the male. Derrick Bailey refers to the

> familiar androcentric assumptions of the Christian tradition. . . [especially] the principle to which the Apostle [Paul] appeals when he directs that women must be veiled as a mark of their subordination when they pray or prophesy, that they must keep silence in church, and that they must not teach or in any other way usurp domination over men.
>
> The principle itself is stated quite categorically in the first epistle to the Corinthians: "the head (*kephalē*) of the woman is the man"; he is "the image (*eikon*) and glory (*doxa*) of God," but she is only "the glory of the man," and must "be in subjection" (*hupotassomai*) as the law demands. In the epistles to the Ephesians and the Colossians . . . it is applied specifically to marriage: "the

For more than eight centuries the Church had striven to inculcate a relatively high ideal of marriage as a relationship instituted and blessed by God; yet its defence of the holy estate against the detractions of heretics and cynics, and its teaching on the sacramental and indissoluble character of the marital union were in fact largely vitiated by other factors which could but conduce to an opposite conception of wedlock. . . .

[These included] the exaltation of virginity as the supreme and truly "religious" state of life; the refusal of marriage to the clergy; the continual insinuation or asseveration that coitus is a defilement and a hindrance to the service of God; the emphasis placed upon the remedial function [relief of men's needs] of matrimony, and the neglect of its relational aspects; and the persistence of a comparatively low view of women.

Marriage . . . [became] but a second best, having nothing good in itself, save only in so far as it provide[d] a remedy for a necessary evil. (Bailey 1959: 163–65 passim)

In the same way, closer identification could be made between woman and Eve than woman and Mary. Eve was the incarnation of mortality, nothing but human. Mary was humanity transcended, semidivine. Devotion to a semidivine female did not have to detract from abhorrence of human females.

Nevertheless, some have seen in the adoration of this figure a premonition of the theme of courtly love about which the minstrels or troubadours sang.

Devotion to Our Lady played its not inconsiderable part in exalting the position of women in general. One wing of the troubadour tradition addressed the Virgin Mother in terms borrowed from the more idealized conventions of their ethos. . . . Woman as the protectress and friend of the trusting servitor finds her apotheosis in the Mary of the *Golden Legend* and similar collections; St Bernard's own upbringing as a feudal vassal in the incipient courtly tradition is raised to a heavenly plane in the famous *Memorare* prayer ("none who sought Thy protection was left unaided"). (Morrall 1970: 129)

Leaving aside the question of the "position of women," we can agree with the author that representations of the Virgin Mother in the idioms of courtly love

---

husband is the head (*kephalē*) of the wife, as Christ also is the head (*kephalē*) of the Church." (1959: 293–94)

were indeed a borrowing from one realm to another. But I wonder if this second realm, the troubadour ethos, did not have a momentum of its own derived from a quite different symbolic application of the male-female relationship.

THE RELEVANCE OF LOVE: VASSAL AND LORD

The examples we have just considered fall into the third of the categories noted at the beginning of this chapter: male-female relationships symbolized the religious potential which Christianity offered. It was specifically the sexual component of male-female interaction which was selected as the basic stereotype; and sexual union could, to put it at its most brief, symbolize the choice between temptation and redemption. However perhaps there was another use of male-female relations as a symbol, a use which also belongs to this third category, but which refers to the domain not of religion but of politics.

The tradition of "love" which arose in the late eleventh century was essentially one of courtly love. "Courtly" had two senses here. First, the scene was usually set in the halls of some lord, and the male lover had as the object of his quest a woman of high birth; second, the terms by which love was sworn and service proved followed very specific rules of behavior (courtesy). It has often been noted that put into practice such declarations of love would be adulterous. C. S. Lewis suggests that we are witnessing the emergence of erotic passion, and that since social practices and church doctrine made such passion (and also the elevation of woman above man) incompatible with the conjugal relationship, an adulterous union was the only logical outcome.

> The unattached knight, as we meet him in the romances, respectable only by his own valour, amiable only by his own courtesy, predestined lover of other men's wives, was therefore a reality; but this does not explain why he loved in such a new way. If courtly love necessitates adultery, adultery hardly necessitates courtly love. . . . We must picture a castle which is a little island of comparative leisure and luxury, and therefore at least of possible refinement, in a barbarous countryside. There are many men in it, and a very few women—the lady, and her damsels. Around these throng the . . . inferior nobles, the landless knights, the squires, and the pages—haughty creatures enough in relation to the peasantry beyond the walls, but feudally inferior to the lady as to her lord—her "men" as feudal language had it. Whatever "courtesy" is in the place flows from her: all female

charm from her and her damsels. There is no question of marriage for most of the court. All these circumstances come very near to being a "cause"; but they do not explain why very similar conditions elsewhere had to wait for Provençal example before they produced like results. . . .

Two things prevented the men of that age from connecting their ideal of romantic and passionate love with marriage.

The first is, of course, the actual practice of feudal society. Marriages had nothing to do with love. . . . All matches were matches of interest, and, worse still, of an interest that was continually changing. When the alliance which had answered would answer no longer, the husband's object was to get rid of the lady as quickly as possible. Marriages were frequently dissolved. The . . . woman . . . was often little better than a piece of property to her husband. So far from being a natural channel for the new kind of love, marriage was rather the drab background against which that love stood out in all the contrast of its new tenderness and delicacy. . . . Any idealization of sexual love, in a society where marriage is purely utilitarian, must begin by being an idealization of adultery.

The second factor is the medieval theory of marriage. . . . [P]assionate love itself was wicked, and did not cease to be wicked if the object of it were your wife. . . . The views of medieval churchmen on the sexual act within marriage . . . are all limited by two complementary agreements. On the one hand, nobody ever asserted that the act was intrinsically sinful. On the other hand, all were agreed that some evil element was present in every concrete instance of this act since the Fall . . . For [Gregory] the act is innocent but the desire is morally evil. . . . Peter Lombard . . . located the evil in the desire and said that it was not a moral evil, but a punishment for the Fall. Thus the act, though not free from evil, may be free from moral evil or sin, but only if it is "excused by the good ends of marriage" . . . [and] passionate love of a man's own wife is adultery. Albertus Magnus . . . sweeps away the idea that the pleasure is evil or a result of the Fall. . . . The real trouble about fallen man is not the strength of his pleasures but the weakness of his reason. . . . The desire, as we now know it, is an evil, a punishment for the Fall, but not a sin. The conjugal act may therefore be not only innocent but meritorious, if it has the right causes—desire of offspring, payment of the marriage debt, and the like. But if desire comes first . . . it remains a mortal sin. . . .

It will be seen that the medieval theory finds room for innocent sexuality: what it does not find room for is passion, whether romantic or otherwise. . . .

The general impression left on the medieval mind by its official teachers was that all love—at least all such passionate and exalted devotion as a courtly poet thought worthy of the name—was more or less wicked. And this impression, combining with the nature of feudal marriage as I have already described it, produced in the poets a certain wilfulness, a readiness to emphasize rather than conceal the antagonism between their amatory and their religious ideals. Thus if the Church tells them that the ardent lover even of his own wife is in mortal sin, they presently reply with the rule that true love is impossible in marriage. If the Church says that the sexual act can be "excused" only by the desire for offspring, then it becomes the mark of the true lover . . . that he served Venus. . . . This cleavage between Church and court . . . is the most striking feature of medieval sentiment. (Lewis 1936: 12–18 passim)

Yet how did a notion of romantic love develop, and how, once given expression, did it become so popular?—for popular it was throughout Europe in the following centuries. Lewis puts his finger on it when he identifies passion. Nevertheless, it seems to me arguable that the poems and songs could only have become popular with such rapidity if they touched on emotions already in existence. Rather than molding new feelings, it is more likely they were giving fresh form to old ones. The question of why a new form should have arisen is still there: but once given expression, there is more explanatory power in supposing that it fed existing sentiments than in postulating an emotional revolution. The problem of explaining why the new idiom spread dissolves if the emotions can be shown to be already widespread.[5] And what could have been these emotions?

Abandoning the idea that the troubadours' love poems were to do in the first place with relations between men and women allows us to look with greater clarity at their most obvious themes. These are the themes of service and reward, of loyalty, allegiance, the durability of trust, the honoring of devotion, the choice and ambiguity of attachment. Such notions could indeed have been at the root of passion, could have been for many a source of emotional conflict. And what aroused them? We do not have to look much further than one of the most basic facts of social structure: the feudal tie. The tie itself was undergoing change, and possibly the emergence of the new idiom had something to do with this. For our own purpose we can see the aptness of representing the tie between lord and vassal as one between lady and lover. The woman is imagined as hard to win, now hot, now cold, now indulgent, now inaccessible. Reward may or may not

5.   That the idioms themselves subsequently gave some shape to male-female relations is another issue.

be forthcoming; service may be rendered to avail or to no avail. Here is a depiction of ambiguities indeed—like those which arise from the feudal relationship with its uneasy compromise between sworn fealty and the contract which can be broken, between service forced upon the inferior because of his position and dependence on the generosity of his overlord. The center of this stage is not a new kind of relationship between men and women but contemporary emotions stemming from feudal contracts. The love poems are about homage and the individual's commitment. The rewards and perils of loyalty are pictured in the knight's enthrallment to a lady. Is it not primarily relations between men, primarily political emotions, which the troubadours are celebrating?

One historian treats chivalry itself as a grand illusion: "In order to forget the painful imperfection of reality, the nobles turn to the continual illusion of a high and heroic life. They wear the mask of Lancelot and of Tristam. It is an amazing self-deception. . . . [For] in the very matter-of-fact considerations on which a match between noble families was based there was little room for the chivalrous fictions of prowess and of service. Thus it came about that the courtly notions of love were never corrected by contact with real life. . . . The ideal of love, such as it was, could not be lived up to, except in a fashion inherently false" (Huizinga [1924] 1955: 80, 128). But the point I am making is not this one. In saying that the romances are not "really" talking about male-female relations per se, I do not mean to imply that they are nothing but an illusion, or that they feed nothing but delusions of grandeur. In an oblique way they deal with important, tough, and extremely realistic issues.

That aspect of the feudal bond which was most charged with emotion was the relationship between fighting men. The subordinate paid homage to his superior: he knelt before him, placed his hands in the hands of his overlord, and said, "I am your man." The vassal had to be personally loyal and obedient to his master; and would be obliged to provide military assistance and attend his lord's court. In return he was given land and retainers, on whom he could call when he was required to give military aid to his overlord. He also received status and prestige from his attachment. In the chronicles, vassals may be depicted as consumed with passion in defense of their master. "Gentle King of St. Denis, rage possesses me in my body / I am your liege-man through faith and through homage / Ready am I to go fighting!"[6]

---

6. Quoted in Brandt (1966). Both this and Morrall (1970) provide information for this section.

The nature of the contract between lord and vassal underwent constant change through time. In the eleventh century it became possible to commute military aid (provision of arms, horses, and men) to a cash payment. The vassal was also required to pay four standard "taxes": to contribute to his lord's ransom, to money his lord needed both when his eldest son was knighted and his eldest daughter married, and toward buying land. By the end of the century, which was when the troubadours' poems of courtly love first assumed popularity, the feudal aristocracy was becoming more exclusive, laying more emphasis on birthright than on the achievement of title through deed. Ceremonies of feudal initiation also became more elaborate, and the blessing of the knight's sword took on the character of a religious rite.[7]

A vassal could set himself up as a lord over others, receiving homage from his inferiors as he paid homage to his own superior. It was possible, in fact, for an individual to pay liege-homage to more than one person, and there were rules to decide which lord had the overriding claims in situations of doubt. Tenant peasants could have more then one master. Moreover, loyalty was in part dependent on reward. Thus, a knight was obliged to be loyal to his feudal superior only so long as he received protection in turn. But even if he was formally protected, there was also the question of wealth. For the victors battle was profit: it meant ransom and booty. Soldiers sought battle. A squire could capture a prisoner, demand ransom, and on receiving this wealth aspire to setting himself up. Knights could be created before battle, to make them fight the harder to earn the reward (booty, ransom) which victory would bring. The knight who distinguished himself might be given a wardship, an heiress, or land, and in turn he would reward his own supporters. But the likelihood of victory also depended on wealth; the largesse, the generosity with which superiors treated their inferiors, had an influence on the loyalty a lord could command. He also had to keep up a certain style of life. Failure to maintain the standard of living appropriate to one's status, and thus to meet obligations to one's own overlord, brought dishonor. Moreover, knights who committed themselves to battle gambled with loss: they could be ruined by the devastation of their land and disgraced by impoverishment. Sums would have to be paid out in ransom, by themselves and by their supporters.

---

7.   The relationship of the knight to Christ was also seen as a quasi-feudal one; and the knight's code of chivalry included defense of the church. If the love poems are related to religions zeal at all, this is a possible area for the genesis of such a relationship.

At every point is discernible the critical factor of choice. Who should be served and who should be rewarded? When should battle be done and when should one desist? To whose ransom should one contribute? The historical chronicles dwell in detail on the shufflings of loyalties, the challenges, the invitations, the constant reassessment of allegiance, and the swearing of fresh fealty. Froissart wrote his famous account in the fourteenth century, but perhaps his minute narrative of petty battles, of conquests and defeats, also retains some echo of political realities which existed earlier. It is full of stories of castles taken and re-taken, towns loyal now to one side now to the other, of rescues and captures. An explicit aim of chronicles of this kind was to apportion fame. But they also give insight into what these constant changes of fortune must have meant. Each capture and rescue, each submission and resistance, served to define loyalty. Loyalty to a particular overlord, whether from an individual, or a whole town, or a province, was under constant review. To condense one of Froissart's narratives: a certain place was taken by a knight on behalf of the Duke of Brittany to whom he owed fealty / to make his possession stronger the Duke went to the King of England and promised to hold the duchy for the King, if he would protect him from the French / the King promised to protect the Duke as a liege-man. One battle set in train a whole process of re-alignments.

Added to the realities of constantly shifting political alliances was the essential ambiguity of loyalty itself. This depended both on the outcome of wars, on victory and defeat, and on the internal relationship between lord and vassal. A switch of loyalty could be the result of a battle; it could also come from a lord's failure to honor service given him, by withholding reward, or failure to meet the obligations of an ally, by not being able to send supporting armies when they were needed. Are there hints, too, of a further ambiguity? If the aristocracy was becoming more entrenched, if entry into the ranks of the great barons was becoming a matter of birth, did this not also alter the basis of the contract between lord and vassal? A contract is a true contract if both sides can break it equally easily. But if the allegiance due to an overlord is demanded as a right, by a superior from an inferior, this calls into question the whole relationship between loyalty and reward. Loyalty was given in the first place for reward (reciprocal protection, advancement, wealth); but it was also now being given because a lord was born a lord and the vassal succeeded to his father's holding. Loyalty might be demanded whatever the quality of reward.[8]

8. Reciprocally, the hereditary expectations of vassals' families must have modified the lord's power to invest an inferior with land as a direct return for obedience and

Commentators have suggested that the ethos of courtly love attempted to elevate women to honorific status, so that ladies of the court would inspire the efforts of knights. Lewis suggests that there were a number of unattached, land-less knights in Provence, without a place in the territorial hierarchy, and devotion to these ladies was one form their loyalty could take. But it has also been pointed out that the world of the poems, the romances, where knights seek to be worthy of the lady's love and direct their exploits to this end, is very different from the world of the chronicles, where there is almost no reference to female inspiration for exploits otherwise described so vividly. One even has to search in Froissart for mention of ladies' favors influencing tournaments. If the romances do have a bearing on the real world, it probably has little to do with events of this nature, and more to do with conflicting emotions and values contained in the feudal relationship itself.

By the code of chivalry the knight was required to show "courtesy" to his equals, to his enemies, and to women. But the woman who is represented as the sought-after object in the romances was not just in turn courteous and demure; she was also merciless. The knight might labor for her love, yet in the end give all and receive nothing in return from her hands but the ennoblement which devotion to her service conferred upon him. If a fundamental problem which the romances treat is the nature of the relationship between service and reward, this was a source for real ambiguities in political life for men at this period, ones related to values which were supposed to engage passion.

Look at the languages of these poems. Lewis' (1936) analysis shows how closely the service of love is modeled on the service of feudal vassal to overlord. My own contention has been, of course, that the "service of love" is *about* the feudal bond. We are observing not the feudalizing of love but rather a love re-lationship between man and woman being used as a symbol for those powerful emotions contained within and enjoined by the feudal bond among men, the eroticizing of feudalism, if you like. In the ethos of courtly love, the lover is the lady's "man." He may address her as "my lord." The premise of their relationship is the courtly style of life: only the courteous can love, and it is love which makes them courteous. The lovers exchange vows on the pattern of the feudal oath, and the lover does homage to his mistress; he is abject, obedient to the lady's slightest wish. He puts faith in the God of Love who can subjugate the cruelest beauties.

---

service (although in theory a vassal's heir still had to renew the holder's contract with the overlord as though on a person to person basis).

His passion is a noble emotion. Love for the lady itself confers nobility (as attachment to an overlord or a sovereign brings prestige). It is not necessary for the man himself to be of noble birth, for grace is bestowed upon him through his service to love by the fact of attachment itself. As from superior to inferior, the lady may show largesse (generosity). Mercy might be another of her qualities, as a vassal would hope for his lord's mercy in judgment on his actions. The revelation of these qualities is also counterpointed by their absence. Thus the lady may be envisaged as inaccessible, merciless. She might yield or withdraw; although once having yielded must be constant to her lover. That the bestowal of favors was a central issue is shown in the belief that "in the after-life of courtly lovers . . . women who had given their favours wisely were the elect; next below them were those who had given their love to all; and lowest were those who had refused all wooers, and who spent eternity sitting on agitated thorns" (Stone 1964: 21). But as we shall see, this particular view point underwent change.

The lady is invariably married to another; what of the husband? In consideration of his position, John Morall (1970) suggests another type of symbolism. He points to the tension which emerged in the feudal system after 1100. The minor vassals and landless knights were demanding a greater share of the establishment than the bigger barons were prepared to give. In almost every Western European country, he writes, there was a confusing shift of loyalties and long and violent outbreaks of turbulent fighting. Many provinces of a disunited France became the scene of petty warfare between one small castle owner and another. Morrall suggests that in the courtly poems the theme of adultery should be taken at its face value. Adultery, real or symbolic, was linked to the challenge which smaller vassals or those of even lower rank were throwing at the greater aristocracy. He quotes love poems addressed to the wife of Henry II. But if the desire were to wrest a prized possession from a superior, to humble the great, then surely the husband's position in the romances would be of paramount importance? It is a striking fact that in many of these poems the husband had little part to play. He was not the lover's true rival.

The conflict was perhaps not primarily to do with seizing power from a superior but with questioning of the values of homage. The essential conflict drawn in the romances lies in the internal tension between lover and the object of his love: whether she will or will not yield, whether he will or will not be faithful. If there are any rivals, these must surely be his equals who are also seeking the woman's favor. And if it was necessary to portray the female as married, this possibly had less to do with the husband's role than with the need to depict the object of loyalty as a person with sovereign status. A married woman was sovereign in her household (she had favors to bestow) in the way that an unmarried female could never be. The status inequality between lady (sovereign) and lover (vassal) was an essential component of the service/reward theme.

Morrall's pointing to this period as one of great unrest supports interpretation along these lines. Personal service (homage) involves rights and obligations. At a time when lesser vassals were engaged in a struggle for power, there must have been many individuals whose political networks put them constantly into dilemma. Was the lord really going to prove his generosity; was the vassal at heart faithful? Even when reward was not forthcoming, what kind of service should be rendered? How far could the lord depend on an established relationship in making demands on his subordinates? There must have been uncertainties on both sides. One should also note that a man of lower rank could only raise himself through being recognized by his superiors. They had it in their power to bestow on him both rank and the wealth he needed to keep himself in the style of the new station he claimed (which would bring with it heavier obligations to provide military aid to his overlord). But this was not an automatic process. A knight's deeds had to be brought to his superior's notice. It was up to the overlord to show generosity toward his inferiors. Largesse was a quality, a state of mind and of feeling: it could not be counted upon. And those who sought to seize power for themselves were putting their fortunes into a very ambiguous position, for ultimately a claim to rank was nothing if it was not recognized.

Possibly these romances suggest one kind of solution to these "problems," and it was a solution most likely to be favored in aristocratic circles: service was an end in itself, and bound together loved one and lover (lord and vassal) irrespective of reward. Indeed, reward lay in the very act of service. For in the twelfth century a note of self-sacrifice apparently crept into the romances. Not only did the loved one impart nobility to the lover but the genuineness of his affection was shown in readiness to endure all even if the love itself was unrequited. In some it was made a point that the desired end was that the love should *not* be consummated: in other words, the tie had become an intrinsic one, the attachment to the lady gave honor to the man, and that was the extent of his reward.[9] This is obviously a solution which favors the lord and encourages

---

9.   Nevill Coghill (1949) sums up Chaucer's later rendering of the *Romance of the rose* thus: the lover is not forbidden to hope for a reward but cannot expect it; all he can demand is mercy.

the perpetuation of an existing rank system. A lesser man derives status from the fact of his relationship to a superior, and he should rely on this come what may. It is indeed an aristocratic doctrine.

Lewis's famous analysis of Guillaume de Lorris' thirteenth-century *Roman de la rose* is all about this tie: it is the internal relationship between lady and lover (that is, lord and vassal) which these romances explore.

> Do not let us be deceived by the allegorical form. That . . . does not mean that the author is talking about non-entities, but that he is talking about the inner world—talking, in fact, about the realities he knows best. No doubt, from a grammatical or logical point of view, the land of Gorre in *Lancelot* is "concrete," and Danger in the *Roman*, being a personification, is "abstract." But no-one . . . has ever been to the land of Gorre, while Guillaume, or any courtly lover of the period—or, for that matter, any lover in any subsequent period—has actually met Danger [stand-offishness]. . . . The "abstract" places and people in the *Romance of the rose* are presentations of actual life. . . .
>
> [The author] removes the heroine entirely. Her character is distributed among personifications. This seems, at first, a startling device, but Guillaume knows what he is about. You cannot really have the lady, and, say, the lady's Pride, walking about on the same stage as if they were entities on the same plane. Nor is it unnatural for a lover to regard his courtship as an adventure, not with a single person, but with that person's varying moods, some of which are his friends and some his enemies. . . . Accordingly, the lover in the *Romance* is concerned not with a single "lady," but with a number of "moods" or "aspects" of that lady who alternately help and hinder his attempts to win her love, symbolized by the Rose. . . . Any protracted wooing involves a conflict not only between the man and the woman but between the woman and herself; it is this second conflict which occupies the most interesting scenes in the *Romance*. (Lewis 1936: 115, 118)

A possible emotional source, then, for the passions engendered in the medieval romances between lady and lover lay in the changing demands made on men in their political life. A love relationship with a high-born woman symbolized vagaries in political loyalties between men. Further, what made the feudal bond so imperative for treatment of this kind were problems and ambiguities in the values on which it was based. There were problems both in identifying which master to serve, and in defining the nature of service to be rendered to one's chosen or allotted overlord. There is some evidence that there were new ambiguities arising in this relationship at the time when the romances began to spread. One last step remains to be blocked in. It is all very well to say that we are dealing with an example of male-female relations symbolizing aspects of relations between men. But why was the former chosen as the symbol? This cannot be answered all at once: it is part of a much bigger question to which we must turn. For the moment we note that if there was an unease about a vassal's responsibilities to his lord and a doubt about the nature of reward and service, stereotypes of women at that time, furnished by the church in particular, provided a model of a being who could be represented as either traitor or protector, the gateway to hell or the portal to heaven. These stereotypes did not lead directly to the image of the courtly lady, whose caprice and whose constancy were of a quite different quality. Yet the attribute of uncertainty was there. Females were ambiguous creatures, and most so in their sexual dealings. They were apt models through which to picture the ambiguities of political allegiance.

ALIKE AND UNLIKE

The time has come to return to my starting point: this was the observation that almost everywhere the conditions of maleness and femaleness are used to make statements about various areas of social life—some of which have a direct bearing on the behavior of men and women toward one another and others of which are concerned with different issues altogether. Stereotypes about what men and women are like are related to certain social values ("governing requires certain qualities: men evince these qualities; women are incapable of governing"), and certain social institutions find their analogy in the supposed relationship of man to woman ("the lower classes are like women, emotional, unreasoning, and not fit to rule"). Once again, there is evident feedback between these two aspects of sexual mythology. Is it possible to say anything about *why* relations between the sexes should be the subject of so emphatic a process of stereotyping, and why the relationship is itself used as a symbol?

One could answer this in many ways. An obvious corollary of some of the themes explored in Chapter Five, and one which has been the subject of many women's liberation writings, is that allocation of certain characteristics to the sexes becomes a rationale for male domination over females. In other words, the way the sexes are depicted directly influences the actual management of male-female interaction in "real life." This is virtually indisputable. But we cannot fully grasp what is going on unless we further realize that the prevalence and tenacity of such stereotyping is also derived from the adaptability of the male-female relationship. To use an analogy: a flag has to be flown the right way up. This is a product of two things. First, a flag contains a design and the design only makes sense if looked at from one particular point of view. Intrinsic to the act of flag-flying, then, is the flag's incorporation of a motif which has to be represented in a certain way. Second, the design on the flag, and the flag itself, is also a symbol of the nation, shipping line, or regiment which flies it. It has to be flown the right way up, because this represents the integrity and honor of that group. Men ruling women attribute to them innate disqualifications for personal mastery; by virtue of their sex they are not fit to dominate. (The flag has to be flown one way because that is the way the design goes.) Men taking precedence over other men represent the inequalities in such a situation through an identification of the inferior with women, or through an analogy between the naturalness of innate inequalities and the naturalness of sexual difference. (The design on the flag makes it necessary for a distinction to be made between "right way up" and "wrong way up." Right way and wrong way in turn become symbols for the identity—victory or defeat—of the group flying it. Preserving the motif becomes necessary to the operation of flying the flag right-way up.)

Oakley (1972: 189) writes: "Western society is organised around the assumption that the differences between the sexes are more important than any qualities they have in common." One of the aims of her book is to find out the extent to which biological characteristics determine differences in intelligence, work capacities and such, between men and women, and the extent to which cultural conditioning (gender definition) is the more significant. She points out that our seeing sex differences as biologically "natural" obscures the extent to which gender is molded by culture. It is a paradox to her that "our society, having achieved most of the equipment and knowledge to dispense with sex differentiation everywhere except in the bedroom and the maternity hospital, nevertheless maintains it as a near universal feature of the social structure" (209). She implies that the extent to which we are able to perceive these differences as culturally based should open our eyes to the many potentialities of male-female interaction. Hers is an extremely sophisticated rendering of the argument that, since many of the imputed differences between the sexes have no biological base, we should therefore be able to get rid of the idea of difference altogether. And this should lead to reform in relations between the sexes themselves.

To my mind this underestimates the dimensions of the problem. Les Hiatt comments, "Male chauvinists and feminists both generally proceed on the assumption that the moral case depends in large measure on how the biological issue is settled" (1971: 71). Whether men should be dominant must depend on proof that they are biologically fit for dominance. Both sides take up a similar view: biology proves that men are / are not necessarily fit. Yet the short answer is always possible: the moral case does not have to depend on biology.

In order to bring out the drift of my own conclusions, let me cite an eminently reasonable summing up of the implications of the "biological" (our biology) differences between the sexes. In Corinne Hutt's words:

> That sex differences do exist is an incontrovertible *biological* fact. Whether such differences should result in differential treatment of males and females is a *social* decision. Equality does not mean similarity. Yet this is a confusion only too evident in the declamations of many feminists: "There are no differences between men and women except for minor anatomical features"; "anything you can do, I can do better." Our society accords the same rights to education, to medical care and to social benefits to all its citizens, whatever their race, colour or creed, or is in principle committed to doing so. Similarly, there can be no justification whatsoever for discriminating between men and women in terms of these fundamental community rights. But these are rights that a society, by consensus, confers upon its members and they are not achieved by the repudiation of biological differences. . . .
>
> On the other hand, there are certain factual reasons why men and women cannot, at present, be considered equivalent employees. . . . A woman's primary role is that of motherhood and most women have some or other of the attributes which fit them for this role. Consequently, the pursuit of a career for the mother of a young family is an arduous and conflict-ridden undertaking. Of course, there are ameliorative procedures that can be introduced—for example, extended maternity leave, state-run playgroups for all under-fives etc.—but these would only dent the tip of the iceberg. The physical, intellectual and emotional demands made upon the mother continue throughout the offspring's childhood, unless one delegates entirely the role of mother to a substitute. . . .
>
> Several results suggest . . . that, despite equality of opportunity, men and women may forge rather different roles for themselves, socially and psychologically. This should occasion not surprise, but relief. It would be quite extraordinary indeed if male and female cognitive styles and orientations were totally at variance with their biological propensities. It is for these reasons that one views with some disquiet another of the oft-repeated demands of some feminist activists—that for twenty-four hour crèches or nurseries to enable women with

young children to continue in their employment. Apart from the adverse effects
that may result from such institutions, there is a logical inconsistency inherent
in such a demand. It lies in the fact that the staff of such nurseries, inevitably
female, would be "condemned" to relentless domesticity and care-taking, the very
occupations of which the feminine liberators are unreservedly contemptuous.
On the contrary, women with families are only able to pursue their careers with
the aid of just such women. (Hutt 1972: 133–38 passim, original emphasis)

We can accept Hutt's conclusions that men and women may forge "rather different roles for themselves" whether or not we take her particular standpoint
that motherhood is a "primary role." What I want to make quite clear is that
this book has not been about the fitness of men or of women for particular jobs,
statuses, roles, or whatever. It is about how societies have constructed and *used*
differences. For we are in danger of underestimating the strength of our own
artifacts.

In so far as we should take into account the evidence of biology, we should
also take into account the evidence of culture or of history. Not perhaps to settle
the moral case but to understand the limits of the extent to which anything can
be settled at all. The "confusion" to which Hutt refers is not just a misfortune
which bogs down any attempt at rationality. These confusions are symbols. The
feminists are not just poor logicians: they are speaking a *social language*. They are
using an interpretation of biology to make statements about humanity and men
and women. In faulting the logic Hutt misses the symbol. Instead of saying the
feminists are wrong, one should ask, why do they use this language? To direct
all our attention to evolutionary antecedents in the make-up of the sexes ignores
the cultural antecedents. The assumption is that if a practice has been identified
as nothing more than a cultural artifact (a "myth") then it can be dispensed with,
since cultures are of our own making. But this can be valid only to the extent
that we are aware of *all* the uses to which the artifact is put. You cannot classify
an axe as a weapon and hope to ban its use if it is also a work tool.

This book has been about uses. It has tried to show some of the ways differences and similarities between the sexes have been molded and used. We are
beyond the point when we can just say gender is mythological, since really men
and women have a common humanity, and that is that. Society makes a language out of these differences and similarities, and the very definition of gender
contributes to and in return receives impetus from this. And if these stereotypes
are used to rationalize actual power relations between the sexes and validate

male domination, they are also used to represent other fundamental aspects of social structure. The woman question is not simply a "whole people" question. It much more complicated than that: it is a "whole society" question. We shall return to this.

Before then, I turn once more to the current liberation debate. Certain interesting points emerge if we consider it as a piece of ethnography. For this forces us to ask *why* so much emphasis should nowadays be put on the biological justification of sex differences. There are two aspects here: the stress on biology and the stress on differences.

Perhaps it is not surprising that a society which seems to place so much *overt* significance on equality should over- rather than under-emphasize natural differences. Equality of opportunity is related above all to occupation. And yet in occupation structures, in jobs and professions, the premise is one of inequality—whether the criteria are those of age, education, experience, type of job, or whatever. The inevitable regretability (for that is how it is seen) of such inequalities is propped up by our interest in the inevitable contrasts of sexual endowments. In a world where it is hardly permitted in public to say, "men are not equal," one is at liberty to say, "men and women are not equal," even if the area is narrowed down to hormones and chromosomes. Complete egalitarianism not just in civil status but also in lifestyles is impossible. The naturalness of sex differences can symbolize the whole contrast between achievement (male) and innate lack of capacity (female). Hence all the talk about why women have produced no great artists and such (which is a way around talking about the unmentionable: men are not equal). For the existence of such genetic contrasts points to the only possible solution of this ideological dilemma. When it is widely acknowledged that equality of opportunity should be available to all, there has to be some accounting for not just the failure of people to use their opportunities but the fact that a society with technologically differentiated skills cannot at heart take such a proposition seriously. Perhaps at the back of our explorations of the meaning of differential sexual endowment is a shadowy combat with this fundamental paradox.

That said, the present debate is possibly about problems deeper than this. In the same way as the medieval romances dealt with what was probably one of the most emotional of contemporary issues, the relationship between service and reward, so the liberation and antiliberation writers use gender to talk about the relationship between the individual and society. And not just in direct terms either. Both sides, in using the language (symbols) of sex relations to make their points in an overt debate, provide combatants for a hidden debate.

Janeway suggests that one of the reasons why we give a central place to sex in our culture lies in its defiance of the rule of machines.

In the world as we know it today there are not many activities other than sex which make intense physical demands and confer great physical rewards of relief and ease. . . . We don't put out to sea in cockleshell craft whose handling requires enormous resources of skill and strength; or to be exact, we do so only for fun and stay home in bad weather. We don't handle plows, or the oxteams or horses which used to pull them, or sow by hand, or harvest in a moving line of scythemen, singing together to keep the rhythm constant. We don't fly falcons we have trained, or hunt the whale with hand-flung harpoons, or the buffalo with bow and arrow. Machines work for us. Our brains are active, our bodies acted upon. And yet it is through our bodies that we feel. Part of the value that we place in the act of sex is because it is an *act*.

And an act which is felt intensely, sparking terror, granting ecstasy. . . . Though its value may change outwardly, sex is protected from too great a loss of seriousness by the physiological intensity of orgastic relief. This unique implosion of joy sets sex off from all other bodily pleasures. As these have faded in intensity, they have fallen toward the condition of sport because they have lost their original purpose of survival: the hunt is no longer a matter of life and death; sowing and the harvest may mean famine or plenty but not to industrial man. Success here is either trivial, distant, or taken for granted. . . .

The value of sex, then, is enhanced because it remains capable of giving intense physical pleasure in a world where other bodily activities have lost a great deal of meaning. Just as women's skills, once so vitally important to feeding and clothing mankind, have deteriorated into hobbies, with needlepoint replacing the spinning wheel, so men's skills and prowess have degenerated into sport. They have become adult play: leisure-time activities which imitate the realities of work. For children, such play is a necessary part of learning to live. In maturity it is a substitute for living. . . .

But there is a social reason too. The narrowing of the world of physical satisfaction as modern man withdraws from his contact with nature has been paralleled by another phenomenon which we have noted before: the dwindling in the variety and extent of personal relationships and social bonds. We need not dwell again on the rise of the nuclear family and the distance from relatives which social mobility produces, on the fact that couples have replaced clans, big houses and tightknit village communities. But we might recall that the most drastic effects of these changes are very recent, with the result that social isolation both is, and is felt to be, at unprecedented heights. . . .

In urban industrial society . . . wider bonds to the community have all but vanished; and we might note that they are non-sexual bonds. The sexual connection, that is, is emphasized by the loss of other social ties just as sexual experience is emphasized by the dwindling of other bodily pleasures. Even the ties of family within the small nuclear household are slacker than they were, for families endure as units for shorter times and the frequency of meeting between adult children and their parents, or between brothers and sisters, has also been affected by social mobility. . . .

For us today, then, the relationship between one man and one woman is becoming the one that sets norms of feeling and behavior. In it is found the greatest, the almost unique, source of physical pleasure—sex, while around it the context of life has been impoverished by the loss of many other affectionate but non-sexual ties, in which warmth was exchanged in other ways from one person to another. . . . In a world full of strangers, how can one count on friends? Only the other member of the couple remains within the reach of responsive emotion. (Janeway [1971] 1972: 263–68 passim, original emphasis)

So we associate sex with nature, and relations between men and women with sex. And in a world increasingly bureaucratic and impersonal, a sexual relationship is seemingly one which above all throws emphasis on the significance of *relationship*, of interpersonal contact. Hence, our efforts to typify the "good sex partnership" as one between two human beings who have respect for each other. Hence, our abhorrence of sex relations which are impersonal (one sex using the other as an object). Is it too far fetched to suppose that we use relations between men and women (primarily in a sexual context but also in others, e.g., sexual partners as coparents, each equally looking after their offspring) as a basic marker of human interaction? A sexual partnership is a relationship as opposed to an impersonal encounter; it is nature against machines; the person against the state; the survival of a natural species against technological exploitation. We have put sex on the side of nature and of biology, and perhaps that is one reason for our efforts to prove that the only genetically determined distinctions between the sexes are those related to the intimate functions of intercourse and reproduction. All the rest is distortion, exploitation. The effect is to throw emphasis on the sexuality of men and women, and on the naturalness of their endowments.

What has happened here? What exactly is the symbol? It is not that of an opposition between the sexes but of their union. Under proper circumstances (for example, when partners recognize each other as persons, which is the premise of relationship) a sexual union between a man and a woman can itself, in its entirety, symbolize the value of human relations against manipulation, which in another idiom is nature against technology. It is not differences between the sexes which generate this symbol but ties between them. The tie exists at once in spite of and because of those differences.

A sex relationship can also embody efforts to assert *individuality* against relationship, self-identity against commitment, independence against dependence; not human beings against machines but man against society. Biology comes into this too; yet the "natural" equality of the sexes leads not to a stress on relationship but to a stress on the uniqueness of individuals who have natural ("genetic") rights against one another. One and the same symbol is thus be used in two very different ways. Both rest on an equation of sexual status with biological status, and on the common humanity (or animality) of people: but the one points to the need for interpersonal communication in a world of machines and impersonal bureaucrats; the other, to the liberation of the individual from social pressures of any kind.

These are uses, then, to which male-female relations are put nowadays. Those who consider that there is a basic equality between the sexes, a common humanity, play down the differences; or rather highlight differences as relevant to one sphere only, coitus and reproduction. Yet this common ground provides a starting point for two divergent conclusions. One is that in defining men and women as equal it is possible for there to be a genuine relationship between them, a union of like minds, of like feelings, of two persons who respect one another. The other is that between equals, defined as persons with their own rights and their own thing to do, the most intimate "relationship," a sexual encounter, can be shown to be a nonrelationship, for the integrity of the person is above all to be protected from the trammels of commitment. If the individual can survive this intimacy, he or she can survive anything. Both these views, and mixtures of them, are to be found among today's feminists. Part of the force of using a biological argument lies not only in attempts to prove the "naturalness" of their position and the distortion imposed by the culture-makers (men) but in the association of a sexual relationship with nature—whether it is technology against nature ("machines destroy relationships") or society against nature ("relationships destroy people").

This is, needless to say, an extreme rendering of viewpoints which people often hold in combination. In claiming equality for the sexes, those who see themselves on the same side of the fence may take now one position and now another. The following two statements come from collections of women's liberation writings.

First,

Yes, sisters, we have a problem as women all right, a problem which renders us powerless and ineffective over the issues of war and peace, as well as over our own lives. And although our problem is Traditional Manhood as much as Traditional Womanhood, we women must begin on the solution.

We must see that we can only solve our problem together, that we cannot solve it individually as earlier Feminist generations attempted to do. We women must organize so that for man there can be no "other woman" when we begin expressing ourselves and acting politically, when we insist to men that they share the housework and child-care, fully and equally, so that we can have independent lives as well.

Human qualities will make us attractive then, not servile qualities. We will want to have daughters as much as we want to have sons. Our children will not become victims of our unconscious resentments and our displaced ambitions. And both our daughters and sons will be free to develop themselves in just the directions they want to go as human beings.

Sisters: men need us, too, after all. And if we just get together and tell our men that we want our freedom as full human beings, that we don't want to live just through our man and his achievements and our mutual offspring, that we want human power in our own right, not just "power behind the throne," that we want neither dominance or submission for anybody, anyplace, in Vietnam or in our own homes, and that when we all have our freedom we can truly love each other.

If men fail to see that love, justice and equality are the solution, that domination and exploitation hurt everybody, then our species is truly doomed; for if domination and exploitation and aggression are inherent biological characteristics which cannot be overcome, then nuclear war is inevitable and we will have reached our evolutionary deadend by annihilating ourselves. (Amatniek 1970: 141)

Second, from Lilith's Manifesto,

Therefore Be It Manifest:

1. The biological dichotomy of sex needs no reinforcement by differential cultural mores. Whatever qualities pertain to humanity pertain to it as a species. If assertiveness, for example, is a virtue in man, it is a virtue also in woman; if forbearance is a virtue in woman, it is likewise a virtue in man. . . .

2. The mutilation of individual whole human beings to fit the half-size Procrustes' beds society assigns selectively to "men" and to "women" serves a purpose far more contrary to the pursuit of freedom than simple divisiveness: because *all* persons can be consigned to one or the other category and their personalities trimmed, by differential social experience, to fit the mold considered appropriate to their sex, *none* can escape; half the human race receives indoctrination and training in the exercise of dominance over others, while the other half receives reciprocal conditioning to servility, all being given to presuppose that a pattern of authority and submission to authority is the universal, inevitable, and biologically determined order of social relationships.

3. All known societies have thus utilized the clear and all-inclusive dichotomy of sex as the chief vehicle for early and continuous limitation on the essentially liberatory free play of human imaginings and aspirations, perverting a benign natural phenomenon to service of the social status quo. Bourgeois society only inherited this tradition—anti-revolutionary by definition—and modified it to suit the special needs and conditions of capitalism; socialist societies have done no more than modify it likewise to their ends. The pursuit of freedom demands that it be utterly transcended.

4. By the nature of revolution as such, not all the forces engaged in it are committed to its fullest possible consummation. That commitment, however, defines the vanguard, whatever other elements may, in the vicissitudes of movement, usurp or be displaced into its position. Should leadership be retained by forces of but limited vision, the revolution must be cut tragically short of its full potential, for commitment to the lesser goals such a pseudo-vanguard does envision will turn against the revolution at the very moment it stands poised to overreach them.

5. It is unthinkable that the revolution now in process be allowed to suffer such curtailment. Heretofore, disappointed survivors of a truncated revolution have known, at least, that the seeds of future revolt remained; no power was capable of exterminating them. The proliferating technology of biochemical manipulation now robs us of even that bitter consolation; no state power, capitalist or socialist, is to be entrusted with it; we can afford no less than total liberation. *This* revolution has got to go for broke: *power to no one, and to every one: to each the power over his/her own life, and no others.* (Women's Majority Union 1970: 528–29, original emphasis)

These writers are on the same side of the fence in the overt debate on women's liberation; but they take up different stands on the hidden debate, the debate over the nature of and the relationship between society and the individual. Although superficially similar they also point to divergent conclusions: the first, that true relationships ("true love") will be possible when human beings are free; the second, that freedom will release the individual from relationships ("power over others"). The same can be shown of some of their opponents.

A different set of people start off on the contrary assumption: that differences between the sexes are natural, fundamental, and wide-ranging, encompassing much more than distinctions in the genital and reproductive matters. Yet those who take this standpoint, that the differences are more significant than the similarities, may end up holding almost the same positions as those who stress the equalities. Sexual differences can be seen as complementary and giving rise to a fundamental interdependence between male and female: the relationship is between unequals but it is valued as a relationship, and is seen to be necessary for the survival of both. Or inequality may lead to a definition of human beings, including men and women, being in opposition to one another, their interests forever contrasting, and to this extent in constant though unequal competition. The degree to which a person emerges "in his own right" depends on his skills in the fight. Again, reference to the biological foundations of inequality justifies either the basic complementarity of the sexes or the eternal struggle between them.

Recall Schneider's definition of sexual intercourse as a symbol of commitment (relationship).

> As a symbol of unity, or oneness, love is the union of the flesh, of opposites, male and female, man and woman. The unity of opposites is not only affirmed in the embrace, but also in the outcome of that union, the unity of blood, the child. For the child brings together and unifies in one person the different biogenetic substances of both parents. . . .
>
> It is love which unites the opposites of male and female, and it is love which preserves the unity of the differentiated and further differentiating parents and their children, as well as the child from his siblings. The one is conjugal love, marked by an erotic component; the other is cognatic love, wholly without erotic aspect; but both are love, which is unifying. And love is what American kinship is all about. (Schneider 1968: 39–40 passim)

An essential precondition for unity is the complementarity (and oppositeness) of the two persons. But natural oppositeness can apparently lead to unhealthy competition.

> Equality [between the sexes] will cause . . . problems. Doctors and nurses, executives and secretaries, producers and actresses, can and do manage because there is a status and dominance difference between them. It is relatively "normal" for men to seek sexual access to females who are their subordinates. Sexual access is not even in itself necessary; . . . polygamy is not necessarily about sex but about dominance. It is an overvaluation of merely sexual intercourse which defines polygamy in terms of sex rather than social access and dominance. But where status dominance does not exist it is possible that some effort at stabilizing the internal sexual power system by coitus or flirtation may result from placing men and women as equals in charged situations concerned with power in the first place. In my own sphere, I have been struck at how predictably academics considering employing a younger female will comment upon her attractiveness *qua* female. It is possible to regard this as an anticipation of possible conflict between woman-as-colleague and woman-as-sexual-object. Nor are women unaware of the importance of attractiveness in securing desirable employment in largely male organizations. Currently there appear to be no solid prospects for significant change in this matter, and it seems but sensible to continue to regard it as a hazard in the search for ways of introducing female influence in the councils of power. (Tiger 1971: 215)

Current discussion over the woman question, then, includes a working out of an intellectual problem as to what is (should be) the relationship between the "individual" and "society." There is an antithesis between our concepts of personal freedom and the requirements of social relationships. Whichever side one takes on the sex question—whether one asserts the basic humanity of men and women or their contrasting endowments—it is possible to use one's stand as a platform from which to plea for the freedom of the individual or for the value of human relationships. Perhaps the hidden debate speaks to a crisis in our notions of the individual and its relationship to society. And perhaps this has been precipitated by, among other things, the technological possibilities of exercising "free will" in ways never dreamed about when freedom was made an acceptable precondition for humanity. The point is simply that the overt debate about male-female relations can be viewed as a vehicle for, a set of symbols for, the discussion of those hidden issues.

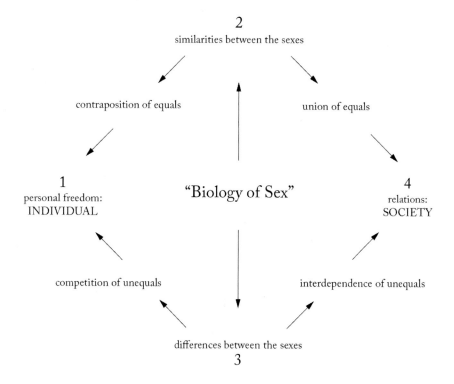

2
similarities between the sexes

contraposition of equals   union of equals

1   "Biology of Sex"   4
personal freedom: relations:
INDIVIDUAL   SOCIETY

competition of unequals   interdependence of unequals

differences between the sexes
3

Overt debate between 2 and 3; hidden debate between 1 and 4.

Figure 2. "The debate over the nature of the sexes, and the debate over the nature of the individual and society"

To the extent it is in anthropologists' professional interests to analyze societies as ongoing concerns, there is nothing new in the observation that they (the anthropologists) tend to emphasize the complementarity of different parts of the social system. As a result, conflict and discrimination may be described as upholding the social order in subtle ways which suggest their desirability rather than the reverse. It may look as though my overworking of the word "symbol" is doing just this, as though I were "reducing" the feminist struggle to "nothing but" an intellectual debate. Doesn't arguing that male-female antagonisms are symbols of something else imply they are not real? No!

If current debates over men and women, and especially sexual relations between them, is in another idiom a debate over the antithesis Europeans make
between a "person" and a "relationship," this does not mean that these debates do
nothing more. On the contrary, I have been describing only an aspect of them. It
does not deny the existence of issues in the politico-economic world concerning
treatment of women or of men. Sexual mythologies continue to have two heads:
they deal with male-female relations, and male-female relations are used to deal
with other things. What my remarks about the latter may explain is something
of the fervor behind the debate, and something of the disappointment that so
much articulateness should seem to have so few results in genuine changes in
people's attitudes. Such outcomes are explicable if we accept the fact that the
woman question is not just about women; it is about women—but it is *also*
about certain paradoxes of our society which alleviation of women's position will
not necessarily alter. In sum, the (overt) debate is likely to have a (hidden) momentum not commensurate with the hoped-for reforms and changes to which
it would seem logically to lead.

In our emphasis on biology we dismiss culture too lightly. The assumption
is that a man-made thing can be unmade. But it can only be unmade if "it" is
properly identified. To say that gender differences between men and women
are basically cultural and not biological in origin does *not* lead to the automatic
conclusion that they are therefore malleable and weak. They may be very strong.
Proving that there is no genetic basis for gender discrimination does not even
begin to approach the problem that such discriminations may be embedded
deeply in society—not just in those institutions which allocate this or that range
of roles to men and women, but in our whole perception of mankind's place in
the world. At the present, the idea of sex and gender is providing a potent focus
for the individual/society problem. Its use will be a vehicle for constant redefi-
nition. In fact, the more we work the concept of gender, whether by denial or
affirmation, the more nourishment we give it. Gender, for us, is like a mandrake.
Pull it up for its poisonous or for its medicinal properties, and you find the root
has human form.

There are two serious points to be made about mythology. The first is a no-
nanthropological one, in the words of a novelist and critic:

> An attempt to define myth [earlier in her book] established that it is bound up
> with emotion, with what we fear may happen and what we hope will come true

and that it therefore prescribes behavior to ward off the worst and produce the best results, in terms of accepted beliefs. What myths tell us about the world is not a description of the way things are, couched in the indicative mood, but instructions for action, imperatives to be followed on pain of "disrupting the order of the universe." Myths therefore exist in a state of tension, a permanent present tense. Though the emotional drives they reveal feed the springs of art, they cannot be criticized or analyzed in the same way as can works of art, because they remain attached to those who believe in them, representing unfulfilled and unresolved desires. They cannot be dispelled logically by being disproved but must be evaluated by methods that allow for their emotional content. At the same time, the fact that myths attract many believers proves that they cannot be dismissed as mere fantasies. They are related to reality through shared feelings and as a response to actual situations which call forth common reactions. . . .

Myths are, first, an attempt to explain the world out there to ourselves so that we understand what is happening and how we are involved in events; but they are also an attempt to manipulate the world so that what is happening can be changed or held at bay. They strive to interpret, to justify or to rectify the way things are, sometimes—illogically—all at once. In the community at large they do this by enunciating beliefs and general assumptions: Women are passive, men are active, women intuitive, men rational—and so on and so on. In one's personal surroundings they prescribe roles and the proper behavior that goes with them: Woman's role is to nurture children, to please men, to support activity but not initiate it. Woman's traditional role bars her from the seats of power. So, by analogy, we find that equivalent roles are taken to justify cutting off other subordinated groups from power. Myth supports the status quo (from which it arises) by calling on sacred texts, ancient wisdom and "things we all know—instinctively." At the same time it tries to satisfy the emotional drives that the status quo leaves unfulfilled. It is deeply ambiguous, caught between what is and what we want to come to pass. . . .

To the extent that we can accept the universal, if uneven alteration in personal and in public life which is taking place now and see it as presenting demands but not as threatening destruction, we shall be better able to deal with it. . . . If we can think objectively about our myths, we won't be so compelled by them and we will be more able to see change as a chance to try out new approaches to problems. Extreme statements, from left and right alike, are inclined to declare that change will mean destruction; which means that such statements are adulterated with some degree of mythic thinking. Of course we must take them seriously (as we take all mythology seriously) for what they tell us about the drive, the determination, the world view and the ability to react with others of those who make them; and when they are made by the powerful, we must assume that the proponents of these views are somewhat more able to act as they wish than are the revolutionary aspirants to power. But I believe we can judge these threats and promises most rationally if we learn to sort out the difference between the emotional expression of mythic imperatives and the logical advancement of a thesis or plan. . . .

And yet . . . we shall never get rid of the social mythology that shapes and explains our world and directs our actions and reactions, whether it is the mythology of the establishment or of a counterculture. Mythology is like gravity, inconvenient at times, but necessary for cohesion. It forms a ground of shared belief on the basis of which groups of people can act together; and we need to be able to act together. Undoubtedly new mythologies incorporating a varying amount of old dogma, are in the making now. A generation ago the "left" thought only in terms of politics; but now a whole pattern of culture, with its special music and literature and dress and attitudes toward life, is growing up within the old order. Its radicalism is cultural and social, not simply political. Nascent revolutions begin by being negative because they react against old values which have lost their force and relevance. Today's radicalism is, tentatively, beginning to set up some positive goals of its own. . . . In its emphasis on humanistic values and the need for closer communion in ways other than sexual and within groups other than those of the family, it has already had a healthy effect on the isolating patterns of the old way of life. To the extent that it deflates the almost lethal overemphasis on sex as the only meaningful close tie between human beings, it will increase the possibility of new kinds of relationships which may enrich our lives just as woman's move out into the world of work produces wider friendships and ties to others. . . .

One might describe these changes as the tendency for woman's place and role to expand and take over man's world: to feminize it, as the first women's movement aimed to do. When we look at the situation this way; we see that men are being pressured from within by women's increased freedom in personal relations and particularly by the control over their lives which the Pill has given them. . . . The more they prize their maleness . . . the more such changes appear to threaten degradation and humiliation, the more they are seen as destructive.

Angry reactions grow out of this internal malaise, this fear of the growing strength of women unchecked by the traditional limits placed on them in the past. It is almost too easy to find examples of aggressive male fantasies in recent fiction . . . and equally easy to find masochistic female fantasies which are quite as disconcerting. . . . But in all such cases, the emotions which power these fantasies of male attacks on women, of sexual rage and sexual submission, should not be dismissed as nonsensical illogic. Exposing them will disprove or discredit them only to those who don't feel the emotions described in such works. [If men writers] . . . tell us that men feel anger and fear for women we'd better believe them. These are mythic emotions, but that should warn us not to think that they can be argued down. To imagine that they can is also an example of mythic thinking, this time the sort that angry women fall into. . . .

I hope that by isolating and examining the idea of social mythology as a field of force operating within and upon human events I have offered some clues to comprehending the world around us, in which the emotional drive that sustains beliefs must be taken seriously even if the beliefs themselves cannot be. Our mythology is a map of feeling which dates back, for each of us, to the earliest, most impressionable stages of life. No social structure will stand if it simply ignores the stresses shown by that map. This does not mean that we must accept the map as right, but rather that, if we seek to change it, we'll do so best if we recognize that we are contending not with disprovable facts, but with treasured emotions, with pride and desire and "age-old" dogma that seems to carry the force of instinct. (Janeway [1971] 1972: 295–307 passim)

Rather than commenting on this, let me juxtapose the second point, an anthropological one. Relations between the sexes are used by many societies, and not least our own, to symbolize fundamental structural features of social life. Briefly, interaction between men and women is a model both for mutual relationship and antagonism, for complementarity and opposition, for nearness and distance, for common interests and competition. One of the reasons why emphasis can be put with equal weight on the natural similarities or on the natural differences is precisely because both coexist. A man and a woman are both alike and unlike; and different cultures elaborate on this combination in different ways. Moreover, they (men and women) need each other for some purposes and not for others, and again cultures elaborate their respective dependence and autonomy.

Amity and enmity; dependency and autonomy. These are the elements of which societies are made. People distance themselves or become intimate; they observe rank or act as peers of one another. Relations between the sexes provide a model for interaction. Our own concern with relationship and personal freedom is but a reformulation of issues most human societies deal with in one idiom or another.

WHY SEX?

Why do many cultures (not all) make so much of sex? Why should relations between the sexes be so frequently the object of mythic attention—and why should it be a powerful symbol? It is here that the primacy we give to sexual (erotic/genital) interaction, very much a possession of our own culture, becomes evident. For many would laugh outright at these questions: the answer seems so obvious. Sex of course! But, if you consider it again, there is no "of course." Sex is only a component of all that goes on between men and women. Well, then, everything else is just an elaboration which flows from sex. But is it?

The stereotypes described in Chapter Two showed how certain societies categorize men and women. Sexual and biological differences may give validity to these stereotypes—and a similar process is found in the definitions of the roles men and women play or the spheres in which they act (Chapter Three). Nevertheless, the end result is not a perception of endless pairs (sexual partners / parents and offspring) but a construction of two blocks. Men are contrasted with or likened to women, and vice versa. Moreover, members of each category can come into interaction with one another, as men and women, in a way which has only the most indirect bearing on sexual partnership or parenthood. Why this elaborate superstructure? Why, if the biological facts of difference and sameness are so obvious, create social categories out of them? Societies which develop pronounced sexual mythologies give a dimension to the contrast between men and women that is almost species-like. Men and women appear as different kinds of creature. From an anthropologist's point of view, however, I wonder if ultimately the contrast is not between two types of *social person*. So when we talk about relations between the sexes, this is what we mean: relations between two varieties of social being.

All societies are built up of contrasts in types of relationships. These may be elaborated to a greater or lesser degree. But the art of social life lies in the recognition of boundaries and knowing how to communicate across them. Many situations can be reduced to a dyadic structure: one type of person in communication with another type—whether between parent and child, shopkeeper and customer, chief and tribute-bearer, our side and their side. And even those relationships which arise between associates defined on grounds of their common characteristics—members of a gang, clansmen, inmates of a college—depend on a latent comparison with others who, by being different, are not members. Social rules are the formulae by which communication is achieved. But the right formulae can only be called into play if a correct identification of the person or persons one is dealing with is made. Interaction with other people is composed of a constant juggling of the contrasts between me / you; common ground / conflicting interests; sameness / difference. And one is not dealing with individuals, but always with a person in a social context, where some formulae are appropriate and others are not. (I speak in an analytical sense here: there may be encounters which society labels as being between "two individuals" but all this means is that a particular set of social conventions are called into play depending on how the society operates the concept of "individual.") We might conclude that when relations between men and women symbolize such basic contrasts, what is mobilized is, above all, the possibility of categorical distinction.

The implications should be apparent. I have given concrete examples of the way male-female relations are used as symbols of political and social relationships. It was obvious in these examples that the particular force of the symbolism was derived in part from the way the society defined men and women in the first place, with a concomitant feedback process, the use of these relations in other contexts modifying the original stereotyping. We should not be surprised that, where the power which men and women have over one another in public affairs becomes a matter for articulate debate, the question of dependency in sexual and domestic matters is also raised. Beyond the legal and social realities, a powerful symbol lies in the equation of women's political subordination to men and their subjugation through housework and sex. And beyond this is the analogy between men/women and superior/inferior males, on which our industrial society is based. There is a further aspect to this symbolic process. In a very general way, and possibly shared by many cultures, contrasts between the sexes can stand for the idea of contrast in general, and communication between them can stand for communication in general. Common humanity but different sex: it is a paradigm for social interaction. Any degree of intimacy, any reach of distance, can be projected onto it. I am not saying that behavior between men and women was the "origin" or "gave rise to" social behavior. Of course not. I am saying that social behavior depends on people's ability to categorize, and that relations between the sexes affords a way of *thinking about* categories.

Nor is it the only way. Attention has been given by anthropologists to peoples' views of the natural world or of their own bodies. The way they place boundaries, between natural species, or between their bodies and external things, contributes to the perception of their own societies. On the same level we must put much thinking about male-female relations. Again let me stress that a prime achievement of sexual mythologies is to produce out of men and women two discrete social categories, two kinds of beings, males and females. This is gender.

Now we are at the point when we can ask, "why sex?" and mean it. That is, we can ask why some societies make (erotic/coital) sex a more important attribute of gender than do others. It is the concept of gender that thus allows us to ask why sex in its "biological" aspect is so important an attribute (of gender) in European societies. Why gender becomes in so many cultures a paradigm for social relationships is another question.

MEN, WOMEN, AND THE IDEA OF A SOCIAL RELATIONSHIP

For more than half a century anthropologists have analyzed connections between the way in which people in different societies delineate the universe or the environment they inhabit and the way in which they think about their own social structures. The same is true of the human body. It provides a repertoire of symbols. Emphasis a society puts on parts of the body, on its wholeness, on its secretions, is a representation in flesh and blood of itself. Society creates the world in its own image. And having done that, like God, can use the world to talk about itself.

There have been various examples of body imagery in this book. The Mae Enga of New Guinea are very concerned about the effects of menstrual blood, and men have to take considerable precautions, both magical and practical, to maintain their physical integrity. Men protect themselves from women in the same way as members of a clan protect themselves from their enemies. An identification is made between the male body and the corporate group of males who form a clan. Relations with members of the opposite sex are necessary, as are relations with other clans, but men are warned to look beyond the benefits which will flow from such contacts and be aware of the dangers also. The boundaries of the male body (the condition of the skin, on which Mae Enga place so much importance) are seen as vulnerable in the same way as the boundary of the clan is (whose territory must be defended). Bemba are concerned with physical wholeness, and some of the implications of this were considered in the last chapter. Here the equation is not between the individual and individual clans maintaining integrity against others but between a person's body and the state, the whole chiefdom, whose integrity is centralized in the paramount chief. The boundary is the Bemba tribe. Other body idioms define internal structures. For example, "The husband is the head of the wife, as Christ is the head of the church": the head is above the trunk and communicates with the lower limbs in the same way as man relates to woman and Christ to his church.

Symbols such as these provide concrete ways for speaking about abstract ideas—about clan solidarity, about the one-ness of the chiefdom, about the subordination of humanity to God. They become vehicles for emotions such as fear, pride, or awe. As Schneider explained in his account of American kinship, they enable people to become committed to their societies. The way the environment is ordered (nature is hostile/supportive; natural species are hierarchically linked or fragmented) represents a domain outside the human body which can be manipulated in the same way. It, too, provides models of boundaries and relationships. And so does gender.

In some contexts relations between men and women can draw attention to facets of the social structure which body or environmental symbols also do. For example, it is not just the condition of their bodies about which Mae Enga men worry but the fact that interaction with women endangers them in particular ways; sexual intercourse for Bemba has implications for the community's health, which is represented in the hearth fire. In addition, gender can be a potent symbol for the notion of a social relationship per se.

Gender is not quite of the same order as a natural species nor yet quite of the same order as the human body. The concept of gender itself assumes a relationship: relations between males and females. When gender becomes a symbol, one kind of social relationship is being used to refer to other kinds of relationships. A fundamental characteristic of gender-thinking is that it produces discrete social categories. In those societies where gender is manipulated it can become a symbol for the existence of social categories in spheres outside the male-female relationship. Unfortunately, this is a proposition which cannot be disproved. Some societies place very low value on gender definitions, and we might assume that male-female relations there are of little symbolic significance. We would expect to find social categories talked about in other ways. Wherever gender is magnified, it probably carries an important symbolic load. That it is used so often suggests its adaptability as a symbol, and this possibly lies in its potential as a symbol for the idea of relationship as such: the form or structure of relationship. The particular content of relationships which the symbols draw attention to will vary, whether it is contests between enemies or paying homage to an overlord or the spiritual submission of man to God.

Relations between the sexes (gender) can deal equally with the definition of boundary and the establishment of communication. These are the elements of which social relationships are made: the definition of persons or groups as discrete social entities and the lines of communication, or the language, between them. As step by step the stereotypes are constructed and the social categories created, so simultaneously are the rules which relate members of one category to the other, for each element of the stereotype carries with it a prescription for behavior.

If all at issue in creating gender were the production of discrete, bounded entities, then the definition of the sexes as unique biological units would suffice. But it never does; rather, each sex is seen as a particular kind of social person. Not only boundary results but also codes for interaction, rules for communication. Gender provides, the anthropologist would say, a paradigm for relationship. Is it a paradox or is it self-evident that in a society like ours, where specialization in most jobs which human beings do leads to an obsession with categories (one has single-stranded relationships with the majority of people one encounters, mostly defined by their occupations, creating situations in which one has to act according rules arising from the categorization of the encounter), that we should make so much of gender? It is a striving for communication: not just at the emotional level which Janeway referred to, but as a sociological necessity. A strict compartmentalization of people's roles is only going to work if the rules for communication are clearly understood. No wonder people get anxious that the *world* will turn topsy-turvy if women do not keep to their place *which means also* if the old channels of communication are obstructed.

But what is there in gender that it can be used as a symbol? For although the relationship between a symbol and what it symbolizes is arbitrary, one does not expect it to be random. There has to be some persuasive link, or the symbol cannot be persuasive. What are the particular properties of gender which makes it so useful as a symbol for communication between distinct social beings?

First, males and females compose a universe (people). Nonmales are females; and nonfemales are males. (I am referring here to gender ascription, not to sexuality.) It may be a world cut in half, but it is still one world. The basic opposition is between male : female, not between male : electricity or female : all the houses in Wales numbered 65. However deeply the line is incised between the two halves, the structure of the opposition relates them. They are two parts of a whole. Sexual mythologies are the last thing one should take at face value, and the extreme contrasts which may be drawn up between the sexes should not blind us. Remember the Fulani cattle camp, with its rope dividing off the areas where men and where women could walk and the dependency of the herd-owning unit on both male and female members. Or purdah in Kanuri which deprives females of almost any access to public life and emphasizes men's domestic needs for women.

Second, in using male-female relations as symbols, society is as it were using itself. It sets up social categories (gender) and social behavior (male-female interaction) to talk about other categories and behaviors. Both the body and the natural world are different, in this respect. For the male-female relationship is also a relationship in its own right. The more the thing used as a symbol is a social artifact (as a relationship is), the more scope there is. Society is free to define the extent to which the sexes are separate but also involved with one another. Interaction between men and women can symbolize relationships of rank, of mutual need (protection/nurture), of competing interest groups, of solidarity in the face of persons of a different social type or equality in spite of differences. If this malleability has an advantage, it also has drawbacks. It is actual relationships, and this means actual people, who are being used. Fulani men and women have in the realities of everyday life to keep to the right side of the camp or there is trouble; Kanuri women have actually to observe the rules of purdah and remain enclosed behind the walls of the compound.

Finally, anthropologists have noted that the most powerful symbols, those which most arouse emotion, frequently refer to the natural world—blood, earth, and so on. The environment and the human body can both be considered "natural." The discrete social categories that form gender can also be made to appear natural. It is here that the manipulation of biology, that is, what the society perceives of as natural endowments, comes in. Differences between the sexes, and their necessity to each other, come to seem inborn. Cultural stereotypes are sex-linked. Whatever a society's concept of biological sex, reproduction and the continuity of social life is seen to depend on the union of a couple who by definition have opposite natural endowments. In short, relations between the sexes are potent as a source of symbolism, not only because of the obviousness of the "biologically determined" differences—the sexual characteristics and functions which differentiate men from women—but the possibility of relationship between them.[10] Both the differences and the necessity for interaction are given a "natural" base. The sexes can stand for contrasts between opposite units; they can stand for connections between complementary halves. Moreover a focus on sexual antithesis or interaction taps areas in which emotions are easily roused, and one of the achievements of a successful symbol is the manipulation of emotion.

Sexual "reality" is not the only kind of reality gender makes available. There is also the social reality of roles, and Chapter Three made some suggestions about the powerful stereotyping drive behind the sex-linking of roles. Perhaps we find it easier to look on roles as culturally defined than we do notions of biology and nature (which we after all place in antithesis to culture). But in both cases it is really that one set of myths or stereotypes produces another. The way in which biology is perceived, the way in which roles are perceived, help define the natures of males and females. We are dealing with constructs (myths) about constructs (gender). Yet they appear to be rooted in the actual world. Reality is touched at two points—in that the myths purport to be about natural attributes (sex) or observable behavior (roles) and in that they refer to existing human beings (men and women).

THE NEW GENDER

Is this not all a variant of what many Women's Liberation writers have said: that the sexes form social classes? In the words of Ti-Grace Atkinson:

> Oppression is an on-going activity. If women are a political class and women are being oppressed, it must be that some other political class is oppressing the class of women. Since the very definition of women entails that only one other class

---

10. Irenäus Eibl-Eibesfeldt (1970: 443), an ethologist, notes the social significance of sex in male-female pair bonding: "the sexual act of humans has acquired a significance in the social life of man which goes beyond the need for reproduction. One argument of the church against birth control . . . is based on the widespread assumption that the sexual act is only in the service of reproduction. This is so in animals. In man, in addition to this function, there is also the important one of maintaining the bond between partners. The sexual act enhances the relationship between people in a way not present in animals." This enhancement of relationship he refers to as a specifically human aspect of sexual behavior.

could be relevant to it, only one other class could possibly be oppressing women: the class of men. (Tanner 1970: 104)

Or the Redstockings Manifesto:

> Women are an oppressed class. Our oppression is total, affecting every facet of our lives. We are exploited as sex objects, breeders, domestic servants, and cheap labor. We are considered inferior beings, whose only purpose is to enhance men's lives. Our humanity is denied. Our prescribed behavior is enforced by the threat of physical violence.
>
> Because we have lived so intimately with our oppressors, in isolation from each other, we have been kept from seeing our personal suffering as a political condition. This creates the illusion that a woman's relationship with her man is a matter of interplay between two unique personalities, and can be worked out individually. In reality, every such relationship is a *class* relationship, and the conflicts between individual men and women are *political* conflicts that can only be solved collectively. (Tanner 1970: 109, original emphasis)

But I do not mean quite the same thing as these writers. Chapter Six pointed to some of the concepts associated with the identification of class in the sense of category with class in the sense of interest group. What follows immediately from these women's perception of female as a class is the assumption that this gives them status as a political group which must fight to defend its rights. This is a particular way of thinking which affects also the very category against which the "class" of women or of men is contrasted: that of human being. A "human being" is also regarded as a class which is an interest group, defined in terms of certain rights, any infringement of or limitations to the exercise of such rights diminishing human status. It is because rights are seen as attributes to be won through political struggle and classes are defined by the rights that they can claim that any identifiable class become a political interest group.

This is our way of looking at people. Midge Decter was perfectly right in summarizing the viewpoint of many liberationist writings as the anguish of self-proclaimed victims (Decter 1973). She suggests that the terror and self-destruction which lies behind this is due to the fact that women have more freedom than they ever had and do not know how to cope. This may indeed be a true identification of the emotional base behind the virulence with which some individuals proclaim their victimization. It does not fully account for the range of idioms on which liberation writers uniformly draw—the concept of rights, the rejection of the notion of persons as objects, the demand for common humanity—nor for the (grudging) acceptance from those who take an opposite standpoint that they are arguing about real things. In the same way as we had to account for the *popularity* of the idea of courtly love in the Middle Ages, we have to account for the readiness of people to take up sides as though the issues *were*, indeed, one of rights, persons, human beings, and so on. To my mind this is explicable only in reference to our cultural milieu; only in reference to our ideas of the way in which people are related to one another; only in reference to our model of society and of relationships. We look upon people as "victims" of society, of technology, of one another. Claiming that women are victims is a special instance of the general case. Indeed, the liberation argument often runs that, just as women are victims of men, men are victims of themselves, behind which lies the unformulated conclusion that human beings are victims. When human beings are singled out as a class (a category perceived as an interest group) they are underprivileged.

Perhaps this stems from feeling that we have indeed, to paraphrase Edmund Leach (1968),[11] let the world run away with us. And although we can condemn "technology" or "social institutions" in the abstract, we know also that ultimately these are of our making. *Things* have got out of control; and this means implicitly, *we* have got out of control. No wonder then that in questioning where things went wrong we should accuse those principles which bind people together—the principles of relationship. The present state of affairs is not the product of any single individual person; therefore, it follows, it must be the result of individuals acting in concert, of individuals forming relationships among themselves which put them at one another's disposal, so that collectively they can perpetrate crimes (on other people, on the environment) that they could never do singly.

This provides some of the emotional drive behind the desire to stress social uniformity, because if there is no social discrimination there can be no power relations between individuals. One logical conclusion is that there can in reality be no relationships. It may not have been the kind of new myth which Janeway was looking for but it is a myth which pinpoints institutionalized relationship per se as the ultimate evil. Decter quotes Shulamith Firestone (1971):

---

11. See Edmund Leach's *A runaway world?* (1968), part of the BBC's Reith Lectures.

The end goal of feminist revolution must be, unlike that of the first feminist movement, not just the elimination of male privilege but of the sex distinction itself: genital differences between human beings would no longer matter culturally. (Decter 1973: 178)

And this leads directly back to my own standpoint. I have been describing what I take to be a particular perception of what people "are like." It is one which might be expected from a culture which fosters the study of relationships (in sociology and anthropology, in psychology, economics, and ethology). We assume we have an objectivity about these things. This sense of objectivity is itself based on our category contrasts nature/culture. This leads into a bog of other category contrasts: naturalness / artifice; biological givens / man-made constructs; unalterable endowments / modifiable society. It is extremely illuminating that one of the arenas in which relationship per se is thrown to the lions should be that of gender.

For many societies, our own not excluded, gender constructs have provided a basic model of what relationship is about. Two beings are set off from one another as discrete social entities, while the very rules for communication between them are being formulated. This is what social life is about; and if we are full of self-disgust (too rich a diet of anthropology and sociology?) about society, what more powerful model to choose than the denial of gender? This is tantamount to saying two things. It says, and in a formula which many liberationists would agree with, individuals should not be cut off from one another by being put into different social classes. But it also says, there can be no communication.

Many would disagree with this second conclusion. Of course. The new myth is that one can interact as individuals, communicate as human beings, without the mediation of society. Spontaneous emotion and self-expression can create new kinds of bonds which depend not on social categories and rules but on a simple consciousness of common humanity. The base point is the self, one's own person, integrity; what are to be given are bits of oneself. The limits of one's potential are set only by the limits of one's body and one's personality. Sympathy must come from the heart, not from a role. Cooperation with others arises from mutual delight, not social responsibility. And this would have begun long ago if men had not created society. Maybe this is good a myth to have. Analytically it is a contradiction in terms. Interaction can only proceed within the framework of rules. Whether these rules are instinctive or learned, or combinations of these, they are a premise of collective life.

Perhaps we should be a little less myopic about what we are doing. There is no such phenomenon, sociologically speaking, as a "natural relationship" between human beings. This is how Decter comments on Firestone's remarks:

> The entire movement in the end speaks with a single voice of its true underlying intention. And that is to create a world, or a culture, in which either literally or to all intents and purposes there would be no men and no women. . . . Obviously, the world of test-tube babies is such a world: if there is no birth, there is no gender. Less obviously, but no less inevitably, a world in which mothers, by a mere and inconvenient quirk of biology, were but the vessels of pregnancy, in which motherhood and fatherhood bespoke essentially the same relation to the offspring of a mechanistically apportioned sexual congress, there would also be no gender—except in a sort of uniformly secondary sense of the term. . . .
>
> There is no more radical nor desperately nihilistic statement to issue forth from the lips of humans than that there are no necessary differences between the sexes. For such differences both issue in and do in themselves constitute the most fundamental principle of the continuation of life on earth.
>
> Denial of that principle—no matter how nobly, or on the other hand, how trivially, uttered—becomes the denial of oneself, one's nature and one's true possibilities: becomes, in other words, the denial of life itself. History has provided us with some examples of this impulse. It has spoken to us through false messiahs, through satanic religions, through a love of suicide, and through a variety of cults dedicated to the redefinition of the meaning of being human. As with Women's Liberation, these messiahs and religions and cults have generally not failed, in their inception anyway, to speak in the language of social justice. And as people learned in the past—and seem to need learn over and over again—should the seeds of such denial take firm root, we shall all of us, men women, and babes in arms, live to reap the whirlwind. (Decter 1973: 178–81 passim)

Maybe the new myth will provide symbols of communication. But it is a depressing signpost that the only possible form of "genuine" communication has to rest on the demonstration that all are equals. This demonstration is made in terms of the intrinsic nature of all human beings, and the common emotions they share and to which they should give spontaneous expression. Societies are usually constructed on the premise that communication takes place between those who are in some respects equal (and therefore able to communicate) and in others unequal, of different social status (and therefore communication is *necessary).* Of course it could be argued that there is no reason why because other societies have deployed gender as a paradigm for communication between persons of different social status, we should continue to do. Using gender uses actual people, and where dominance is an issue real oppression may ensue. But inequalities exist outside the spheres of dominance/subordination. Indeed, it is also arguable that the recognition of inequalities, as well as equality, between persons, has been a major factor in the development of individuality as a concept. One cannot treat people alike because, at the least, and leaving aside questions of personality and such, everyone holds a particular constellation of social statuses. This person was educated at X, has both parents still alive, works at Y; that person has three children, was brought up by Z, expects to leave his present job. If we want to treat people as individuals there is as much chance of doing so by taking into account all the facets of his or her social roles as in denying that social roles are relevant and supposing one is talking to a unit identical to oneself in the rights it can claim.

Something is missing. "Society" can be thought of as a kind of creative entity "doing" this or that with symbols, or "representing" itself to itself in this or that way. But have not all the pointers been that when we talk about society and its constructs we are likely to mean men's social life and their vision of the world? This brings us back in another way to the question of dominance. The book started with the observation that sexual mythologies validate male claims to dominance. We have said that they do rather more, and that they impinge not just on the way men and women behave toward on another but are idioms in terms of which other social relationships may be thought about, and possibly the very idea of social relationship itself. But if society—and social categorization, no less—is a male construct, then is this not saying by a rather circuitous route exactly the same thing: men manipulate their relations with women in their own interests? Yet it would be a sexist/mythic/cultural conclusion, resting on the specific idea that men and women are naturally opposed interest groups, to only equate such a construction (society) with the living struggles of the moment. The conclusion simply does not go deep enough or far enough into the problems that liberationist and other feminist writers have identified.

That may be put in other terms, and I take myself as an example. Anthropologists are taught to step a little way outside their own (and their brothers') societies but not out of society altogether.

Afterword

Judith Butler

Marilyn Strathern's early book, retrospectively titled *Before and after gender*, gives us a chance to rethink our idea about 1970s feminism in the British context, and to consider once again how important anthropological reflection has been for the conceptualization of sex, gender, sexual and social relations, institutions, and systems, and to rethink our notions of what is old and what is new in gender studies. An extraordinarily accomplished and highly praised anthropologist, Strathern pushes the boundaries of her field with an eclectic set of readings, her juxtaposition of de Beauvoir and ethnographic findings, her insistence on treating novels much in the same way as she treats ethnographic details, treatises on the subjection of women, and popular argument about the sexes, including important feminist publications by Kate Millet, Germaine Greer, and the Redstockings Collective. In a way, Strathern's writing enacts a certain freedom of thought, roaming as it will among various texts and claims, calm and deliberate, and always thoughtful. If there is a metonymic procedure by which various texts and reports from different cultures and times are brought to bear upon one another through a successive set of reflections, it certainly proceeds with uncommon rigor. For what keep appearing are ways of perceiving and making sense of women, the relation between the sexes, the category of sex, and socio-political norms such as equality, freedom, and interdependency. She is also writing against the backdrop of the prodigious effect of structuralist anthropology and its rendition of the "exchange of women" and the prevalent conception within feminism that women have been treated as objects, and that they should be treated as persons. Strathern wonders why it is we think that we must conceptualize the issue within such terms, and examines marriage exchanges to show us that women were all along treated, and treating themselves, as something more and different than mute objects. It has been one feminist tactic to oppose the exchange of women on the grounds that women are objectified as they are given away in marriage, treated as gifts and goods. And yet, Strathern discerns another sense of "exchange" that seems important for feminist reflections on how the differences between the sexes are conceptualized and treated. It is difficult to say how an earlier publication of these essays might have affected the subsequent development of feminist and gender studies but it seems clear that our conceptions of gender might have been framed within a relational understanding, and that this could have side-stepped some arguments about biological facts, the status of women as objects, and the importance of identities that seemed—and seem—so often to get in the way of open and thoughtful feminist reflection on gender.

The structuralist account often gave rise to readings in which the exchange of women was lifted out of its social context, acquiring a formal structure that backgrounded the other social relations and important symbols at work in the marriage exchange. Lévi-Strauss obviously moved in that direction in his own "Principles of Kinship," which accelerated the connection between the exchange of women, and the exchange of signs, such that the incest taboo honored and reproduced by exogamy paralleled those founding linguistic acts by which all human communication proceeds. And yet, extracting the relation between the sexes from all other social relations committed an error, facilitating a formal grasp of the exchange at the expense of considerable complexity. Strathern writes here that "anthropologists can only 'make sense' of acts which characterize relations between the sexes by considering many other aspects of the social life of the people as well." For instance, both Bemba men and Mae Enga bachelors take elaborate sexual precautions before marrying and engaging in sexual relations. This makes sense once we realize that sexual potency carries a certain danger within that society. So those who seek recourse to the formal model of sexual exchange lose this nuance. But so, too, do those who seek to explain sexual preparations and practices as flowing from natural causes.

Strathern is less interested in the pugnacious declaration that there are no natural differences between the sexes than in drawing attention to a related problem, namely, that however those natural differences are identified, they are always conceived in some way, relying on a conceptual scheme. This raises an epistemological question: is it possible to know and verify the differences between the sexes that hold for all cultures and all time, if every effort to determine what those salient differences might be is delivered through a specific cultural formulation? Note that this is not an ontological claim; such as, there are no natural differences. Rather, it is epistemological, namely, noting that differences such as these are always conceptualized and, moreover, one sex is always conceptualized in relation to one another and to other social relations as well. For this reason, we cannot precisely isolate and extract those differences from the conceptual frame in which they are posited without at the same time losing our capacity to apprehend the phenomena in question. That mistaken procedure of abstraction presumes that we are only interested in one question and its answer: are there natural differences between the sexes, yes or no? Abstracting those differences from the way they are conceived rests then on a methodological contradiction: we can conceive—affirm or deny—the differences between the sexes on the condition that we do not conceive of them.

Indeed, in Strathern's view, "the line between what is natural and what is cultural is drawn in different places depending on the viewpoint of the observer." As a result, the question of how best to delimit those spheres always makes implicit reference to the observational standpoint and way of conceiving. That viewpoint, however, is not simply an idiosyncratic perspective of the individual but rather a mode of perception formed and saturated by an idiomatic conceptualization of the facts. We might, as she points out, refer to the "facts" of sexual reproduction, but what then have we achieved? Have we then come to the end of the road? To consider that unequivocal assertion of facts as the end of a discussion is precisely to miss the point that those facts are presented and arranged within a cultural way of knowing, and that facts do not appear without being organized in some way. We tend to note the facts that are culturally organized and call them biological, and that claim is less false then simply partial. We still have to ask, under what conditions, and through what linguistic or visual medium, do biological facts appear as such? If there is an organization that precedes and conditions that appearance, or that requires that appearance, then the "fact" might be said to represent in a condensed form that entire organization. It can still be a fact, but what we mean by "facts" has perhaps become more complex regarded in this way.

Strathern is writing in these pages against all kinds of popular and academic arguments that are worrying about the question of natural differences, but also trying to take account of stereotypes. If there is a stereotype of what a woman or a man is, is that precisely because there are recurrent instances, and as a result they form the basis for a generalization? Or is it rather that there are unthinking habits of mind that tend to explain and organize different kinds of behavior and appearance in stereotypical ways that rule out the possibility of seeing variation and complexity? Strathern cautions against the use of "stereotype" in explanations of why women and men may be different in a given society. If we claim that women are stereotyped, and that these stereotypes limit them and, as a result, stereotypes should be eradicated, we may fail to grasp the way in which stereotypes change in the course of being embodied. The stereotype does not have a single meaning; it can, for instance, be inhabited in ways that enable women to express their desires or attain their goals. Indeed, embodiment is an animated vector for changing aims and intentions. Once a stereotype is embodied, it can be diverted from its original purpose, since embodiment can change or redirect the stereotype that is inhabited. Similarly, forms of male cross-dressing deliberately take on women's clothing because certain acts can only be properly performed by a woman. The pertinent question is not what cross-dressing signifies, considered on its own. The question, rather, is what purpose does it serve, or what aims does it seek to realize, within a specific and complex set of social relations.

In the cases that Strathern relates with lively description, we see that the stereotype is linked with mimicry, that it can be taken on by women for their own purposes, and that it can serve as a condition for performing certain rituals and commenting on the relation between the sexes. Strathern points out that the Iatmul clans of Papua New Guinea ritualize forms of cross-dressing whenever a nephew is to be honored for his action or achievement. The relationship between uncle and nephew is established by the woman who is the mother—the mother is the organizing kinship link. So men dress up, miming the actions of women—we might say, "miming the local stereotype"—because it is only from her position—and by virtue of her position—that the act of honoring can be performed. This miming activity articulates the ties between the clans, a tie that depends on the mother and wife. Strathern makes clears that mimicry can also be full of ridicule and disparagement, at which point the mimicry functions to comment upon what women do, articulating popular conceptions of their conduct. Mimicry thus serves different functions depending on the organization of kinship and its relation to broader social relations. Before decrying stereotypes as simply wrong or defending them as reasonable generalizations on the basis of recurrent experience, we might ask what function do stereotypes serve in relation to kinship and what meanings do they carry? Analyzing the stereotype as a fixed image is not the same as considering how it is embodied, who embodies it, and for what purposes. It is interesting to see the bivalent character of this imitation—idealizing and degrading the imitated. It may well be that when women embody or enact a stereotype, they are engaged in imitating what others think of them, showing how well they can do it, but also offering a critical commentary on the imitation itself. The mimicry of women by men is pervasively ambivalent, underscoring, as Strathern suggests, the ambivalence in the relation between the sexes. Perhaps we might add: the mimicry of women by women may also signify an ambivalence of that sex in relation to the dominant conception of its sex.

Although social scientists might simply ask, what are the roles with which women are typically associated, and can we give natural grounds for those roles, or secure necessary social functions for that role? They might then form a weighty list that satisfies the question of why there are such roles. But with that list of roles, they would not offer any understanding of what significance those roles might have. To determine the significance of sex roles, one might ask first how they are perceived and valued. The perception enters into the very understanding of the role, how it is enacted and perceived. So the social scientist who enumerates those roles and asks after their justification or purpose has already committed himself to a specific perception of roles as more or less necessary, as more or less fixed. His hypothesis encodes a certain fantasy about what women are, and how they should be, and the list fortifies his fantasy. Simone de Beauvoir reminds us that descriptions of women are imbued with fantasy. Women might be angels or whores, enchantresses, or weak creatures. Whatever the role, the symbol, the codified fantasy, these are the means, Strathern tells us, through which women's nature is described. Hence, we are asked to reconsider descriptions of roles as codifications of fantasy.

Here again, as with the debate about natural differences, a consequential epistemological claim is underway: a woman is perceived a certain way, and that perception includes elements of fantasy, and this perception not only forms how she is defined and described but it also weighs upon her. She has a relation to this fantasy, which is not the same as being the fantasy. This makes mimicry possible, including self-mimicry, but also critical commentary on the perception/fantasy that weighs upon her or is encountered as an obstacle and obstruction. That fantasy-imbued perception is part of the "situation" into which she emerges. To be a woman is to be in a situation. One cannot take the woman out of the situation without losing sight of the woman. The perception and fantasy of which we speak is part of the conceptual scheme that describes sex, sex difference, what women are, and what they do. It is a form of epistemological overload. It does not belong to any particular individual; it crosses individual perception and constitutes a cultural pattern of knowing, a conceptual way of knowing. There is no easy way to distinguish concept, fantasy, and perception; they blend as they define and prescribe what women are and what they should do. The consequence is that so many of the ontological claims about women—who they are, what they want, what they can and cannot do or know—are already framed within this perceptual field, one that is saturated with fantasy. What we might call a phantasm of who they are is precisely what women encounter in numerous daily theaters of self-reflection—in work, in intimate life, in politics, the descriptions of anthropologists and psychologists. They meet this phantasm as they might meet a stranger, a stranger who oddly shares their name, in numerous daily theaters where they find a reference to who they are. This incommensurability is the condition of both mimicry and critical reflection.

Strathern offers a gentle but persistent reminder to Marxist feminism that the gendered division of labor also depends upon perception, and that it serves other functions besides consolidating inequality. She is not praising the division of labor but she does think that a closer look will give us clues about forms of tacit interdependency that we might wish to value. That closer look involves a shift in perception. Some argue, for instance, that the very existence of different tasks for men and women are distributed on the basis of natural capacities, as if powerful inferences about capacities ground and justify differential tasks. If we look more closely or carefully at, for instance, aboriginal societies, we find, in Strathern's words, that "this is more a matter of gender (what males and females are perceived to be capable of doing) than of sex (their biological capacities)." She then writes, "an outsider can perhaps 'see' that if the division of labor makes certain jobs the exclusive concern of one sex, then the two sexes are necessarily dependent on one another. But this may or may not be openly recognized." Indeed, to see how interdependency operates is not to presume that there are "conscious assertions of mutuality." Although the explicit discourse may well assert the inferiority or weakness of women, the gendered division of labor bespeaks an interdependency between the sexes that is not always avowed. Such

an insight, however, can be a powerful one for women who, situated in an inferior position, nevertheless "know" that they are indispensable, and that interdependency is the implicit and greater truth at work in social relations between
the sexes. Influenced by psychoanalysis to some degree, Strathern allows us to
consider that proclamations about dominance have to be contextualized within
social relations that admit to interdependency in other ways. In her view, "it is
highly unusual in human societies to find interdependence between the sexes as
an explicit value governing all aspects of social life. Even if it is acknowledged
in economic terms (and it need not be) it may be denied in those political or
religious dogmas which give the male ultimate dominance. This means, however, that those areas in which interdependence is recognized puts ammunition
into the hands of the dominated." Of course, one wonders as well what happens
to those figures, whether intersex, hermaphroditic, two-spirited peoples, or the
berdache, who are positioned on the margin or fall outside both gender categories, or who operate as mediating spirits or forces between the two, combining
elements of each and adding more? Do such figures not only call into question
the exclusive claims of dominance but the exhaustive terms of binary gender as
well?

The question of the status of binary gender as a conceptual scheme is not
one that Strathern poses in the 1970s, and that is fully understandable. And yet,
her text proves prescient. She gives us a way to think about the stranglehold
of binary thinking. We are asked to greet critically various loud claims of male
dominance / female subordination and see how the division proclaimed presupposes—and disavows—conditions of interdependency. She asks us as well
to rethink the very relation between persons and objects, one that surfaced in
feminism when women were said to be treated like objects when they should be
treated as persons. The distinction between person and object belongs to a very
specific cultural way of seeing and thinking. The subject is understood as acting,
the object, as acted upon, but is this the only way to parse such terms? Is the
organic object not living, producing effects on its own? Do tools not sometimes
organize and prepare their own use? And are subjects not acted upon by others,
by cultural forces, by stereotypes in general? What if we were to understand
human agency as affected, animate, and dependent, doing and done to? How
would that then alter the ideals for which we struggle in this world?

If we believe that subjects "do" and that objects simply "are" a certain way, we
make assumptions about doing and being that miss out on the way in which are
we done by things or by one another, done in, and undone. For Strathern, our

ideas of subject and object derive from a very culturally specific way in which humans act, with or without instruments, on nature, on forms of dominion over nature that condition the way we think about relations of domination between kinds of people. According to this scheme, unlimited action and unconditioned freedom are ideals of personhood, and the object domain signifies lack of freedom, matter that must yield. For Strathern, operating within an ethos in which interdependency may well prove to be the most important feminist value, the ideal of unlimited freedom and mastery is yet another way to disavow an abiding and valuable interdependency among people. The value of interdependency cannot be thought within the framework that allocates unlimited freedom to master to men and lifeless, yielding matter or recalcitrance and frigidity, to women. In fact, we might extend her analysis to think about biological processes and organic objects and networks, all of which produce effects, are acted upon and acting, and constitute part of the larger network of life processes to which both persons and objects belong and upon which they necessarily depend.

To take this value of interdependency seriously means that we have to know where to find it when we analyze structures of inequality, and that we have to find ways to avow it within feminist emancipatory discourses. The critique of inequality is supplemented by the affirmation of interdependency or mutuality. Strathern rightly worries that any limitation on freedom is regarded as "subjugation" within certain kinds of emancipatory models. That we do limit our consumption of goods, or that we check ourselves when violence becomes an option are all forms of living with others in a shared world that ought not to be devalued. The challenge to our conceptual schemes is a large one, and remains perfectly timely. Do we see persons as separate and differentiated entities, or are they always relationally positioned? If a person is produced, as it were, from a set of relations (and kinship is only one anthropological model of how this works), then to what extent does a person come to represent a set of constituting relations?

The focus on relationship is central to Strathern's views on gender as well. Gender as a term does not refer to my gender or your gender much less to our gender presentations or gender identities. These are all permutations of gender, to be sure, but gender, as a term, designates a set of relationships. It is not an attribute of personhood or, rather, more precisely, what appears as an attribute of a person represents a set of relationships condensed or congealed into the attribute. In other words, gendered attributes are representations of broader relations between men and women as well as their relations to any number of social practices. In Strathern's words, "when gender becomes a symbol, one kind of social relationship is being used to refer to other kinds of relationships." Gender not only names men and women but the relations that bring those categories into being. Gender does not have a mimetic relation to sex, and though it can operated in the description of biological differences, it is not tied to biological differences in patterned ways. Gender would be those relationships that produce and reproduce the categories of gender. Strathern at that time names "men" and "women" but we may want to name more. Whatever counts as the "sex" of a person is perceived in such a way that a kind of social person is produced through that perception. That perception is part of a broader conceptual scheme, referenced earlier in our discussion of natural differences and stereotypes. The relationship between the sexes is regulated in various ways, and it is through such regulated transactions that gendered differences are reproduced.

For Strathern, gender is not a way of thinking about persons but a paradigm for thinking about social relationships. Of course, there have been better and worse ways of doing that. If we become discrete persons or even discrete genders, we may imagine ourselves as cut off from one another, as distinct and individual, even relatively free of gender norms or relatively free to elect gender as we see fit. Such views, however, fail to understand the individual as a social form, not only acted upon by norms but also defined in relation to others. If we start with methodological individualism, then, have we at that moment affirmed nonrelationality as the point of departure for social descriptions? That nonrelational perspective has implications not only for how we describe the relation between men and women, but for how we understand gender as naming a complex set of interrelationships perceived and institutionalized in distinct ways. But the failure to grasp those complex interrelationships continues the practice of disavowing interdependency. To orient ourselves in order to perceive, and communicate, how lives are implicated in each other and broader living and social processes, requires a shift in disposition, a different way of seeing the world. The wager here is that our descriptions become better, but so too do feminist aspirations become more clear. The point is not to wage a war of one sex against another, or even to ground women in a disposition of their own. Indeed, in my view, a complex constellation of gender may well confront us with forms of interrelationships that move beyond the binary of gender.

For Strathern in these early years, the task is rather to combat those forms of mastery, individualism, and the disavowal of interdependency at a conceptual level not because all such matters can be resolved through thought alone. Rather,

the conceptual is presupposed by the practical field of social relations, and actively structures what we take to be the most basic units of analysis. When iden-
titarian logics steep themselves in conceptual separatism, as it were, they limit
the aspirations of feminism itself. The very modes by which one group is defined, or defines itself, over and against another fails to grasp that such distinctions are part of a social world in which interdependent groups are organized.
That insight shifts both our descriptive and normative approaches. Those limiting conceptual frames keep us from understanding the complex and sometimes
antagonistic field of interdependency and opening lines of communication and
exchange that take on conflict while affirming relationality. Strathern's early
probing and challenging makes this subtle and far-reaching suggestion time
and again, and in different ways, that interdependency, understood as the social condition so often occluded by accepted conceptual frames, can be grasped
and pursued through other ways of perceiving the broader picture of difference.
At stake is not only how any of us perceive the terrain of social relations but
how that perceiving enables and informs a new making of the social world that
makes it our contentious and common task.

References

Amatniek, Kathie. 1970. "Funeral oration for traditional womanhood." In *Voices from women's liberation*, edited by Leslie B. Tanner, 138–42. New York: Signet Books.

Antoun, Richard T. 1968. "The modesty of women in Arabic Muslim villages: A study in the accommodation of tradition." *American Anthropologist* 70 (4): 671–97.

Ardener, Edwin. 1972. "Belief and the problem of women." In *The interpretation of ritual*, edited by Jean Sybil La Fontaine, 135–58. London: Tavistock Publications.

Bailey, Derrick S. 1959. *The man-woman relationship in Christian thought.* London: Longmans.

Bateson, Gregory. (1936) 1958. *Naven: A survey of the problems suggested by a composite picture of the culture of a New Guinea tribe drawn from three points of view.* Stanford, CA: Stanford University Press.

Berndt, Catherine H. (1970) 1986. "Digging sticks and spears; Or, the two sex model." In *Woman's role in Aboriginal society*, edited by Fay Gale, 64–84. Canberra: Australian Institute of Aboriginal Studies.

Brandt, William J. 1966. *The shape of medieval history: Studies in modes of perception.* New Haven, CT: Yale University Press.

Callan, Hilary. 1970. *Ethology and society: Towards an anthropological view.* Oxford: Oxford University Press.

Catlin, George E. G. 1929. "Introduction." In *The rights of woman and the subjection of women*, by Mary Wollstonecraft and John Stuart Mill, xi–xxxix. London: J. M. Dent and Sons.

Cobbe, Frances P. (1881) 1894. *The duties of women*. London: T. Fisher Unwin.

Coghill, Nevill. 1949. *The poet Chaucer*. Oxford: Oxford University Press.

Cohen, Abner. 1969. *Custom and politics in urban Africa: A study of Hausa migrants in Yoruba town*. London: Routledge and Kegan Paul.

Cohen, Ronald. 1971. *Dominance and defiance: A study of marital instability in an Islamic African society*. Washington, DC: American Anthropological Association.

Collins, Wilkie. (1859–60) 1969. *The woman in white*. London: J. M. Dent & Sons.

Dalla Costa, Mariarosa. 1972. "Women and the subversion of the community." In *The power of women and the subversion of the community*, edited by Selma James, 19–49. Bristol: Falling Wall Press.

De Beauvoir, Simone. 1972. *The second sex*. Translated by H. M. Parshley. New York: Penguin Books.

Decter, Midge. 1973. *The new chastity and other arguments against Women's liberation*. London: Wildwood House.

Dunbar, Roxanne. 1970. "Female liberation as the basis for social revolution." In *Sisterhood is powerful: An anthology of writings from the Women's Liberation Movement*, edited by Robin Morgan, 477–92. New York: Vintage Books.

Dunbar, Roxanne, and Lisa Leghorn. 1970. "The man's problem." In *Voices from Women's Liberation*, edited by Leslie B. Tanner, 313–15. New York: Signet Books.

Eibl-Eibesfeldt, Irenäus. 1970. *Ethology: The biology of behaviour*. New York: Holt, Rinehart and Winston.

Epstein, Arnold L. [Bill]. 1967. "Injury and liability: Legal ideas and implicit assumptions." *Mankind* 6: 376–83.

Fawcett Society. 1967. "Women in a changing world." Report of a conference held at the Fawcett Society, London.

Firestone, Shulamith. 1971. *The dialectic of sex*. New York: Bantam Books.

Forge, Anthony. 1966. "Art and environment in the Sepik." *Proceedings of the Royal Anthropological Institute for 1965*: 23–31.

Fortes, Meyer. (1949) 1970. "Time and social structure. An Ashanti case study." In *Time and social Structure, and other essays*, 1–32. London: The Athlone Press.

————. 1950. "Kinship and marriage among the Ashanti." In *African systems of kinship and marriage*, edited A. R. Radcliffe-Brown and D. Forde, 252–84. Oxford: Oxford University Press.

Friedan, Betty. (1963) 1965. *The feminine mystique*. New York: Penguin Books.

Gale, Fay, ed. (1970) 1986. *Woman's role in Aboriginal society*. Canberra: Australian Institute of Aboriginal Studies.

Gibbs, James. 1969. "Law and personality: Signposts for a new direction." In *Law in culture and society*, edited by Laura Nader, 176–207. Chicago: Aldine.

Gissing, George. (1893) n.d. *The odd women*. London: Nelson and Sons.

Goodale, Jane C. 1971. *Tiwi wives: A study of the women of Melville Island in North Australia*. Seattle: University of Washington Press.

Goody, Esther. 1962. "Separation and divorce among the Gonja." In *Marriage in tribal societies*, edited by Meyer Fortes, 14–54. Cambridge: Cambridge University Press.

————. 1973. *Contexts of kinship: An essay in the family sociology of the Gonja of Northern Ghana*. Cambridge: Cambridge University Press.

Greer, Germaine. 1970. *The female eunuch*. London: MacGibbon & Kee.

Hiatt, Betty. (1970) 1986. "Woman the gatherer." In *Woman's role in Aboriginal society*, edited by Fay Gale, 4–15. Canberra: Australian Institute of Aboriginal Studies.

Hiatt, Les. R. 1971. "Feminism." *Quadrant* 15 (5): 65–71.

Hogbin, Ian. 1970. *The island of menstruating men: Religion in Wogeo, New Guinea*, Scranton, PA: Chandler.

Hope, Alec D. 1970. *A midsummer eve's dream: Variations on a theme, by William Dunbar*. Canberra: Australian National University Press.

Huizinga, J. (1924) 1955. *The waning of the Middle Ages*. Translated by F. Hopman. Penguin Books.

Hutt, Corinne. 1972. *Males and females*. Harmondsworth: Penguin Books.

James, Selma, ed. 1972. *The power of women and the subversion of the community*. Bristol: Falling Wall Press.

Janeway, Elizabeth. (1971) 1972. *Man's world, woman's place: A study in social mythology*. London: Michael Joseph.

Kaberry, Phyllis. 1939. *Aboriginal woman, sacred and profane*. London: George Routledge & Sons, Ltd.

La Fontaine, Jean S. 1962. "Gisu marriage and affinal relations." In *Marriage in tribal societies*, edited by Meyer Fortes, 88–120. Cambridge: Cambridge University Press.

————. 1972. "Ritualization of women's life-crises in Bugisu." In *The inter-pretation of ritual*, edited by J. S. La Fontaine, 159–86. London: Tavistock Publications.

Leach, Edmund. 1968. *A runaway world?* The Reith Lectures. London: BBC Books.

Lewis, C. S. 1936. *The allegory of love: A study in medieval tradition*. Oxford: Oxford University Press.

Lopata, Helena Z. 1971. *Occupation: Housewife*. Oxford: Oxford University Press.

Mead, Margaret. 1935. *Sex and temperament in three primitive societies*. George Routledge & Sons, Ltd.

————. (1950) 1962. *Male and female. A study of the sexes in a changing world*. New York: Penguin Books.

Meggitt, Mervyn. 1964. "Male-female relationships in the Highland of New Guinea." *American Anthropologist* 66: 204–24.

Mill, John Stuart. (1869) 1970. "The subjection of women." In *Essays on sex equality*, edited by Alice S Rossi, 123–242. Chicago: University of Chicago Press.

Millett, Kate. (1969) 1971. *Sexual politics*. London: Rupert Hart-Davis.

Morgan, Robin, ed. 1970. *Sisterhood is powerful: An anthology of writings from the Women's Liberation Movement*. New York: Vintage Books.

Morrall, John B. 1970. *The medieval imprint: The founding of the Western European tradition*. London: Penguin Books.

Oakley, Ann. 1972. *Sex, gender and society*. London: Maurice Temple Smith.

O'Neill, William L. 1969. *The woman movement: Feminism in the United States and England*. London: George, Allen and Unwin.

Rendel, Margherita, et al. 1968. *Equality for women*, Fabian research series 268. London: The Fabian Society.

Richards, Audrey I. 1956. *Chisungu: A girl's initiation ceremony among the Bemba of Northern Rhodesia*. London: Faber & Faber.

Richardson, Maurice. 1969. "Introduction." In *The woman in white*, by Wilkie Collins, v–ix. London: J. M. Dent and Sons.

Rossi, Alice S., ed. 1970. *Essays on sex equality: John Stuart Mill, Harriet Taylor Mill*. Chicago: University of Chicago Press.

Rowbotham, Sheila. 1971. *Women's Liberation and the new politics*. Spokesman pamphlet, no. 17. Nottingham: Bertrand Russell Peace Foundation.

Schneider, David. 1968. *American kinship: A cultural account*. Englewoods-Cliff, NJ: Prentice Hall.

Schreiner, Olive. (1883) 1971. *The story of an African farm*. London: Penguin Books.

Stanner, W. E. H. 1965. "Religion, totemism and symbolism." In *Aboriginal man in Australia*, edited by R. M. and C. H. Berndt, 207–37. Sydney: Angus and Robertson.

Stenning, Derrick J. 1959. *Savannah nomads: A study of the Wodaabe pastoral Fulani of Western Bornu Province, Northern Region, Nigeria*. Oxford: Oxford University Press.

Stone, Brian, trans. 1964. *Medieval English verse*. London: Penguin Books.

Tanner, Leslie B., ed. 1970. *Voices from Women's Liberation*. New York: Signet Books.

Tiger, Lionel. 1971. *Men in groups*. London: Panther.

Wells, H. G. (1909) 1910. *Ann Veronica: A modern love story*. London: T. Fisher Unwin.

White, Isobel M. (1970) 1986. "Aboriginal women's status: A paradox resolved." In *Woman's role in Aboriginal society*, edited by Fay Gale, 36–49. Canberra: Australian Institute of Aboriginal Studies.

Women's Majority Union (Seattle, Washington). 1970. "Lilith's manifesto —1969". In *Sisterhood is powerful: An anthology of writings from the Women's Liberation Movement*, edited by Robin Morgan, 527–29. New York: Vintage Books.

Young, Michael, and Peter Willmott. (1957) 1962. *Family and kinship in East London*. London: Penguin Books.

Index of Names

Hau Books is committed to publishing the most distinguished texts in classic and advanced anthropological theory. The titles aim to situate ethnography as the prime heuristic of anthropology, and return it to the forefront of conceptual developments in the discipline. Hau Books is sponsored by some of the world's most distinguished anthropology departments and research institutions, and releases its titles in both print editions and open-access formats.

www.haubooks.com

Supported by
Hau-N. E. T.
Network of Ethnographic Theory

University of Aarhus – EPICENTER (DK)
University of Amsterdam (NL)
University of Bergen (NO)
Brown University (US)
California Institute of Integral Studies (US)
University of Campinas (BR)
University of Canterbury (NZ)
University of Chicago (US)
University College London (UK)
University of Colorado Boulder Libraries (US)
CNRS – Centre d'Études Himalayennes (FR)
Cornell University (US)
University of Edinburgh (UK)
The Graduate Institute, Geneva Library (CH)
University of Helsinki (FL)
Indiana University Library (US)
Johns Hopkins University (US)
University of Kent (UK)
Lafayette College Library (US)
London School of Economics and Political Science (UK)
Institute of Social Sciences of the University of Lisbon (PL)
University of Manchester (UK)
The University of Manchester Library (UK)
Max-Planck Institute for the Study of Religious and Ethnic
Diversity at Göttingen (DE)
Musée de Quai Branly (FR)
Museu Nacional – UFRJ (BR)
Norwegian Museum of Cultural History (NO)
University of Oslo (NO)
University of Oslo Library (NO)
Pontificia Universidad Católica de Chile (CL)
Princeton University (US)
University of Queensland (AU)
University of Rochester (US)
Universidad Autónoma de San Luis Potosi (MX)
SOAS, University of London (UK)
University of Sydney (AU)
University of Toronto Libraries (CA)

www.haujournal.org/haunet